Word 2007 Document Automation with VBA and VSTO

Scott Driza

Word 2007 Document Automation with VBA and VSTO

Scott Driza

Wordware Publishing, Inc.

Library of Congress Cataloging-in-Publication Data

Driza, Scott.
   Word 2007 document automation with VBA and VSTO / by Scott Driza.
      p. cm.
   Includes index.
   ISBN-13: 978-1-59822-047-6 (pbk.)
   ISBN-10: 1-59822-047-0
   1. Microsoft Word--Handbooks, manuals, etc. 2. Microsoft Visual Basic for
applications--Handbooks, manuals, etc. 3. Microsoft Visual studio--Handbooks,
manuals, etc. I. Title.
   Z52.5.M52D78 2009
   005.52--dc22   2009002853

ISBN-13: 978-1-59822-047-6
ISBN-10: 1-59822-047-0
10 9 8 7 6 5 4 3 2 1
0903

All inquiries for volume purchases of this book should be addressed to Wordware Publishing, Inc., at the above address. Telephone inquiries may be made by calling:

(972) 423-0090

For Debra, Connor, and Finley.

Contents

Acknowledgments

I'd like to thank my wife for supporting me through various projects over the past couple years — especially this book. I also need to thank my son, Connor, for being my little buddy and sneaking out to "help" me write this book when he should've been sleeping. I'm also grateful for my sunny little daughter, Finley, who routinely smashed the keyboard to let me know that I should've been paying more attention to her.

I'm also thankful for all our current dogs (Peanut, Skye, and Fergie) and our beloved Shani who isn't with us any longer.

I owe more to my parents, Steve and Dolores Driza, than they can possibly know. I'm also indebted to my brother, Steve Driza, and my sister, Sue Fadden, and their spouses and children. They have helped me tremendously.

This book is the result of extensive collaboration with Tae Chung. He picked up the torch and turned a large pile of notes, half-written chapters, and images into a cohesive book. Tae is responsible for everything good about the book. Any mistakes or omissions are my responsibility. Beth Kohler and Tim McEvoy have been great to work with and I can only hope to be lucky enough to work with them again in the future.

The most credit for the material covered in this book belongs to Melvin Helfand (the father of modern Word programming). His innovative thoughts and our close working relationship through the years showed me what is possible with a bit of creativity and persistence.

Special thanks to Carl Bucaro, who has assisted me on a variety of Word-related projects over the years.

I've also had the pleasure of knowing some incredible people in the technology arena: Tim Probst, John Lind, Richard Astle, Stephen Haynes, Bayard Woodworth, Ted Yates, Harry Kimura, Dr. William Sun, Joe Chang, Binh Li, Jason Williams, and Bill Gravelle.

Special thanks to some of the finest business people, professionals, and executives I've seen in action: Scott McNulla, Jeff Hallberg, Lou Pizante, Jason Connolly, Chris Randazzo, Bill McFarlane, Ryder Smith, Lauren Ingersoll, Mark Emanuelson, Bret Schaefer, Richard Hernandez, Craig Crawford, Greg Spires, John Michals, and Steve Regan.

Thanks throughout the years to: Bob Rockwell, Thaddeus Murphy, Shannon Farley, Tom Struble, J.B. Trew, Randy Lee, Bryan Gaston, Anna Kim, Jennifer Mathwig, Mark Strachota, Leo Irakliotis, Art Hogue, Andy Longo, Doug Melton, Brian Howard, Chuck Cornell, Arthur LeFrancois, Mark Shaklette, Craig Grotts, Dann O'Brien, David Lehman, John Nix, Richard and Melissa Brown, Tom Parry, Linda and Danny Cannon, Steve Bender and Dawn Brandewie, Nancy and Jerry Brandewie, Alfred Brophy, Lee Cannon, Rodney Cooke and Page Dobson, Robert T. Keel and Martha Kulmacz, Cheyenne Dupree, Donnie Wachtman, Brad Warren, Jude Henry, Jeff Flesner, and Keith and Ashleigh Muse.

... and, my best friend of all, Dr. Thomas Edward Wyatt.

Introduction

Welcome to the biggest change in Microsoft Word since WYSIWYG. As you probably already know, Office 2007 is a major change from previous Office versions. If you are entirely new to Microsoft Office, you should find Word 2007 very intuitive. Microsoft spent many millions of dollars working with users to ensure that the experience was as positive as possible. For example, when clicking on objects such as images, text, or spreadsheet areas, special context-sensitive "Ribbons" will appear to assist you.

The preparation of documents has always been a tedious process, especially when lengthy documents were typed page by page. And remember — the typewriter *was* a revolutionary instrument. Even though early word processors were a major advance over the typewriter, by today's standards they are both terribly inefficient. Yet, despite all of the recent advancements in office workflow solutions, most organizations still prepare documents in an outdated fashion. At best they may have an off-the-shelf-solution. These are notoriously difficult to work with, may not even let an organization use their own documents, and sometimes don't even allow the file to be exported to standard formats.

Luckily, Word 2007 is the most advanced word processor ever developed. In fact, most people will not even scratch the surface in terms of the functionality available to them. This book covers Visual Basic for Applications (VBA), the underlying programming language embedded behind the Office suite of applications. In addition, roughly the second half of the book covers Visual Studio Tools for Office, which is the latest and greatest Office programming utility to come out of Redmond.

Who Is This Book For?

This book appeals to a few different types of Word users. One audience is the advanced Word user who is looking to automate the preparation of documents (business and legal). In an effort not to bore these users, we've tried to be brief when covering simple, well-known concepts. Following a similar vein, an effort has been made to distinguish particularly useful concepts or, in some cases, even snippets of code where applicable.

Another audience for this book includes competent programmers who are unfamiliar with document automation and the Word object model. In many ways, document automation programming may be more difficult for seasoned programmers. Especially those programmers accustomed to dealing with relational data and simple reports. Document automation is usually like creating "crazy" reports in that they often have a much larger number of decision trees and customization.

Good luck!

Chapter 1

What's New in Word 2007

Introduction

Word 2007 is Microsoft's biggest application change since going from "green screens" to "what you see is what you get" (WYSIWYG). The traditional Word menu bars and buttons have been replaced with the "Ribbon." Collectively, the new look is called the "Fluent User Interface," but in practice, most people (erroneously) refer to the entire collection of changes as the Ribbon.

The Ribbon contains the same functionality as the menu bars and command buttons, but it is a more intuitive and more elegant solution that is the result of many millions of dollars of testing and is designed to make Word simpler to use. It helps users quickly find the correct commands and enhances their productivity. In turn, this results in the easy creation of professional-looking documents. Word 2007 contains rich review functions, commenting, and comparison capabilities that allow for easier collaboration than ever. Most importantly from an automation perspective, advanced data integration ensures that documents are updated from various sources of business information.

What's On the Ribbon?

There are three basic components to the Ribbon:

▼ **Tabs** — Each tab is related to a specific type of work that you do in Word. Tabs group commands and buttons that are related to that type of work.

▼ **Groups** — Each tab has several groups that show related items together. For example, Font is a group that contains commands for formatting text.

▼ **Commands** — A command is a button, a box to enter information, or a menu. The most commonly used commands have the largest buttons. Some examples of commands are the Bold button and Font list.

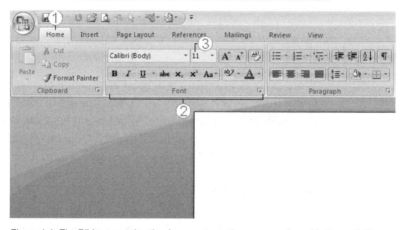

Figure 1-1: The Ribbon contains the document creation commands and buttons. 1) The Home tab. 2) The Font group. 3) The Point Size box.

The most commonly used commands in Word are located on the Home tab. There is a convenient feature of the Ribbon that allows you to use more screen space for your document. You can hide the Ribbon temporarily by double-clicking the active tab. The groups disappear so that you have more room on screen. Whenever you want to see all of the commands again, double-click the active tab to bring back the groups.

The Microsoft Office Button

Although most people don't like the new user interface at first (it is natural to resist change), after using it for a couple weeks you'll find that many of the changes are significant improvements. Some of Word's most important commands and features have little or nothing to do with the authoring experience. In addition to the document creation process, users typically spend a lot of time doing things like sharing, protecting, printing, and e-mailing. In previous versions of Word, these commands were all nested in various command menus and there was no central location where users could go to perform actions on the document. Word 2007 introduces the Microsoft Office button, which provides that central starting point. The Office button helps users find these valuable features and it simplifies the core authoring experience by allowing the Ribbon to be used solely for creating documents.

The Mini Toolbar

The Mini toolbar is a small floating toolbar that appears right next to the text that is highlighted. This allows users to easily click on buttons to make changes to the text such as bold, italic, or font size without having to mouse up to the Ribbon and back to the text again. This seems like a relatively minor change, but the savings are tremendous during the course of writing a lengthy document.

In order to display the Mini toolbar, highlight some text and then cursor (mouse) over it. When the Mini toolbar first appears, it is transparent. Move the mouse over the Mini toolbar to make it appear solid (as shown in Figure 1-2), then click on its buttons and controls to format text.

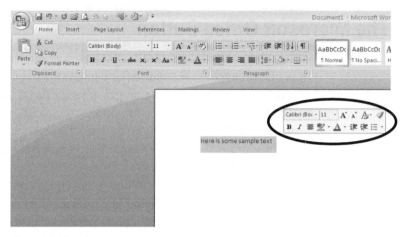

Figure 1-2: The Mini toolbar

Dialog Launchers

Dialog boxes are a key part of the Fluent User Interface. Most of the traditional Word dialog boxes remain untouched in Word 2007. When you first look at a group, you may not see all of the commands that were available in the previous version of Word. Rest assured, you can still access these commands from the dialogs. You'll notice that most of the groups have a small triangle icon in the lower-right corner. This is called the dialog box launcher. When you click it, you'll see more commands and options related to that group. Sometimes those options will appear in the form of a dialog box that will look similar to those in previous versions of Word. Others may appear in a task pane.

Note: The actual display of the groups is dependent on the screen resolution you're using. Larger monitors and higher screen resolutions will display more commands.

The Quick Access Toolbar

The Quick Access Toolbar, located next to the Microsoft Office button, contains commands used to save or print a file and to undo or redo commands. However, the most important feature of this toolbar is that you can customize it to fit your needs.

You customize the toolbar by right-clicking it and choosing Customize Quick Access Toolbar. Alternatively, click the Office button and choose Word Options, then choose Customize to see a dialog that contains a list of available commands that can be added to the Quick Access Toolbar. This dialog is equivalent to Tools | Options in previous versions of Word. A final method of adding commands to the Quick Access Toolbar is by right-clicking a command on any toolbar and choosing Add to Quick Access Toolbar.

Keyboard Shortcuts

Keyboard shortcuts have a new name: Key Tips. Press and hold the Alt key briefly and the Key Tip badges appear for each of the Ribbon tabs, the Quick Access Toolbar commands, and the Microsoft Office button. Press the Key Tip for the particular tab you want to display and you will then see Key Tips for all commands for that tab. From there, you can press the Key Tip for the exact command you want.

All of the old shortcuts that started with the Ctrl key (for example, Ctrl+C for copy or Ctrl+V for paste) remain the same as in previous versions of Word. But the Ribbon comes with important new shortcuts. This change has two big advantages over previous versions:

▼ Shortcuts for every single button on the Ribbon.

▼ Shortcuts that often require fewer keys.

> **Note:** You can also still use the old Alt+ shortcuts that accessed menus and commands; however, in some cases the old menus may not be available. The Alt+ keyboard shortcuts won't display screen reminders for you, so you'll need to know the full shortcut to use them.

On-Demand Tabs

One of the coolest features is the on-demand tab functionality in Word 2007. Most developers are familiar with the IntelliSense feature, which displays context-sensitive information based on the cursor location and surrounding information. In a similar fashion, on-demand tabs appear only when you need them. For example, imagine you are working with a document that has an inline image and you want to add a caption to the image.

1. Click on the image with your mouse cursor.
2. The Picture Tools tab appears. Click that tab.
3. Additional groups and commands appear for working with pictures, such as the Picture Styles group.

When you navigate away from the picture, the Picture Tools tab disappears and the other groups come back.

> **Note:** On-demand tabs appear for other activity areas, like tables, drawings, diagrams, and charts.

Document Themes

Document themes are basically a step up from styles. Styles are a way to apply consistent formatting throughout your document. Themes extend the concept and include the definitions of colors, fonts, and graphic effects for a document. Themes allow you to apply one or more of these elements by selecting the palette, font, or styling from one of the galleries in the Themes group.

Themes provide a mechanism by which you can propagate changes consistently across an entire document without having to redefine the individual styles.

Note: The theme functionality ceases if a piece of the theme is altered. This means the document will no longer be theme-aware. For example, suppose a font is changed directly or one of the standard colors is chosen from the bottom of the color picker. This information can be used to update the style definition, but it will still mean the document is no longer theme-aware.

Themes exist and can be distributed independently of an individual document as they have their own file format (.thmx). This format can be shared among Word, Excel, PowerPoint, and Outlook e-mail messages. Pretty much anything that can be inserted into a document is automatically themed to match the overall document. You can also use similar themes for reports in Access, diagrams in Visio, and even project plans in Microsoft Project.

Developer Enhancements

Word 2007 introduces some enhancements that will hopefully make a developer's life easier. There are new features that apply to all of the core applications in the 2007 Microsoft Office system, and some that are specific to Word. The shared enhancements include the new user interface discussed above, new Microsoft Office Open XML Formats (Office XML Formats), and the ability to easily attach custom XML data to a file. Word 2007 dramatically improves the native XML capabilities, including a new default file format that is written almost entirely in XML.

Content Controls

Content controls are predefined blocks of content that can be positioned anywhere in the document. These are completely new in Word 2007 and are thus not backward compatible. Content controls can be used for standard form documentation and can be used to map XML data to specific pieces of a document. This XML data can be mapped using the Word 2007 XML Format. Directly mapping content improves upon some of the problems encountered when working directly with XML in Word 2003.

XML Mapping

This feature enables users to create a link between a document and an XML file. You can add structured custom data (stored in one or more XML files) to the document and map the data to specific content controls and thus different portions of the document. The improved Word 2007 XML format allows easy programmatic access to this data. Most importantly from an architecture perspective, this model creates separation between the document formatting and custom XML data.

Document Building Blocks

These are exactly what they sound like: predefined pieces of content. In most cases, this is text such as a cover page, a header/footer, or a legal clause in a contract. These custom building blocks facilitate document automation and result in easily created, professional-looking Word documents.

Everyone can take advantage of the document building blocks to ease the pain of creating documents, but savvy users and developers can leverage them to an even larger extent by creating and using custom building blocks. Obviously, Word doesn't limit you to the base building blocks included in the application.

Word XML Format

Word XML format is based on the Open Packaging Conventions. The main purpose is to divide the file into logical document components, each of which defines a specific piece. The improvements in this area mean that you can programmatically alter something in the file, such as the header or footer, without accidentally modifying any other XML document parts. The XML data is now encapsulated in its own part, so manipulating the end result using the custom XML is now easier.

Conclusion

Microsoft Word 2007 is a great improvement over previous versions. Microsoft spent millions of dollars researching and improving the way the application looks and works. In some cases users will take a little time to get accustomed to the changes, but most organizations have found the transition easier than they anticipated. This chapter reviewed some of the most important improvements and changes to Word 2007. The following chapter will show how to automate documents without programming.

Chapter 2

Automation without Programming

Introduction

The new version of Microsoft Word is easy to use, but it is an amazingly complex tool. A novice Windows user can generally create a simple document right out of the box. At the opposite end of the spectrum, I've also seen experienced programmers spend countless hours trying to format tables and struggle with the proper application of styles. There are innumerable ways to accomplish many common tasks. In most instances, the "right" method may boil down to a question of preference. Document automation is a prime example of this. There is no "right" way to automate a document. The "right" way is dictated by the customer.

Most of the topics covered in this chapter are widely known and widely covered, at least to some extent, by most books about Microsoft Word. However, these other books rarely cover these topics in the context of document automation. Hopefully, this chapter will introduce you to some novel ways of using common Word functionality to make your life (or the lives of your users) easier. Most of the topics covered are not unique to Word 2007, but they are covered in the context of Word 2007, so the menu paths may be different if you are using a previous version of Word.

Because of the relative simplicity of each of these topics, even relative Word novices can benefit by implementing one or more of them. In many cases, the simple techniques described here may be all the document automation they need.

Why Templates?

Many, if not most, non-retail businesses require the use of documents that are frequently and repetitively prepared. Typically, each time a new document is needed, a Word user will open a recent version of the same document, and click Office button | Save As to save the document under a new name. There is, of course, nothing intrinsically wrong with this approach — as long as you remember to delete from the Save As file any changes made to the basic document that were specific to the last transaction. However, time and again we have seen examples where changes made for a particular transaction or situation were adopted as new standard provisions without much thought being given to the effect of the changes on other transactions or situations. In other cases, metadata specific to a completely separate transaction has been discovered in a document. These unfortunate oversights boil down to a simple misuse of Microsoft Word. If a document is reused with that much frequency, it should be turned into a template.

Fortunately, Word provides a simple way to preserve frequently used documents through its template feature. Templates are essentially the shell of a document in a basic, mostly untouchable form. After a document is saved as a template, new documents can be created that are essentially copies of the templated document. The template (and its accompanying VBA code) stays in the background in its original form. You can, of course, edit the template at any time. However, the use of a template eliminates the likelihood of inadvertent changes to standardized documents.

Templates also open the door to numerous other forms of customization and automation. For example, a custom template can have a different font and different margin sizes than found in your "normal" template — the template Word runs by default. As to automation, you will see how templates are an integral part of most of the projects outlined in this book.

How Do You Create a Template?

Creating a template is simple. Word 2007 allows you to save templates with or without macros. For our purposes, we do not need macros in the template, so just do the following (see Figure 2-1):

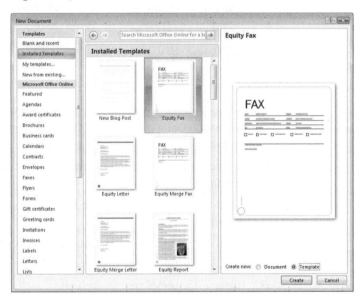

Figure 2-1

1. Create the document you want to save as a template.
2. Click **Office button | Save As**.
3. From the list of choices, choose **Word Template**.

As you can see, creating a template is very easy.

Using Templates

Templates provide the best mechanism to create consistent, properly formatted documentation. Word 2007 has dramatically improved the ability to create documents based on templates. You'll notice that Word now includes hundreds of templates by default. In addition, you can use Microsoft Office Online to get the latest form documents Microsoft makes available. You also have the option to choose templates from other locations. To create a document based on a template:

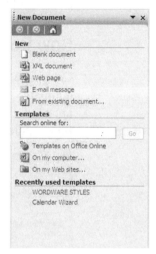

Figure 2-2

1. Click **Office button | New**.

2. This will open up the New Document dialog, as shown in Figure 2-2.

3. This gives you the following options for creating a new document:

   ■ Create a new blank document based on the Normal template.

   ■ Create a new document based on an existing document.

   ■ Look for templates from Microsoft Office Online.

   ■ Browse for templates installed on your computer.

   ■ Browse for templates on web sites.

Workgroup Templates

If more than one person is going to use a template and you have a network, you should consider installing your templates on your network server and accessing them through the workgroup templates feature. This will avoid the necessity of updating each computer every time a template is added or changed.

To allow your PCs to access templates located on a network, each PC must be set up to recognize workgroup templates. Assume that your network location for templates is "J:\Wordtemplates." It's a little more cumbersome to get to the File Locations dialog in Word 2007 (see Figure 2-3):

Figure 2-3

1. Click **Office button | Word Options | Advanced**, then scroll to the General section and click the **File Locations** button.

2. Highlight the line **Workgroup templates**, and click **Modify**.

3. In the Modify Location dialog box that opens, go to the network drive ("J") and find and highlight the **Wordtemplates** folder.

4. Click **OK** twice.

Even if you are not networked, you might want to set up a special templates folder on the C: drive as a container for workgroup templates (or user templates) so that they will be easy to find and edit. The user templates setting can be found in the same dialog as the workgroup templates setting.

Note: Although workgroup templates can be used by multiple people at the same time (since each is working with a copy of the template, and not the original), template modifications cannot be saved to the network drive if anyone has a document open that was created with the template.

AutoCorrect

This is another widely known feature whose automation benefit is relatively unknown. Many Word users know about the AutoCorrect feature of Word — they associate the feature with the automatic correction of common spelling errors. For example, if you type the word "agian", AutoCorrect will correct the spelling and change the word to "again". This feature can be turned off if desired to prevent the undesired "fixing" of words.

Somewhat less well known is the ability of AutoCorrect to speed typing of documents. This is accomplished via the use of customized AutoCorrect lists. The concept is very simple: Define a set combination of characters as a shortcut for a complete paragraph and you can easily automate the insertion of complete clauses.

Using AutoCorrect

Assume, for example, that the name of your company is "North American First Widgets and Capital Formation Company, Incorporated." To avoid having to type that name numerous times:

1. Click **Office button | Word Options | Proofing | AutoCorrect Options**.
2. In the box labeled "Replace:", type **nafw** (see Figure 2-4).
3. In the box labeled "With:", type **North American First Widgets and Capital Formation Company, Incorporated**.
4. Click **Add** and then **OK**.

Now you can type the name of your company merely by typing the letters "nafw" and hitting the Spacebar or Enter or typing a punctuation mark. Doing so will cause AutoCorrect to expand the entry to the full name.

Figure 2-4

The Downside of AutoCorrect

AutoCorrect clearly has a place in reducing the amount of typing for many phrases. There is a downside, however. You have to remember the abbreviation you used to trigger AutoCorrect. In common practice, it seems to work really well for a limited number of frequently used entries (eight to ten). After that, we found users spending significant amounts of time trying to remember what letters to type to activate the AutoCorrect. The lack of an easy-to-use interface further complicates this problem.

AutoText

From the perspective of document automation, AutoText, a cousin of AutoCorrect, is much more versatile and can begin to provide some real and meaningful document automation.

With AutoText, a large block of text (as opposed to the relatively short phrase or sentence with AutoCorrect) is typically saved under a one-word name. That text can be, for example, the entire body of a letter. Accordingly, if you have five or six form letters, the body of each can be saved in AutoText and retrieved merely by typing a single word. Variables within the body of such letters can be stored as blank lines and filled in after the AutoText is inserted.

In Word 2007, AutoText is not part of the standard Ribbon commands. Before you begin working through the steps below, click the **Microsoft Office** button, then click **Word Options** and **Customize**. In the Choose commands from list, click on **Commands Not in the Ribbon**, then click **AutoText**, **Add**, and then **OK**.

Creating AutoText

To create AutoText, follow these steps:

1. Type the following sentence: **The quick brown fox jumped over the Land Rover**.

2. Select (highlight) the entire sentence and press **Ctrl+C** to copy the text. Include the paragraph mark if you want your AutoText to be a separate paragraph and/or contain the formatting in which it was originally typed.

3. Click the **AutoText** command on the Ribbon to open the dialog shown in Figure 2-5. Then click on **OK** to save the current selection to the AutoText Gallery.

Figure 2-5

4. In the Create New Building Block dialog box that appears, type **brownfox** as the name for your AutoText and click **OK**.

Retrieving Your AutoText

To retrieve the AutoText you just created:

1. Place your cursor at the point where you want to insert your AutoText.
2. Click the **AutoText** item from the Quick Access Toolbar on the Ribbon.
3. From the list of AutoText items that appears, click once on the name of the AutoText you want to insert (in our example, **brownfox**).

Practical Limitations

In practice AutoText works great for about 20 to 30 entries, which is more than enough for most businesses. Beyond that, however, you may find that either there are simply too many to remember or you need to scroll through the list of AutoText entries trying to remember which keyword you used to describe the passage you want.

Find and Replace

Why Use Find and Replace?

When automating document creation, something you might overlook is using Word's Find and Replace functions to update either a template created document (as we recommend) or even the last used version of your form letter. If similar documents are needed with only slight changes to information that is used more than once, Find and Replace will eliminate the duplicate typing.

The first key to keep in mind is to use easily recognized catch words as your "find" words. If you set up a form as a template and you want to use Find and Replace to update it, we recommend that the words you use should be both easily recognizable and not likely to be confused with intended words.

Tip: You may even want to enclose the words in some sort of bracket {},[],() or pipes ||.

Our recommendation is that you use all capital letters for the words to be replaced, and that those words prompt you to make the change. In any event, it is important that the words to be replaced not mislead the user into overlooking the replacement.

Caution: Make sure your words are unique and will not occur naturally elsewhere in the letter. Consider using [LASTNAME] instead of "last"; otherwise, you may replace something inadvertently, such as "send in your payment prior to the *last* day of the month."

Consider the following letter as a simple example:

```
[PREFIXNAME] [FIRSTNAME] [LASTNAME]
[CUSTOMERADDRESS]
[CITYSTATEZIP]

Dear [PREFIXNAME] [LASTNAME],

We are pleased to enclose the Widgets you ordered from us.
[PREFIXNAME] [LASTNAME], we know that you have a choice of Widget
suppliers, and appreciate your choosing us.

If you have any questions or need any help with your Widgets,
please do not hesitate to call your personal sales rep, Joe Smith.

Sincerely yours,
```

Here, the key benefit of the Find and Replace comes from being able to avoid typing the intended [PREFIXNAME] and [LASTNAME] more than once.

Find and Replace Instructions

Using Find and Replace is one of the more common Word actions and most users are familiar with their use. The Find and Replace dialog box is shown in Figure 2-6. Nevertheless, for completeness, here are the instructions:

1. On the Home tab, click **Replace** or (our preference) press **Ctrl+H**.
2. In the Find what: section of the dialog box that appears, type **[PREFIXNAME]**. (Note that if prior to opening the Find and Replace dialog box you selected this word, it would have automatically been copied into the Find what: section.)
3. In the Replace with: section of the dialog box, type **Mr.**
4. Click **Replace All**.

Repeat this process for each word you want replaced.

Figure 2-6

Assuring Replacement

You can assure that every word required to be replaced is actually replaced by typing a list of the words to be replaced at the beginning of the document or template. Follow this list with either a page break (Control+Enter or choose Page Break from the Insert tab) or a section break. When you are done with the word replacement, delete the page and/or section containing the list.

Section Breaks

It's easy to use section breaks to bundle multiple documents. Frequently, more than one document is sent to a customer at the same time. So, for example, a sales order is likely to be accompanied by a thank you letter, and a sales proposal is likely to have a brief cover letter. If you prepare legal documents, chances are that each document is part of a package of documents.

If you bundle each of the related documents into a single document, using section breaks between each document, then, assuming that you use Find and Replace or one of the other methods of updating variable information described in this book, you will be able to type all of the documents at once and never have to type the same information twice. So, for example, if you use Find and Replace to insert a customer's name, it will appear in each of the bundled documents.

Why Use Section Breaks?

As mentioned above, you can use page breaks to separate multiple documents. Why then do we recommend the use of section breaks? The answer is because section breaks are much more flexible than mere page breaks in that they can be used to vary formatting, allow different margins on the same page, mix columns and text on the same page, and have different headers and footers on different pages of the same document. Most important, however, from the context of document automation and assembly is the relative ease with which each document can be given its own page numbers (see below).

You can use section breaks to change the layout or formatting of a page or pages in your document. For example, you can lay out part of a single-column page as two columns. You can separate the chapters in your document so that the page numbering for each chapter begins at 1. You can also create a different header or footer for a section of your document. In Word 2007, you can choose many page layouts from the gallery of new page designs.

Inserting a Section Break

To insert a section break, just place your cursor where you want a new section and open the Page Layout tab, then click **Page Layout | Breaks | Next Page**, as shown in Figure 2-7.

Note that Next Page, rather than Continuous, is the appropriate choice for bundling multiple documents. If, on the other hand, you want to perform one of the other tasks enabled by section breaks (such as having mixed columns and text on the same page), choose a Continuous section break. The other types of section breaks are Even Page and Odd Page, which are probably most suitable for separating the chapters of a book or long paper where it is desired that all chapters start on either a left-hand page or a right-hand page.

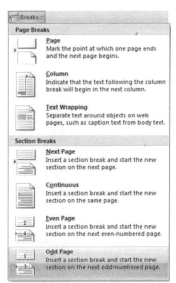

Figure 2-7

Page Numbers

No discussion of section breaks would be complete without a reference to page numbers. As mentioned above, page numbers are one of the principal reasons for using section breaks to bundle multiple related documents. Page numbers also cause the most problems for those who attempt such bundling. The reason is the tendency of Word to continue page numbers from one document to the next notwithstanding the section break between documents. Word does, however, provide an easy way around this problem. Just follow the steps outlined below to properly insert page numbers using the Insert tab:

1. Start on the first page of your bundled document.

2. Choose **Insert | Page Number** from the Ribbon, as shown in Figure 2-8.

3. You can then graphically navigate to see how the page number will appear. Figure 2-8 shows some of the options available when you choose Bottom of Page.

Figure 2-8

4. Once the page numbers have been added, you can specify whether or not they will appear on the first page of sections by using the options in the Header & Footer Tools Design tab, as shown in Figure 2-9. You can open the Header & Footer Tools Design tab by double-clicking in the header or footer section of the document.

Figure 2-9

Listing the steps makes this sound more complicated than it really is. When you actually try it, you will see that it is easy to do. We suggest that you try it by first actually bundling two or more documents (using Section Break | Next Page between documents), and then inserting page numbers following the method described above.

Provision Banks

A "provision bank" is our term for a single document that holds a number of different provisions or bodies of language. Assume, for example, that your business has 50 different form letters, with most of them used only once or twice a year. You could set up a template for each of the form letters and/or store them in AutoText. But a provision bank may be an easier solution, particularly for those letters that are infrequently used.

Storing infrequently used provisions (or even those you use every day) in a single document gives you the assurance that you will always be able to find the provision you need. Provision banks are particularly recommended for attorneys as a method of storing specially drafted contract or other document provisions.

Organizing a Provision Bank

If you only have a few provisions in your provision bank, you won't have to worry about how it is organized. If, on the other hand, your provision bank has many provisions, then organization becomes necessary. We recommend that each provision be given a meaningful descriptive title, and that the provisions then be organized in alphabetical order.

Save as a Template

In order to be assured that your provision bank is not inadvertently changed, make sure that you save it as a template.

Add a Hyperlinked Index

If you accumulate a large provision bank, it may be helpful to add a hyperlinked index at the beginning. This will enable you to immediately move to any hyperlinked provision.

To add a hyperlink:

1. First, insert a bookmark (using **Insert | Bookmark**) at the spot you want to go to — typically, the start of a particular provision. The name of the bookmark must be a single word or a group of words with no spaces between them.

2. Scroll back up to the beginning of the provision bank document (or better yet, press **Ctrl+Home**).

3. Click **Insert | Hyperlink** (or press **Ctrl+K**).

4. In the Insert Hyperlink dialog box that appears, click on the button labeled **Bookmark**.

5. In the Select Place in Document dialog box that opens, click on the name of your new bookmark and then click **OK**. (This closes the Select Place in Document dialog box and takes you back to the Insert Hyperlink dialog box.)

6. In the Text to display: text box, type in a descriptive title for the hyperlinked provision.

7. In the text box labeled Address: you should see a pound sign (#) followed by the name of your bookmark.

8. Click **OK**. You should now see your hyperlink at the beginning of the provision bank document.

Field Basics

What Is a Field?

Many documents you create may contain information, such as the date, author or reviewer, or page number, that needs to be updated frequently. Word provides the option of creating fields that automatically update selected information. In Word, many different types of fields are available for insertion into a document. Word fields are hidden codes that store variable information. You have seen fields in operation every time you insert page numbers using one of the techniques described above. Although you seem to see a page number, you are in fact seeing a Page field that changes the page number as and when necessary due to the addition or deletion of text.

You have also seen a field if you used the Insert | Date command and checked the box labeled Update automatically. In that case, a Word field acts in the background to change the date to the current date every time you reopen the document. There are over 80 types of fields embedded within Word. However, for the purpose of this introductory chapter, only a handful are relevant. As the Word Help files are very comprehensive regarding the use of fields, please consult them for the individual details of the field you wish to use.

How Do You View a Field?

Although Word fields are normally hidden, you can view them at any time by selecting the text containing the field and pressing Alt+F9.

1. Choose **Insert | Date & Time** from the Ribbon.
2. From the Available formats list, click on the third one from the top, which formats a date like this: January 1, 2009.

3. Check the box labeled **Update automatically**.

4. Click **OK**. This has the effect of inserting a Date field with the current date.

5. Select the entire date you just inserted.

6. Press **Alt+F9**.

You should now see the field code, which should look like this:

```
{ DATE \@ "MMMM d, yyyy" }
```

Note: Notice the brackets on either side of the field code. These are not the same as the "{" brackets you can type with your PC. You can't type a field code. It has to be inserted using one of the techniques described below.

The first word in the field code is the field type — in this case Date. It is followed by a formatting switch that sets the format of the date as the full name of the month, the day as a number, and the full year as a number.

You can view some of the other date formatting switches by choosing a different format when inserting the date. Alt+F9 acts as a toggle switch. So, if you want to see the field code as text, select the code and press Alt+F9 again.

As an aside, we always found the field name "Time" odd as a method of inserting a date, particularly because there is also a Date field that will insert a date. The difference is that the Time field will insert both dates and times, as well as combinations.

Inserting Field Codes

Since the brackets surrounding a field code cannot be directly typed in, you have to find another way to insert a Word field. Actually, we are going to show you two ways; the first is the method most people use, which was probably intended by Microsoft as the primary method, and the second is a method we find both quicker and easier to use. Either method is fine.

1. Click on **Insert | Quick Parts | Field**.

2.   In the dialog box that appears, choose **User Information** from the Categories drop-down.

3.   In the Field names section of the dialog box, click on **UserName**.

4.   Click **OK**.

If you have the field codes displayed (Alt+F9), you should see the following field: {USERNAME *MERGEFORMAT}. This should change the field to your name, or the name of the registered Windows user whose session is active. (If it doesn't, go to Office button | Word Options | Popular Tools | Options | User Information, type your name in the box labeled User name, and click OK.)

As with the Date field, the first word in the field, UserName, is the field type, and the part after the * is a formatting switch that formats the name in the same manner as the Word document.

Word includes the Mergeformat switch if you select the check box labeled Preserve formatting during updates when using Insert | Quick Parts | Field. Our experience with the Mergeformat switch has been less than positive (sometimes the results have surprised us). We prefer the Charformat switch described below for its greater reliability and control.

Although the Insert | Quick Parts | Field procedure described above may be helpful for people not familiar with Word fields, we prefer the greater control and, for us, speed of the manual process that follows:

1.   Click **Ctrl+F9** (most manipulation of fields involves the use of F9).

    This has the effect of inserting field brackets, which look like this: "{ }". It also has the effect of toggling the View Field Codes command (Alt+F9) so that all field codes are visible.

2.   Place your cursor between the two brackets of the field code you have inserted and type **UserName *charformat**.

3.   Underline the first letter of the field name (i.e., the "U" in UserName).

4. Select the field and press **Alt+F9**. This should toggle the field to display your name as above.

Note: The Charformat switch has formatted your name with the same formatting as the first letter of the field name — in this case, your name is underlined.

Commonly Used Fields

Word 2007 has a total of 77 different fields. In this chapter, we've decided to introduce some fields that can have a big impact with relatively little effort. Before we explore the options of combining Word fields with VBA code, we'll introduce a few of the fields and include them in a real-world application.

One of the key considerations when designing templates is to make sure users will enter data in the right place. The reason templates are so popular is that difficult document creation can be simplified so that, in some cases, even entry-level clerks can complete large, complex documents. These documents can then face a review process, rather than have an expensive resource draft the documents from scratch.

The MacroButton Field

I was reluctant at first, but I am finally giving in and admitting the usefulness of this "creative" way of using the MacroButton field. Strictly speaking, the MacroButton field can be used to run code (macros) when a user clicks on a certain place in the document. However, it can also be used as a placeholder to allow the entry of text. (Which is how we will use it here.) The MacroButton field code lets you create placemarkers in your template that users can click on to enter text. You can include prompts that essentially tell the end user exactly what is expected in the field. When a user clicks the MacroButton, the appropriate prompt is highlighted. Once they've typed the text, the prompt and the field code disappear, to be replaced by the actual text that the user typed. A good example of this technique can be found by exploring the Word fax and letter templates.

1. To create a MacroButton field, position your cursor where the text should appear and choose **Insert | Quick Parts | Field**.

2. From the Categories list, choose **Document Automation**, and from the Field names list, choose **MacroButton**.

3. Now enter a value in the Display text box, such as **TypeNameHere**. This is the text the end user will see.

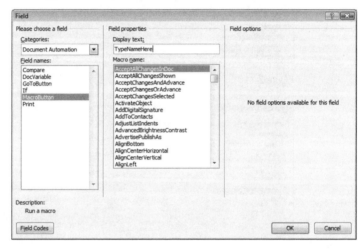

Figure 2-10

4. Now notice the list of macro names in the list box below. The MacroButton, by default, wants to run a macro when the user clicks it. In order to avoid this unwanted behavior, you must "clear out" the macro that is specified by Word (see Figure 2-11). Do this by clicking the **Field Codes** button. Simply replace the default macro with two double quotes (""), as shown in Figure 2-12, and you are ready to use the MacroButton.

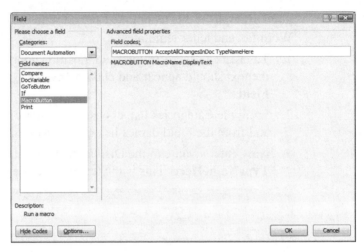

Figure 2-11

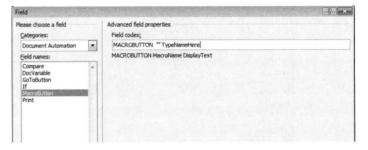

Figure 2-12

5. Click **OK** to finish and you'll see the words appear in the document. If you see the field code {MACROBUTTON YourNameHere}, press Alt+F9 to toggle the display of field codes. Save your template and test the result.

Caution: Make sure you use the double quotes. If you inadvertently have a macro with the name you used as the display text, you may wind up running that instead.

You can have multiple MacroButton fields in a given template; just be sure to keep them properly differentiated. You can also surround the text with specific symbols or characters to provide the user with a visual cue that the field requires editing. Another tip to ensure that fields are not glossed over is to save the document with Field Code shading turned on for all fields. Use **Office button | Word Options | Advanced**, then scroll to the Show document content section and choose **Show field codes instead of their values** to make your field codes stand out even more.

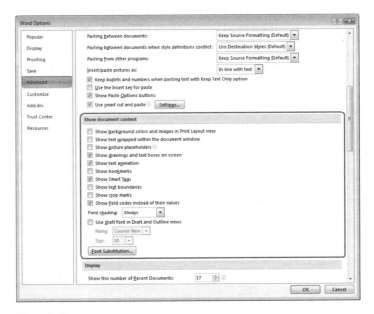

Figure 2-13

The AutoTextList Field

The AutoTextList field code lets you create a drop-down list of AutoText entries. Users select an item from the list to insert that item into the document. Type the entries you want for your drop-down list (single lines or even paragraphs) in a new document. Select them all, and create a new named style for them by choosing the New Style button from the Styles palette. We'll assume you've typed a list of companies and given it the style name CompanyList.

1. One at a time, select each entry and set it as an AutoText entry by choosing **Insert | Quick Parts | Field** and choosing **AutoText** from the Field names list. Click the **Field Codes** button and then the **Options** button. Type the name that will identify this entry in the list, and then click

Add to Field and **OK**. When you're done, you can delete the entries or discard the document. When you select words or phrases as entries, don't include the trailing paragraph marker.

2. To create the AutoTextList to display your entries, choose **Insert | Quick Parts | Field**. From the Categories list, choose **Links and References**, and from the Field names list, choose **AutoTextList**. Then click the Field Codes button to show the codes. Complete the text area so it looks like this:

```
AUTOTEXTLIST "Company list" \s "CompanyList" \t "Right-click to
select a company"
```

The first part of the command is the text that will appear in the document. The part after the \s switch is the name of the style you created. The part after the \t switch is ToolTip text that appears when you hold your mouse over the field code.

Note that once you type the first few letters of a designated AutoText item, the full text will pop up in a floating tip. Pressing Enter will fill in the whole thing.

3. Click **OK** to continue and save the document before testing it.

4. Test the ToolTip text by holding your mouse pointer over the words CompanyList, then right-clicking the field code and choosing an entry from the list.

There are a couple of issues to watch out for, however. First, any feature that displays a right-click menu will override this list, so, for example, make sure Track Changes is turned off before you insert CompanyList. Second, right-clicking the inserted name to access the AutoText list won't work for a name marked as a spelling error. Right-clicking this word will display the spelling pop-up menu.

You can use this AutoTextList field code for selectable lists in document templates, too. Create your list separately, then save the AutoTextList field code itself as an AutoText entry. You can insert the text anywhere you need it.

Prompting for Data Entry

Fill-in Fields

There are two Word field codes that can be used to prompt a user for data entry in a more formal manner than the MacroButton field. These fields are the Ask and Fill-in field codes. These field codes create prompt dialogs for text entry. The resultant dialogs are small and unprofessional looking, similar to using InputBoxes. The main difference between the two is that Fill-in responses appear in one position in the document, and Ask data can be used in multiple places in the document. They're both useful for creating forms and legal contracts.

1. Creating a Fill-in field is easy. You simply click where you want the data to appear and choose **Insert | Quick Parts | Field**. From the Categories list, choose **Mail Merge**, and from the Field names list, choose **Fill-in**.

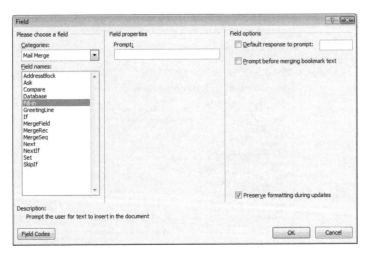

Figure 2-14

2. Once you've entered the prompt and default text, click the **Field Codes** button. This provides a useful method to review the exact syntax of the field code. Once you've reviewed the field code text for accuracy (you can edit here as well), click **OK**. When you see the prompt dialog box appear, click **OK** to accept it. For each entry you expect, create one Fill-in field in the place that the data will appear.

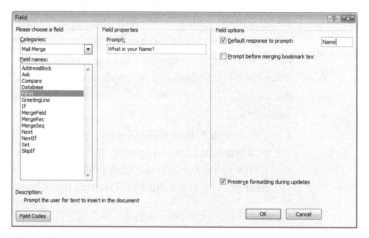

Figure 2-15

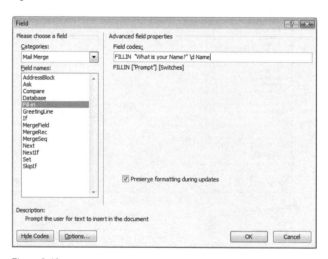

Figure 2-16

3. When you're done, save the document as a template using **Office button | Save As**, and from the Save as type list, choose Word 97-2003 Template (*.dot) or Word Template (*.dotx). Close the document.

Whenever you create a document based on this template, you'll be prompted to enter the data. Once you enter the data, click OK to move to the next input dialog.

Ask Fields

In addition to the Fill-in field, the Ask field lets you prompt the user and then place the resultant data in one or more places in the document. Unlike Fill-in fields, however, Ask fields aren't automatically updated when you create a document based on a template that contains them. Instead, you must update the fields manually, as we'll discuss later. When you create an Ask field, you specify a bookmark name under which to store the data, and then you create references to the bookmark text wherever that data should appear in the document.

Here's how to create an Ask field and place the resulting text in two places in a document.

1. Begin by choosing **Insert | Quick Parts | Field**. From the Field names list, choose **Ask**. Next, fill in the Prompt text box with the prompt you want the user to see (Figure 2-17). The Bookmark name should contain the name of the bookmark that you want to be populated (Figure 2-18). The list box below will contain a list of all the available bookmarks in the document or template that you are creating. You can optionally specify a default response and choose to prompt the user before merging the information to the bookmark.

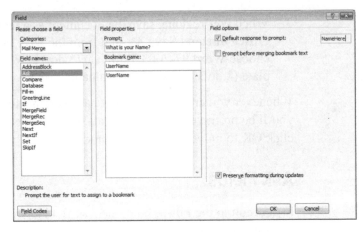

Figure 2-17

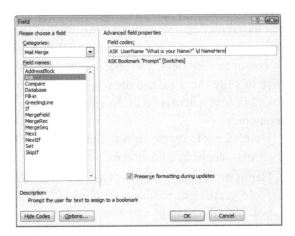

Figure 2-18

2. Click **OK**. A prompt dialog will open; click **OK** to accept it.

3. To create the fields for displaying the text, click in the first position that the name should appear. **Choose Insert | Quick Parts | Field**. From the Categories list, choose **Links and References**, and from the Field names list, choose **Ref**. Click the **Field Codes** button and complete the text area like so: **REF UserName**. This creates a cross-reference to the bookmark called UserName, which is the bookmark name you created in the Ask field.

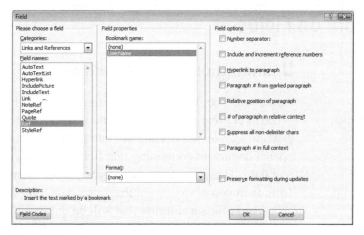

Figure 2-19

4. In the document, you'll see your name appear where you placed the Ref field. Repeat this process to add another Ref field where you want the data to appear a second time. When you're done, save the document either as a regular file or as a template.

5. To test the field, open the file (or create a document based on the template) and update the field codes by choosing **Home | Select | Select All** (or pressing Ctrl+A), then press **F9**. You'll be prompted for your name, and it will then appear in both places in the document.

You can request multiple pieces of text by creating a different Ask field code for each and allocating a different bookmark name to each. You can also automate field code updating by recording these steps as a macro stored in the file. If you name the macro AutoOpen, it will run whenever the file is opened.

More on Fields

Unlinking or Locking a Field

As you can see, fields are an exciting feature of Microsoft Word. Yet there are times when they are a real pain. For example, if you use a Time or Date field, then every time you open a document containing that field it will update to the current date. Typically, however, if you send a letter dated March 15th, then you always want that letter dated the same date.

Word offers a solution that will be quite useful when we get into VBA. That solution involves "unlinking" fields, as follows:

1. Choose **Home | Select | Select All** or, better yet, use the keyboard shortcut, Ctrl+A. Either method has the effect of selecting the entire document.

2. Press **Ctrl+Shift+F9**.

3. Click anywhere on the document to deselect the text.

This procedure has the effect of turning the field codes into regular text and making the field codes disappear. As an alternative, you can lock the fields (i.e., prevent them from being updated or changed) by selecting all of the text as above and pressing Ctrl+F11. Once locked, they can be unlocked by selecting the text and pressing Ctrl+Shift+F11.

Locking is the better alternative if you expect to want to use the fields to update a document after it has been prepared. We, on the other hand, have generally used the unlinking process. You decide which is easier.

Updating Fields

Updating is the process of making sure the value of a field is current. To update a field on a document, select the text containing the field and press F9. If, on the other hand, you open a new document under a template, it will (at least since Word 97) automatically update all fields in the same manner as if you selected the text and pressed F9. Prior to Word 97 it was necessary to use a specialized program called an AutoNew macro to update fields.

Although such a macro is no longer necessary to update fields, we will use it when we get to VBA. Certain fields, specifically the Date and Time fields (and possibly others), automatically update every time a document is opened, whether or not it is a new document. Page fields, used to insert page numbers, automatically update each time text is added or deleted to the extent that a page number is changed.

More on Switches

You have already seen the Date switch — a backslash and an at sign (@) followed by the date format in quotes with "MMMM" representing the month fully written out, "dd" representing the day of the month, and "yyyy" representing the year.

You have further seen the \Charformat switch, which formats the field result's font and font size and whether the field result is bold, italic, and/or underlined; all based upon the first letter in the field. The \Mergeformat switch formats the field result in the same manner as the rest of the paragraph in which it is located. This switch does not, for example, allow the field result to be bolded unless the entire paragraph is bolded.

However, Word will on occasion automatically insert the \Mergeformat switch by itself — which is why we generally add the \Charformat switch to every field. The \Charformat switch does not affect the case of the field result. To do that you have to add *Upper, |*Lower, *Caps, or *FirstCap to the field, generally after the \Charformat switch.

Number Switches

Numbers are formatted using a backslash followed by a pound sign (#) and then the format in quotes. If you want to format a number with two decimal places, you would use \#"0.00". On the other hand, if you are looking for a whole number without a decimal point, you can probably do without a number switch. Lawyers frequently use both words and figures to describe a number. The *CardText switch will write out as text all numbers up to 999,999.99.

By way of an example, we will use the NumPages field, which counts the number of pages in a document. If a document has 35 pages, the field {NUMPAGES *CardText} ({NUMPAGES}) should update to "thirty-five (35)".

A couple of other useful number switches are the *Ordinal and *OrdText switches. The *Ordinal switch returns an ordinal number such as 1st or 2nd. The *OrdText switch converts an ordinal number to text. Accordingly, {Page * OrdText } ({Page * Ordinal }), where the page number is 5, should update to "fifth (5th)".

Dollar Switches

Somewhat more important (at least for us) are the dollar switches. For our example here, we will use a Ref field — one that refers to a bookmark. So, {REF loanamount \#$,0.00}, where loanamount is One Thousand Dollars, will return"$1,000.00". If the loan amount were Five Million Three Hundred Thousand Five Hundred and Forty Dollars and Fifteen Cents, the field result would appear as "$5,300,540.15".

The *DollarText switch will convert numerical dollars into text up to $999,999.99. Continuing with our first example, {REF loanamount *DollarText (REF loanamount \#$,0.00)}, where loanamount is again $1,000, will return "One Thousand Dollars ($1,000.00)".

Content Controls

Word 2007 introduces a new feature that developers and power users can add to their arsenal: content controls. Content controls are Word-based controls that you can use to customize templates, forms, and documents. For example, you can use a traditional ComboBox (albeit, one with a much more fluid presentation in the Word UI) that provides a restricted set of choices for the user of the form.

Content controls can provide instructional text for users, and you can set the controls to disappear when users type in their own text. You can find the content controls for your document on the Developer tab. Figure 2-20 shows the Developer tab and the out-of-the-box content controls. To create a content control through the UI, select the text that you want to turn into a content control and then choose the content control type you want from the Controls section of the Developer tab on the Ribbon. This creates a content control around the selected text.

Figure 2-20

Content Control XML Support

Word 2003 was the first version of Word to support XML interaction by providing the ability to attach an XML schema to a document. Once a schema is attached, you can map elements from an XML file, provided they conformed to the schema. XML schema provides a higher-level test in addition to well-formedness called validation. An XML document must be "valid" according to the schema. This functionality creates an enhanced, easy-to-use document structure that provides easy access to data.

While XML schema was a great first step, there are still limitations; notably, the presentation and custom XML data are linked through the Word application surface. This approach means that end users can accidentally delete part of the XML structure used to define the document, thereby invalidating the document's XML structure according to its schema. Fortunately, Word 2007 addresses this issue with the addition of content controls.

XML Mapping

In order to understand how the XML functionality works in conjunction with content controls, let's look at a quick example. We can start by simply inserting some plain text controls onto the surface of a blank document. As you can see in Figure 2-21, I've entered the following text controls: Company Name, Street Address, and City, State and Zip.

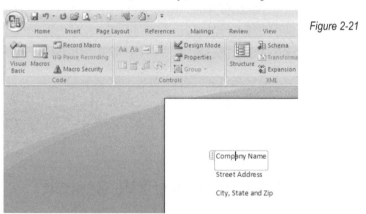

Figure 2-21

You'll notice that the fields look like blank text by default when they are not selected. We'll then map XML elements into these fields with the following steps:

1. Create the text controls shown in Figure 2-21 and then save the document as a Word 2007 Macro Enabled document. This will give the document the .docx file extension. I simply saved the document to C:\wordware\ chapter2\sample.docx, but feel free to save the document anywhere you'd like.

2. The next step is to create a simple data storage document in XML. This can be done by creating a new document, inserting the necessary XML elements, and saving the document as an XML file. I'll create a simple, one-record document (shown below) called Customer that contains elements beneath the root node called CompanyName, StreetAddress, and CityStateZip. This provides content to the structured XML that we will map to the Word content controls.

```xml
<?xml version="1.0"?>
<Customer>
  <CompanyName>Microsoft</CompanyName>
  <StreetAddress>123 Main Street</StreetAddress>
  <CityStateZip>Berwyn, Illinois 60402</CityStateZip>
</Customer>
```

Figure 2-22

3. We will then save the document as an XML file (with the .xml extension). In this case, I have saved the XML file to C:\wordware\chapter2\test.xml.

4. In order to access the XML mapping, we'll need to add a new data store. Data stores are objects that attach data to a Document object. The data can then be retrieved into the document or parsed by calling the CustomXMLPart.Add method of the CustomXMLParts collection in our VBA code.

5. We're going to jump ahead just slightly and write a little VBA code for demonstration purposes. We'll take a deeper look at invoking the methods once we begin discussing VBA. This method instantiates an empty data store object that can be accessed by the document. Please note that calling this method merely creates an empty data store instance. In order to use this empty data store, you'll need to *load* data into the object. We can load a custom XML part from an XML file into the data store object by calling the CustomXMLPart.Load method of the CustomXMLPart object in our VBA code, passing a valid path to the XML file into the parameter.

Based on our example, Figure 2-23 shows the code necessary to map the XML data into the document. We can enter this code in the ThisDocument module of our sample.docx document. Open the Microsoft Visual Basic editor and run the Visual Basic for Applications (VBA) code from Figure 2-23 to add a data store to your document.

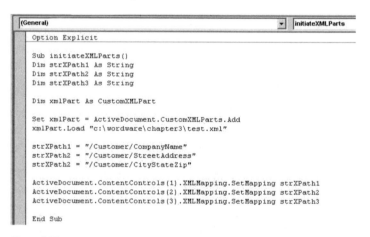

```
(General)                                                    ▼  initiateXMLParts

    Option Explicit

    Sub initiateXMLParts()
    Dim strXPath1 As String
    Dim strXPath2 As String
    Dim strXPath3 As String

    Dim xmlPart As CustomXMLPart

    Set xmlPart = ActiveDocument.CustomXMLParts.Add
    xmlPart.Load "c:\wordware\chapter3\test.xml"

    strXPath1 = "/Customer/CompanyName"
    strXPath2 = "/Customer/StreetAddress"
    strXPath2 = "/Customer/CityStateZip"

    ActiveDocument.ContentControls(1).XMLMapping.SetMapping strXPath1
    ActiveDocument.ContentControls(2).XMLMapping.SetMapping strXPath2
    ActiveDocument.ContentControls(3).XMLMapping.SetMapping strXPath3

    End Sub
```

Figure 2-23

Using Content Controls for Document Automation

You've just seen a quick example of how Word's new content controls can be used for document-based solutions. It should also be easy to imagine how content controls could be used for document automation, including structured document assembly, data capture/extraction, and document construction. Content controls offer template creators another tool to structure arbitrary pieces of a Word 2007 document by using semantics, content restrictions, and behaviors.

There are numerous types of content controls, including text blocks, drop-down menus, combo boxes, calendar controls, and pictures. As you've seen, you can map these content controls to elements in an XML file. Using XML Path Language (XPath), you can programmatically map content in an XML file to a content control. This enables you to write a simple and short application to manipulate and modify data in a document.

Conclusion

As you've seen, Microsoft Word 2007 is easier to use than any previous version, but it is also an amazingly complex tool. Although novice Windows users can generally create a simple document right out of the box, there are many advanced features that even experienced programmers spend countless hours trying to perfect. Remember, there is no "right" way to automate a document. You need to make a careful assessment of what you are trying to accomplish and then use the most efficient route to get to the end result.

Chapter 3

Introduction to VBA

Introduction

In the previous chapter we introduced some Word automation concepts that are available without resorting to programming. The bulk of this book focuses on automation using either VBA or VSTO. This chapter will introduce you to the programming language behind Microsoft Word 2007 and the entire suite of Office 2007 applications as well. This language is called Visual Basic for Applications (VBA), and is used to programmatically automate things such as document creation. Microsoft has been using VBA in Word since version 97, so there is already a wealth of information available. If you are already familiar with VBA, you may want to skim this chapter as a refresher. If you are new to VBA, please read this chapter thoroughly and be sure to acquaint yourself with the Visual Basic Editor (VBE). Also, please pay special attention to the Tips, Notes, and Cautions. These flags have helpful information and, in many cases, may help you avoid pitfalls. Remember, this chapter is meant only as an introduction to VBA; the following chapters are meant to give you a deeper understanding of the VBA programming language.

A Quick Introduction to the Visual Basic Editor (VBE)

VBA has an easy-to-use interface called the Visual Basic Editor (VBE). In order to access the VBE, you first need to display the Developer tab, which you can do by opening an Office 2007 system application, such as Word 2007. Click the **Microsoft Office button**, and then click **Word Options**. The Popular panel of the Word Options dialog box is shown. Click the **Show Developer tab in the Ribbon** check box, as shown in Figure 3-1, then click **OK**. Once the Developer tab is displayed, you can access the Visual Basic Editor in Word by choosing the Visual Basic button (or pressing **Alt+F11**). If you've only been a Word user up until now, the first thing you will notice (see Figure 3-2) is that the VBE doesn't resemble anything close to a document. The VBE is a very powerful development environment.

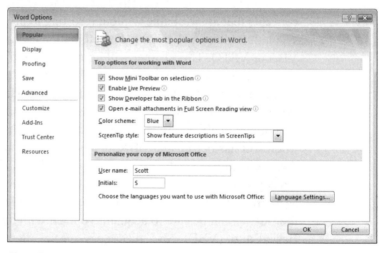

Figure 3-1

The Visual Basic Editor application window is divided into three smaller windows when you first enter it. On the left are the Project Explorer and Properties windows. And to the right, the main window is the Code window. This is where you'll be writing the majority of your code. You can add other debugging windows to monitor variable values while you step through code. We will be discussing the debugging windows later.

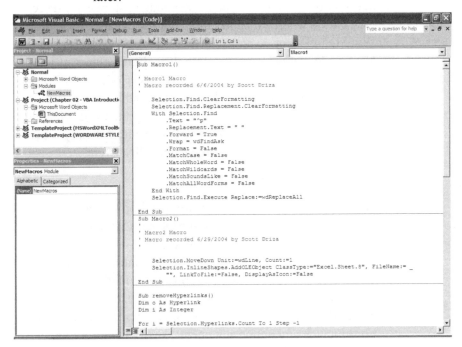

Figure 3-2: The Visual Basic Editor

VBE Component Basics

The Visual Basic Editor contains a number of development tools that were once found only in advanced development environments. Each of these components appears in a different window and each window may be resized, moved, or docked (by double-clicking on the title bar or by choosing Tools | Options | Docking). If you need to view Help for an individual window within VBE, position your cursor within the window and press F1. Each of these windows is described below.

Code Window

As mentioned previously, the main window that occupies the majority of the screen is the Code window, shown in Figure 3-2. This is where you enter the VBA code that lies behind a Word template or document. The Code window displays the VBA code that is associated with the selected object. If you are viewing an object, you can display the Code window by double-clicking the object. For example, add a UserForm, then double-click the UserForm to display the Code window (the process of double-clicking will also automatically create a subroutine for the UserForm_DoubleClick event).

Object List and Procedure List

At the top of the Code window are two drop-downs. The drop-down on the left is called the Object List. It contains a list of all objects in the active module. For instance, when the active module is a UserForm, all of the controls on the UserForm will appear in this drop-down. Finally, most modules also contain a General section. The General section is a place where general declarations can be typed. These declarations include any option statements, such as Option Explicit (to force variable declaration) or Option Compare Text (to compare text rather than ASCII character values). The drop-down on the right is the Procedure and Event List. This list contains all of the available events for the current object.

Project Explorer

In the upper-left corner is the Project Explorer window, shown in Figure 3-3. In Word, this window has a tree struc-ture that represents all open documents and templates. These documents and templates are projects as far as VBA is con-cerned. A project is basically a warehouse for objects and the code behind them. You can click on any of the small plus signs to expand the branch; this will expose any of the five possible nodes: ThisDocument, UserForms, Modules, Class Modules, and References. In addition, there are two small but-tons at the top of the window that can be used to switch between viewing a form and its accompanying code.

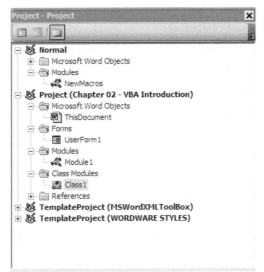

Figure 3-3: The Project Explorer window

ThisDocument

The ThisDocument section contains the properties of the actual document or template. This section operates in a very similar manner to a standard code module. If you are familiar with any of the recent Word macro viruses, you probably have seen how they use this section to propagate.

UserForms

The UserForms branch contains any customized UserForms attached to the document or template. The term "UserForm" is often used interchangeably with "dialog box" (generally, in the VBA vernacular, a *UserForm* is one that is custom created, and a *dialog box* is one that is built into the program). It may help to think of a UserForm as a blank object that can be turned into a dialog box through the use of controls and code. Controls facilitate certain tasks by executing the code behind the control's events. The actual UserForm is manipulated by changing its properties or by adding controls from the Toolbox (Edit | Toolbox). Properties and the VBA Toolbox will be discussed toward the end of this chapter. To insert a UserForm into the document, choose **Insert | UserForm**, as shown in Figure 3-4.

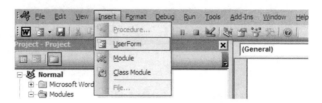

Figure 3-4: Select UserForm from the Insert menu.

Modules

Modules are basically storage areas for procedures (functions and subroutines). Modules come in different varieties. There are class modules and code modules, and technically forms are modules as well. Variables may also be declared outside of procedures in the Modules section.

Class Modules

Class modules are a specialized form of module that allow for the creation of an object. Class modules can be used in creative ways to capture events for many intrinsic objects that are dynamically created or accessed.

References

The References section allows for one project (usually a document) to call procedures in another project (usually the template used to create that document). You will see that references are invaluable for using Office automation. In Word, all documents will contain a reference to the template that was used to create them.

Tip: Do not confuse a reference displayed in the Project Explorer with one that shows up in the Tools|References section. References in Word's Project Explorer are generally other templates. References in the Tools | References section refer to the object libraries available to the project (usually DLL files).

Properties Window

The Properties window appears immediately below the Project window (see Figure 3-5). This window displays the design time properties for the object that has the focus.

Tip: The object may have other properties that do not display in the Properties window. Several objects have properties that are only available at run time.

As a general rule, you can think of properties as the adjectives of an object; they determine an object's characteristics. Common properties include height, width, background color, and font. In addition to these simple properties, all controls have advanced properties that allow greater manipulation to achieve desired results.

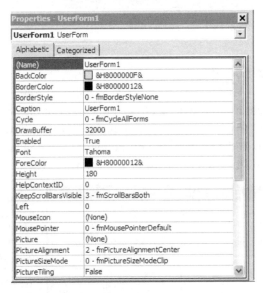

Figure 3-5: The Properties window of the selected object

Note: Some properties may be changed only at run time and thus will not show up in the Properties window, while others are read-only and do not allow the alteration of their values.

VBE Top-Level Menu Bar

Like all Microsoft products, there is a top-level menu bar that provides access to all of the application's features. The VBE is no different. Figure 3-6 shows the top-level menus associated with the VBE. This menu bar provides access to many of the same top-level menus you will find in Word. Most Windows users are familiar with all of the commands that are typically contained in the File menu such as Save, Insert, Cut, Copy, Paste, Find, Redo, Undo, and Help. Below the menu bar is a row of buttons, contained on the Standard toolbar, that include Run, Reset, Break, and Design Mode. The Standard toolbar also has shortcut buttons to display the Properties window, Project Explorer, Toolbox, and Object Browser.

Figure 3-6: Top-level menus of the Visual Basic Editor

VBE Toolbars

Toolbar buttons can be clicked to carry out the corresponding action. If you desire, you can also select the Show ToolTips option in the General tab of the Options dialog box to display tooltips for each of the toolbar buttons.

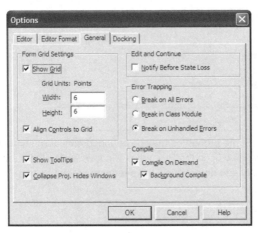

Figure 3-7: To display tooltips for each button in the toolbar, check the Show ToolTips check box found in Tools | Options | General tab.

Edit Toolbar

Figure 3-8 shows the Edit toolbar. This toolbar contains buttons that access some commonly used menu items for editing code. You should make an attempt to become very familiar with this toolbar. Even many experienced programmers waste valuable time searching for information that is available at the click of a button. The Edit toolbar is broken up into four sections divided with vertical bars: Shortcuts, Indents, Comments, and Bookmarks. Following is a brief description of what each of these buttons does.

Figure 3-8: The Edit toolbar

The Shortcut Buttons

List Properties/Methods The first button on the Edit toolbar opens a box in the Code window that indicates the available properties and methods for the object indicated by the cursor.

List Constants The second button opens a box in the Code window listing the valid constants for the property preceding the equal sign (=).

Quick Info This button illustrates the proper syntax for a variable, function, method, or procedure based on the location of the cursor within the name of the variable, function, method, or procedure.

Parameter Info This button displays information about the parameters of the function indicated by the cursor location.

Complete Word This button automatically completes the word you are typing with the characters that Visual Basic inputs through Microsoft's IntelliType feature.

The Indent Buttons

 Indent This button shifts all lines in the current selection to the next tab stop.

 Outdent This button shifts all lines in the current selection to the previous tab stop.

The Comment Buttons

 Toggle Breakpoint This button sets or removes a breakpoint (a temporary halt in the programming code during run time) at the current line. A breakpoint is equivalent to the Stop command. A red indicator will appear to the left of the code (the margin indicator bar) and the line of code will be white on a red background, as shown in Figure 3-9.

Figure 3-9: A breakpoint indicated by the red highlight and button in the margin indicator bar

---

Note: Breakpoints cause normally executing code to enter break mode and display the VBE at the line where the breakpoint occurs. At this point you can use the buttons on the Debug toolbar to step through the code.

 Comment Block This button adds the comment character (') to the beginning of each line of a selected block of text.

Note: Comments allow you to communicate with future programmers (including yourself!). You can store any type of information in a comment, but it is usually best to include the purpose of the procedure and the name of the creator. Comments also often include the date the procedure was created. This may come in handy if you are searching for a procedure based on a specific version.

 Uncomment Block This button removes the comment character from each line of a selected block of text.

The Bookmark Buttons

Bookmarks provide a convenient way to navigate through a VBA project and are indicated by a blue, rounded rectangle next to the code in the margin indicator bar (see Figure 3-10). Bookmarks may be added in a few different ways in VBA. One is to select **Edit | Bookmarks | Toggle Bookmark**. You can also right-click the margin indicator bar next to the appropriate line of code and select Toggle Bookmark. Of course, the easiest method is to use the Toggle Bookmark button on the Edit toolbar.

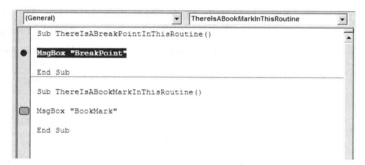

Figure 3-10: A bookmark indicated by the light-blue rectangle in the margin indicator bar

 Toggle Bookmark This button toggles a bookmark on or off for the active line in the Code window.

 Next Bookmark This button moves the focus of the editor to the next bookmark in the bookmark order.

 Previous Bookmark This button moves the focus of the editor to the previous bookmark in the bookmark order.

 Clear All Bookmarks This button removes all bookmarks.

Debug Toolbar

The Debug toolbar is shown in Figure 3-11. This toolbar contains buttons for some commonly used debugging features.

Figure 3-11: The Debug toolbar

Design Mode This button turns Design mode off and on. The Design mode allows you to edit objects in the VBA project.

Run This button runs the current selection. This may be a procedure if the cursor is in a procedure, a UserForm if the UserForm is the currently active selection, or a macro.

Break This button stops execution of a program while it is running and switches to break mode.

Reset This button resets the project. All variables will lose their values and control will return to the user.

Toggle Breakpoint This button operates similarly to the Toggle Bookmark button in that it sets or removes a breakpoint at the current line.

Stepping Through a Project

The Debug toolbar provides access to some of the most powerful debugging techniques available. Stepping through a project (halting at each line of code) allows you to monitor variable values, loops, and program flow. Each button of the Debug toolbar also has a corresponding keystroke combination. The next line to be executed will be highlighted in yellow, with a yellow arrow displayed in the margin indicator bar, as shown in Figure 3-12.

Figure 3-12: A project shown halted in debug mode is indicated by the yellow highlight and arrow in the margin indicator bar.

Tip: You can monitor variables using one of the windows discussed below, or you can simply position your cursor atop the variable to display the value via control tip text.

Step Into (F8) This button executes code one line at a time.

Step Over (Shift+F8) This button executes code one procedure or line at a time in the Code window.

Step Out (Ctrl+Shift+F8) This button executes the remaining lines of a procedure in which the cursor lies.

Monitoring Project Values

Oftentimes your program may run without encountering an error, but the end result will be incorrect in some way. This is most likely due to a logic flaw in your code. Keeping track of a variable's value and stepping through a project may show you where the flaw occurs. VBA is especially robust when it comes to monitoring values. In this section, we discuss the monitoring options available through the Debug toolbar.

Locals Window This button displays the Locals window, shown in Figure 3-13. The Locals window allows you to monitor all variables in any procedure. In break mode, the Locals window displays each variable and its corresponding value (at that given time) in the current procedure on a separate line. The topmost line is the name of the module. If you expand the variable, you will see a list of the global variables.

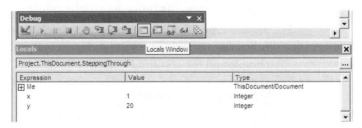

Figure 3-13: The Locals window is displayed after the Locals Window button in the Debug toolbar is clicked.

Watches Window This button displays the Watches window, shown in Figure 3-14. Sometimes you will want to watch more than just the values of a variable. The Watches window allows you to monitor the result of any expression or the value of an object's property.

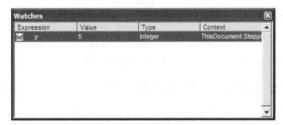

Figure 3-14: The Watches window of the Visual Basic Editor

You will need to set up watch expressions in order to monitor either of these through the Watches window. In order to set up a watch, use the following procedure:

1. Select the expression by placing the cursor inside the word for single-word expressions or by highlighting the entire expression.

2. Select **Debug | Add Watch** or right-click the selection and select **Add Watch** to display the Add Watch dialog box.

3. If the expression isn't shown in the Expression text box, you may enter the expression manually. The value you enter can be any valid variable name, a property, a user-defined function name, or a valid VBA expression.

4. Use the Context section to specify where the variable is used, including the procedure and module.

5. Set the type of watch to specify how VBA will react. The following table displays the different watch types you can choose and the resulting behavior.

Watch Type	Explanation
Watch Expression	The expression will be displayed in the window in break mode.
Break When Value Is True	VBA will stop executing and enter break mode when the expression value becomes True.
Break When Value Changes	VBA will stop executing and enter break mode when the expression value changes.

6. Click **OK**.

The Watches window allows you to view the values of a given expression, but doesn't allow you to manipulate that value. If you need to manipulate a value, you can use the Immediate window.

Immediate Window This button displays the Immediate window, which is displayed in Figure 3-15. The Immediate window can be used to test experimental statements to see how they affect a procedure, to change the value of a variable or property, or to run other procedures. You can type lines of code in the Immediate window just as you would in the Code window.

Figure 3-15: The Immediate window and Immediate Window button of the Debug toolbar

Note: VBA will try to execute the code after the Enter key is pressed.

Quick Watch This button displays the Quick Watch dialog box (shown in Figure 3-16) with the current value of the selected expression.

Figure 3-16: The Quick Watch dialog box

Call Stack This button displays the Call Stack dialog box, which lists the currently active procedure calls (procedures in the project that have started but are not completed).

Tip: Understanding the call stack can be a good way to prevent problems. In a large project you may show and hide several UserForms. Remember that the procedure that shows a UserForm doesn't finish executing.

UserForm Toolbar

The UserForm toolbar is shown in Figure 3-17. This toolbar contains buttons that are useful for working with forms.

Figure 3-17: The UserForm toolbar

Note: The UserForm toolbar is used to manipulate an existing form. To add a UserForm, either use the Insert UserForm button on the Standard toolbar or select Insert | UserForm.

Bring To Front This button moves the selected control(s) to the front of all other controls on a form.

Send To Back This button moves the selected control(s) behind all other controls on a form.

Group This button is used to create a group of controls. Draw a box around the controls that you wish to group together and click this button to form a group.

Note: Groups are useful to work with when aligning controls to a form. You can also select a control, press Shift, and continue selecting controls to cut or copy a number of controls.

Ungroup This button ungroups the controls that were previously grouped.

Alignment

The Alignments drop-down is shown in Figure 3-18. In order for any application to be successful, the user must easily understand it. One of the most frequent mistakes programmers make is to design an unfriendly interface. Jagged edges, unaligned controls, poor color choices, and inconsistency all lead to design disaster. Fortunately, Microsoft provides many tools to help you get your design RIGHT! Following are the choices available from the Alignments drop-down on the UserForm toolbar.

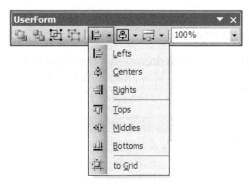

Figure 3-18: Alignment choices from the Alignments drop-down on the UserForm toolbar

Lefts Aligns the horizontal position of the selected controls according to the leftmost edges.

Centers Aligns the horizontal position of the selected controls according to the centers of each control.

Rights Aligns the horizontal position of the selected controls according to the rightmost edges.

Tops Aligns the vertical position of the selected controls according to the top of each control.

Middles Aligns the vertical position of the selected controls according to the middle of each control.

Bottoms Aligns the vertical position of the selected controls according to the bottom of each control.

To Grid Aligns the top left of the selected controls to the closest grid line.

Centering

The Centering drop-down is shown in Figure 3-19. The options in this drop-down allow you to center controls on the form either horizontally or vertically.

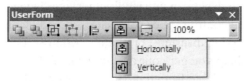

Figure 3-19: The Centering drop-down on the UserForm toolbar

Make Same Size

The Make Same Size drop-down is shown in Figure 3-20. The options in this drop-down allow you to adjust the control's width, height, or both at the same time.

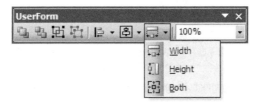

Figure 3-20: The Make Same Size drop-down on the UserForm toolbar

Zoom

The Zoom drop-down is shown in Figure 3-21. Choose a setting from the list to reduce or enlarge the display of all controls on the UserForm. You can set any magnification from 10 to 200 percent.

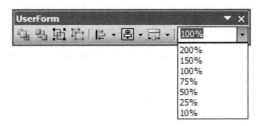

Figure 3-21: The Zoom drop-down on the UserForm toolbar

Object Browser

Figure 3-22 shows the Object Browser. You may access the Object Browser by selecting **View | Object Browser** or by pressing **F2**. The Object Browser is used to browse through all available objects in your project. It displays each object's properties, methods, and events. You can also see the procedures and constants available from the different object libraries in your project. The Object Browser is capable of displaying all objects, including objects you create as well as objects from other applications.

Figure 3-22: The Object Browser. The shortcut keystroke for the Object Browser is F2.

The Object Browser becomes especially useful when you add a reference to an external object. In the upper-left corner of the Object Browser is a drop-down that allows you to select a single library for viewing. This allows you to determine exactly what properties, methods, and events pertain to the newly referenced object.

The Visual Basic Environment

Procedures

Procedures encompass both functions and subroutines. These can be distinguished by the syntax in which they appear.

This procedure is a subroutine:

```
Sub Subroutine1()
    'Underlying Code
End Sub
```

This procedure is a function:

```
Function Function1() As Integer
    'Underlying code and return value
End Function
```

There are two ways to insert a procedure into a code module. The first is to choose the appropriate module and then choose **Insert | Procedure**, which opens the dialog box shown in Figure 3-23.

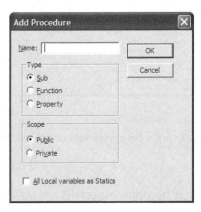

Figure 3-23: The Add Procedure dialog box

The second (and easier) method is just to type either "Sub" for a subroutine or "Function" for a function followed by the appropriate name in the Code window. When you press Enter, the VBE automatically creates an "End Sub" (or "End Function") and moves the cursor to the preceding line. Now you can simply start typing your code.

You can think of procedures as all of the different actions that your program can execute. You can manipulate your code to trigger different procedures depending on different events. Generally, you want your procedures to perform only one specific event so that you can reuse procedures to accomplish the same tasks with different code. For example, you may have a project that has multiple UserForms that all have a button that will determine the number of loaded UserForms at any one time and also gives the name of the active UserForm. Rather than writing procedures behind each command button, you could have publicly declared procedures in a module that would be available to all of the UserForms. This also makes it easier to add additional UserForms. The ability to reuse portions of your code in different areas is referred to as the *modularity* of your code. Following is a brief description of functions and subroutines.

Functions

Functions can be either private or public. This is referred to as *scope* and is relevant with all procedures and applies in a very similar manner to variables. The best programming practice is to declare them private, which means they will be locally available, unless you are going to access them from other modules. Scope refers to the visibility of functions, subs, or variables to other modules. The Visual Basic Editor doesn't require you to declare the function as private or public, but it is good programming practice to declare everything explicitly from the outset so others can determine your intent. By default, functions are private unless declared otherwise.

The main difference between functions and subroutines is that functions can return a value to the calling procedure while subroutines cannot. To return a value from a function, we must assign a variable that returns the value. See the following example:

```
Private Sub ShowMsg()
    MsgBox "The number is " & NumReturn(4)
End Sub
Private Function NumReturn(iNumber As Integer) As Integer
```

```
        NumReturn = iNumber * 5
End Function
```

In the above example, the subroutine ShowMsg calls a message box (a built-in VBA feature) and displays the result of the NumReturn function when the number 4 is passed as an argument. The function multiplies the integer 4 by the number 5 and returns an integer, 20, that will be displayed in the message box. Also, notice the ampersand (&) is used to tie together the language and the number. This sign can be used to tie together different information. This is known as *concatenation* and will be discussed periodically throughout this book.

Subroutines

Subroutines are identical to functions concerning scope. Subroutines may be declared as either public or private. The main difference is that subroutines do not return values. However, you can call subroutines from other subroutines. There will be instances where you call subroutines to manipulate either module-level or public variables that might be used by other functions or subroutines. While this is not good programming practice, it is important to remember if you will be trying to interpret the code of others. Please look closely at the following example:

```
Option Explicit
Public iNumber As Integer
Private Sub ShowMsg()
        iNumber = 4
        NumChange
        MsgBox "The number is " & iNumber
End Sub
Private Sub NumChange()
        iNumber = (iNumber * 5)
End Sub
```

Running the ShowMsg subroutine here produces the same result as the function shown previously, namely, a message box with the number 20 displayed in it. Here, the number 4 is also multiplied by 5, but we are using a subroutine to modify a public variable. We dimension (declare) the variable public at the module level so it will be available to both procedures. The ShowMsg subroutine sets the variable iNumber equal to 4 and then runs the embedded subroutine NumChange, which multiplies the variable by 5. Then ShowMsg finishes by displaying the message box with the number 20. Notice, however, that if the variable were declared within the ShowMsg subroutine, a compile error (variable not defined) would result because NumChange would not be able to "see" the variable. Its scope would then be limited to only the procedure in which it is declared.

Parameters and Arguments

Anything following either a sub or a function that is enclosed in brackets is a parameter of that procedure. The value of a parameter is called its *argument*. If you begin typing a predefined VBA function that requires arguments (i.e., has parameters), you'll notice that some of the arguments are included in brackets while others are not. See Figure 3-24.

Figure 3-24: Example of a function with required and optional parameters. Optional parameters are enclosed in brackets ([ ]) while required parameters are not.

Anything that is not enclosed in brackets is a required parameter. If an argument is not assigned to such a parameter, the procedure will fail. It almost goes without saying that if a parameter is optional (included in brackets), then it is not necessary to assign an argument to it.

When declaring a function, you will want to assign a variable type for the return value as well as define any parameters that will be used in the function. See the example in Figure 3-25 for declaring parameters.

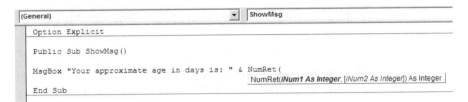

Figure 3-25: The NumRet function indicating it has the required parameter, iNum1, and an optional parameter, iNum2

Notice that we have an optional parameter, *iNum2*, in our function. The IntelliType feature shows both parameters. The optional parameter is in brackets, as illustrated above.

UserForms

UserForms are the medium through which you will interact with users. Think of these as your own customizable dialog boxes. Broadly defined, they are objects. They have properties and methods that allow you to change the way they look and act. (We'll discuss these properties and methods shortly.) To create a UserForm, simply choose **Insert | UserForm** as shown in Figure 3-26.

Figure 3-26: Create a UserForm in your project by selecting Insert | UserForm.

The first thing you should always do after inserting a UserForm is give it a distinct name. If you have a project with multiple UserForms, you don't want to get confused by names like UserForm1, UserForm2, and so on. Because they are objects and can be confused with other types of objects, a simple naming convention for forms is to have the first three letters be "frm." The importance of standard naming conventions cannot be overstated. For example, there will be instances where you will need to create collections. One of the easiest ways to do so is to loop through certain variables, controls, etc., and add those with a certain prefix.

Adding Controls to a UserForm with the VBA Toolbox

A UserForm by itself is capable of doing basically nothing. In order to make a UserForm useful it is necessary to bring out the VBA Toolbox to insert any of the various controls that can be found on it. Select **View | Toolbox** to display the dialog box shown in Figure 3-27.

Figure 3-27: The Toolbox dialog

It's a good idea to become familiar with the sizing, shaping, and removal of controls. Notice that when you click on a control, the Properties window will show the properties of the control rather than the properties of the UserForm. You can change any of these before the program is run (design time) or you can include code that will change any of these properties while the program is running (run time).

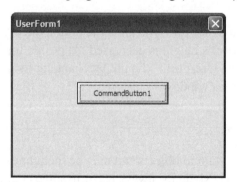

Figure 3-28: UserForm1 with one CommandButton control

To see how a UserForm can be changed at run time, try the following example:

1. Insert a UserForm, like the one shown in Figure 3-28, and put a CommandButton near the top.

2. In the design environment, double-click on the CommandButton; this should take you to the Code window behind the UserForm. Insert the following subroutine for the CommandButton1_Click event:

```
Private Sub CommandButton1_Click()
    Me.Height = Me.Height - 5
End Sub
```

3. You can return to the UserForm by clicking the UserForm icon at the top of the Project Explorer window. Note that you can easily change between a UserForm and its code by using this method. Now, run the UserForm either by pressing **F5** with the UserForm highlighted or by pressing the Run Macro button (▶) in the Standard toolbar, as shown in Figure 3-29.

Figure 3-29: You can run the UserForm by pressing the Run Macro button.

Notice that every time you click the button the event fires and the UserForm's height is decreased. At design time you could decrease the UserForm's height by changing its property in the Properties window.

Methods

Methods pertain to objects and may be thought of as the verbs of the object. Methods always perform some action. Figure 3-30 shows how methods and properties are displayed in the Object Browser. You can access the Object Browser in the VBE by pressing **F2** or selecting **View | Object Browser**.

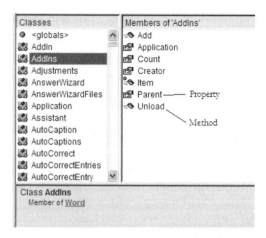

Figure 3-30: Viewing methods and properties in the Object Browser window

Let's illustrate by taking a look at the ActiveDocument object, which represents the document with the focus in a Word session. Its methods are comprised of the same things you might manually do when interacting with a document: Save, SaveAs, Close, etc. Methods often involve the use of arguments, many of which may not be required for the method to execute. The Close method uses the following syntax:

```
ActiveDocument.Close(SaveChanges, [OriginalFormat],
[RouteDocument])
```

In the above example, the only required argument is *SaveChanges*. If you try to execute the Close method without passing a valid argument, an error will be generated. There are two valid ways of passing arguments. One is by separating the arguments by commas. However, the better alternative is to use named arguments. Using named arguments will make your code much easier for a future programmer to read because he or she can see what arguments are being used. Another advantage is that named arguments may be declared in any order. Named arguments use the name of the argument followed by a specific operator (:=) and the value for the argument. For example:

```
ActiveDocument.Close SaveChanges:=wdDoNotSaveChanges
```

A final note is that optional arguments will always show up in brackets ([ ]) to indicate that they are not required. Optional arguments may be passed the same as required arguments. Optional arguments will also always appear at the end of the arguments section.

Properties

While you can think of methods as the verbs of the object, properties can be thought of as the adjectives that describe the object. Height, width, color, and border style are all general examples of properties. They have much the same syntax as methods in that they appear immediately following a period after an object's name. For example:

```
ActiveDocument.Name
```

Properties entail two additional dimensions that methods do not. Properties can be either read-only or both read and write. The above example is a read-only property. This means that it can only return the value of the Name property as it exists in the active document.

However, there are some objects where the Name property is both read and write. The Font object is an example of an object with a read/write Name property. You can use Font.Name to return the value of the current font, or you could use Font.Name=Arial to set the current font. All properties may be set using the "=" operator.

What perplexes most beginners is that some properties may do double duty as objects. Again, Font is a good example. Font is a property of the ActiveDocument object in addition to being its own object. In other words, it represents a property of the ActiveDocument, and it is an object with its own individual properties, such as Bold.

Modules

Modules are the areas where the code is stored. This makes modules the storage house for your code. It is important to note that there are a few different types of modules: "regular" modules, form modules, ThisDocument modules, and class modules. Choosing Module from the Insert menu creates what is normally referred to as a "module." It can be referenced globally throughout the project.

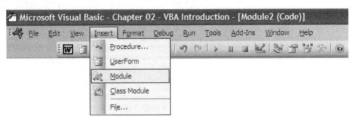

Figure 3-31: Inserting a module through the Insert menu

Another example of a module is the code that exists behind a form. This is often referred to as a form module. The form is just the graphical representation of all the properties that make up the form. These properties are given a default value so there is something to initialize (and it saves you the trouble of building one from scratch!).

Every document and template will contain a ThisDocument module that contains the code underlying the actual document. It also contains properties that can be manipulated in the Properties window or by code. ThisDocument is also an object in Word.

Lastly, there are class modules. Class modules may also be inserted through the use of the Insert menu. For now, you can think of them as special-duty modules that enable you to create your own objects.

Modules may be imported or exported through the use of the File menu in the Visual Basic Editor. This allows you to reuse code that you create in other projects. The same is true of UserForms and class modules. Modules that are exported will have the file extension .bas.

Events

The most important thing to know about VBA programming is that it is event driven. All of your code will be triggered by predefined things that the user can do. Clicking on a button, scrolling on a page, and expanding a drop-down list are all examples of events. The upper right-hand corner of the Code window in the VBE contains a drop-down list that contains all the events that correspond to whatever object is in the accompanying object drop-down to the immediate left (see Figure 3-32).

Figure 3-32: All the events (shown in the drop-down on the right) associated with the UserForm object

These events are triggered by certain user actions. Some events are intuitive, such as clicking, but for other events, you may have to resort to the Microsoft Help files. When programming, always make sure that you capture the action that you intend the user to follow.

In addition, Word provides some automatic events that come in handy when creating a template system. You can trigger code to execute whenever a document is opened, closed, or created by choosing **File | New**.

Class Modules

Class modules give programmers the ability to create and manipulate their own classes of objects. Class modules are extremely powerful and useful. One of the main benefits of class modules is that they lend themselves to modularity. That is, once you've created your own custom object replete with properties and methods, you'll find that you can probably reuse it in another project.

Another advantage of class modules is that they embody the idea of encapsulation. In other words, you can control the manipulation of the data that your object represents. Rather than manipulating the raw data, you will be using the properties and methods of your object to control the process.

Figure 3-33: The procedures of a class module are shown in the drop-down to the right.

Although class modules define the properties and methods of the object, those properties and methods do not manipulate the object by themselves. To actually manipulate the data, you will be instantiating the object, calling its methods, and setting its properties. Although class modules can be difficult to understand, it's easy to think of them as an intermediate part of programming. Class modules are simply a means to create your own objects. You can then use those objects in your project as you would use any of the built-in objects.

Conclusion

This chapter introduced you to Visual Basic for Applications, the programming language behind the Microsoft Office 2007 programs. If you are new to VBA, you should refer to this chapter often, as it can serve as a refresher. Although the examples were very basic, they will help you build confidence as you proceed through the book. This chapter also covered the Visual Basic Editor and many of its components, in addition to touching on the elements of VBA programming, including events, modules, functions, and subroutines. Now that you've gotten your feet wet, please read the following chapters closely.

Chapter 4

Word 2007 and VBA

Introduction

In this chapter we take a look at many of Word's features that are important in the development of automated Word solutions. Throughout this book, we will discuss the means necessary to integrate all of these features through VBA, XML, and code-behind documents using Visual Studio 2008. Now it's time to see how Word interacts with VBA. Word 2007 has the most extensive set of customization options of all Office applications.

You will need to understand these options for the automated documents that you create. Almost anything that can be done normally in Word can be controlled programmatically. Remember that the goal of document automation is to create documents quickly and to ensure that the finished document is free of errors.

Word Macros

Macros are small chunks of VBA code that programmatically perform tasks. Macros give the everyday user the power to automate routine tasks at the touch of a button. Each of Word's built-in functions is controlled by its own macro(s) (more on this later). Rather than utilizing a proprietary macro language, Microsoft implemented VBA, which is syntactically identical to Visual Basic, so that users could learn a language that could be used across applications.

How Macros Work

We've already noted that macros are basically just small chunks of code. Every time a macro is recorded, Word stores the resulting VBA code in the appropriate template. Each macro is stored as a separate subroutine. You can also attach your custom macros to buttons or keystrokes, or you can tie the macro to predefined events. Once a macro is recorded, you can manipulate the code in the VBE. This means the macro can be modified to call other macros, open dialog boxes, return values (turned into a function), or even open and work with other applications.

To perform any of these tasks, you must understand VBA. Using both VBA and the Word Object Model, you can dive deep down into Word and control some of the most advanced Word functions programmatically. VBA also includes functions, statements, and access to type libraries that enable you to perform various file manipulations, store data, etc. If VBA doesn't provide the functionality that you require, you may need to investigate code behind documents (an older approach) or the new VSTO solutions offered in Visual Studio 2008.

Recording a Macro

The easiest way to create a macro is to use the Macro Recorder (**Developer tab | Record Macro**). Once you name your macro and click **OK**, you simply carry out your task as you normally would. When you are finished, click **Stop Recording**. The Macro Recorder records each step you perform and translates the step into VBA code. You can then view and modify the procedure in the Visual Basic Editor.

Tip: Keep in mind that there are limitations on what you can record. For instance, the Macro Recorder is not able to track your tasks as you switch between applications. However, just because the Macro Recorder isn't capable of recording such a task, please don't think that it's impossible for VBA to complete such a task. As you will see, VBA is capable of doing almost anything you can do manually.

Planning Macros

Before recording any macro, it is advisable to plan out the steps necessary to accomplish exactly what you want. The Macro Recorder will often record much more than just the bare minimum code. If you record a macro and perform trial and error until you get it right, your recorded code will be a bloated mess. Of course, you can always edit the macro, but it's better to start with a plan.

When you choose Record Macro from the Developer tab, the Record Macro dialog box appears, as shown in Figure 4-1. The text box at the top is where you type the name for your new macro.

Make sure that you assign an appropriate name to the macro. Word will automatically assign a generic name, such as "Macro1." The best convention is to enter a short, descriptive name so that in the future you will know exactly why the macro was created. If the OK button is not enabled, you have probably entered an invalid name. Macro names must begin with a letter and cannot have any spaces.

The default location to store a macro is in the Normal template. This will make the macro available to all documents because the Normal template is a global template. Every time you open Word the macro will be available. If you store the macro in a different document, it will only be available when that document is active. If you store the macro in a different template, it will be available when a document based on that template is open. Although macros usually reside in a standard module named NewMacros, it is possible to place macros in the ThisDocument module of a document.

The Description text box allows for the entry of a description of the macro. This text will appear in the VBA code that the Macro Recorder creates. This text will be commented out so the compiler doesn't generate an error when it comes across the text. Commented code is always preceded by an apostrophe. Finally, you will notice in Figure 4-1 that you can assign the macro to a toolbar or to the keyboard.

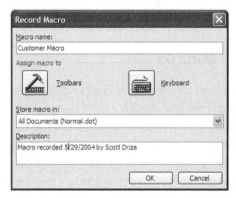

Figure 4-1: You can set your newly recorded macro to a toolbar or to the keyboard.

Shortcut Keys

Shortcut keys provide a convenient way to make your macros available to a user. The downfall is that there is no graphical representation of the macro (a button). Many users remember the days when everything was handled by shortcut keys. Early word processing applications were notorious for having confusing key combinations, but the more modern WYSIWYG interfaces alleviated the need to have the cardboard key indicator sitting above the function keys. These functions are mostly still available through the key combinations, but most users prefer mouse-driven applications.

With all this in mind, there will still be times when you want to have keystroke-driven macros. For example, the

Word toolbars can seem pretty cluttered without having custom macros on them, and if you start adding your own toolbars and buttons, you may overwhelm users. Save the toolbar buttons for the most frequently used macros. If users hunt around to learn the keystroke combination for a macro once or twice, they will remember it.

Assigning a keystroke combination is very easy. Figure 4-2 shows the dialog box that is displayed when you choose to assign the macro to the keyboard (**Office button | Word Options | Customize | Customize** (located at the bottom left of the window)).

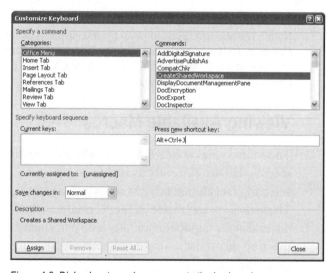

Figure 4-2: Dialog box to assign a macro to the keyboard

The Save changes in drop-down lists the available documents and templates where the key assignment may be saved. Save your changes in a global template if you want to make the change universally available. Again, it is best to save these types of customizations in the Normal template.

The Current keys section displays the current key assignment for the highlighted macro. This section is updated once a key combination is entered in the Press new shortcut key section and the Assign button is clicked. You can use the Remove button to remove individual keystroke settings. Also, you can use Reset All to remove all of the custom keyboard combinations. Finally, be sure not to overwrite any existing keystroke combinations. Combinations that are already assigned will appear directly below the Press new shortcut key text box.

Tip: Remember that you can always remove toolbars, buttons, or keystroke combinations that you don't want. Also, you can easily print a list of shortcut keys. Select Developer tab | Macros and select Word commands from the Macros in drop-down list. Then, in the Macro name box, click ListCommands and then click the Run button. In the List Commands dialog box, choose Current keyboard settings and click OK. Then print the document.

Note: The shortcut keys mentioned in the Help files all refer to a standard U.S. keyboard layout. Foreign keyboards may not match the keys on a U.S. keyboard, so you may have to make adjustments when using shortcut keys.

Viewing Available Macros

The Macros dialog box (shown in Figure 4-3) displays all macros that are currently available and can be accessed by selecting **Developer tab | Macros** or by pressing **Alt+F8**. These macros can reside in the Normal template, an active document, or a global template. You can change the option in the drop-down list to make only certain documents' macros available.

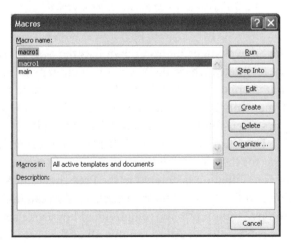

Figure 4-3: The Macros dialog box showing available macros

Choosing a macro and pressing the **Edit** button opens the Visual Basic Editor and displays the code behind the chosen macro. Notice that the code contains the commented text, which was automatically created by the Macro Recorder. You are free to edit this code and alter the macro in any way you choose. Frequently, Office programmers find themselves stuck trying to write complex routines only to remember that they can use the Macro Recorder to provide the necessary code.

Macro Errors

Your recorded macro may not run correctly in every situation. Word will generate an error if the macro is unable to run. There may be certain options or settings that have changed since the macro was recorded. For example, a macro that searches for hidden text won't run properly if there is no hidden text to be displayed.

Note: Always write the error number down. You can then search for that specific error message in the Help files.

Macro Organizer

Word provides a great tool to move macros from one Word project to another. This tool, which can be accessed with the Organizer button in the Macros dialog box (**Developer tab | Macros | Organizer**), is also capable of moving modules, class modules, and UserForms in the same manner (see Figure 4-4). The other tabs of the Organizer window facilitate the transfer of styles, AutoText, and toolbars from one Word project to another.

Each document or template represents a single project. The Organizer allows you to move parts of these projects. If you have some very useful macros in one template, you can use the Organizer to transfer them to a new project. This is much easier than cutting and pasting large blocks of text in the VBE.

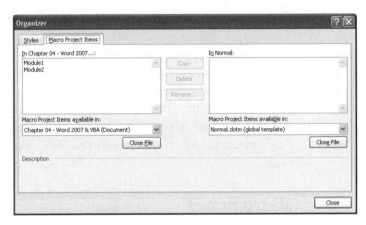

Figure 4-4: The Organizer window

Macro Security

Although macros were originally meant to automate certain tasks such as certain keystrokes or mouse clicks, they can also be designed to do far more complex tasks. This is what makes macros such a great tool, but at the same time, a potential security risk. Since any developer can write code that will run many commands on your computer, a hacker can easily create a document with a malicious macro attached to it that is designed to spread a virus to your computer when opened. According to your needs as a user, you should adjust the security settings of Word. The Trust Center window (shown in Figure 4-5) is where you can specify these security settings. It can be accessed by selecting **Office button | Word Options | Trust Center | Trust Center Settings | Macro Settings**.

If you don't see a warning when opening a document that contains macros, the security level for Word is probably set to Low. Setting the security level to Medium will warn you that a document or add-in contains macros.

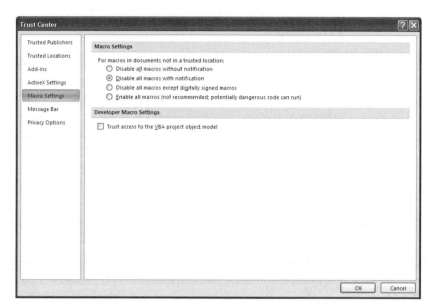

Figure 4-5: Macro Settings on the Trust Center window

Note: If you or someone you have designated as a trusted source developed the macros, you will not be warned. If you designate a macro developer as a trusted source, Word will open the document and enable the macros.

You can easily remove someone from the trusted source list. If you have no one listed in the list of trusted sources, Word will prompt you every time you open a document or load an add-in that contains macros.

In unfamiliar documents, you should confirm that the macros were signed and check the source of the document. In the VBE, simply choose Digital Signature from the Tools menu.

Caution: Documents stored in the folder where a user's templates reside will not trigger a warning. You can set a default location for user templates on the File Locations tab in the Options dialog box. By default, this location is implicitly trusted. You won't see a warning when you open documents or templates that contain macros from this location.

Warnings

If you open a document or load an add-in that contains digitally signed macros but the digital certificate has not been authenticated, you will receive a warning. This warning appears in the Security Warning box if the security level for Microsoft Word is set to High or Medium. For example, if the macro developer has created his or her own digital certificate, you will receive this warning. This type of unauthenticated certificate can be forged to falsify the identity of the certificate's source. For example, a malicious user might create a certificate named "Microsoft Corporation." The only warning you have that the certificate is false is this specific warning. As a general rule, professional software developers should always use authenticated certificates. You should only accept unauthenticated certificates from individual co-workers or friends. Don't accept one from a source you don't know!

If you are in an Office development team for a large organization, the best bet is to set the Word security level to High and select the Always trust macros from this source check box to enable your macros. Remember, even a setting of Medium will not require you to add the macro developer to the list of trusted sources if it is digitally signed. Word macro viruses are extremely prevalent; if you do not know who authored a macro, do not enable that macro. Do not even open the document until you have verified the source is safe.

Word's AutoMacros

Word contains many macros that run automatically. Although these are often referred to as "AutoMacros," they are simply events that can drive the execution of VBA code. Following are Word's most frequently used AutoMacros.

AutoExit

This macro runs whenever you exit the Word application. An AutoExit macro should be stored in either the Normal template or any other globally available template. Remember that a macro is only available if the document or template to which it is attached is available. The Normal and global templates are available at all times.

AutoClose

This is the appropriate macro to run when closing an individual template or document instead of the entire application. When this macro is stored in a template, it will run any time a document based on that template is closed.

AutoNew

This macro runs when a new document is created based on the template that contains the macro.

AutoOpen

This macro runs anytime a template or document is opened.

Differentiating Word's Document Events

The names AutoClose, AutoNew, and AutoOpen have been kept the same in Word 2007 for compatibility with versions of Word all the way back to Word 97. You can also use events to control macro execution under the same circumstances. The Document_New event corresponds to the AutoNew macro. The Document_Open event corresponds to the AutoOpen macro. Finally, the Document_Close macro corresponds to the AutoClose macro. As you will see, these events and macros can act differently depending on where they are placed.

You write procedures to respond to these events in the ThisDocument module or in a standard code module, such as NewMacros. Use the following steps to create an event procedure:

1. In the VBE, open the Project Explorer window, choose a project, and double-click **ThisDocument**. ThisDocument is located in the Microsoft Word Objects folder.

2. Select **Document** from the Object drop-down list and select an event from the Procedure drop-down list. This will add an empty subroutine to the ThisDocument module.

3. You can then add whatever VBA code you want to control the triggering of that event. The code below uses the MsgBox function to display information to the user. When it is placed in the Normal project, it will run when a new document based on the Normal template is created:

```
Private Sub Document_New()
    MsgBox "A new document has been created."
End Sub
```

Event procedures in the Normal template do not have a global scope. More precisely, event procedures residing in the Normal template will only be fired if the document is attached to the Normal template. This difference in functionality can be very important when choosing which way to automate your documents.

Note: If there are AutoMacros in both the document and the attached template, only the AutoMacro in the document will execute. Conversely, if a project has an event procedure in both the document and its attached template, both event procedures will run.

Changing Word's Built-in Macros

You can tweak Word so that it can only be used for specific purposes or so that only specific templates are available to users by writing subroutines that are named the same as a command in Word. These subroutines will replace Word's automatic commands. This can be extremely useful when developing a customized documentation system. To see a list of the names of all Word commands, choose Word Commands from the Macros in list box.

The following code illustrates how Word's built-in macros can be manipulated:

```
Private Sub FileNew()
```

```
        MsgBox "Sorry, you do not have permission to create
        a new document"
End Sub
```

This example shows how you can programmatically control one of Word's built-in functions. Figure 4-6 shows the Macros dialog and the Word commands that can be overwritten. The appendix contains a complete listing of all Word commands.

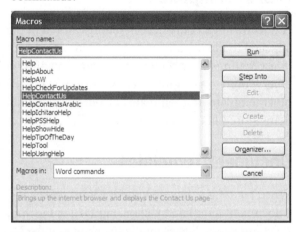

Figure 4-6: The Macros dialog box displaying built-in Word commands

Note: Use the same syntax that appears in the Macros dialog box. For example:

```
        Sub FileCloseOrCloseAll ( )
```

Templates

Word documents are all based on a template. In the VBE, every Word document will have a reference to the template that created it. The template is basically the storage facility for all the document settings such as UserForms, modules, class modules, AutoText, styles, fonts, menus, page settings, and formatting.

There are two basic types of templates: global templates and document templates. Global templates are available to all documents. The most common global template is the Normal template. This is the default template from which all new blank documents are created. Templates contain settings that are available only to documents attached to that template. A document created from a template can use the settings from both that template and any global template. Word provides numerous document templates, and you can also create your own template.

Global Templates

A document can only access settings stored in the template attached to the document or in the Normal template. In order to use settings from another template, you must either load the other template as a global template or attach a reference to the other template. If a template is loaded as a global template, items stored in that template are available to all documents.

Document Templates

When creating a new document, Word makes it easy to select a document template by choosing **Office button | New** and selecting a template from the list shown in the New Document window. It is also easy to add a custom document template to this list for easy access in the future. There are two areas where these templates can reside in the Templates list: the User templates and Workgroup templates directories. These directories can be located by selecting **Office button | Word Options | Advanced** and clicking the **File Locations** button in the General section.

If you use Word 2007 to change the location in which your new templates are saved, you also change the location in which all Office 2007 program templates are saved. From within Word, click **Office button | Word Options | Advanced** and click the **File Locations** button under the General section. Figure 4-7 shows the resultant dialog. This is where you can modify your user templates by clicking **Modify**. In the Modify Location dialog box, change the setting in the Folder name list or the Look in list to the folder in which you want to save your new templates.

Figure 4-7: The File Locations dialog box is accessed by clicking the File Locations button in the General section of the Word Options window.

The Workgroup templates directory should be on a shared network drive. This way the templates can be centrally maintained and administered. You also want to make sure that users do not inadvertently alter the templates.

Tip: Your network files should be read-only. You should also have the systems administrator deny access to anyone without the appropriate permissions.

The User templates folder is where individual users can maintain custom templates. Templates stored in this folder will appear on the Templates list. This directory is usually mapped to a user's C: drive. There may be instances when you want to take advantage of this location. The Workgroup templates directory may be a convenient location to install templates in an organization that has remote users.

Caution: Any document (.doc) file that you save in the Templates folder also acts as a template.

Note: When saving a template, Word automatically switches to the User templates location. If you save a template in a different location, the template will not appear in the Templates list.

Storing Templates in the Startup Folder

Any templates that you load in a Word session are unloaded when you close Word. To load a template each time you start Word, copy the template to the Startup folder. This location is shown in Figure 4-8. To find that location, select **Office button | Word Options | Advanced | File Locations**.

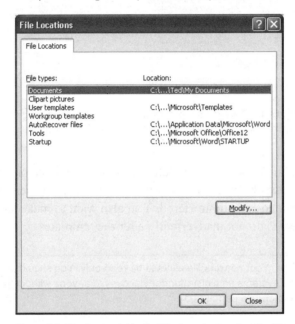

Figure 4-8: The Startup folder for Word can be found on the File Locations dialog box.

Tip: This path is usually C:\Windows\Application Data\Microsoft\ Word\STARTUP.

Using Command-Line Switches

Word allows certain arguments it calls "switches" to be passed to it when loading. By passing switches to Word you can alter its behavior. These can be passed by going to the Microsoft Windows Start menu, clicking **Run**, and typing **winword** followed by the various switches you would like to pass. The following table lists the command-line switches that apply to Word.

Switch	Description
/a	This switch prevents add-ins and global templates (including the Normal template) from being loaded.
/laddinpath	This switch loads a specific Word add-in.
/m	This switch prevents any AutoExec (automatically executing) macros from running.
/m macroname	This switch runs a specific macro and prevents Word from running any AutoExec macros.
/n	This switch prevents Word from opening a document when Word is started.
/t templatename	This switch starts Word with a new document based on the specified template rather than the Normal template.
/w	When this switch is passed, documents opened in each instance of Word will not appear as choices in the Window menu of the other documents.
(no switch)	A new Word window is opened with a blank document using the existing instance of the Word application.

Tip: You can also prevent AutoMacros from running by holding down Shift while Word is starting. When starting Word from the Office shortcut bar, immediately press Shift after clicking the Word button.

Loading Add-Ins

Add-ins are supplemental programs that you install to extend the capabilities of Word by adding custom commands and specialized features. When you load an add-in, it remains loaded for the current Word session only. If you quit and then restart Word, the add-in is not automatically reloaded. Like templates, you must store the add-in in your startup folder to have it available when Word is restarted. Once you have added the add-in to the Startup folder, go to **Office button | Word Options | Add-Ins** and choose **Word Add-ins** from the Manage drop-down, then click **Go**.

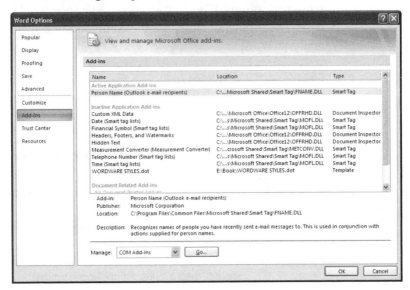

Figure 4-9

In the Templates and Add-ins dialog box (that appears in Figures 4-10 through 4-13), you may add a template, XML schema, XML expansion pack, or linked cascading style sheet for Word to automatically load by clicking the various "Add" buttons and navigating to your file.

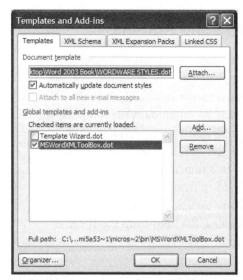

Figure 4-10: Click the Add button to add a template to the startup list.

Figure 4-11: Click the Add Schema button to add a custom XML schema to the startup list.

Figure 4-12: Click the Add button to add an XML expansion pack to the startup list.

Figure 4-13: Click the Add button to add a linked CSS to the startup list.

Unloading Templates and Add-ins

To conserve memory and increase the speed of Word, it's a good idea to unload templates and add-in programs you don't often use. When you unload a template or add-in that's located in your Startup folder, Word unloads the template for the current Word session but automatically reloads it the next time you start Word. When you unload a template or add-in located in any other folder, it is unavailable until you reload it. To delete a template or add-in from Word, you must remove the template or add-in by using the Templates and Add-ins dialog box. You choose the item from the list and then click the **Remove** button.

Fields

Fields are used as placeholders for data that might change in a document and for creating form letters and labels in mail merge documents. Some of the most common fields are the Page field, which is inserted when you add page numbers, and the Date field, which is inserted when you click Date & Time on the Insert tab and then select the Update automatically check box. The Field dialog box (shown in Figure 4-14) can be accessed by selecting **Insert tab | Quick Parts | Field**. There is a more thorough description of Word's fields in Chapter 2.

Fields are inserted automatically when you create an index or table of contents by choosing commands from the References tab on the Ribbon. You can change the corresponding options of a specific field by selecting a field and changing options in the Field options area of the Field dialog box (as shown in Figure 4-15). You can also use fields to automatically insert document information (such as the author or file name), to perform calculations, to create links and references to other documents or items, and to perform other special tasks.

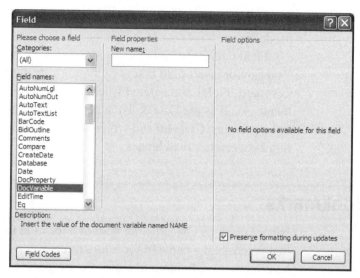

Figure 4-14: The Field dialog box

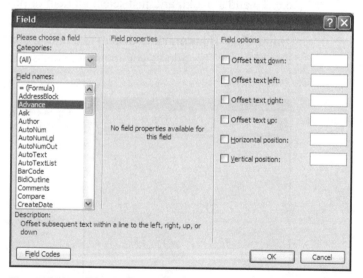

Figure 4-15: Change the options of a specific field in the Field options area.

To display the results of field codes, such as the results of calculations, hide the field codes by clicking **Office button | Word Options | Advanced** and then clearing the Show field codes instead of their values check box. Fields are somewhat like formulas in Microsoft Excel — the field code is like the formula, and the field result is like the value that the formula produces.

Field codes appear between curly brackets or braces ({ }). You cannot insert field braces by typing characters on the keyboard. Fields are inserted when you use particular commands, such as the Date & Time command on the Insert tab, or by pressing **Ctrl+F9** and typing the appropriate information between the field braces.

Bookmarks

A bookmark can be either an item or a location in a document that you assign a name to for future reference. Bookmarks can be used to quickly jump to a specific location in a document, create cross-references, mark page ranges for index entries, etc. To add a bookmark, just select an item or position the cursor at a specific location and in the Insert tab's Links group, click **Bookmark** to display the dialog box shown in Figure 4-16. This allows you to assign your selection a bookmark name.

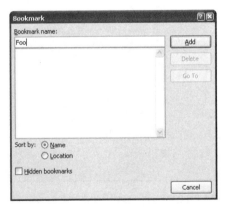

Figure 4-16: To add a bookmark, give your bookmark a name and click Add.

Normally, bookmarks aren't visible in your document. If you want to display bookmarks when you're working in a document, you will need to turn them on just as you would to see Word's fields (**Office button | Word Options | Advanced | Show bookmarks**). After turning on the visibility of bookmarks, you'll notice that Word uses brackets to represent bookmarks around an item or an I-beam to represent a book-mark at a location.

Note: Unlike field codes, you cannot print bookmarks.

Bookmarks are frequently used in document automation as placeholders for various reasons. Sometimes bookmarks are used as entry points for specific information. Other times, bookmarks are used to mark areas where text will be pasted. As you will see throughout this book, I personally prefer to use Word's fields when applicable. Fields allow you to see and print the code that contains both the formatting and infor-mation that will be inserted into the document. When you are working with complex documents, it is often easier to insert text using DocVariable fields rather than using bookmarks. However, I've used bookmark examples throughout the book as well. This way, you will be exposed to the different ways in which text can be inserted and documents can be automated.

Word VBA Tips

Before we get to the substance of actually writing code in the following chapters, there are a couple items to note. These will come in handy as you progress in your VBA develop-ment. The rest of this chapter discusses topics involving locking your VBA code, preventing unauthorized interference with your code, and distributing your code to users via templates.

Locking Your VBA Code

In many instances, you will want to prevent unauthorized users from accessing your VBA code. The process of locking your VBA code is very straightforward: First, open the Visual Basic Editor. This is accomplished either by pressing **Alt+F11** or by choosing **Visual Basic** from the Developer tab. Once in the VBE, right-click on the project name in the Project window on the left and select **TemplateProject properties** from the pop-up menu. (You can also access this dialog via **Tools | Project Properties**.) You will then see the Project Properties dialog box, as shown in Figure 4-17.

Figure 4-17: Access the Project Properties dialog box to "lock" your code.

Note: Initially, your project will have a generic "project" name. You should rename your project before protecting it. You'll notice that the Project Properties window changes to indicate the proper name of your project.

There are several options available on the General tab of the Project Properties dialog. You can include a brief project description, specify a help file, and specify the context ID for the help file if you would like to be directed to a specific topic within the help file. VBA also supports conditional compilation. You can use conditional compilation to run blocks of code selectively; for example, run debugging statements comparing the speed of different approaches to the same programming task, or localizing an application for different languages. Conditional compiler constants are set in code with the #Const directive. This directive is used to mark blocks of code to be conditionally compiled with the #If…Then…#Else directive.

In order to protect your project, you will want to select the Protection tab and select the Lock project for viewing check box as shown in Figure 4-18. You will then enter the same password in the Password and Confirm password boxes. Once you've entered your password, simply click **OK** and you are ready to go.

Figure 4-18: Check the Lock project for viewing check box and supply a password to lock your code.

Please keep in mind that it is fairly easy to create (or otherwise obtain) a brute force password cracking program. Brute force programs simply continue creating different passwords and trying to crack the password. If you've gone through the trouble of setting up a password, please make sure to use one of sufficient length and complexity. The following table lists the amount of time a brute force program (running on a P4 2000 machine) will take to crack a Word VBA password.

4 character lower- or uppercase letters	a few seconds
4 character lower- and uppercase letters	a few seconds
4 character lower- and uppercase letters and numbers	a few seconds
5 character lower- or uppercase letters (e.g., passb)	under 60 seconds
5 character lower- and uppercase letters (e.g., passB)	approx 6 minutes
5 character lower- and uppercase letters and numbers (e.g., Pasb1)	approx 15 minutes
8 character lower- or uppercase letters	approx 58 hours
8 character lower- and uppercase letters	approx 21 months
8 character lower- and uppercase letters and numbers	approx 7 years
10 character lower- or uppercase letters	approx 5 years

10 character lower- and uppercase letters	approx 4648 years
10 character lower- and uppercase letters and numbers	approx 26984 years

Tip: It's a good practice to keep the original copy of the template unlocked. There is always the chance that you'll forget the password and you'll be locked out of your own project.

Preventing User Macro Interference

One common problem with Word projects is that savvy users will figure out how to force a hard stop with the Ctrl+Break key combination. This is easily thwarted by inserting the following code into the appropriate procedures. One note of caution: It is best to insert this code once the routines have been thoroughly tested. If you're accustomed to stopping your infinite loops with Ctrl+Break, these few lines will cause you headaches and reboots.

```
Sub SomeRoutine()
Application.EnableCancelKey = wdCancelDisabled
' code here
Application.EnableCancelKey = wdCancelInterrupt
End Sub
```

Distributing VBA Macros

Here is a fairly common scenario: A user (perhaps you) creates a couple of specific macros that have a high degree of value to other users in his or her organization. This presents the problem of distributing these macros so that they run properly on other people's machines.

By default, Word stores macros in the Normal template unless you specify a different location. In many cases, an organization may have a default, or shared, Normal template. In other cases, users have created their own macros and saved them in their Normal template. The Normal template also includes extra menu items or toolbars, keyboard shortcuts, AutoText entries, etc. This is why it is almost never a good option to simply replace someone's Normal template.

Generally, macros fall into two categories: (1) macros that are specific to a certain document or set of documents, and (2) generic macros that usually pertain to certain formatting or general business use situations.

The rest of this book is largely dedicated to the first type of macro. These macros become part of the template and are distributed as part of the template. This is usually accomplished by distributing that template to the users. This can be accomplished by putting it in either the Workgroup templates folder or the User templates folder. These locations can be viewed in the File Locations dialog box, as shown in Figure 4-19.

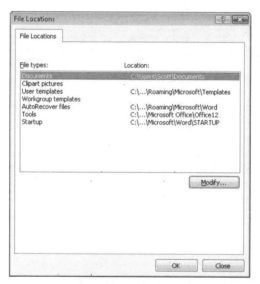

Figure 4-19: The File Locations dialog box is accessed from Office button | Word Options | Advanced | General | File Locations.

If you have a template full of generic macros, you can make them available to your users by propagating the template to the user's Word Startup folder. Keep in mind that this will allow you to distribute all items specific to the template, including any additional menu items, toolbars, and keyboard shortcuts that you want to set up to make it easier to access the macros. This folder can be identified by going to **Office button | Word Options | Advanced | General | File Locations**. The template will be available once it is copied to this directory. The template is considered an add-in and will be loaded automatically upon startup. You can see the list of your add-ins by choosing **Office button | Word Options | Add-Ins** (see Figure 4-20).

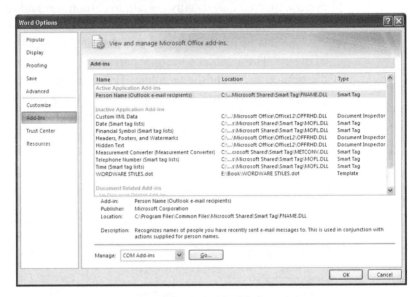

Figure 4-20: View the list of your add-ins in the Word Options window.

Tip Each situation is different. You may discover that it is easier to point your users' Workgroup templates path and their Startup path to a location on the server (easily done using user profiles).

Conclusion

This chapter introduced many of Word's features that will be important in the proper development of a Word document automation system. Throughout this book, we will continue to discuss the means necessary to integrate all of these features together through VBA. There is no way to touch on every possible use of Word because Word 2007 has the most extensive set of customization options of all Office applications. Please also refer to Chapter 6, "The Word 2007 Object Model."

Chapter 5

The VBA Programming Language

Introduction

This chapter provides an overview of some commonly used VBA programming tools including message boxes, input boxes, arrays, collections, string functions, string statements, and variable declarations. An emphasis on interacting with the user is maintained throughout the chapter. This guide is best used as a reference source while programming. It's important to note that the syntax of VBA has not changed significantly since the earlier versions of Word. You may be able to leverage code from previous versions of Word, but please note that any user interface-specific code will need to be rewritten since the Word 2007 UI has changed completely!

Variables

Variables are a basic element of almost every programming language. In its simplest form, a *variable* is simply a memory address where information is stored. In VBA, variables are created by dimensioning them. Dimensioning a variable is done in several different ways, but the main thing to keep in mind is that the process of dimensioning a variable tells the computer how large of a memory chunk to allocate for a specific variable.

Note: This brings up the first point of good VBA programming. Your programs should always require explicit variable declaration. This book assumes you are using the Option Explicit statement. By contrast, implicit variable declaration simply requires that you type the name of the variable, and when the code is compiled the variable will be assigned to a variant data type, which is the largest type of VBA variable and consumes the most memory. Another downfall of implicit variable declaration is that your variable names are not checked. In other words, if you use "Name" as a variable in one spot and later misspell it as "Neme" the computer thinks this is a new variable and assigns it its own memory address.

Variable Declaration

Explicit variable declaration requires that you specify both the type and scope of the variable. We mentioned above that variables can be assigned different amounts of space in memory, but a variable can also be available at different times during the execution of a program (scope). In other words, you can limit or expand the procedures that may utilize a specific variable. Let's look at the syntax for some variable declarations.

Local Variable Declaration

A locally declared variable is available only to the procedure in which it is called. In the following example, iLocal is dimensioned locally and would not be available to another procedure. This is helpful when you want to use the same name in different procedures (note that this is not recommended). Also notice that the variable was assigned to the integer data type. (We'll discuss the different types of variables in a bit.)

```
Sub Test()
Private iLocal As Integer
End Sub
```

Module-Level Variable Declaration

The next scope option is the module-level private scope. As we saw in the previous chapter, modules are where the code is stored and may be behind UserForms, standard modules, or even class modules. A privately declared variable outside of a procedure is available only to the procedures and functions in that specific module.

Global-Level Variable Declaration

The final scope of a variable is that of a public variable. The Public keyword indicates that the variable is available to all procedures and functions within the project. These must be declared in a module. This is useful when you want a variable to be utilized throughout the executing life of the project.

Static Variables

Another concern with variables is when they should be extinguished. When a procedure or function quits running, typically any local variables are extinguished. In other words, they lose their value and no longer occupy a memory address. However, a local variable may be declared with the Static keyword. This enables a variable that would normally be extinguished to maintain its value even if no code is executing.

You may be wondering, "Why not use a public variable?" A public variable loses its value when all of the code in the project finishes executing. You can run a complex macro in a document, but once that macro finishes, all variables are extinguished except for static ones. This allows your code to remember values from the execution of one procedure to the next.

In some cases, a public variable can accomplish exactly what a static variable can, but good programming dictates that you use the most restrictive scope available. The following code demonstrates the differences:

```
'at the module level
Public iState As Integer
Sub PublicVariable()
    iState = iState + 1
    MsgBox iState
End Sub
Sub StaticVariable()
    Static iVar As Integer
iVar + 1
    MsgBox iVar
End Sub
```

Note: Make sure you follow consistent variable naming conventions. The most common convention calls for the first one to three characters to describe the type of variable, followed by a meaningful variable name. Some programmers go even further and use a character to indicate the scope of the variable.

Types of Variables

Byte

Bytes are stored as single, unsigned, 8-bit (8 bits = 1 byte) numbers. Bytes range in value from 0 to 255. The byte data type best represents binary data. Although they are infrequently used, bytes are the smallest of all VBA data types.

Note: Trying to assign a value of more than 255 to a byte results in an overflow error, as shown in Figure 5-1.

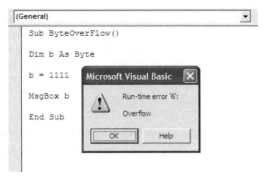

Figure 5-1: An overflow as a result of assigning a value larger than 255 to a byte

Boolean

Booleans are stored as 16-bit (2-byte) numbers. However, Booleans can only be True or False. Numeric values correlate to Boolean values as follows: 0 becomes False and all other values, whether positive or negative, become True (see Figure 5-2). A Boolean False becomes 0 and a Boolean True becomes –1 when Booleans are converted to numeric types.

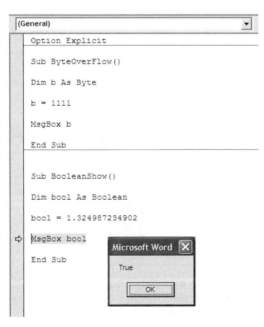

Figure 5-2: Any value for a Boolean type other than 0 will return True.

Note: Use either True or False to assign a value to Boolean variables. Programmers sometimes use Yes/No, On/Off, X/O combinations. In previous versions of the Visual Basic language, 0 was recognized as False and all non-zero values were True.

Integer

Integers are stored as 16-bit (2-byte) whole numbers ranging from –32,768 to 32,767. The type declaration character for integers is the percent sign (%).

Long

Longs are stored as 32-bit (4-byte) whole numbers ranging in value from –2,147,483,648 to 2,147,483,647. The type declaration character for the long is the ampersand character (&).

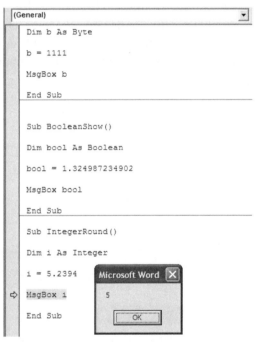

```
(General)

    Dim b As Byte

    b = 1111

    MsgBox b

    End Sub


    Sub BooleanShow()

    Dim bool As Boolean

    bool = 1.324987234902

    MsgBox bool

    End Sub

    Sub IntegerRound()

    Dim i As Integer

    i = 5.2394

    MsgBox i

    End Sub
```

Microsoft Word
5
OK

Figure 5-3: In this case, a rounded value of 5 is returned since integers and long types require whole numbers.

Note: Keep in mind that integers and longs require whole numbers. Many beginning programmers encounter unexpected errors using these data types for values that require fractional precision. Figure 5-3 shows that assigning an integer a fractional value doesn't generate an error, but rather results in the number being rounded to a whole number.

Note: Longs are sometimes referred to as long integers. This is due to the fact that many 16-bit integers were upgraded to longs when the 32-bit versions of Windows were released.

Single

Singles are stored as 32-bit (4-byte) floating-point numbers, ranging in value from –3.402823E38 to –1.401298E–45 for negative values and from 1.401298E–45 to 3.402823E38 for positive values. The type declaration character for single variables is the exclamation point (!).

```
Sub SingleShow()

Dim s As Single

s = 3.12309309213903

MsgBox s

End Sub
```

Microsoft Word

3.123093

OK

Figure 5-4: Single type returning a truncated value due to its value restrictions

Double

Doubles are stored as 64-bit (8-byte) floating-point numbers ranging in value from –1.79769313486231E308 to –4.94065645841247E–324 for negative values and from 4.94065645841247E–324 to 1.79769313486232E308 for positive values. The type declaration character for the double variable type is the number sign (#).

Currency

Variables of the currency type are stored as 64-bit (8-byte) numbers in an integer format, scaled by 10,000 to give a fixed-point number with 15 digits to the left of the decimal point and 4 digits to the right. This representation provides a range of –922,337,203,685,477.5808 to 922,337,203,685,477.5807. The type declaration character for currency is the "at" sign (@).

Note: If you are using calculations involving money, you should be using the currency data type.

Date

Date type variables are stored as 64-bit (8-byte) floating-point numbers that represent dates ranging from 1 January 100 to 31 December 9999 and times from 0:00:00 to 23:59:59. Any recognizable literal date values can be assigned to date variables. Date literals must be enclosed within number signs (#) like this: #January 1, 1993# or #1 Jan 93#.

Date variables display dates according to the short date format recognized by your computer. VBA works with dates as serial numbers using December 31, 1899 as an arbitrary starting point. This means that 1 corresponds to December 31, 1899; 2 corresponds to January 1, 1900; 3 corresponds to January 2, 1900; and so on. See Figure 5-5 to see how August 1, 2004 is displayed according to an absolute numeric value. Times display according to the time format (either 12-hour or 24-hour) recognized by your computer.

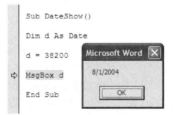

```
Sub DateShow()

    Dim d As Date

    d = 38200

    MsgBox d

    End Sub
```

Microsoft Word

8/1/2004

OK

Figure 5-5: The serial number of 38200 is congruent to the date 8/1/2004.

Note: When other data types are converted to date, values to the left of the decimal represent date information while values to the right of the decimal represent time. Midnight is 0 and noon is 0.5. Negative whole numbers represent dates before 31 December 1899.

Object

Object variables are stored as 32-bit (4-byte) addresses that refer to objects. Using the Set statement, a variable declared as an object can have any object reference assigned to it.

Note: Although a variable declared with the object type is flexible enough to contain a reference to any object, binding to the object referenced by that variable is always late binding and IntelliSense will not be available. To force early binding, assign the object reference to a variable declared with a specific object variable type.

String

The most common variable in Word programming is probably the string data type. A string contains a combination of characters. These may be text characters or specially recognized VBA constants that indicate certain controls such as Tab or Return. Strings can contain blank spaces, each representing a character. The important thing about strings is that they must always be enclosed in quotation marks. Strings can be either fixed length or variable length. To define a string as fixed length, the VBA multiplication sign (*) is used and the corresponding number indicates the length of the string. A fixed-length string can range from one to approximately 64K (2^{16}) characters. A variable-length string can contain up to approximately two billion (2^{31}) characters.

Note: A public fixed-length string can't be used in a class module.

The codes for string characters range from 0 to 255. The first 128 characters (0 to 127) of the character set correspond to the letters and symbols on a standard U.S. keyboard. These first 128 characters are the same as those defined by the ASCII character set. The second 128 characters (128 to 255) represent special characters, such as letters in international alphabets, accents, currency symbols, and fractions. The type declaration character for the string variable type is the dollar sign ($).

Figure 5-6 shows an example using a fixed-length string. Notice that the message box displays "7 Chars" even though the variable was set equal to a longer string. The second line of the message box contains the length of the string. Due to its declaration, the string is still actually 15 characters wide and occupies the same amount of memory.

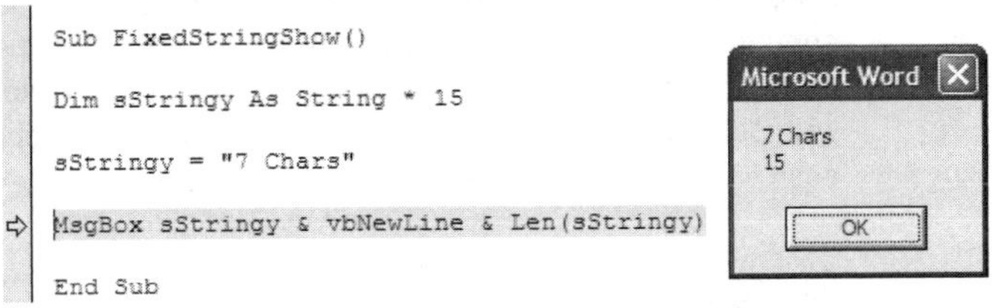

```
Sub FixedStringShow()

Dim sStringy As String * 15

sStringy = "7 Chars"

MsgBox sStringy & vbNewLine & Len(sStringy)

End Sub
```

Microsoft Word ☒

7 Chars
15

OK

Figure 5-6: A message box displaying the contents of fixed-length string variable sStringy and its length

Variant

The variant data type is the default data type for all variables that are not explicitly declared as some other type. There is no type declaration character for the variant data type. Variant is a special data type that can contain any kind of data except a fixed-length string. It is important to note that variants can even support user-defined data types. In addition, variants can also contain the special values Empty, Error, Nothing, and Null.

Note: You can determine what type of data is being stored in a variant by using the VarType or TypeName functions.

Variants can hold numeric data including integers or real numbers with values ranging from $-1.797693134862315E308$ to $-4.94066E-324$ for negative values and from $4.94066E-324$ to $1.797693134862315E308$ for positive values. Generally, numeric variant data is maintained in its original data type within the variant. For example, if you assign the numerical value "2584" to a variant type variable, any subsequent operations will treat the variant as an integer. However, if an arithmetic operation causes a variant containing a byte, an integer, a long, or a single to exceed the normal range for the original data type, the result is promoted within the variant to the next larger data type. Therefore, a byte is promoted to an integer, an integer is promoted to a long, and longs and singles are promoted to doubles. An error will be generated when variant variables containing currency, decimal, and double values exceed their respective ranges.

Note: Although it is not encouraged, you can use the variant data type to work with data in a more flexible way. If a variant variable contains digits, they may be either the string representation of the digits or their actual value, depending on the context. For example:

```
Dim varVar As Variant
varVar = 90210
```

In the example in the above note, varVar contains a numeric representation — the actual value 90210. This can be used as a string if inserted into another string. The following message box will use varVar as a string:

```
MsgBox "Beverly Hills " & varVar
```

Arithmetic operators also work as expected on variant variables that contain numeric values or string data that can be interpreted as numbers. If you use the + operator to add varVar to a variable of a numeric type, the result is an arithmetic sum.

Other Variant Values

The value Empty indicates a variant that hasn't been initialized (assigned an initial value). A variant containing Empty is 0 if it is used in a numeric context and a zero-length string ("") if it is used in a string context.

Caution: Don't confuse Empty with Null. Null indicates that the variant variable is intentionally absent of value.

In a variant, Error is a special value used to indicate that an error condition has occurred in a procedure. However, unlike with other kinds of errors, normal application-level error handling does not occur. This allows you, or the application itself, to take some alternative action based on the error value. Error values are created by converting real numbers to error values using the CVErr function.

User-Defined Variable Types

User-defined variable types are declared at the module level using the Type statement. This statement is used to define a user-defined data type containing one or more elements. User-defined variables are frequently used when working with external procedures (DLL functions). It is important to understand how to set up your own variable types. Following is the syntax for the Type statement:

```
[Private|Public] Type varname
    elementname [([subscripts])] As type
    [elementname [([subscripts])] As type]
    . . .
End Type
```

The Type statement has the following parts:

Public	This is an optional part used to declare user-defined types that are available to all procedures in all modules in all projects.
Private	This is an optional part used to declare user-defined types that are available only within the module where the declaration is made.
varname	This required argument contains the name of the user-defined type. It follows standard variable naming conventions.
elementname	This is required and contains the name of an element of the user-defined type. Element names also follow standard variable naming conventions, except that keywords can be used.
subscripts	When not explicitly stated in lower, the lower bound of an array is controlled by the Option Base statement. The lower bound is 0 if no Option Base statement is present.
type	The data type is a required element and may be byte, Boolean, integer, long, currency, single, double, date, string (for variable-length strings), string * length (for fixed-length strings), object, variant, another user-defined type, or an object type.

Once you have declared a user-defined type using the Type statement, you can declare a variable of that type anywhere within the scope of the declaration. Use Dim, Private, Public, ReDim, or Static to declare a variable of a user-defined type. In standard modules and class modules, user-defined types are public by default. This visibility can be changed using the Private keyword. Line numbers and line labels aren't allowed in Type...End Type blocks. User-defined types are often used for data records, which frequently consist of a number of related elements of different data types.

The following example shows a user-defined type:

```
Type PuppyData
    PuppyCode As Integer
    KennelName As String
End Type
Dim Shani As PuppyData
Shani.PuppyCode = 10
Shani.Name = "Wyndrunhr"
```

Constants

If you are going to use frequently occurring values in a particular project, or you need to depend on certain values that are difficult to remember or have no obvious meaning, your code will benefit from using constants. Constants also make your code easier to read and maintain. You can use constants, represented by meaningful names, to take the place of a number or string that doesn't change throughout a project. There are two types of constants — intrinsic and user-defined.

Note: You cannot assign new values to constants.

Intrinsic Constants

These constants (system-defined constants) are provided by applications and controls. Other applications that provide object libraries, such as Microsoft Access, Microsoft Excel, and Microsoft Word, also provide intrinsic constants. The Object Browser is usually the best place to get a list of the constants provided by individual object libraries. Visual Basic constants are listed in the Visual Basic for Applications type library.

Note: Visual Basic continues to recognize constants created in earlier versions of Visual Basic or Visual Basic for Applications. You can upgrade your constants to those listed in the Object Browser. Constants listed in the Object Browser don't have to be declared in your application.

User-Defined Constants

These constants are declared and set using the Const statement. By declaring a constant, you can assign a meaningful name to a value and use it consistently throughout your code. After a constant is declared, it cannot be modified or assigned a new value.

You can declare a constant within a procedure or at the top of a module in the Declarations section. Module-level constants are private by default. To declare a public module-level constant, precede the Const statement with the Public keyword. You can explicitly declare a private constant by preceding the Const statement with the Private keyword to make it easier to read and interpret in your code. The following example declares the Public constant conAge as an integer and assigns it the value 34:

```
Public Const conAge As Integer = 34
```

Constants can be declared as one of the following data types: Boolean, byte, integer, long, currency, single, double, date, string, or variant. Because you already know the value of a constant, you can specify the data type in a Const statement. You can declare several constants in one statement. To specify a data type, you must include the data type for each constant.

Note: In earlier versions of Visual Basic, constant names were usually all caps with underscores. For example:
```
NUMBER_EMPLOYEES
```

Intrinsic constants are now qualified to avoid the confusion when constants with the same name exist in more than one object library and that may have different values assigned to them. There are two ways to qualify constant names: by prefix and by library reference.

The intrinsic constants supplied by all objects appear in a mixed-case format, with a two-character prefix indicating the object library that defines the constant. Constants from the Visual Basic for Applications object library are prefaced with "vb" and constants from the Microsoft Excel object library are prefaced with "xl." The following examples illustrate how prefixes for custom controls vary, depending on the type library:

```
vbTileHorizontal
xlDialogBorder
```

You can also qualify the reference to a constant by using the following syntax:

```
[libname.] [modulename.]constname
```

Collections

A collection object is an ordered set of items that can be referred to as a unit. The collection object provides a convenient way to refer to a group of related items as a single object. The items, or members, in a collection need only be related by the fact that they exist in the collection. Members of a collection don't have to share the same data type.

A collection can be created the same way as other objects. For example:

```
Dim X As New Collection
```

Once a collection is created, members can be added using the Add method and removed using the Remove method. Specific members can be returned from the collection using the Item method, while the entire collection can be iterated using the For Each...Next statement.

Arrays

Arrays are helpful for obvious reasons: It is easier to make a declaration such as lFinCharge(1-10) than declare ten different variables for the interest charge on each of ten years. There will be situations when you do not know how many items you will need in the index. VBA allows you to create a dynamic array that can contain any number of values. Furthermore, you can use the ReDim statement to change the number of its contents. Be aware, though, that the ReDim statement will destroy all existing data unless it is used in conjunction with the Preserve statement.

```
ReDim Preserve JoeArray(100)
```

By default, the subscripts of arrays start with 0. In other words, the lower bound of the array is 0 and the number specified in the Dim statement determines the upper bound. You can change the lower bound for your arrays using the Option Base statement. The following line of code will make all of your arrays start with 1:

```
Option Base 1
```

Note: You can also change the lower bound by specifying it in the Dim statement:
```
Dim JoeArray(5 to 500) as String
```

Multidimensional Arrays

VBA also supports the capability to create multidimensional arrays. You can create arrays with one or more dimensions (the maximum is 60). It is easiest to think of two-dimensional arrays in terms of rows and columns, and three-dimensional arrays like a cube, and so on. These rows and columns make up the array's matrix. The syntax for the Dim statement is basically the same, except for the inclusion of the extra dimensions. See Figure 5-7 for a graphical explanation.

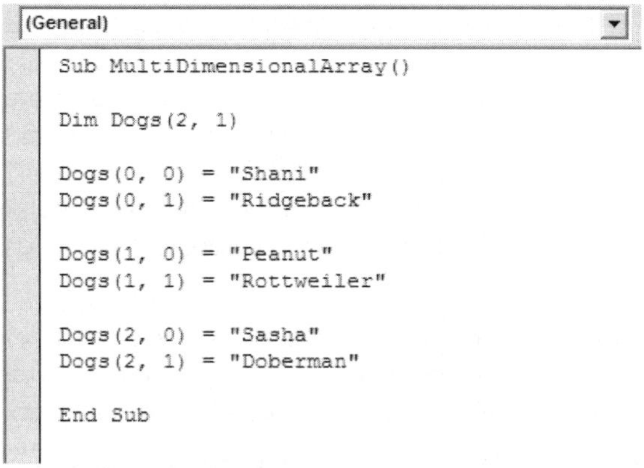

```
(General)                                                    ▼

    Sub MultiDimensionalArray()

    Dim Dogs(2, 1)

    Dogs(0, 0) = "Shani"
    Dogs(0, 1) = "Ridgeback"

    Dogs(1, 0) = "Peanut"
    Dogs(1, 1) = "Rottweiler"

    Dogs(2, 0) = "Sasha"
    Dogs(2, 1) = "Doberman"

    End Sub
```

Figure 5-7: This code declares an array of size 3 x 2 and sets each array slot with values from the table.

The code in Figure 5-7 sets up an array that can be represented by the following table:

Dog's Name	Dog Type
Shani	Ridgeback
Peanut	Rottweiler
Sasha	Doberman

Displaying Information to the User

One of the best ways to interact with users (as well as visually see what your code is doing without stepping through the code) is through message boxes and input boxes. Message boxes are a great way to display errors, tips, and other information.

Message Boxes

The MsgBox function displays a message in the form of a dialog box, waits for the user to click a button, and returns an integer indicating which button the user clicked. Following is the syntax for the MsgBox function:

```
MsgBox(prompt[, buttons] [, title] [, helpfile, context])
```

The MsgBox function syntax has these named arguments:

prompt	This parameter is required. This text will be displayed as the message in the dialog box (maximum length of ~1024 characters). You can make the prompt appear on separate lines by using a carriage return character (Chr(13)), a linefeed character (Chr(10)), or a carriage return/linefeed character combination (Chr(13) and Chr(10)) between each line.
buttons	This parameter is optional. It is either a constant or numeric expression that specifies buttons to display, the icon style to use, the identity of the default button, and the modality of the message box.
title	This parameter is optional. This text will be displayed in the title bar of the dialog box. If you omit *title*, the application name is placed in the title bar.
helpfile	This parameter is also optional. This string expression identifies the Help file to use to provide context-sensitive help for the dialog box. Note: If *helpfile* is provided, *context* must also be provided.
context	This is used in conjunction with the *helpfile* parameter. It is a numeric expression that represents the Help context number assigned to the appropriate Help topic. Note: If *context* is provided, *helpfile* must also be provided.

Button Settings

As you will see in many examples throughout the book, using the appropriate button combination is important when interacting with users. Pay careful attention to the standard Microsoft conventions.

In the table below, Group1 describes the number and type of buttons displayed in the dialog box, Group2 describes the icon style, Group3 determines which button is the default, and Group4 determines the modality of the message box. When adding numbers to create a final value for the *buttons* argument, use only one number from each group.

	Constant	Value	Description
Group1	vbOKOnly	0	An OK button is displayed.
	vbOKCancel	1	OK and Cancel buttons are displayed.
	vbAbortRetryIgnore	2	Abort, Retry, and Ignore buttons are displayed.

	Constant	Value	Description
	vbYesNoCancel	3	Yes, No, and Cancel buttons are displayed.
	vbYesNo	4	Yes and No buttons are displayed.
	vbRetryCancel	5	Retry and Cancel buttons are displayed.
Group2	vbCritical	16	A Critical Message icon is displayed.
	vbQuestion	32	A Warning Query icon is displayed.
	vbExclamation	48	A Warning Message icon is displayed.
	vbInformation	64	An Information Message icon is displayed.
Group3	vbDefaultButton1	0	The first button is default.
	vbDefaultButton2	256	The second button is default.
	vbDefaultButton3	512	The third button is default.
	vbDefaultButton4	768	The fourth button is default.
Group4	vbApplicationModal	0	Application modal forces the user to respond before continuing in the current application.
	vbSystemModal	4096	System modal suspends all applications until the user responds to the message box.
	vbMsgBoxHelpButton	16384	This adds a Help button to the message box.
	vbMsgBoxSetForeground	65536	Specifies the message box window as the foreground window.
	vbMsgBoxRight	524288	Makes all text right aligned.
	vbMsgBoxRtlReading	1048576	Specifies that the text should appear as right-to-left reading on Hebrew and Arabic systems.

Note: These button constants are specified by the VBA programming language. This means that you can use the constants in place of the actual values.

Return Values

If you are using message boxes to get information from the user, you must obtain a return value and have the code react accordingly. The following example shows you how to concatenate the above button constants and work with the return value. Return values are also constants, so you can use either the numeric value or the built-in VBA constant.

```
Sub MessageBox()
Dim sPrompt As String, sTitle As String
```

```
Dim iButtons As Integer, iResponse As Integer
sPrompt = "Eating Lunch Today?" & Chr(13) & "(It's Chicken!)"
iButtons = vbYesNo + vbInformation + vbDefaultButton1
sTitle = "Cafeteria"
iResponse = MsgBox(sPrompt, iButtons, sTitle)
If iResponse = vbYes Then
    MsgBox "See you there!", vbOKOnly, "Tasty"
Else
    MsgBox "Your loss!", vbOKOnly, "Dummy"
End If
End Sub
```

The following table describes the available return values in VBA:

Constant	Value	Description
vbOK	1	OK
vbCancel	2	Cancel
vbAbort	3	Abort
vbRetry	4	Retry
vbIgnore	5	Ignore
vbYes	6	Yes
vbNo	7	No

When the *helpfile* and *context* parameters are provided, the user can press F1 to view the Help topic corresponding to the context. Some host applications, Microsoft Excel for example, also automatically add a Help button to the dialog box. If the dialog box displays a Cancel button, pressing the Esc key has the same effect as clicking Cancel. If the dialog box contains a Help button, context-sensitive help is provided for the dialog box. However, no value is returned until one of the other buttons is clicked.

Note: To specify more than the first named argument, you must use MsgBox in an expression. To omit some positional arguments, you must include the corresponding comma delimiter.

Input Boxes

Message boxes provide a great deal of functionality and allow you to get feedback from the end user. Sometimes, though, you will want to obtain more from a user than just the numeric value of the button selected. In this case, you will probably want to work with an input box. Input boxes display a prompt in a dialog box, wait for the user to input text or click a button, and return a string containing the contents of the text box. The syntax is:

InputBox(*prompt*[, *title*] [, *default*] [, *xpos*] [, *ypos*] [, *helpfile*, *context*])

The InputBox function has these named arguments:

prompt	This parameter is required. This text will be displayed as the message in the dialog box (maximum length of ~1024 characters). You can make the prompt appear on separate lines by using a carriage return character (Chr(13)), a linefeed character (Chr(10)), or a carriage return/linefeed character combination (Chr(13) and Chr(10)) between each line.
title	This parameter is optional. This text will be displayed in the title bar of the dialog box. If you omit *title*, the application name is placed in the title bar.
default	This optional parameter represents the text that will be displayed by default in the text box. If you omit *default*, the text box is displayed empty.
xpos	This optional numeric parameter specifies, in twips, the horizontal distance of the left edge of the dialog box from the left edge of the screen. If *xpos* is omitted, the dialog box is horizontally centered.
ypos	This optional numeric parameter specifies, in twips, the vertical distance of the upper edge of the dialog box from the top of the screen. If *ypos* is omitted, the dialog box is vertically positioned approximately one-third of the way down the screen.
helpfile	This parameter is also optional. This string expression identifies the Help file to use to provide context-sensitive help for the dialog box. Note: If *helpfile* is provided, *context* must also be provided.
context	This is used in conjunction with the *helpfile* parameter. It is a numeric expression that represents the Help context number assigned to the appropriate Help topic. Note: If *context* is provided, *helpfile* must also be provided.

If the *helpfile* and *context* parameters are provided, the user can press F1 to view the Help topic corresponding to the context. Some host applications, for example, Microsoft Excel, also automatically add a Help button to the dialog box. If the user clicks OK or presses Enter, the InputBox function returns whatever is in the text box. If the user clicks Cancel, the function returns a zero-length string ("").

The following example displays the InputBox shown in Figure 5-8. If the user enters the correct password, a message box is displayed, indicating "You're right!" If an incorrect value is entered, a "Nope!" message box is displayed.

```
Sub InputboxShow()
Dim sPassword As String
sName = InputBox("What is the secret password?", "Example", "Hint
- leaps buildings in a single leap")
If sName = "Superman" Then
    MsgBox "You're right!", vbOKOnly, "Example"
Else
    MsgBox "Nope!", vbOKOnly, "Example"
End If
End Sub
```

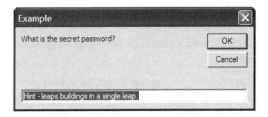

Figure 5-8: The InputBox

Note: If you want to specify more than just the first named argument, you must use the InputBox statement in an expression. If you want to omit one or more of the positional arguments, you must include a comma delimiter and a space.

String Functions

The most frequently used variable type when working with documents is the string. Oftentimes, strings must be manipulated prior to being inserted into a document. For instance, you may want to trim trailing or leading spaces from a name, or you may want to extract information contained in a list. VBA provides many built-in string functions to accomplish your desired goals.

Note: Remember to provide explicit comments for your code when performing complicated string manipulations. Since string manipulations may be achieved by using different combinations of code, it is oftentimes much more time consuming to figure out existing code than to redo the code.

The following are some commonly used VBA string functions.

LCase(*string*)

This function takes one argument and returns a string that has been converted entirely to lowercase. The *string* argument may be any valid string. The following example sets SName to "john g. doe":

```
SName = LCase("John G. Doe")
```

UCase(*string*)

This function takes one argument and returns a string that has been converted entirely to uppercase. The *string* argument may be any valid string. The following example sets SName to "JOHN G. DOE":

```
SName = UCase("John G. Doe")
```

StrConv(*string, conversion*)

This function takes two arguments and changes a string's character set or case. The *string* argument may be any valid string. The *conversion* argument may be either an integer value or a constant. See the following table for the conversion argument.

vbUpperCase	1	Converts all characters to uppercase.
vbLowerCase	2	Converts all characters to lowercase.
vbProperCase	3	Converts the first character of every word in the string to uppercase and all other characters to lowercase.
vbWide	4	Converts narrow characters to wide characters. (Far East versions only)
vbNarrow	8	Converts wide characters to narrow characters. (Far East versions only)
vbKatakana	16	Converts Hiragana characters to Katakana characters. (Japanese versions only)
vbHiragana	32	Converts Katakana characters to Hiragana characters. (Japanese versions only)
vbUnicode	64	Converts the string to Unicode using the default code page of the system.
vbFromUnicode	128	Converts the string from Unicode to the default code page of the system.

The following example sets sSentence to "John Is A Nice Guy":

```
sSentence = StrConv("joHn iS a nIcE guY", vbProperCase)
```

StrComp(*string1, string2, [compare]*)

The StrComp function compares two strings on either a binary or text basis. Both *string* arguments may be any valid string. The optional third argument is a constant that controls the basis for the comparison. If this argument is omitted, the function uses the default *compare* argument of 0 (binary). Please refer to the table in the InStr section later in this chapter for the constants for the *compare* argument.

Comparison	Return Value
string1 = string2	0
string1 < string2 (alphabetically)	−1
string1 > string2 (alphabetically)	1
either string1 or string2 is Null	Null

In the following examples, iNum1 returns 1 and iNum2 returns 0:

```
iNum1 = StrComp("john", "JOHN", vbBinaryCompare)
iNum2 = StrComp("john", "JOHN", vbTextCompare)
```

String(*number, character*)

The String function returns a string filled with the specified number of characters. The *number* argument is any valid numeric expression (long) that indicates the length of the string. The *character* argument is the ANSI character code of the string to repeat or a one-character string.

In the following examples, sString1 returns "ddddd" and sString2 returns "!!!!!":

```
sString1 = String(5, "d")
sString2 = String(5, 33)
```

Space(*number*)

The Space function returns a string full of the specified number of spaces. The *number* argument may be any valid long data type.

Here, sString returns "   " (five spaces):

```
sString = Space(5)
```

Len(*string*)

The Len function returns a long representing the number of characters in a string. The argument is any valid string.

Here, lNum returns 5:

```
lNum = Len("Billy")
```

InStr([*start*], *string1*, *string2*, [*compare*])

The InStr function returns a long representing the position of *string2* as it appears in *string1*. The optional *start* argument may be any valid numeric expression that determines where in *string1* the function will start searching for *string2*. The optional *compare* argument may be any of the constants defined in the following table. If either of the *string* arguments are Null, the function returns a Null.

Constant	Value	Description
vbBinaryCompare	0	A case-sensitive comparison (default).
vbTextCompare	1	A case-insensitive comparison.
vbDatabaseCompare	2	Based on an Access database sort order.

In the following example lNum returns 3:

```
lNum = InStr(1, "Johnny", "h", vbBinaryCompare)
```

Mid(*string*, *start*, [*length*])

The Mid function returns a string from within another string. The *string* argument may be any valid string. The *start* argument is a long data type indicating the position within *string* to start. The optional *length* argument indicates the total number of characters to return. If it is omitted, the remainder of the string is returned.

Note: Do not confuse this with the Mid statement. Although the names are the same, the syntax is different.

Here, sString returns "hnny":

```
sString = Mid("Johnny", 3)
```

Left(*string*, *length*)

The Left function returns a string representing the specified number of characters taken from the left side of the *string* argument. The *string* argument may be any valid string and the *length* argument may be any valid long. If the *length* argument is longer than the length of the *string* argument, the entire string is returned.

Here, sFName returns "Bill":

```
sFName = Left("Billy Bucknerd", 4)
```

Right(*string, length*)

The Right function returns a string representing the specified number of characters taken from the right side of the string argument. The *string* argument may be any valid string and the *length* argument may be any valid long. If the *length* argument is longer than the length of the *string* argument, the entire string is returned.

Here, sLName returns "nerd":

```
sLName = Right("Billy Bucknerd", 4)
```

Trim(*string*)

The Trim function trims (removes) both the leading and trailing spaces from a string. The *string* argument may be any valid string.

Here, sName returns "Peanut" (without any spaces):

```
sName = Trim("  Peanut    ")
```

Tip: This is a helpful function when you are searching for a value that may contain spaces. For instance, suppose you want to perform some action if a user doesn't enter a value in a text box; you can use the Trim function to avoid logic errors if the user should enter a few blank spaces accidentally.

LTrim(*string*)

The LTrim function trims the leading spaces from a string. The *string* argument may be any valid string.

Here, sName returns "Peanut   " (with three blank spaces at the end):

```
sName = LTrim(" Peanut    ")
```

RTrim(*string*)

The RTrim function trims the trailing spaces from a string.
The *string* argument may be any valid string.

Here, sName returns " Peanut" (with three blank spaces
at the beginning):

```
sName = RTrim(" Peanut    ")
```

Chr(*charcode*)

The Chr function returns the character associated with the
specified character code. The *charcode* argument is a number
that corresponds to a character. This function is often useful
when programmatically inserting text that is difficult or confusing to represent in VBA.

The following two examples are equivalent, and return the
word "Washington" enclosed in quotes:

```
MsgBox Chr(34) & "Washington" & Chr(34)
MsgBox """Washington"""
```

Note: Some of VBA's intrinsic functions have two versions, one
that returns a variant and one that returns a string. Unless a "$"
character is the last character of the function, a variant will be
returned. Variants are easier to work with because incongruent
data types are automatically converted. However, you may want to
use the string versions if: (1) you want to minimize memory
requirements, as strings are smaller than variants; (2) you want to
detect when data of one type is converted to another; or (3) you
write data directly to random access files.

String Statements

The following statements are often useful for manipulating
strings. Unlike functions, statements do not return a value and
are used to manipulate data directly. Pay close attention to the
syntax of the following statements.

Option Compare {Binary|Text|Database}

This statement, when used, must appear in a module before any variable or constant declarations.

Option Compare Binary

By using this setting, all strings will be compared on a sort order derived from the machine's internal binary representations. This is the default setting. It results in a case-sensitive comparison of all strings.

Option Compare Text

By using this setting, all strings will be compared on a case-insensitive base. This option is often helpful when trying to match user input to fixed data. Oftentimes, users will spell data correctly, but they may not capitalize appropriately.

Option Compare Database

This setting, which can only be used with Microsoft Access, results in string comparisons based on the sort order determined by the database.

Mid(*stringvar, start, [length]*) = *string*

The Mid statement replaces a portion of a string with another string. The *stringvar* argument may be any valid string. The *start* argument is a long indicating where in the string to start. The optional *length* argument is a long indicating the number of characters to replace (if omitted, the entire string is replaced). The number of characters replaced is always equal to or less than the number of characters in the *stringvar* argument.

This example incorporates the Option Compare statement and returns "Cpt. Bill J. Smith":

```
Option Compare Text 'should appear before variable declaration
sName = "sgt. Bill J. Smith"
If Left(sName, 4) = "SGT." Then
```

```
MID(SNAME, 1, 4)"Cpt."
End if
```

RSet

The RSet statement right aligns a string and replaces the characters of the existing string. The string will contain the same number of characters as the original.

In this example, " Puppy" is returned:

```
sName = "sgt. Bill J. Smith"
RSet sName = "Puppy"
```

LSet

This statement left aligns a string and replaces the characters of the existing string. This statement operates the same as the statement above except that it is left aligned and returns "Puppy   ".

```
sName = "sgt. Bill J. Smith"
LSet sName = "Puppy"
```

Conclusion

This chapter served as an introduction to VBA variables and variable declaration. Variables are an integral part of programming in any language. We also looked at constants and their use. Of course, in most programming you need to interact with the user in some fashion; to this end we discussed the MsgBox and InputBox functions. Although both of these functions are very basic, you will probably find yourself working with them at some point. Finally, because your Word programming will undoubtedly involve working with string variables, we discussed numerous functions that can be used to manipulate strings.

Chapter 6

The Word 2007 Object Model

Introduction

Document automation requires that you be well versed in the Word 2007 object model. You may use this chapter to familiarize yourself with some of the most commonly used Word objects. Included are several snippets of code that are frequently encountered when working with Word documents. The Word 2007 object model is the largest object model of all the Office applications.

The Application Object

As you've already seen, an object is something that is characterized by its properties and methods. Below is a complete listing of the properties, methods, and events for the Word.Application object. Don't let this list intimidate you; the majority of your work will be with a much smaller subset of this list. As you will see, some of these are also top-level objects themselves. Instead of covering each of these in detail, we'll discuss the most commonly used objects.

Properties of the Word 2007 Application Object

ActiveDocument	Returns a Document object that represents the active document (the document with the focus). If there are no documents open, an error occurs. Read-only.
ActiveEncryptionSession	Returns a Long that represents the encryption session associated with the active document. Read-only.
ActivePrinter	Returns or sets the name of the active printer. Read/write String.
ActiveWindow	Returns a Window object that represents the active window (the window with the focus). If there are no windows open, an error occurs. Read-only.
AddIns	Returns an AddIns collection that represents all available add-ins, regardless of whether they're currently loaded. Read-only.
AnswerWizard	Returns an AnswerWizard object that contains the files used by the online Help search engine.
Application	Returns an Application object that represents the Microsoft Word application.
ArbitraryXMLSupportAvailable	Returns a Boolean that represents whether Microsoft Word accepts custom XML schemas. True indicates that Word accepts custom XML schemas.
Assistance	Returns an Assistance object that represents the Microsoft Office Help Viewer. Read-only.
Assistant	Returns an Assistant object that represents the Microsoft Office Assistant.
AutoCaptions	Returns an AutoCaptions collection that represents the captions that are automatically added when items such as tables and pictures are inserted into a document. Read-only.
AutoCorrect	Returns an AutoCorrect object that contains the current AutoCorrect options, entries, and exceptions. Read-only.
AutoCorrectEmail	Returns an AutoCorrect object that represents automatic corrections made to e-mail messages.
AutomationSecurity	Returns or sets an MsoAutomationSecurity constant that represents the security setting Microsoft Word uses when programmatically opening files.
BackgroundPrintingStatus	Returns the number of print jobs in the background printing queue. Read-only Long.

BackgroundSavingStatus	Returns the number of files queued up to be saved in the background. Read-only Long.
Bibliography	Returns a Bibliography object that represents the bibliography reference sources stored in Microsoft Office Word. Read-only.
BrowseExtraFileTypes	Set this property to "text/html" to allow hyperlinked HTML files to be opened in Microsoft Word (instead of the default Internet browser). Read/write String.
Browser	Returns a Browser object that represents the Select Browse Object tool on the vertical scroll bar. Read-only.
Build	Returns the version and build number of the Word application. Read-only String.
CapsLock	True if the Caps Lock key is turned on. Read-only Boolean.
Caption	Returns or sets the text displayed in the title bar of the application window. Read/write String.
CaptionLabels	Returns a CaptionLabels collection that represents all the available caption labels. Read-only.
CheckLanguage	True if Microsoft Word automatically detects the language you are using as you type. Read/write Boolean.
COMAddins	Returns a reference to the COMAddins collection that represents all the Component Object Model (COM) add-ins currently loaded in Microsoft Word.
CommandBars	Returns a CommandBars collection that represents the menu bar and all the toolbars in Microsoft Word.
Creator	Returns a 32-bit integer that indicates the application in which the specified object was created. Read-only Long.
CustomDictionaries	Returns a Dictionaries object that represents the collection of active custom dictionaries. Read-only.
CustomizationContext	Returns or sets a Template or Document object that represents the template or document in which changes to menu bars, toolbars, and key bindings are stored. Read/write.
DefaultLegalBlackline	True for Microsoft Word to compare and merge documents using the Legal blackline option in the Compare and Merge Documents dialog boxes. Read/write Boolean.
DefaultSaveFormat	Returns or sets the default format that will appear in the Save as type box in the Save As dialog box. Read/write String.
DefaultTableSeparator	Returns or sets the single character used to separate text into cells when text is converted to a table. Read/write String.

Dialogs	Returns a Dialogs collection that represents all the built-in dialog boxes in Word. Read-only.
DisplayAlerts	Returns or sets the way certain alerts and messages are handled while a macro is running. Read/write WdAlertLevel.
DisplayAutoCompleteTips	True if Word displays tips that suggest text for completing words, dates, or phrases as you type. Read/write Boolean.
DisplayDocumentInformationPanel	Returns or sets a Boolean that represents whether the document properties panel is displayed. Read/write.
DisplayRecentFiles	True if the names of recently used files are displayed on the File menu. Read/write Boolean.
DisplayScreenTips	True if comments, footnotes, endnotes, and hyperlinks are displayed as tips. Text marked as having comments is highlighted. Read/write Boolean.
DisplayScrollBars	True if Word displays a scroll bar in at least one document window. False if there are no scroll bars displayed in any window. Read/write Boolean.
Documents	Returns a Documents collection that represents all the open documents. Read-only.
DontResetInsertionPointProperties	Returns or sets a Boolean that represents whether Microsoft Office Word maintains the formatting properties of the text at that position of the insertion point after running other code. Read/write.
EmailOptions	Returns an EmailOptions object that represents the global preferences for e-mail authoring. Read-only.
EmailTemplate	Returns or sets a String that represents the document template to use when sending e-mail messages. Read/write.
EnableCancelKey	Returns or sets the way that Word handles Ctrl+Break user interruptions. Read/write WdEnableCancelKey.
FeatureInstall	Returns or sets how Microsoft Word handles calls to methods and properties that require features not yet installed. Read/write MsoFeatureInstall.
FileConverters	Returns a FileConverters collection that represents all the file converters available to Microsoft Word. Read-only.
FileDialog	Returns a FileDialog object that represents a single instance of a file dialog box.
FindKey	Returns a KeyBinding object that represents the specified key combination. Read-only.

FocusInMailHeader	True if the insertion point is in an e-mail header field (the To: field, for example). Read-only Boolean.
FontNames	Returns a FontNames object that includes the names of all the available fonts. Read-only.
HangulHanjaDictionaries	Returns a HangulHanjaConversionDictionaries collection that represents all the active custom conversion dictionaries.
Height	Returns or sets the height of the active document window. Read/write Long.
International	Returns information about the current country/region and international settings. Read-only Variant.
IsObjectValid	True if the specified variable that references an object is valid. Read-only Boolean.
KeyBindings	Returns a KeyBindings collection that represents customized key assignments, which include a key code, a key category, and a command.
KeysBoundTo	Returns a KeysBoundTo object that represents all the key combinations assigned to the specified item.
LandscapeFontNames	Returns a FontNames object that includes the names of all the available landscape fonts.
Language	Returns an MsoLanguageID constant that represents the language selected for the Microsoft Word user interface.MsoLanguageID can be one of these MsoLanguageID constants.
Languages	Returns a Languages collection that represents the proofing languages listed in the Language dialog box (on the Tools menu, click Language, and then click Set Language).
LanguageSettings	Returns a LanguageSettings object, which contains information about the language settings in Microsoft Word.
Left	Returns or sets a Long that represents the horizontal position of the active document, measured in points. Read/write.
ListGalleries	Returns a ListGalleries collection that represents the three list template galleries.
MacroContainer	Returns a Template or Document object that represents the template or document in which the module that contains the running procedure is stored.
MailingLabel	Returns a MailingLabel object that represents a mailing label.
MailMessage	Returns a MailMessage object that represents the active e-mail message.

MailSystem	Returns the mail system (or systems) installed on the host computer. Read-only WdMailSystem.
MAPIAvailable	True if MAPI is installed. Read-only Boolean.
MathCoprocessorAvailable	True if a math coprocessor is installed and available to Microsoft Word. Read-only Boolean.
MouseAvailable	True if there is a mouse available for the system. Read-only Boolean.
Name	Returns the name of the specified object. Read-only String.
NewDocument	Returns a NewFile object that represents a document listed on the New Document task pane.
NormalTemplate	Returns a Template object that represents the Normal template.
NumLock	Returns the state of the Num Lock key. True if the keys on the numeric keypad insert numbers and False if the keys move the insertion point. Read-only Boolean.
OMathAutoCorrect	Returns an OMathAutoCorrect object that represents the auto correct entries for equations. Read-only.
OpenAttachmentsInFullScreen	Returns or sets a Boolean that represents whether Microsoft Word opens e-mail attachments in Reading mode. Read/write.
Options	Returns an Options object that represents application settings in Microsoft Word.
Parent	Returns an Object that represents the parent object of the specified Application object.
Path	Returns the disk or web path to the specified object. Read-only String.
PathSeparator	Returns the character used to separate folder names. This property returns a backslash (\). Read-only String.
PortraitFontNames	Returns a FontNames object that includes the names of all the available portrait fonts.
PrintPreview	True if print preview is the current view. Read/write Boolean.
RecentFiles	Returns a RecentFiles collection that represents the most recently accessed files.
RestrictLinkedStyles	Returns or sets a Boolean that represents whether Microsoft Office Word allows linked styles. Read/write.
ScreenUpdating	True if screen updating is turned on. Read/write Boolean.
Selection	Returns the Selection object that represents a selected range or the insertion point. Read-only.

ShowStartupDialog	True to display the task pane when starting Microsoft Word. Read/write Boolean.
ShowStylePreviews	Returns or sets a Boolean that represents whether Microsoft Office Word shows a preview of the formatting for styles in the Styles dialog box. Read/write.
ShowVisualBasicEditor	True if the Visual Basic Editor window is visible. Read/write Boolean.
ShowWindowsInTaskbar	True displays opened documents in the task bar, the default Single Document Interface (SDI). False lists opened documents only in the Window menu, providing the appearance of a Multiple Document Interface (MDI). Read/write Boolean.
SmartTagRecognizers	Returns a SmartTagRecognizers collection for an application.
SmartTagTypes	Returns a SmartTagTypes collection that represents the Smart Tag types for the Smart Tag components installed in Microsoft Word.
SpecialMode	True if Microsoft Word is in a special mode (for example, CopyText mode or MoveText mode). Read-only Boolean.
StartupPath	Returns or sets the complete path of the Startup folder, excluding the final separator. Read/write String.
StatusBar	Displays the specified text in the status bar. Write-only String.
SynonymInfo	Returns a SynonymInfo object that contains information from the thesaurus on synonyms, antonyms, or related words and expressions for the specified word or phrase.
System	Returns a System object, which can be used to return system-related information and perform system-related tasks.
TaskPanes	Returns a TaskPanes collection that represents the most commonly performed tasks in Microsoft Word.
Tasks	Returns a Tasks collection that represents all the applications that are running.
Templates	Returns a Templates collection that represents all the available templates — global templates and those attached to open documents.
Top	Returns or sets the vertical position of the active document. Read/write Long.
UsableHeight	Returns the maximum height (in points) to which you can set a Microsoft Word document window. Read-only Long.
UsableWidth	Returns the maximum width (in points) to which you can set a Microsoft Word document window. Read-only Long.

UserAddress	Returns or sets the user's mailing address. Read/write String.
UserControl	True if the document or application was created or opened by the user. Read-only Boolean.
UserInitials	Returns or sets the user's initials, which Word uses to construct comment marks. Read/write String.
UserName	Returns or sets the user's name, which is used on envelopes and for the Author document property. Read/write String.
VBE	Returns a VBE object that represents the Visual Basic Editor.
Version	Returns the Microsoft Word version number. Read-only String.
Visible	True if the specified object is visible. Read/write Boolean.
Width	Returns or sets the width of the application window, in points. Read/write Long.
Windows	Returns a Windows collection that represents all document windows. Read-only.
WindowState	Returns or sets the state of the specified document window or task window. Read/write WdWindowState.
WordBasic	Returns an automation object (Word.Basic) that includes methods for all the WordBasic statements and functions available in Word version 6.0 and Word for Windows 95. Read-only.
XMLNamespaces	Returns an XMLNamespaces collection that represents the XML schemas in the schema library.

Methods of the Word 2007 Application Object

Activate	Activates the specified object.
AddAddress	Adds an entry to the address book. Each entry has values for one or more tag IDs.
AutomaticChange	Performs an AutoFormat action when there is a change suggested by the Office Assistant. If no AutoFormat action is active, this method generates an error.
BuildKeyCode	Returns a unique number for the specified key combination.
CentimetersToPoints	Converts a measurement from centimeters to points (1 cm = 28.35 points). Returns the converted measurement as a Single.
ChangeFileOpenDirectory	Sets the folder in which Word searches for documents.
CheckGrammar	Checks a string for grammatical errors. Returns a Boolean to indicate whether the string contains grammatical errors. True if the string contains no errors.
CheckSpelling	Checks a string for spelling errors. Returns a Boolean to indicate whether the string contains spelling errors. True if the string has no spelling errors.
CleanString	Removes nonprinting characters (character codes 1–29) and special Word characters from the specified string or changes them to spaces (character code 32). Returns the result as a String.
CompareDocuments	Compares two documents and returns a Document object that represents the document that contains the differences between the two documents, marked using tracked changes.
DDEExecute	Sends a command or series of commands to an application through the specified dynamic data exchange (DDE) channel.
DDEInitiate	Opens a DDE channel to another application and returns the channel number.
DDEPoke	Uses an open DDE channel to send data to an application.
DDERequest	Uses an open DDE channel to request information from the receiving application and returns the information as a String.
DDETerminate	Closes the specified DDE channel to another application.
DDETerminateAll	Closes all DDE channels opened by Microsoft Word.

DefaultWebOptions	Returns the DefaultWebOptions object that contains global application-level attributes used by Microsoft Word whenever you save a document as a web page or open a web page.
GetAddress	Returns an address from the default address book.
GetDefaultTheme	Returns a String that represents the name of the default theme plus the theme formatting options Microsoft Word uses for new documents, e-mail messages, or web pages.
GetSpellingSuggestions	Returns a SpellingSuggestions collection that represents the words suggested as spelling replacements for a given word.
GoBack	Moves the insertion point among the last three locations where editing occurred in the active document (the same as pressing Shift+F5).
GoForward	Moves the insertion point forward among the last three locations where editing occurred in the active document.
Help	Displays installed help information.
HelpTool	Changes the pointer from an arrow to a question mark, indicating that you'll get context-sensitive Help information about the next command or screen element you click. If you click text, Word displays a box describing current paragraph and character formats. Pressing Esc turns the pointer back to an arrow.
InchesToPoints	Converts a measurement from inches to points (1 inch = 72 points). Returns the converted measurement as a Single.
Keyboard	Returns or sets the keyboard language and layout settings.
KeyboardBidi	Sets the keyboard language to a right-to-left language and the text entry direction to right-to-left.
KeyboardLatin	Sets the keyboard language to a left-to-right language and the text entry direction to left-to-right.
KeyString	Returns the key combination string for the specified keys (for example, Ctrl+Shift+A).
LinesToPoints	Converts a measurement from lines to points (1 line = 12 points). Returns the converted measurement as a Single.
ListCommands	Creates a new document and then inserts a table of Word commands along with their associated shortcut keys and menu assignments.
LoadMasterList	Loads a bibliography source file.

LookupNameProperties	Looks up a name in the global address book list and displays the Properties dialog box, which includes information about the specified name.
MergeDocuments	Compares two documents and returns a Document object that represents the document that contains the differences between the two documents, marked using tracked changes.
MillimetersToPoints	Converts a measurement from millimeters to points (1 millimeter = 2.835 points). Returns the converted measurement as a Single.
MountVolume	You have requested Help for a Visual Basic keyword used only on the Macintosh. For information about the MountVolume method of the Application object, consult the language reference Help included with Microsoft Office Macintosh Edition.
Move	Positions a task window or the active document window.
NewWindow	Opens a new window with the same document as the specified window. Returns a Window object.
NextLetter	You have requested Help for a Visual Basic keyword used only on the Macintosh. For information about the NextLetter method of the Application object, consult the language reference Help included with Microsoft Office Macintosh Edition.
OnTime	Starts a background timer that runs a macro at a specified time.
OrganizerCopy	Copies the specified AutoText entry, toolbar, style, or macro project item from the source document or template to the destination document or template.
OrganizerDelete	Deletes the specified style, AutoText entry, toolbar, or macro project item from a document or template.
OrganizerRename	Renames the specified style, AutoText entry, toolbar, or macro project item in a document or template.
PicasToPoints	Converts a measurement from picas to points (1 pica = 12 points). Returns the converted measurement as a Single.
PixelsToPoints	Converts a measurement from pixels to points. Returns the converted measurement as a Single.
PointsToCentimeters	Converts a measurement from points to centimeters (1 centimeter = 28.35 points). Returns the converted measurement as a Single.
PointsToInches	Converts a measurement from points to inches (1 inch = 72 points). Returns the converted measurement as a Single.
PointsToLines	Converts a measurement from points to lines (1 line = 12 points). Returns the converted measurement as a Single.

PointsToMillimeters	Converts a measurement from points to millimeters (1 millimeter = 2.835 points). Returns the converted measurement as a Single.
PointsToPicas	Converts a measurement from points to picas (1 pica = 12 points). Returns the converted measurement as a Single.
PointsToPixels	Converts a measurement from points to pixels. Returns the converted measurement as a Single.
PrintOut	Prints all or part of the specified document.
ProductCode	Returns the Microsoft Word globally unique identifier (GUID) as a String.
PutFocusInMailHeader	Places the insertion point in the To line of the mail header if the document in the active window is an e-mail document.
Quit	Quits Microsoft Word and optionally saves or routes the open documents.
Repeat	Repeats the most recent editing action one or more times. Returns True if the commands were repeated successfully.
ResetIgnoreAll	Clears the list of words that were previously ignored during a spelling check.
Resize	Sizes the Word application window or the specified task window.
Run	Runs a Visual Basic macro.
ScreenRefresh	Updates the display on the monitor with the current information in the video memory buffer.
SetDefaultTheme	Sets a default theme for Microsoft Word to use with new documents, e-mail messages, or web pages.
ShowClipboard	Displays the Clipboard task pane.
ShowMe	Displays the Office Assistant or the Help window when there is more information available.
SubstituteFont	Sets font-mapping options.
ToggleKeyboard	Switches the keyboard language setting between right-to-left and left-to-right languages.

Events of the Word 2007 Application Object

DocumentBeforeClose	Occurs immediately before any open document closes.
DocumentBeforePrint	Occurs before any open document is printed.
DocumentBeforeSave	Occurs before any open document is saved.

DocumentChange	Occurs when a new document is created, when an existing document is opened, or when another document is made the active document.
DocumentOpen	Occurs when a document is opened.
DocumentSync	Occurs when the local copy of a document that is part of a document workspace is synchronized with the copy on the server.
EPostageInsert	Occurs when a user inserts electronic postage into a document.
EPostageInsertEx	Occurs when a user inserts electronic postage into a document.
EPostagePropertyDialog	Occurs when a user clicks the E-postage Properties (Envelopes and Labels dialog box) button or Print Electronic Postage toolbar button.
MailMergeAfterMerge	Occurs after all records in a mail merge have merged successfully.
MailMergeAfterRecordMerge	Occurs after each record in the data source successfully merges in a mail merge.
MailMergeBeforeMerge	Occurs when a merge is executed before any records merge.
MailMergeBeforeRecordMerge	Occurs as a merge is executed for the individual records in a merge.
MailMergeDataSourceLoad	Occurs when the data source is loaded for a mail merge.
MailMergeDataSourceValidate	Occurs when a user validates mail merge recipients by clicking Validate in the Mail Merge Recipients dialog box.
MailMergeDataSourceValidate2	Occurs when a user validates mail merge recipients by clicking the Validate addresses link button in the Mail Merge Recipients dialog box.
MailMergeWizardSendToCustom	Occurs when the custom button is clicked during step six of the Mail Merge Wizard.
MailMergeWizardStateChange	Occurs when a user changes from a specified step to a specified step in the Mail Merge Wizard.
NewDocument	Occurs when a new document is created.
Quit	Occurs when the user exits Microsoft Office Word.
WindowActivate	Occurs when any document window is activated.
WindowBeforeDoubleClick	Occurs when the editing area of a document window is double-clicked, before the default double-click action.
WindowBeforeRightClick	Occurs when the editing area of a document window is right-clicked, before the default right-click action.
WindowDeactivate	Occurs when any document window is deactivated.

WindowSelectionChange	Occurs when the selection changes in the active document window.
WindowSize	Occurs when the application window is resized or moved.
XMLSelectionChange	Occurs when the parent XML node of the current selection changes.
XMLValidationError	Occurs when there is a validation error in the document.

Using Events with the Application Object

Each time Word is started, an instance of the Application object is created. This is the top-level object in Microsoft Word (as in most other Office applications). This object exposes properties and methods that manipulate the entire Word environment, including the appearance of the application window. You can either work with the Word application model directly, or you can set an object variable equal to the Word Application object. When working with Word, either directly or through automation, use the Application object only to manipulate the properties and methods that pertain directly to Word. In most instances, you will be working with a subobject such as a document.

```
Application.WindowState = wdWindowStateMaximize
```

Tip: When using automation, you should use an early bound object variable to instantiate the Word object model.

Sometimes properties actually return lower level objects. These objects are called *accessors*. If these accessors are global, you can work with the object directly and do not need to include the "Application" qualifier. You can use the Object Browser to see what objects are globally available (click <globals> in the Classes drop-down), or you can use the shortcut keystroke (Ctrl+J) to display an IntelliSense window that will list the globally available properties and functions.

Each of the following examples returns the same Name property:

```
MsgBox Application.ActiveDocument.Name
MsgBox ActiveDocument.Name
MsgBox Application.NormalTemplate.Name
MsgBox NormalTemplate.Name
```

Figure 6-1 shows that pressing Ctrl+J displays an IntelliSense pop-up window in the Visual Basic Editor:

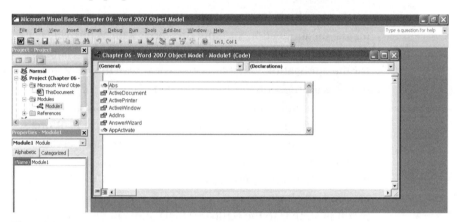

Figure 6-1

Intercepting Application Events

You can respond to certain application-level events using AutoMacros as discussed in Chapter 4. However, there may be times when you need to respond to other application events outside of the context of a particular document or template. In this case, it will be necessary to use the Application object model. This involves creating an Application type object declared with WithEvents. The WithEvents keyword declaration allows the object to respond to the exposed events via a class module.

Responding to Application Events

If you open a template, press Alt+F11, and double-click on Microsoft Word Objects in the Project Explorer window of the VBA environment, you'll see a built-in class module called ThisDocument. If you open this, you can use the list boxes on the toolbar to help you create document event procedures.

It would make sense for there to be another built-in class module called ThisApplication, but Microsoft chose to leave this out. In essence, however, a class is simply a container object that allows you to create properties, which are objects in their own right, and then create properties and methods for those objects.

From a high-level viewpoint there are two essential elements: an application variable (declared with WithEvents) to receive the events and a class module to serve as a container for the application variable. The easiest way to create application event procedures is to create an add-in. (We discussed loading and unloading add-ins in Chapter 4.) Essentially, this means creating a template (.dot) file and storing it in Word's startup directory so that it is global. Once you have created the add-in, open it in Word, go to the VBE, and insert a class module. Rename the class module from Class1 to ThisApplication. I've chosen to use "ThisApplication" because it shows that it is similar to the built-in ThisDocument class module. But note that the ThisApplication object is simply a container and doesn't actually represent an application. It represents all the properties of the Class object, and we are free to define those properties however we choose.

Next, insert the following code in the class module:

```
Option Explicit
Public WithEvents oApp As Word.Application
```

Using the WithEvents keyword indicates that the oApp object variable will respond to the events triggered by the Word.Application object. In essence, we are merely mirroring the Word application by creating another object that refers to its instantiation. Because oApp is declared publicly, it is a property of the Class object ThisApplication. Keep in mind that we haven't yet assigned oApp to an instance of the Word application (we'll do that in a minute). The WithEvents keyword can only be used in class modules and can only refer to OLE-compliant objects. All we've done so far is declared the variable of which the type is a Word Application object and used the WithEvents keyword to declare that the variable will respond to events. As far as memory is concerned, we're still not concerned because the oApp object doesn't actually exist yet.

It is now time to insert a normal code module by selecting **Insert | Module**. In the module, insert the following code:

```
Option Explicit
Dim oAppClass As New ThisApplication
```

Where ThisApplication is the name of the class module. The statement creates an object variable named oAppClass that references (it is actually a pointer to) the Class object named ThisApplication that you created earlier. The New keyword in the declaration creates a new instance of the Class object and makes it available via early binding. This means that the object is created in real time versus compile time, and that an instance of the class is loaded into memory. Now add the following code in the same module.

```
Public Sub AutoExec()
Set oAppClass.oApp = Word.Application
End Sub
```

The oApp object is available via IntelliSense because it is a property of the Class object oAppClass. It was declared as a public variable when we inserted it into the class module. The above code creates an instance of the oApp object and loads it into memory. At this point, the variable actually refers to an instance of the live Word.Application object. Essentially, the creation and allocation of this variable is what makes the oApp object exist in the first place. Keep in mind the subtle nuance — now there is an actual Word application instance, whereas previously there was only a declaration of a variable of a specific type

If you insert an AutoExec procedure, you can respond every time Word is loaded. When Word is launched, it also launches its accompanying add-ins and they are automatically loaded into memory. When it loads the add-in with the Application variable and accompanying events, those events will be triggered and, in turn, the AutoExec macro will be fired.

You can go back now to the ThisApplication class module. The class module contains two list boxes on the toolbar. If you pull down the one on the left and change the selection from (General) to oApp, a procedure called oApp_Quit() will be created. The list box on the right contains several other application events that can be utilized.

Note: Although these are all application events, some of them can only be triggered by a document.

The Document Object

The Document object represents a document. It is a member of the Documents collection, which is a collection of all open documents in the active instance of Word. You can use the Documents collection to reference a specific instance of a document using the Documents(*index*) syntax, where *index* can be either the document's name or its index number. Keep in mind that it is often best to use the actual name of a document instead of the numerical index property because as documents are opened and closed, the index values of the Documents collection change. The following is a complete listing of the properties, methods, and events that pertain to the Document object.

Properties of the Document Object

ActiveTheme	Returns the name of the active theme plus the theme formatting options for the specified document. Read-only String.
ActiveThemeDisplayName	Returns the display name of the active theme for the specified document. Read-only String.
ActiveWindow	Returns a Window object that represents the active window (the window with the focus). Read-only.
ActiveWritingStyle	Returns or sets the writing style for a specified language in the specified document. Read/write String.
Application	Returns an Application object that represents the Microsoft Word application.

AttachedTemplate	Returns a Template object that represents the template attached to the specified document. Read/write Variant.
AutoFormatOverride	Returns or sets a Boolean that represents whether automatic formatting options override formatting restrictions in a document where formatting restrictions are in effect.
AutoHyphenation	True if automatic hyphenation is turned on for the specified document. Read/write Boolean.
Background	Returns a Shape object that represents the background image for the specified document. Read-only.
Bibliography	Returns a Bibliography object that represents the bibliography references contained within a document. Read-only.
Bookmarks	Returns a Bookmarks collection that represents all the bookmarks in a document. Read-only.
BuiltInDocumentProperties	Returns a DocumentProperties collection that represents all the built-in document properties for the specified document.
Characters	Returns a Characters collection that represents the characters in a document. Read-only.
ChildNodeSuggestions	Returns an XMLChildNodeSuggestions collection that represents the list of allowed elements for the document.
ClickAndTypeParagraphStyle	Returns or sets the default paragraph style applied to text by the Click and Type feature in the specified document. Read/write Variant.
CodeName	Returns the code name for the specified document. Read-only String.
CommandBars	Returns a CommandBars collection that represents the menu bar and all the toolbars in Microsoft Word.
Comments	Returns a Comments collection that represents all the comments in the specified document. Read-only.
Compatibility	True if the compatibility option specified by the *Type* argument is enabled. Compatibility options affect how a document is displayed in Microsoft Word. Read/write Boolean.
ConsecutiveHyphensLimit	Returns or sets the maximum number of consecutive lines that can end with hyphens. Read/write Long.
Container	Returns the object that represents the container application for the specified document. Read-only Object.
Content	Returns a Range object that represents the main document story. Read-only.

ContentControls	Returns a ContentControls collection that represents all the content controls in a document. Read-only.
ContentTypeProperties	Returns a MetaProperties collection that represents the metadata stored in a document, such as author name, subject, and company. Read-only.
Creator	Returns a 32-bit integer that indicates the application in which the specified object was created. Read-only Long.
CurrentRsid	Returns a Long that represents a random number that Word assigns to changes in a document. Read-only.
CustomDocumentProperties	Returns a DocumentProperties collection that represents all the custom document properties for the specified document.
CustomXMLParts	Returns a CustomXMLParts collection that represents the custom XML in the XML data store. Read-only.
DefaultTableStyle	Returns a Variant that represents the table style that is applied to all newly created tables in a document. Read-only.
DefaultTabStop	Returns or sets the interval (in points) between the default tab stops in the specified document. Read/write Single.
DefaultTargetFrame	Returns or sets a String indicating the browser frame in which to display a web page reached through a hyperlink. Read/write.
DisableFeatures	True disables all features introduced after the version specified in the DisableFeaturesIntroducedAfter property. The default value is False. Read/write Boolean.
DisableFeaturesIntroducedAfter	Disables all features introduced after a specified version of Microsoft Word in the document only. Read/write WdDisableFeaturesIntroducedAfter.
DocumentInspectors	Returns a DocumentInspectors collection that enables you to locate hidden personal information, such as author name, company name, and revision date. Read-only.
DocumentLibraryVersions	Returns a DocumentLibraryVersions collection that represents the collection of versions of a shared document that has versioning enabled and that is stored in a document library on a server.
DocumentTheme	Returns an OfficeTheme object that represents the Microsoft Office theme applied to a document. Read-only.
DoNotEmbedSystemFonts	True for Microsoft Word to not embed common system fonts. Read/write Boolean.
Email	Returns an Email object that contains all the e-mail-related properties of the current document. Read-only.

EmbedLinguisticData	True for Microsoft Word to embed speech and handwriting so that data can be converted back to speech or handwriting. Read/write Boolean.
EmbedSmartTags	True for Microsoft Word to save the Smart Tag information in a document. Read/write Boolean.
EmbedTrueTypeFonts	True if Word embeds TrueType fonts in a document when it is saved. Read/write Boolean.
EncryptionProvider	Returns a String specifying the name of the algorithm encryption provider that Word uses when encrypting documents. Read/write.
Endnotes	Returns an Endnotes collection that represents all the endnotes in a document. Read-only.
EnforceStyle	Returns or sets a Boolean that represents whether formatting restrictions are enforced in a protected document.
Envelope	Returns an Envelope object that represents an envelope and envelope features in a document. Read-only.
FarEastLineBreakLanguage	Returns or sets a WdFarEastLineBreakLanguageID that represents the East Asian language to use when breaking lines of text in the specified document or template. Read/write.
FarEastLineBreakLevel	Returns or sets a WdFarEastLineBreakLevel that represents the line break control level for the specified document. Read/write.
Fields	Returns a Fields collection that represents all the fields in the document. Read-only.
Final	Returns or sets a Boolean that indicates whether a document is final. Read/write.
Footnotes	Returns a Footnotes collection that represents all the footnotes in a document. Read-only.
FormattingShowClear	True for Microsoft Word to show clear formatting in the Styles and Formatting task pane. Read/write Boolean.
FormattingShowFilter	Sets or returns a WdShowFilter constant that represents the styles and formatting displayed in the Styles and Formatting task pane. Read/write Boolean.
FormattingShowFont	True for Microsoft Word to display font formatting in the Styles and Formatting task pane. Read/write Boolean.
FormattingShowNextLevel	Returns or sets a Boolean that represents whether Word shows the next heading level when the previous heading level is used. Read/write.

FormattingShowNumbering	True for Microsoft Word to display number formatting in the Styles and Formatting task pane. Read/write Boolean.
FormattingShowParagraph	True for Microsoft Word to display paragraph formatting in the Styles and Formatting task pane. Read/write Boolean.
FormattingShowUserStyleName	Returns or sets a Boolean that represents whether to show user-defined styles. Read/write.
FormFields	Returns a FormFields collection that represents all the form fields in the document. Read-only.
FormsDesign	True if the specified document is in form design mode. Read-only Boolean.
Frames	Returns a Frames collection that represents all the frames in a document. Read-only.
Frameset	Returns a Frameset object that represents an entire frames page or a single frame on a frames page. Read-only.
FullName	Returns a String that represents the name of a document, including the path. Read-only.
GrammarChecked	True if a grammar check has been run on the specified range or document. Read/write Boolean.
GrammaticalErrors	Returns a ProofreadingErrors collection that represents the sentences that failed the grammar check in the specified document. Read-only.
GridDistanceHorizontal	Returns or sets a Single that represents the amount of horizontal space between the invisible gridlines that Microsoft Word uses when you draw, move, and resize AutoShapes or East Asian characters in the specified document. Read/write.
GridDistanceVertical	Returns or sets a Single that represents the amount of vertical space between the invisible gridlines that Microsoft Word uses when you draw, move, and resize AutoShapes or East Asian characters in the specified document. Read/write.
GridOriginFromMargin	True if Microsoft Word starts the character grid from the upper-left corner of the page. Read/write Boolean.
GridOriginHorizontal	Returns or sets a Single that represents the point, relative to the left edge of the page, where you want the invisible grid for drawing, moving, and resizing AutoShapes or East Asian characters to begin in the specified document. Read/write.

GridOriginVertical	Returns or sets a Single that represents the point, relative to the top of the page, where you want the invisible grid for drawing, moving, and resizing AutoShapes or East Asian characters to begin in the specified document. Read/write.
GridSpaceBetweenHorizontalLines	Returns or sets the interval at which Word displays horizontal character gridlines in print layout view. Read/write Long.
GridSpaceBetweenVerticalLines	Returns or sets the interval at which Word displays vertical character gridlines in print layout view. Read/write Long.
HasMailer	You have requested Help for a Visual Basic keyword used only on the Macintosh. For information about the HasMailer property for the Document object, consult the language reference Help included with Microsoft Office Macintosh Edition.
HasPassword	True if a password is required to open the specified document. Read-only Boolean.
HasVBProject	Returns a Boolean that represents whether a document has an attached Microsoft Visual Basic for Applications project. Read-only.
HTMLDivisions	Returns an HTMLDivisions collection that represents the HTML DIV elements in a web document.
Hyperlinks	Returns a Hyperlinks collection that represents all the hyperlinks in the specified document. Read-only.
HyphenateCaps	True if words in all capital letters can be hyphenated. Read/write Boolean.
HyphenationZone	Returns or sets the width of the hyphenation zone, in points. Read/write Long.
Indexes	Returns an Indexes collection that represents all the indexes in the specified document. Read-only.
InlineShapes	Returns an InlineShapes collection that represents all the InlineShape objects in a document. Read-only.
IsMasterDocument	True if the specified document is a master document. Read-only Boolean.
IsSubdocument	True if the specified document is a subdocument of a master document. Read-only Boolean.
JustificationMode	Returns or sets the character spacing adjustment for the specified document. Read/write WdJustificationMode.
KerningByAlgorithm	True if Microsoft Word kerns half-width Latin characters and punctuation marks in the specified document. Read/write Boolean.

Kind	Returns or sets the format type that Word uses when automatically formatting the specified document. Read/write WdDocumentKind.
LanguageDetected	Returns or sets a value that specifies whether Word has detected the language of the specified text. Read/write Boolean.
ListParagraphs	Returns a ListParagraphs object that represents all the numbered paragraphs in a document. Read-only.
Lists	Returns a Lists collection that contains all the formatted lists in the specified document. Read-only.
ListTemplates	Returns a ListTemplates collection that represents all the list formats for the specified document. Read-only.
LockQuickStyleSet	Returns or sets a Boolean that represents whether users can change which set of Quick Styles is being used. Read/write.
LockTheme	Returns or sets a Boolean that represents whether a user can change a document theme. Read/write.
MailEnvelope	Returns an MsoEnvelope object that represents an e-mail header for a document.
Mailer	You have requested Help for a Visual Basic keyword used only on the Macintosh. For information about the Mailer property for the Document object, consult the language reference Help included with Microsoft Office Macintosh Edition.
MailMerge	Returns a MailMerge object that represents the mail merge functionality for the specified document. Read-only.
Name	Returns the name of the specified object. Read-only String.
NoLineBreakAfter	Returns or sets the kinsoku characters after which Microsoft Word will not break a line. Read/write String.
NoLineBreakBefore	Returns or sets the kinsoku characters before which Microsoft Word will not break a line. Read/write String.
OMathBreakBin	Returns or sets a WdOMathBreakBin constant that represents where Microsoft Office Word places binary operators when equations span two or more lines. Read/write.
OMathBreakSub	Returns or sets a WdOMathBreakSub constant that represents how Microsoft Office Word handles a subtraction operator that falls before a line break. Read/write.
OMathFontName	Returns or sets a String that represents the name of the font used in a document to display equations. Read/write.
OMathIntSubSupLim	Returns or sets a Boolean that represents the default location of limits for integrals. Read/write.

OMathJc	Returns or sets a WdOMathJc constant that represents the default justification — left, right, centered, or centered as a group — of a group of equations. Read/write.
OMathLeftMargin	Returns or sets a Single that represents the left margin for equations. Read/write.
OMathNarySupSubLim	Returns or sets a Boolean that represents the default location of limits for n-ary objects other than integrals. Read/write.
OMathRightMargin	Returns or sets a Single that represents the right margin for equations. Read/write.
OMaths	Returns an OMaths collection that represents the OMath objects within the specified range. Read-only.
OMathSmallFrac	Returns or sets a Boolean that represents whether to use small fractions in equations contained within the document. Read/write.
OMathWrap	Returns or sets a Single that represents the placement of the second line of an equation that wraps to a new line. Read/write.
OpenEncoding	Returns the encoding used to open the specified document. Read-only MsoEncoding.
OptimizeForWord97	True if Microsoft Office Word optimizes the current document for viewing in Microsoft Word 97 by disabling any incompatible formatting. Read/write Boolean.
OriginalDocumentTitle	Returns a String that represents the document title for the original document after running a legal-blackline document compare function. Read-only.
PageSetup	Returns a PageSetup object that is associated with the specified document. Read-only.
Paragraphs	Returns a Paragraphs collection that represents all the paragraphs in the specified document. Read-only.
Parent	Returns an Object that represents the parent object of the specified Document object.
Password	Sets a password that must be supplied to open the specified document. Write-only String.
PasswordEncryptionAlgorithm	Returns a String indicating the algorithm Microsoft Word uses for encrypting documents with passwords. Read-only.
PasswordEncryptionFileProperties	True if Microsoft Word encrypts file properties for password-protected documents. Read-only Boolean.

PasswordEncryptionKeyLength	Returns a Long indicating the key length of the algorithm Microsoft Word uses when encrypting documents with passwords. Read-only.
PasswordEncryptionProvider	Returns a String specifying the name of the algorithm encryption provider that Microsoft Word uses when encrypting documents with passwords. Read-only.
Path	Returns the disk or Web path to the document. Read-only String.
Permission	Returns a Permission object that represents the permission settings in the specified document.
PrintFormsData	True if Microsoft Word prints onto a preprinted form only the data entered in the corresponding online form. Read/write Boolean.
PrintFractionalWidths	True if the specified document is formatted to use fractional point spacing to display and print characters. Read/write Boolean.
PrintPostScriptOverText	True if Print field instructions (such as PostScript commands) in a document are to be printed on top of text and graphics when a PostScript printer is used. Read/write Boolean.
PrintRevisions	True if revision marks are printed with the document. False if revision marks aren't printed (that is, tracked changes are printed as if they'd been accepted). Read/write Boolean.
ProtectionType	Returns the protection type for the specified document. Can be one of the following WdProtectionType constants: wdAllowOnlyComments, wdAllowOnlyFormFields, wdAllowOnlyReading, wdAllowOnlyRevisions, or wdNoProtection.
ReadabilityStatistics	Returns a ReadabilityStatistics collection that represents the readability statistics for the specified document or range. Read-only.
ReadingLayoutSizeX	Sets or returns a Long that represents the width of pages in a document when it is displayed in reading layout view and is frozen for entering handwritten markup.
ReadingLayoutSizeY	Sets or returns a Long that represents the height of pages in a document when it is displayed in reading layout view and is frozen for entering handwritten markup.
ReadingModeLayoutFrozen	Sets or returns a Boolean that represents whether pages displayed in reading layout view are frozen to a specified size for inserting handwritten markup into a document.
ReadOnly	True if changes to the document cannot be saved to the original document. Read-only Boolean.

ReadOnlyRecommended	True if Microsoft Office Word displays a message box whenever a user opens the document, suggesting that it be opened as read-only. Read/write Boolean.
RemoveDateAndTime	Sets or returns a Boolean indicating whether a document stores the date and time metadata for tracked changes.
RemovePersonalInformation	True if Microsoft Word removes all user information from comments, revisions, and the Properties dialog box upon saving a document. Read/write Boolean.
Research	Returns a Research object that represents the research service for a document. Read-only.
RevisedDocumentTitle	Returns a String that represents the document title for a revised document after running a legal-blackline document compare function. Read-only.
Revisions	Returns a Revisions collection that represents the tracked changes in the document or range. Read-only.
Saved	True if the specified document or template has not changed since it was last saved. False if Microsoft Word displays a prompt to save changes when the document is closed. Read/write Boolean.
SaveEncoding	Returns or sets the encoding to use when saving a document. Read/write MsoEncoding.
SaveFormat	Returns the file format of the specified document or file converter. Read-only Long.
SaveFormsData	True if Microsoft Word saves the data entered in a form as a tab-delimited record for use in a database. Read/write Boolean.
SaveSubsetFonts	True if Microsoft Word saves a subset of the embedded TrueType fonts with the document. Read/write Boolean.
Scripts	Returns a Scripts collection that represents the collection of HTML scripts in the specified object.
Sections	Returns a Sections collection that represents the sections in the specified document. Read-only.
Sentences	Returns a Sentences collection that represents all the sentences in the document. Read-only.
ServerPolicy	Returns a ServerPolicy object that represents a policy specified for a document stored on a server running Microsoft Office SharePoint Server 2007. Read-only.
Shapes	Returns a Shapes collection that represents all the Shape objects in the specified document. Read-only.

SharedWorkspace	Returns a SharedWorkspace object that represents the document workspace in which a specified document is located.
ShowGrammaticalErrors	True if grammatical errors are marked by a wavy green line in the specified document. Read/write Boolean.
ShowRevisions	True if tracked changes in the specified document are shown on the screen. Read/write Boolean.
ShowSpellingErrors	True if Microsoft Word underlines spelling errors in the document. Read/write Boolean.
ShowSummary	True if an automatic summary is displayed for the specified document. Read/write Boolean.
Signatures	Returns a SignatureSet collection that represents the digital signatures for a document.
SmartTag	Returns a SmartTag object that represents the settings for a Smart Tag solution.
SmartTags	Returns a SmartTags object that represents a Smart Tag in a document.
SmartTagsAsXMLProps	True for Microsoft Word to create an XML header containing Smart Tag information when a document containing Smart Tags is saved as HTML. Read/write Boolean.
SnapToGrid	True if AutoShapes or East Asian characters are automatically aligned with an invisible grid when they are drawn, moved, or resized in the specified document. Read/write Boolean.
SnapToShapes	True if Microsoft Word automatically aligns AutoShapes or East Asian characters with invisible gridlines that go through the vertical and horizontal edges of other AutoShapes or East Asian characters in the specified document. Read/write Boolean.
SpellingChecked	True if spelling has been checked throughout the specified range or document. False if all or some of the range or document has not been checked for spelling. Read/write Boolean.
SpellingErrors	Returns a ProofreadingErrors collection that represents the words identified as spelling errors in the specified document or range. Read-only.
StoryRanges	Returns a StoryRanges collection that represents all the stories in the specified document. Read-only.
Styles	Returns a Styles collection for the specified document. Read-only.
StyleSheets	Returns a StyleSheets collection that represents the web style sheets attached to a document.

StyleSortMethod	Returns or sets a WdStyleSort constant that represents the sort method to use when sorting styles in the Styles task pane. Read/write.
Subdocuments	Returns a Subdocuments collection that represents all the subdocuments in the specified document. Read-only.
SummaryLength	Returns or sets the length of the summary as a percentage of the document length. Read/write Long.
SummaryViewMode	Returns or sets the way a summary is displayed. Read/write WdSummaryMode.
Sync	Returns a Sync object that provides access to the methods and properties for documents that are part of a document workspace.
Tables	Returns a Tables collection that represents all the tables in the specified document. Read-only.
TablesOfAuthorities	Returns a TablesOfAuthorities collection that represents the tables of authorities in the specified document. Read-only.
TablesOfAuthoritiesCategories	Returns a TablesOfAuthoritiesCategories collection that represents the available table of authorities categories for the specified document. Read-only.
TablesOfContents	Returns a TablesOfContents collection that represents the tables of contents in the specified document. Read-only.
TablesOfFigures	Returns a TablesOfFigures collection that represents the tables of figures in the specified document. Read-only.
TextEncoding	Returns or sets the code page, or character set, that Microsoft Word uses for a document saved as an encoded text file. Read/write MsoEncoding.
TextLineEnding	Returns or sets a WdLineEndingType constant indicating how Microsoft Word marks the line and paragraph breaks in documents saved as text files. Read/write.
TrackFormatting	Returns or sets a Boolean that represents whether to track formatting changes when Track Changes is turned on. Read/write.
TrackMoves	Returns or sets a Boolean that represents whether to mark moved text when Track Changes is turned on. Read/write.
TrackRevisions	True if changes are tracked in the specified document. Read/write Boolean.
Type	Returns the document type (template or document). Read-only WdDocumentType.

UpdateStylesOnOpen	True if the styles in the specified document are updated to match the styles in the attached template each time the document is opened. Read/write Boolean.
UseMathDefaults	Returns or sets a Boolean that represents whether to use the default math settings when creating new equations. Read/write.
UserControl	True if the document was created or opened by the user. Read/write Boolean.
Variables	Returns a Variables collection that represents the variables stored in the specified document. Read-only.
VBASigned	True if the Microsoft Visual Basic for Applications (VBA) project for the specified document has been digitally signed. Read-only Boolean.
VBProject	Returns the VBProject object for the specified template or document.
WebOptions	Returns the WebOptions object, which contains document-level attributes used by Microsoft Word when you save a document as a web page or open a web page. Read-only.
Windows	Returns a Windows collection that represents all windows for the specified document. Read-only.
WordOpenXML	Returns a String that represents the flat XML format for the Word Open XML contents of the document. Read-only.
Words	Returns a Words collection that represents all the words in a document. Read-only.
WritePassword	Sets a password for saving changes to the specified document. Write-only String.
WriteReserved	True if the specified document is protected with a write password. Read-only Boolean.
XMLHideNamespaces	Returns a Boolean that represents whether to hide the XML namespaces in the list of elements in the XML Structure task pane.
XMLNodes	Returns an XMLNodes collection that represents the collection of all XML elements within a document.
XMLSaveDataOnly	Sets or returns a Boolean that represents whether a document is saved with the XML markup or as text only.
XMLSaveThroughXSLT	Sets or returns a String that specifies the path and file name for the Extensible Stylesheet Language Transformation (XSLT) to apply when a user saves a document.

XMLSchemaReferences	Returns an XMLSchemaReferences collection that represents the schemas attached to a document.
XMLSchemaViolations	Returns an XMLNodes collection that represents all nodes in the document that have validation errors.
XMLShowAdvancedErrors	Returns or sets a Boolean that represents whether error message text is generated from the built-in Microsoft Word error messages or from the Microsoft XML Core Services (MSXML) 5.0 component included with Office.
XMLUseXSLTWhenSaving	Returns a Boolean that represents whether to save a document through an Extensible Stylesheet Language Transformation (XSLT). True saves a document through an XSLT.

Methods of the Document Object

AcceptAllRevisions	Accepts all tracked changes in the specified document.
AcceptAllRevisionsShown	Accepts all revisions in the specified document that are displayed on the screen.
Activate	Activates the specified document so that it becomes the active document.
AddToFavorites	Creates a shortcut to the document or hyperlink and adds it to the Favorites folder.
ApplyDocumentTheme	Applies a document theme to a document.
ApplyQuickStyleSet	Changes the set of quick styles listed.
ApplyTheme	Applies a theme to an open document.
AutoFormat	Automatically formats a document.
AutoSummarize	Creates an automatic summary of the specified document and returns a Range object.
CanCheckin	True if Microsoft Word can check in a specified document to a server. Read/write Boolean.
CheckConsistency	Searches all text in a Japanese language document and displays instances where character usage is inconsistent for the same words.
CheckGrammar	Begins a spelling and grammar check for the specified document or range.
CheckIn	Returns a document from a local computer to a server, and sets the local document to read-only so that it cannot be edited locally.

CheckNewSmartTags	Accesses the Microsoft Office web site for available Smart Tag recognizer and action files.
CheckSpelling	Begins a spelling check for the specified document or range.
Close	Closes the specified document.
ClosePrintPreview	Switches the specified document from print preview to the previous view.
Compare	Displays revision marks that indicate where the specified document differs from another document.
ComputeStatistics	Returns a statistic based on the contents of the specified document. Long.
Convert	Converts file to the newest file format and enables all new features.
ConvertNumbersToText	Changes the list numbers and ListNum fields in the specified document to text.
ConvertVietDoc	Reconverts a Vietnamese document to Unicode using a code page other than the default.
CopyStylesFromTemplate	Copies styles from the specified template to a document.
CountNumberedItems	Returns the number of bulleted or numbered items and ListNum fields in the specified Document object.
CreateLetterContent	Creates and returns a LetterContent object based on the specified letter elements. LetterContent object.
DataForm	Displays the Data Form dialog box, in which you can add, delete, or modify records.
DeleteAllComments	Deletes all comments from the Comments collection in a document.
DeleteAllCommentsShown	Deletes all revisions in a specified document that are displayed on the screen.
DeleteAllEditableRanges	Deletes permissions in all ranges for which the specified user or group of users has permission to modify.
DeleteAllInkAnnotations	Deletes all handwritten ink annotations in a document.
DetectLanguage	Analyzes the specified text to determine the language that it is written in.
DowngradeDocument	Downgrades a document to the Word 97-2003 document format so that it can be edited in a previous version of Microsoft Office Word.

EndReview	Terminates a review of a file that has been sent for review using the SendForReview method or that has been automatically placed in a review cycle by sending a document to another user in an e-mail message.
ExportAsFixedFormat	Saves a document as PDF or XPS format.
FitToPages	Decreases the font size of text just enough so that the document will fit on fewer pages.
FollowHyperlink	Displays a cached document if it has already been downloaded. Otherwise, this method resolves the hyperlink, downloads the target document, and displays the document in the appropriate application.
ForwardMailer	You have requested Help for a Visual Basic keyword used only on the Macintosh. For information about the ForwardMailer method for the Document object, consult the language reference Help included with Microsoft Office Macintosh Edition.
FreezeLayout	In Web view, fixes the layout of the document as it currently appears so that line breaks remain fixed and ink annotations do not move when you resize the window.
GetCrossReferenceItems	Returns an array of items that can be cross-referenced based on the specified cross-reference type.
GetLetterContent	Retrieves letter elements from the specified document and returns a LetterContent object.
GetWorkflowTasks	Returns a WorkflowTasks collection that represents the workflow tasks assigned to a document.
GetWorkflowTemplates	Returns a WorkflowTemplates collection that represents the workflow templates attached to a document.
GoTo	Returns a Range object that represents the start position of the specified item, such as a page, bookmark, or field.
LockServerFile	Locks the file on the server, preventing anyone else from editing it.
MakeCompatibilityDefault	Sets the compatibility options.
ManualHyphenation	Initiates manual hyphenation of a document, one line at a time.
Merge	Merges the changes marked with revision marks from one document to another.
Post	Posts the specified document to a public folder in Microsoft Exchange.
PresentIt	Opens PowerPoint with the specified Word document loaded.

PrintOut	Prints all or part of the specified document.
PrintPreview	Switches the view to print preview.
Protect	Returns or sets the protection type for the document associated with the specified routing slip. Read/write WdProtectionType.
Range	Returns a Range object by using the specified starting and ending character positions.
RecheckSmartTags	Removes Smart Tags recognized by the grammar checker and rechecks the document content against all Smart Tag recognizers.
Redo	Redoes the last action that was undone (reverses the Undo method). Returns True if the actions were redone successfully.
RejectAllRevisions	Rejects all tracked changes in the specified document.
RejectAllRevisionsShown	Rejects all revisions in a document that are displayed on the screen.
Reload	Reloads a cached document by resolving the hyperlink to the document and downloading it.
ReloadAs	Reloads a document based on an HTML document, using the specified document encoding.
RemoveDocumentInformation	Removes sensitive information, properties, comments, and other metadata from a document.
RemoveLockedStyles	Purges a document of locked styles when formatting restrictions have been applied in a document.
RemoveNumbers	Removes numbers or bullets from the specified document.
RemoveSmartTags	Removes all Smart Tag information from a document.
RemoveTheme	Removes the active theme from the current document.
Repaginate	Repaginates the entire document.
Reply	Opens a new e-mail message — with the sender's address on the To line — for replying to the active message.
ReplyAll	Opens a new e-mail message — with the sender's and all other recipients' addresses on the To and Cc lines, as appropriate — for replying to the active message.
ReplyWithChanges	Sends an e-mail message to the author of a document that has been sent out for review, notifying them that a reviewer has completed review of the document.
ResetFormFields	Clears all form fields in a document, preparing the form to be filled in again.

RunAutoMacro	Runs an auto macro that's stored in the specified document. If the specified auto macro doesn't exist, nothing happens.
RunLetterWizard	Runs the Letter Wizard on the specified document.
Save	Saves all the documents in the Documents collection.
SaveAs	Saves the specified document with a new name or format. Some of the arguments for this method correspond to the options in the Save As dialog box (File menu).
SaveAsQuickStyleSet	Saves the group of quick styles currently in use.
Select	Selects the contents of the specified document.
SelectAllEditableRanges	Selects all ranges for which the specified user or group of users has permission to modify.
SelectContentControlsByTag	Returns a ContentControls collection that represents all the content controls in a document with the tag value specified in the *Tag* parameter. Read-only.
SelectContentControlsByTitle	Returns a ContentControls collection that represents all the content controls in a document with the title specified in the *Title* parameter. Read-only.
SelectLinkedControls	Returns a ContentControls collection that represents all content controls in a document that are linked to the specific custom XML node in the document's XML data store as specified by the *Node* parameter. Read-only.
SelectNodes	Returns an XMLNodes collection that represents all the nodes that match the *XPath* parameter in the order in which they appear in the document or range.
SelectSingleNode	Returns an XMLNode object that represents the first node that matches the *XPath* parameter in the specified document.
SelectUnlinkedControls	Returns a ContentControls collection that represents all content controls in a document that are not linked to an XML node in the document's XML data store. Read-only.
SendFax	Sends the specified document as a fax, without any user interaction.
SendFaxOverInternet	Sends a document to a fax service provider, which faxes the document to one or more specified recipients.
SendForReview	Sends a document in an e-mail message for review by the specified recipients.
SendMail	Opens a message window for sending the specified document through Microsoft Exchange.

SendMailer	You have requested Help for a Visual Basic keyword used only on the Macintosh. For information about the SendMailer method for the Document object, consult the language reference Help included with Microsoft Office Macintosh Edition.
SetDefaultTableStyle	Specifies the table style to use for newly created tables in a document.
SetLetterContent	Inserts the contents of the specified LetterContent object into a document.
SetPasswordEncryptionOptions	Sets the options Microsoft Word uses for encrypting documents with passwords.
ToggleFormsDesign	Switches form design mode on or off.
TransformDocument	Applies the specified Extensible Stylesheet Language Transformation (XSLT) file to the specified document and replaces the document with the results.
Undo	Undoes the last action or a sequence of actions, which are displayed in the Undo list. Returns True if the actions were successfully undone.
UndoClear	Clears the list of actions that can be undone for the specified document.
Unprotect	Removes protection from the specified document.
UpdateStyles	Copies all styles from the attached template into the document, overwriting any existing styles in the document that have the same name.
UpdateSummaryProperties	Updates the keyword and comment text in the Properties dialog box (File menu) to reflect the AutoSummary content for the specified document.
ViewCode	Displays the code window for the selected Microsoft ActiveX control in the specified document.
ViewPropertyBrowser	Displays the property window for the selected Microsoft ActiveX control in the specified document.
WebPagePreview	Displays a preview of the current document as it would look if saved as a web page.

Events of the Document Object

BuildingBlockInsert	Occurs when you insert a building block into a document.
Close	Occurs when a document is closed.
ContentControlAfterAdd	Occurs after adding a content control to a document.
ContentControlBeforeContentUpdate	Occurs before updating the content in a content control, only when the content comes from the Office XML data store.
ContentControlBeforeDelete	Occurs before removing a content control from a document.
ContentControlBeforeStoreUpdate	Occurs before updating the document's XML data store with the value of a content control.
ContentControlOnEnter	Occurs when a user enters a content control.
ContentControlOnExit	Occurs when a user leaves a content control.
New	Occurs when a new document based on the template is created. A procedure for the New event will run only if it is stored in a template.
Open	Occurs when a document is opened.
Sync	Occurs when the local copy of a document that is part of a document workspace is synchronized with the copy on the server.
XMLAfterInsert	Occurs when a user adds a new XML element to a document. If more than one element is added to the document at the same time (for example, when cutting and pasting XML), the event fires for each element that is inserted.
XMLBeforeDelete	Occurs when a user deletes an XML element from a document. If more than one element is deleted from the document at the same time (for example, when cutting and pasting XML), the event fires for each element that is deleted.

Using Properties and Methods

The ActiveDocument property is used to return the Document object that represents the document with the focus. The ActiveDocument property is read-only, so it cannot be used to give the focus to a particular document (use the Activate method to give focus to a particular document). If there are no documents open, an error will occur if this property is referenced. You can avoid this error by checking to see that a document is actually open by using the Count property of the Documents collection. For example:

```
If Documents.Count > 0 then
    MsgBox ActiveDocument.Name
Else
    MsgBox "There are no documents open!"
End If
```

You will find that working with the Documents object is usually the starting point for your Word programming. Therefore, we will spend a few pages covering how to work with the most common properties and methods of the Documents object.

Opening Documents

You can open existing Word documents using the Open method of the Documents object.

```
Documents.Open(FileName, ConfirmConversions, ReadOnly,
AddToRecentFiles, PasswordDocument, PasswordTemplate, Revert,
WritePasswordDocument, WritePasswordTemplate, Format)
```

The Open function syntax has these named arguments:

FileName	This is the name of the document to be opened (paths are accepted).
ConfirmConversions	Set this to True if you want to display the Convert File dialog box (non-Word format files only).
ReadOnly	Set this to True to open the document as read-only.

AddToRecentFiles	Set this to True to add the file name to the list of recently used files.
PasswordDocument	This allows you to enter the password for opening the document.
PasswordTemplate	This allows you to enter the password for opening the template.
Revert	This parameter is used to control what happens if the file is already open. Set it to True to discard any unsaved changes to the open document and reopen the file. A value of False will activate the open document.
WritePasswordDocument	This allows you to enter a password for saving changes to the document.
WritePasswordTemplate	This allows you to enter a password for saving changes to the template.
Format	This indicates which type of file converter to use when opening the document: wdOpenFormatAuto (default) wdOpenFormatDocument wdOpenFormatRTF wdOpenFormatTemplate wdOpenFormatText wdOpenFormatUnicodeText

Here is a brief code snippet that shows the two different ways you can use the Open method to work with documents. The first line is how you would normally open a document if you were working in a macro. The second and third lines show how you would work with the same document if you were using automation. In this case, you would set a variable equal to the document and work directly with the variable.

```
Documents.Open("C:\Wordware\Sample.doc")
Dim oDoc as Document
Set oDoc = Documents.Open("C:\Wordware\Sample.doc")
```

Programmatically Creating New Documents

Use the Add method to create a new empty document and add it to the Documents collection. By default, the Add method bases newly created documents on the Normal template. Several different collection objects use the Add method to add another member to their collection. The syntax is:

```
Documents.Add(Template, NewTemplate)
```

The *Template* argument refers to the name of the template to be used for the new document. The default for this argument is the Normal template. If *NewTemplate* is True, Word will create the new document as a template. The default value of the *NewTemplate* argument is False.

The following line of code creates a new document based on the Normal template:

```
Documents.Add
```

You can also set an object variable equal to a document using the Add method:

```
Dim oDoc as Document
Set oDoc = Documents.Add("C:\Wordware\MyTemplate.dot")
```

Saving Documents

If you've worked with any Windows application, you are familiar with saving files. Using VBA code to save documents is no different from manually saving them from the Microsoft Office button. The first time you save a document, you'll be using the SaveAs method. This method allows you to specify all of the things you do when you choose to save your document for the first time manually. You can enter a file name, choose a directory, choose a file type, etc.

Once a document has been saved, you can use the Save method. This operates in an identical manner to clicking Save from the Microsoft Office button. The user will not be prompted and the file will save in the same format with which it was opened. If you use the Save method when working with a file that has never been saved, the Save As dialog box will appear and prompt the user for a name.

You can immediately save a newly created document using the following syntax:

```
Documents.Add.SaveAs FileName:="C:\Wordware\SaveTheDoc.doc"
```

You can also save all open documents (without looping through the Documents collection) by using the Save method with the Documents collection:

```
Documents.Save NoPrompt:=True
```

Closing Documents

Closing a document is accomplished by executing the Close method of the appropriate Documents object. Programmatically using the Close method is no different than closing documents manually. The syntax is:

```
Documents.Close(SaveChanges, OriginalFormat, RouteDocument)
```

The Close function syntax has these arguments:

SaveChanges	This argument specifies the save action for the document. Use one of the following wdSaveOptions constants: wdDoNotSaveChanges wdPromptToSaveChanges wdSaveChanges
OriginalFormat	This specifies the save format for the document. Use one of the following wdOriginalFormat constants: wdOriginalDocumentFormat wdPromptUser wdWordDocument
RouteDocument	Set this argument to True to route the document to the next recipient. If the document doesn't have a routing slip attached, this argument is ignored.

If there have been changes to the document, Word will prompt the user with a message box inquiring whether changes should be saved, as shown in Figure 6-2.

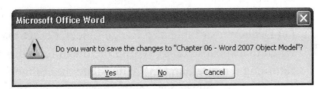

Figure 6-2: The save changes message box

Note: You can prevent VBA from displaying this message box by setting the *SaveChanges* argument to False or by using the built-in constant wdDoNotSaveChanges, as shown in the following code snippet:

```
Documents("SaveTheDoc.doc").Close
SaveChanges:=wdDoNotSaveChanges
```

Caution: Watch out when using the Close method of the ActiveDocument object. If your template works with other documents, this code may operate correctly during normal execution. But if it runs when you are testing your project, your template may close and you will lose your changes.

The following example enumerates the Documents collection to determine whether the document named ShaniDog.doc is open. If this document is contained in the Documents collection, the document is activated; otherwise, it's opened.

```
For Each doc In Documents
If doc.Name = "ShaniDog.doc" Then found = True
    Next doc
If found <> True Then
    Documents.Open FileName:="C:\Wordware\ShaniDog.doc"
Else
    Documents("ShaniDog.doc").Activate
End If
```

The Range Object

A common undertaking when working with Microsoft Word is to programmatically select a specific area within a document and do something with that area. These areas may be tables, sections, paragraphs, or even words. The Range object provides a convenient way to work with these different areas of a document.

Working with ranges generally involves these three steps: (1) Declare a variable as a Range object, (2) set that variable equal to a specific range within the document (this involves returning a range), and (3) manipulate the Range variable according to your needs. (Note that if you are only going to be working with the area once, you do not need to create a variable to contain the range.) Once you have a range specified, you can work with the different methods and properties of the Range object to control how the document will look, respond, etc.

Note: Range objects are contiguous areas within a document defined by starting and ending positions.

Below is a complete listing of the properties and methods that pertain to the Range object.

Properties of the Range Object

Application	Returns an Application object that represents the Microsoft Word application.
Bold	True if the range is formatted as bold. Read/write Long.
BoldBi	True if the font or range is formatted as bold. Returns True, False, or wdUndefined (for a mixture of bold and non-bold text). Can be set to True, False, or wdToggle. Read/write Long.
BookmarkID	Returns the number of the bookmark that encloses the beginning of the specified range; returns 0 (zero) if there is no corresponding bookmark. Read-only Long.
Bookmarks	Returns a Bookmarks collection that represents all the bookmarks in a document, range, or selection. Read-only.
Borders	Returns a Borders collection that represents all the borders for the specified object.
Case	Returns or sets a WdCharacterCase constant that represents the case of the text in the specified range. Read/write.
Cells	Returns a Cells collection that represents the table cells in a range. Read-only.
Characters	Returns a Characters collection that represents the characters in a range. Read-only.
CharacterStyle	Returns a Variant that represents the style used to format one or more characters. Read-only.
CharacterWidth	Returns or sets the character width of the specified range. Read/write WdCharacterWidth.

Columns	Returns a Columns collection that represents all the table columns in the range. Read-only.
CombineCharacters	True if the specified range contains combined characters. Read/write Boolean.
Comments	Returns a Comments collection that represents all the comments in the specified document, selection, or range. Read-only.
ContentControls	Returns a ContentControls collection that represents the content controls contained within a range. Read-only.
Creator	Returns a 32-bit integer that indicates the application in which the specified object was created. Read-only Long.
DisableCharacterSpaceGrid	True if Microsoft Word ignores the number of characters per line for the corresponding Range object. Read/write Boolean.
Document	Returns a Document object associated with the specified range. Read-only.
Duplicate	Returns a read-only Range object that represents all the properties of the specified range.
Editors	Returns an Editors object that represents all the users authorized to modify a selection or range within a document.
EmphasisMark	Returns or sets the emphasis mark for a character or designated character string. Read/write WdEmphasisMark.
End	Returns or sets the ending character position of a range. Read/write Long.
EndnoteOptions	Returns an EndnoteOptions object that represents the endnotes in a range.
Endnotes	Returns an Endnotes collection that represents all the endnotes in a range. Read-only.
EnhMetaFileBits	Returns a Variant that represents a picture representation of how a range of text appears.
Fields	Returns a Fields collection that represents all the fields in the range. Read-only.
Find	Returns a Find object that contains the criteria for a find operation. Read-only.
FitTextWidth	Returns or sets the width (in the current measurement units) in which Microsoft Word fits the text in the current selection or range. Read/write Single.
Font	Returns or sets a Font object that represents the character formatting of the specified object. Read/write Font.

FootnoteOptions	Returns a FootnoteOptions object that represents the footnotes in a selection or range.
Footnotes	Returns a Footnotes collection that represents all the footnotes in a range. Read-only.
FormattedText	Returns or sets a Range object that includes the formatted text in the specified range or selection. Read/write.
FormFields	Returns a FormFields collection that represents all the form fields in the range. Read-only.
Frames	Returns a Frames collection that represents all the frames in a range. Read-only.
GrammarChecked	True if a grammar check has been run on the specified range or document. Read/write Boolean.
GrammaticalErrors	Returns a ProofreadingErrors collection that represents the sentences that failed the grammar check on the specified document or range. Read-only.
HighlightColorIndex	Returns or sets the highlight color for the specified range. Read/write WdColorIndex.
HorizontalInVertical	Returns or sets the formatting for horizontal text set within vertical text. Read/write WdHorizontalInVerticalType.
HTMLDivisions	Returns an HTMLDivisions object that represents an HTML division in a web document.
Hyperlinks	Returns a Hyperlinks collection that represents all the hyperlinks in the specified range. Read-only.
ID	Returns or sets the identification name for the specified range. Read/write String.
Information	Returns information about the specified range. Read-only Variant.
InlineShapes	Returns an InlineShapes collection that represents all the InlineShape objects in a range. Read-only.
IsEndOfRowMark	True if the specified range is collapsed and is located at the end-of-row mark in a table. Read-only Boolean.
Italic	True if the font or range is formatted as italic. Read/write Long.
ItalicBi	True if the font or range is formatted as italic. Read/write Long.
Kana	Returns or sets whether the specified range of Japanese language text is Hiragana or Katakana. Read/write WdKana.
LanguageDetected	Returns or sets a value that specifies whether Microsoft Word has detected the language of the specified text. Read/write Boolean.

LanguageID	Returns or sets a WdLanguageID constant that represents the language for the specified range. Read/write.
LanguageIDFarEast	Returns or sets an East Asian language for the specified object. Read/write WdLanguageID.
LanguageIDOther	Returns or sets the language for the specified range. Read/write WdLanguageID.
ListFormat	Returns a ListFormat object that represents all the list formatting characteristics of a range. Read-only.
ListParagraphs	Returns a ListParagraphs collection that represents all the numbered paragraphs in the range. Read-only.
ListStyle	Returns a Variant that represents the style used to format a bulleted list or numbered list. Read-only.
NextStoryRange	Returns a Range object that refers to the next story. Read-only Range.
NoProofing	True if the spelling and grammar checker ignores the specified text. Read/write Long.
OMaths	Returns an OMaths collection that represents the OMath objects within the specified range. Read-only.
Orientation	Returns or sets the orientation of text in a range when the Text Direction feature is enabled. Read/write WdTextOrientation.
PageSetup	Returns a PageSetup object that's associated with the specified range. Read-only.
ParagraphFormat	Returns or sets a ParagraphFormat object that represents the paragraph settings for the specified range. Read/write.
Paragraphs	Returns a Paragraphs collection that represents all the paragraphs in the specified range. Read-only.
ParagraphStyle	Returns a Variant that represents the style used to format a paragraph. Read-only.
Parent	Returns an Object that represents the parent object of the specified Range object.
ParentContentControl	Returns a ContentControl object that represents the parent content control for the specified range. Read-only.
PreviousBookmarkID	Returns the number of the last bookmark that starts before or at the same place as the specified range. Read-only Long.
ReadabilityStatistics	Returns a ReadabilityStatistics collection that represents the readability statistics for the specified document or range. Read-only.
Revisions	Returns a Revisions collection that represents the tracked changes in the range. Read-only.

Rows	Returns a Rows collection that represents all the table rows in a range. Read-only.
Scripts	Returns a Scripts collection that represents the collection of HTML scripts in the specified object.
Sections	Returns a Sections collection that represents the sections in the specified range. Read-only.
Sentences	Returns a Sentences collection that represents all the sentences in the range. Read-only.
Shading	Returns a Shading object that refers to the shading formatting for the specified object.
ShapeRange	Returns a ShapeRange collection that represents all the Shape objects in the specified range. Read-only.
ShowAll	True if all nonprinting characters (such as hidden text, tab marks, space marks, and paragraph marks) are displayed. Read/write Boolean.
SmartTags	Returns a SmartTags object that represents a Smart Tag in a document.
SpellingChecked	True if spelling has been checked throughout the specified range or document. False if all or some of the range or document has not been checked for spelling. Read/write Boolean.
SpellingErrors	Returns a ProofreadingErrors collection that represents the words identified as spelling errors in the specified range. Read-only.
Start	Returns or sets the starting character position of a range. Read/write Long.
StoryLength	Returns the number of characters in the story that contains the specified range. Read-only Long.
StoryType	Returns the story type for the specified range, selection, or bookmark. Read-only WdStoryType.
Style	Returns or sets the style for the specified object. Read/write Variant.
Subdocuments	Returns a Subdocuments collection that represents all the subdocuments in the specified range or document. Read-only.
SynonymInfo	Returns a SynonymInfo object that contains information from the thesaurus on synonyms, antonyms, or related words and expressions for the contents of a range.
Tables	Returns a Tables collection that represents all the tables in the specified range. Read-only.
TableStyle	Returns a Variant that represents the style used to format a table. Read-only.

Text	Returns or sets the text in the specified range or selection. Read/write String.
TextRetrievalMode	Returns a TextRetrievalMode object that controls how text is retrieved from the specified Range. Read/write.
TopLevelTables	Returns a Tables collection that represents the tables at the outermost nesting level in the current range. Read-only.
TwoLinesInOne	Returns or sets whether Microsoft Word sets two lines of text in one and specifies the characters that enclose the text, if any. Read/write WdTwoLinesInOneType.
Underline	Returns or sets the type of underline applied to a range. Read/write WdUnderline.
WordOpenXML	Returns a String that represents the XML contained within the range in the Microsoft Office Word Open XML format. Read-only.
Words	Returns a Words collection that represents all the words in a range. Read-only.
XML	Returns a String that represents the XML text in the specified object.
XMLNodes	Returns an XMLNodes collection that represents the XML elements in the specified range — including any elements that are only partially within the range. Read-only.
XMLParentNode	Returns an XMLNode object that represents the parent XML node of a range. Read-only.

Methods of the Range Object

AutoFormat	Automatically formats a document. Use the Kind property to specify a document type.
Calculate	Calculates a mathematical expression within a range or selection. Returns the result as a Single.
CheckGrammar	Begins a spelling and grammar check for the specified range.
CheckSpelling	Begins a spelling check for the specified document or range.
CheckSynonyms	Displays the Thesaurus dialog box, which lists alternative word choices, or synonyms, for the text in the specified range.
Collapse	Collapses a range or selection to the starting or ending position. After a range or selection is collapsed, the starting and ending points are equal.
ComputeStatistics	Returns a Long that represents a statistic based on the contents of the specified range.

ConvertHangulAndHanja	Converts the specified range from hangul to hanja or vice versa.
ConvertToTable	Converts text within a range to a table. Returns the table as a Table object.
Copy	Copies the specified range to the clipboard.
CopyAsPicture	The CopyAsPicture method works the same way as the Copy method.
CreatePublisher	You have requested Help for a Visual Basic keyword used only on the Macintosh. For information about the CreatePublisher method of the Range object, consult the language reference Help included with Microsoft Office Macintosh Edition.
Cut	Removes the specified object from the document and places it on the clipboard.
Delete	Deletes the specified number of characters or words.
DetectLanguage	Analyzes the specified text to determine the language that it is written in.
EndOf	Moves or extends the ending character position of a range to the end of the nearest specified text unit.
Expand	Expands the specified range or selection. Returns the number of characters added to the range or selection. Long.
ExportAsFixedFormat	Saves a portion of a document as PDF or XPS format.
ExportFragment	Exports the selected range into a document for use as a document fragment.
GetSpellingSuggestions	Returns a SpellingSuggestions collection that represents the words suggested as spelling replacements for the first word in the specified range.
GoTo	Returns a Range object that represents the start position of the specified item, such as a page, bookmark, or field.
GoToEditableRange	Returns a Range object that represents an area of a document that can be modified by the specified user or group of users.
GoToNext	Returns a Range object that refers to the start position of the next item or location specified by the *What* argument.
GoToPrevious	Returns a Range object that refers to the start position of the previous item or location specified by the *What* argument.
ImportFragment	Imports a document fragment into the document at the specified range.
InRange	Returns True if the range to which the method is applied is contained in the range specified by the *Range* argument.
InsertAfter	Inserts the specified text at the end of a range.
InsertAlignmentTab	Inserts an absolute tab that is always positioned in the same spot, relative to either the margins or indents.

InsertAutoText	Attempts to match the text in the specified range or the text surrounding the range with an existing AutoText entry name.
InsertBefore	Inserts the specified text before the specified range.
InsertBreak	Inserts a page, column, or section break.
InsertCaption	Inserts a caption immediately preceding or following the specified range.
InsertCrossReference	Inserts a cross-reference to a heading, bookmark, footnote, or endnote, or to an item for which a caption label is defined (for example, an equation, figure, or table).
InsertDatabase	Retrieves data from a data source (for example, a separate Microsoft Office Word document, a Microsoft Office Excel worksheet, or a Microsoft Office Access database) and inserts the data as a table in place of the specified range.
InsertDateTime	Inserts the current date or time, or both, either as text or as a Time field.
InsertFile	Inserts all or part of the specified file.
InsertParagraph	Replaces the specified range with a new paragraph.
InsertParagraphAfter	Inserts a paragraph mark after a range.
InsertParagraphBefore	Inserts a new paragraph before the specified range.
InsertSymbol	Inserts a symbol in place of the specified range.
InsertXML	Inserts the specified XML into the document at the specified range, replacing any text contained within the range.
InStory	True if the range to which this method is applied is in the same story as the range specified by the *Range* argument.
IsEqual	True if the range to which this method is applied is equal to the range specified by the *Range* argument.
LookupNameProperties	Looks up a name in the global address book list and displays the Properties dialog box, which includes information about the specified name.
ModifyEnclosure	Adds, modifies, or removes an enclosure around the specified character or characters.
Move	Collapses the specified range to its start or end position and then moves the collapsed object by the specified number of units.
MoveEnd	Moves the ending character position of a range.
MoveEndUntil	Moves the end position of the specified range until any of the specified characters are found in the document. If the movement is forward in the document, the range is expanded.

MoveEndWhile	Moves the ending character position of a range while any of the specified characters are found in the document.
MoveStart	Moves the start position of the specified range.
MoveStartUntil	Moves the start position of the specified range until one of the specified characters is found in the document.
MoveStartWhile	Moves the start position of the specified range while any of the specified characters are found in the document.
MoveUntil	Moves the specified range until one of the specified characters is found in the document.
MoveWhile	Moves the specified range while any of the specified characters are found in the document.
Next	Returns a Range object that represents the specified unit relative to the specified range.
NextSubdocument	Moves the range to the next subdocument.
Paste	Inserts the contents of the clipboard at the specified range.
PasteAndFormat	Pastes the selected table cells and formats them as specified.
PasteAppendTable	Merges pasted cells into an existing table by inserting the pasted rows between the selected rows. No cells are overwritten.
PasteAsNestedTable	Pastes a cell or group of cells as a nested table into the selected range.
PasteExcelTable	Pastes and formats a Microsoft Excel table.
PasteSpecial	Inserts the contents of the clipboard.
PhoneticGuide	Adds phonetic guides to the specified range.
Previous	Returns the previous range relative to the specified range.
PreviousSubdocument	Moves the range to the previous subdocument.
Relocate	In outline view, moves the paragraphs within the specified range after the next visible paragraph or before the previous visible paragraph.
Select	Selects the specified range.
SetListLevel	Sets the list level for one or more items in a numbered list.
SetRange	Sets the starting and ending character positions for an existing range.
Sort	Sorts the paragraphs in the specified range.
SortAscending	Sorts paragraphs or table rows in ascending alphanumeric order.
SortDescending	Sorts paragraphs or table rows in descending alphanumeric order.

StartOf	Moves or extends the start position of the specified range or selection to the beginning of the nearest specified text unit. This method returns a Long that indicates the number of characters by which the range or selection was moved or extended. The method returns a negative number if the movement is backward through the document.
SubscribeTo	You have requested Help for a Visual Basic keyword used only on the Macintosh. For information about the SubscribeTo method of the Range object, consult the language reference Help included with Microsoft Office Macintosh Edition.
TCSCConverter	Converts the specified range from Traditional Chinese to Simplified Chinese or vice versa.
WholeStory	Expands a range to include the entire story.

Utilizing the Range Object

Returning Ranges

Before working with a Range variable, you obviously have to return a Range object. This section describes some simple ways to access the Range object. Usually, you will be setting an object variable equal to the newly declared range; this way you can work with the Range object throughout the lifetime of the variable.

Using the Range Method

One way to create a Range object in a document is to use the Range method (available from a Documents object). The Range method requires both starting and ending positions. Following is the syntax of the Range method:

```
Documents(1).Range(Start, End)
```

Start is the starting character position and *End* is the ending character position.

The *Start* and *End* arguments require integer character position values. These values begin with 0 (zero) corresponding to the beginning of a document. Every character in the document will be counted, including nonprinting characters.

Note: Hidden characters are counted even if they're not displayed. If starting and ending positions are not specified, the entire document is returned as a Range object.

Using the Range Property

Another way to create a Range object is to use the Range property of an object in the document. This property returns a Range object that represents the portion of a document that's contained in the specified object. The Range property is read-only.

The Selection Object

Another useful object, very similar to the Range object, is the Selection object. However, the Selection object has one key difference: There can only be one Selection object per pane in a document window, and only one Selection object can be active at any given time. You will find the Selection object especially useful when you are interacting with users. You can then use the Selection object to refer to any text that the user may highlight in a document. This enables you to create intelligent macros that apply certain properties to areas that the user selects. Following are the properties and methods of the Selection object.

Properties of the Selection Object

Active	True if the selection in the specified window or pane is active. Read-only Boolean.
Application	Returns an Application object that represents the Microsoft Word application.
BookmarkID	Returns the number of the bookmark that encloses the beginning of the specified selection. Read-only Long.
Bookmarks	Returns a Bookmarks collection that represents all the bookmarks in a document, range, or selection. Read-only.
Borders	Returns a Borders collection that represents all the borders for the specified object.

Cells	Returns a Cells collection that represents the table cells in a selection. Read-only.
Characters	Returns a Characters collection that represents the characters in a document, range, or selection. Read-only.
ChildShapeRange	Returns a ShapeRange collection representing the child shapes contained within a selection.
Columns	Returns a Columns collection that represents all the table columns in a selection. Read-only.
ColumnSelectMode	True if column selection mode is active. Read/write Boolean.
Comments	Returns a Comments collection that represents all the comments in the specified selection. Read-only.
Creator	Returns a 32-bit integer that indicates the application in which the specified object was created. Read-only Long.
Document	Returns a Document object associated with the specified selection. Read-only.
Editors	Returns an Editors object that represents all the users authorized to modify a selection within a document.
End	Returns or sets the ending character position of a selection. Read/write Long.
EndnoteOptions	Returns an EndnoteOptions object that represents the endnotes in a selection.
Endnotes	Returns an Endnotes collection that represents all the endnotes contained within a selection. Read-only.
EnhMetaFileBits	Returns a Variant that represents a picture representation of how a selection or range of text appears.
ExtendMode	True if Extend mode is active. Read/write Boolean.
Fields	Returns a read-only Fields collection that represents all the fields in the selection.
Find	Returns a Find object that contains the criteria for a find operation. Read-only.
FitTextWidth	Returns or sets the width (in the current measurement units) in which Microsoft Word fits the text in the current selection. Read/write Single.
Flags	Returns or sets properties of the selection. Read/write WdSelectionFlags.
Font	Returns or sets a Font object that represents the character formatting of the specified object. Read/write.

FootnoteOptions	Returns a FootnoteOptions object that represents the footnotes in a selection.
Footnotes	Returns a Footnotes collection that represents all the footnotes in a range, selection, or document. Read-only.
FormattedText	Returns or sets a Range object that includes the formatted text in the specified range or selection. Read/write.
FormFields	Returns a FormFields collection that represents all the form fields in the selection. Read-only.
Frames	Returns a Frames collection that represents all the frames in a selection. Read-only.
HasChildShapeRange	True if the selection contains child shapes. Read-only Boolean.
HeaderFooter	Returns a HeaderFooter object for the specified selection. Read-only.
HTMLDivisions	Returns an HTMLDivisions object that represents an HTML division in a web document.
Hyperlinks	Returns a Hyperlinks collection that represents all the hyperlinks in the specified selection. Read-only.
Information	Returns information about the specified selection. Read-only Variant.
InlineShapes	Returns an InlineShapes collection that represents all the InlineShape objects in a selection. Read-only.
IPAtEndOfLine	True if the insertion point is at the end of a line that wraps to the next line. Read-only Boolean.
IsEndOfRowMark	True if the specified selection or range is collapsed and is located at the end-of-row mark in a table. Read-only Boolean.
LanguageDetected	Returns or sets a Boolean that specifies whether Microsoft Word has detected the language of the selected text.
LanguageID	Returns or sets the language for the specified object. Read/write.
LanguageIDFarEast	Returns or sets an East Asian language for the specified object. Read/write WdLanguageID.
LanguageIDOther	Returns or sets the language for the specified object. Read/write WdLanguageID.
NoProofing	True if the spelling and grammar checker ignores the specified text. Returns wdUndefined if set to True for only some of the specified text. Read/write Long.
OMaths	Returns an OMaths collection that represents the OMath objects within the current selection. Read-only.

Orientation	Returns or sets the orientation of text in a selection when the Text Direction feature is enabled. Read/write WdTextOrientation.
PageSetup	Returns a PageSetup object that's associated with the specified selection. Read-only.
ParagraphFormat	Returns or sets a ParagraphFormat object that represents the paragraph settings for the specified selection. Read/write.
Paragraphs	Returns a Paragraphs collection that represents all the paragraphs in the specified selection. Read-only.
Parent	Returns an Object that represents the parent object of the specified Selection object.
PreviousBookmarkID	Returns the number of the last bookmark that starts before or at the same place as the specified selection or range; returns 0 (zero) if there is no corresponding bookmark. Read-only Long.
Range	Returns a Range object that represents the portion of a document that's contained in the specified object.
Rows	Returns a Rows collection that represents all the table rows in a range, selection, or table. Read-only.
Sections	Returns a Sections collection that represents the sections in the specified selection. Read-only.
Sentences	Returns a Sentences collection that represents all the sentences in the selection. Read-only.
Shading	Returns a Shading object that refers to the shading formatting for the specified selection.
ShapeRange	Returns a ShapeRange collection that represents all the Shape objects in the selection. Read-only.
SmartTags	Returns a SmartTags object that represents a Smart Tag in a selection. Read-only.
Start	Returns or sets the starting character position of a selection. Read/write Long.
StartIsActive	True if the beginning of the selection is active. Read/write Boolean.
StoryLength	Returns the number of characters in the story that contains the specified selection. Read-only Long.
StoryType	Returns the story type for the specified selection. Read-only WdStoryType.

Style	Returns or sets the style for the specified object. To set this property, specify the local name of the style, an integer, a WdBuiltinStyle constant, or an object that represents the style. For a list of valid constants, consult the Microsoft Visual Basic Object Browser. Read/write Variant.
Tables	Returns a Tables collection that represents all the tables in the specified selection. Read-only.
Text	Returns or sets the text in the specified selection. Read/write String.
TopLevelTables	Returns a Tables collection that represents the tables at the outermost nesting level in the current selection. Read-only.
Type	Returns the selection type. Read-only WdSelectionType.
WordOpenXML	Returns a String that represents the XML contained within the selection in the Microsoft Office Word Open XML format. Read-only.
Words	Returns a Words collection that represents all the words in a selection. Read-only.
XML	Returns a String that represents the XML text in the specified object.
XMLNodes	Returns an XMLNodes collection that represents the collection of all XML elements within a selection — including those elements that are only partially within the selection.
XMLParentNode	Returns an XMLNode object that represents the parent node of a selection.

Methods of the Selection Object

BoldRun	Adds the bold character format to or removes it from the current run.
Calculate	Calculates a mathematical expression within a selection. Returns the result as a Single.
ClearCharacterAllFormatting	Removes all character formatting (formatting applied either manually or through character styles) from the selected text.
ClearCharacterDirectFormatting	Removes character formatting (formatting that has been applied manually using the buttons on the Ribbon or through the dialog boxes) from the selected text.
ClearCharacterStyle	Removes character formatting that has been applied through character styles from the selected text.
ClearFormatting	Removes text and paragraph formatting from a selection.
ClearParagraphAllFormatting	Removes all paragraph formatting (formatting applied either manually or through paragraph styles) from the selected text.

ClearParagraphDirectFormatting	Removes paragraph formatting that has been applied manually (using the buttons on the Ribbon or through the dialog boxes) from the selected text.
ClearParagraphStyle	Removes paragraph formatting that has been applied through paragraph styles from the selected text.
Collapse	Collapses a selection to the starting or ending position. After a selection is collapsed, the starting and ending points are equal.
ConvertToTable	Converts text within a range to a table. Returns the table as a Table object.
Copy	Copies the specified selection to the clipboard.
CopyAsPicture	The CopyAsPicture method works the same way as the Copy method.
CopyFormat	Copies the character formatting of the first character in the selected text.
CreateAutoTextEntry	Adds a new AutoTextEntry object to the AutoTextEntries collection, based on the current selection.
CreateTextbox	Adds a default-size text box around the selection.
Cut	Removes the specified object from the document and moves it to the clipboard.
Delete	Deletes the specified number of characters or words.
DetectLanguage	Analyzes the specified text to determine the language that it is written in.
EndKey	Moves or extends the selection to the end of the specified unit.
EndOf	Moves or extends the ending character position of a range or selection to the end of the nearest specified text unit.
EscapeKey	Cancels a mode such as extend or column select (equivalent to pressing the Esc key).
Expand	Expands the specified range or selection. Returns the number of characters added to the range or selection. Long.
ExportAsFixedFormat	Saves the current selection as PDF or XPS format.
Extend	Turns on extend mode, or if extend mode is already on, extends the selection to the next larger unit of text.
GoTo	Moves the insertion point to the character position immediately preceding the specified item, and returns a Range object (except for the wdGoToGrammaticalError, wdGoToProofreadingError, or wdGoToSpellingError constant).

GoToEditableRange	Returns a Range object that represents an area of a document that can be modified by the specified user or group of users.
GoToNext	Returns a Range object that refers to the start position of the next item or location specified by the *What* argument. If you apply this method to the Selection object, the method moves the selection to the specified item (except for the wdGoToGrammaticalError, wdGoToProofreadingError, and wdGoToSpellingError constants).
GoToPrevious	Returns a Range object that refers to the start position of the previous item or location specified by the *What* argument. If applied to a Selection object, GoToPrevious moves the selection to the specified item. Range object.
HomeKey	Moves or extends the selection to the beginning of the specified unit. This method returns an integer that indicates the number of characters the selection was actually moved, or it returns 0 (zero) if the move was unsuccessful.This method corresponds to functionality of the Home key.
InRange	True if the selection to which the method is applied is contained within the range specified by the *Range* argument.
InsertAfter	Inserts the specified text at the end of a range or selection.
InsertBefore	Inserts the specified text before the specified selection.
InsertBreak	Inserts a page, column, or section break.
InsertCaption	Inserts a caption immediately preceding or following the specified selection.
InsertCells	Adds cells to an existing table.
InsertColumns	Inserts columns to the left of the column that contains the selection.
InsertColumnsRight	Inserts columns to the right of the current selection.
InsertCrossReference	Inserts a cross-reference to a heading, bookmark, footnote, or endnote, or to an item for which a caption label is defined (for example, an equation, figure, or table).
InsertDateTime	Inserts the current date or time, or both, either as text or as a Time field.
InsertFile	Inserts all or part of the specified file.
InsertFormula	Inserts an = (Formula) field that contains a formula at the selection.
InsertNewPage	Inserts a new page at the position of the insertion point.
InsertParagraph	Replaces the specified selection with a new paragraph.
InsertParagraphAfter	Inserts a paragraph mark after a selection.
InsertParagraphBefore	Inserts a new paragraph before the specified selection or range.

InsertRows	Inserts the specified number of new rows above the row that contains the selection. If the selection isn't in a table, an error occurs.
InsertRowsAbove	Inserts rows above the current selection.
InsertRowsBelow	Inserts rows below the current selection.
InsertStyleSeparator	Inserts a special hidden paragraph mark that allows Microsoft Word to join paragraphs formatted using different paragraph styles, so lead-in headings can be inserted into a table of contents.
InsertSymbol	Inserts a symbol in place of the specified selection.
InsertXML	Inserts the specified XML into the document at the cursor, replacing any selected text.
InStory	True if the selection to which this method is applied is in the same story as the range specified by the *Range* argument.
IsEqual	True if the selection to which this method is applied is equal to the range specified by the *Range* argument.
ItalicRun	Adds the italic character format to or removes it from the current run.
LtrPara	Sets the reading order and alignment of the specified paragraphs to left-to-right.
LtrRun	Sets the reading order and alignment of the specified run to left-to-right.
Move	Collapses the specified selection to its start or end position and then moves the collapsed object by the specified number of units. This method returns a Long value that represents the number of units by which the selection was moved, or it returns 0 (zero) if the move was unsuccessful.
MoveDown	Moves the selection down and returns the number of units it has been moved.
MoveEnd	Moves the ending character position of a range or selection.
MoveEndUntil	Moves the end position of the specified selection until any of the specified characters are found in the document.
MoveEndWhile	Moves the ending character position of a selection while any of the specified characters are found in the document.
MoveLeft	Moves the selection to the left and returns the number of units it has been moved.
MoveRight	Moves the selection to the right and returns the number of units it has been moved.
MoveStart	Moves the start position of the specified selection.

MoveStartUntil	Moves the start position of the specified selection until one of the specified characters is found in the document. If the movement is backward through the document, the selection is expanded.
MoveStartWhile	Moves the start position of the specified selection while any of the specified characters are found in the document.
MoveUntil	Moves the specified selection until one of the specified characters is found in the document.
MoveUp	Moves the selection up and returns the number of units that it has been moved.
MoveWhile	Moves the specified selection while any of the specified characters are found in the document.
Next	Returns a Range object that represents the next unit relative to the specified selection.
NextField	Selects the next field.
NextRevision	Locates and returns the next tracked change as a Revision object.
NextSubdocument	Moves the selection to the next subdocument.
Paste	Inserts the contents of the clipboard at the specified selection.
PasteAndFormat	Pastes the selected table cells and formats them as specified.
PasteAppendTable	Merges pasted cells into an existing table by inserting the pasted rows between the selected rows. No cells are overwritten.
PasteAsNestedTable	Pastes a cell or group of cells as a nested table into the selection.
PasteExcelTable	Pastes and formats a Microsoft Excel table.
PasteFormat	Applies formatting copied with the CopyFormat method to the selection.
PasteSpecial	Inserts the contents of the clipboard.
Previous	Moves the selected text by the specified number of units and returns a Range object relative to the collapsed selection.
PreviousField	Selects and returns the previous field.
PreviousRevision	Locates and returns the previous tracked change as a Revision object.
PreviousSubdocument	Moves the selection to the previous subdocument.
ReadingModeGrowFont	Increases the size of the displayed text one point size when the document is displayed in Reading mode.
ReadingModeShrinkFont	Decreases the size of the displayed text one point size when the document is displayed in Reading mode.
RtlPara	Sets the reading order and alignment of the specified paragraphs to right-to-left.

RtlRun	Sets the reading order and alignment of the specified run to right-to-left.
Select	Selects the specified text.
SelectCell	Selects the entire cell containing the current selection.
SelectColumn	Selects the column that contains the insertion point, or selects all columns that contain the selection.
SelectCurrentAlignment	Extends the selection forward until text with a different paragraph alignment is encountered.
SelectCurrentColor	Extends the selection forward until text with a different color is encountered.
SelectCurrentFont	Extends the selection forward until text in a different font or font size is encountered.
SelectCurrentIndent	Extends the selection forward until text with different left or right paragraph indents is encountered.
SelectCurrentSpacing	Extends the selection forward until a paragraph with different line spacing is encountered.
SelectCurrentTabs	Extends the selection forward until a paragraph with different tab stops is encountered.
SelectRow	Selects the row that contains the insertion point, or selects all rows that contain the selection.
SetRange	Sets the starting and ending character positions for the selection.
Shrink	Shrinks the selection to the next smaller unit of text.
ShrinkDiscontiguousSelection	Cancels the selection of all but the most recently selected text when a selection contains multiple, unconnected selections.
Sort	Sorts the paragraphs in the specified selection.
SortAscending	Sorts paragraphs or table rows in ascending alphanumeric order.
SortDescending	Sorts paragraphs or table rows within the selection in descending alphanumeric order.
SplitTable	Inserts an empty paragraph above the first row in the selection.
StartOf	Moves or extends the start position of the specified range or selection to the beginning of the nearest specified text unit. This method returns a Long that indicates the number of characters by which the range or selection was moved or extended. The method returns a negative number if the movement is backward through the document.
ToggleCharacterCode	Switches a selection between a Unicode character and its corresponding hexadecimal value.

TypeBackspace	Deletes the character preceding a collapsed selection (an insertion point).
TypeParagraph	Inserts a new, blank paragraph.
TypeText	Inserts the specified text.
WholeStory	Expands a selection to include the entire story.

Working with the Selection Object

Returning Selections

There are generally two methods you will use to return a Selection object. The first is to use the Selection property of an object to return the Selection object. If no characters are selected, the Selection property will represent the cursor location when used with the Application object. The following example selects the entire first paragraph of the active document, collapses the selection to the first line, and moves the insertion point to the end of that line.

```
Paragraphs(1).Range.Select
Selection.EndKey Unit:=wdLine, Extend:=wdMove
```

The second way you can create a Selection object is to use the Select method of an object. The Selection property only applies to the Application object, the Pane object, and the Window object. The Select method can be used with many different types of objects. This versatility makes it the preferred way of returning a Selection object.

Working with Selections

The Select method selects the content of a document and requires a variable that represents a Document object. The following example selects the ActiveDocument object, which is a member of the Documents collection, and displays the name of the first bookmark in that document.

```
ActiveDocument.Select
MsgBox Selection.Bookmarks(1).Name
```

When you are working with Selection objects, you can use the Type property to return the selection type. This is very convenient if you only want to work with certain types of selections. You can also use the Information property to return information about the selection. Keep in mind that you can use the Range property to return a Range object from the Selection object. The Selection object also includes numerous methods to expand, collapse, and move within the selection.

Note: There can be only one Selection object per window pane; however, you can have multiple Range objects. Many Word programmers prefer working with Range objects for that reason.

Word 2007 XML Objects

The Word 2007 object model has five objects and five collections that programmatically support XML-related actions. For information on the members of those objects and collections, see the Word 2007 online programming help.

XMLChildNodeSuggestion Object

The XMLChildNodeSuggestion object and the XMLChildNodeSuggestions collection represent one or more elements that are possible as children of the currently selected element according to the XML document's corresponding attached schema. You can navigate the XMLChildNodeSuggestions collection using an ordinal index number or an element name. For example:

```
ActiveDocument.ChildNodeSuggestions.Item(Index:=1).Insert
ActiveDocument.ChildNodeSuggestions. _
Item(Index:="sales_order").Insert
```

Properties of the XMLChildNodeSuggestion Object

Application	Returns an Application object that represents the Microsoft Word application.
BaseName	Returns a String that represents the name of the element without any prefix.
Creator	Returns a 32-bit integer that indicates the application in which the specified object was created. Read-only Long.
NamespaceURI	Returns a String that represents the Uniform Resource Identifier (URI) of the schema namespace for the specified object. Read-only.
Parent	Returns an Object that represents the parent object of the specified XMLChildNodeSuggestion object.
XMLSchemaReference	Returns an XMLSchemaReference object that represents the XML schema to which the specified XMLChildNodeSuggestion object belongs.

Methods of the XMLChildNodeSuggestion Object

Insert	Inserts an XMLNode object that represents an XML element node.

XMLNamespace Object

The XMLNamespace object and the XMLNamespaces collection represent one or more registered namespace URIs in the user's schema library. You can navigate the XMLNamespaces collection using an ordinal index number or a namespace URI. For example:

```
Application.XMLNamespaces.Item(Index:=1).AttachToDocument
Document:=ActiveDocument
Application.XMLNamespaces.Item _
(Index:="myCompany.schemas.com.sales_order").AttachToDocument _
Document:=ActiveDocument
```

Properties of the XMLNamespace Object

Alias	Returns a String that represents the display name for the specified object.
Application	Returns an Application object that represents the Microsoft Word application.
Creator	Returns a 32-bit integer that indicates the application in which the specified object was created. Read-only Long.

DefaultTransform	Returns an XSLTransform object that represents the default Extensible Stylesheet Language Transformation (XSLT) file to use when opening a document from an XML schema for a particular namespace.
Location	Returns or sets a String that represents the physical location of the namespace of an XML schema in the schema library. Read/write.
Parent	Returns an Object that represents the parent object of the specified XMLNamespace object.
URI	Returns a String that represents the Uniform Resource Identifier (URI) of the associated namespace.
XSLTransforms	Returns an XSLTransforms collection that represents the Extensible Stylesheet Language Transformation (XSLT) files specified for use with a schema.

Methods of the XMLNamespace Object

| AttachToDocument | Attaches an XML schema to a document. |
| Delete | Deletes the specified XML schema from the list of available XML schemas. |

XMLNode Object

The XMLNode object and the XMLNodes collection represent one or more elements in an XML document, range, and even child nodes of a containing element. You can navigate the XMLNodes collection by ordinal index number only, for example:

```
MsgBox Prompt:=ActiveDocument.XMLNodes.Item(Index:=1).BaseName
```

Properties of the XMLNode Object

Application	Returns an Application object that represents the Microsoft Word application.
Attributes	Returns an XMLNodes collection that represents the attributes for the specified element.
BaseName	Returns a String that represents the name of the element without any prefix.
ChildNodes	Returns an XMLNodes collection that represents the child elements of a specified element.

ChildNodeSuggestions	Returns an XMLChildNodeSuggestions collection that represents the list of child elements for a specified element.
Creator	Returns a 32-bit integer that indicates the application in which the specified object was created. Read-only Long.
FirstChild	Returns a DiagramNode object that represents the first child node of a parent node. Read-only.
HasChildNodes	Returns a Boolean that represents whether an XML node has child nodes. Read-only.
LastChild	Returns an XMLNode object that represents the last child node of an XML element.
Level	Returns a WdXMLNodeLevel constant that represents whether an XML element is part of a paragraph, is a paragraph, or is contained within a table cell or contains a table row. Read-only.
NamespaceURI	Returns a String that represents the Uniform Resource Identifier (URI) of the schema namespace for the specified object. Read-only.
NextSibling	Returns an XMLNode object that represents the next element in the document that is at the same level as the specified element.
NodeType	Returns a WdXMLNodeType constant that represents the type of node.
NodeValue	Returns or sets a String that represents the value of an XML element. Read/write.
OwnerDocument	Returns a Document object that represents the parent document of the specified XML element.
Parent	Returns an Object that represents the parent object of the specified XMLNode object.
ParentNode	Returns an XMLNode object that represents the parent element of the specified element.
PlaceholderText	Sets or returns a String that represents the text displayed for an element that contains no text.
PreviousSibling	Returns an XMLNode object that represents the previous element in the document that is at the same level as the specified element.
Range	Returns a Range object that represents the portion of a document that is contained in the specified object. Read-only.
SmartTag	Returns a SmartTag object that represents the Smart Tag associated with an XML element.
Text	Returns or sets the text contained within the XML element. Read/write String.
ValidationErrorText	Returns a String that represents the description for a validation error on an XMLNode object.

ValidationStatus	Returns a WdXMLValidationStatus constant that represents whether an element or attribute is valid according to the attached schema.
WordOpenXML	Returns a String that represents the XML for the node in the Microsoft Office Word Open XML format. Read-only.
XML	Returns a String that represents the text, with or without XML markup, that is contained within an XML node. Read-only.

Methods of the XMLNode Object

Copy	Copies the specified XML element, excluding XML markup, to the clipboard.
Cut	Removes the specified XML element from the document and places it on the clipboard.
Delete	Deletes the specified XML element from an XML document.
RemoveChild	Removes a child element from the specified element.
SelectNodes	Returns an XMLNodes collection that represents all the child elements that match the *XPath* parameter, in the order in which they appear within the specified XML element.
SelectSingleNode	Returns an XMLNode object that represents the first child element that matches the *XPath* parameter within the specified XML element.
SetValidationError	Changes the validation error text displayed to a user for a specified node and forces Word to report a node as invalid.
Validate	Validates an individual XML element against the XML schemas that are attached to a document.

XMLSchemaReference Object

The XMLSchemaReference object and the XMLSchema-References collection represent one or more schemas for each unique namespace that is attached to a document. You can navigate the XMLSchemaReferences collection using an ordinal index number or a namespace URI, for example:

```
ActiveDocument.XMLSchemaReferences.Item(Index:=1).Reload
ActiveDocument.XMLSchemaReferences.Item _
(Index:="myCompany.schemas.com.sales_order").Reload
```

Properties of the XMLSchemaReference Object

Application	Returns an Application object that represents the Microsoft Word application.
Creator	Returns a 32-bit integer that indicates the application in which the specified object was created. Read-only Long.
Location	Returns a String that represents the physical location of an XML schema. Read-only.
NamespaceURI	Returns a String that represents the Uniform Resource Identifier (URI) of the schema namespace for the specified object. Read-only.
Parent	Returns an Object that represents the parent object of the specified XMLSchemaReference object.

Methods of the XMLSchemaReference Object

Delete	Deletes the specified XML Schema Reference.
Reload	Reloads the XML schemas that are referenced in a document.

XSLTransform Object

The XSLTransform object and the XSLTransforms collection represent one or more transforms registered for Word only. You can navigate the XSLTransforms collection by using an ordinal index number or by using an alias. If no transform is found with that alias, then Word attempts to use the transform's ID. For example:

```
MsgBox Application.XMLNamespaces.Item _
    (Index:=1).XSLTransforms.Item(Index:=1).Location
MsgBox Application.XMLNamespaces.Item _
    (Index:=" myCompany.schemas.com.sales_order") _
    .XSLTransforms.Item(Index:="Elegant Memo").Location
```

Note: The Word 2007 XML object model was designed to resemble the existing Microsoft XML (MSXML) parser document object model. If you are familiar with the MSXML parser, you should find the Word XML object model familiar and intuitive. In fact, Word XML validation and parsing is done with MSXML in the background; Word 2007 uses Microsoft XML v5.0, an incremental update to the existing Microsoft XML v4.0 (Microsoft XML Core Services).

Properties of the XSLTransform Object

Application	Returns an Application object that represents the Microsoft Word application.
Count	Returns a Long that represents the number of XSLTransforms in the collection. Read-only.
Creator	Returns a 32-bit integer that indicates the application in which the specified object was created. Read-only Long.
Parent	Returns an Object that represents the parent object of the specified XSLTransforms object.

Methods of the XSLTransform Object

Add	Returns an XSLTransform object that represents an Extensible Stylesheet Language Transformation (XSLT) added to the collection of XSLTs for a specified schema.
Item	Returns an XSLTransform object in a collection.

The Find and Replace Objects

You can use either the Selection or the Range object to return Find and Replace objects. The Find method returns True if the find operation is successful and obviously False when unsuccessful. There is a slight difference depending on whether you return the Find object from the Selection or the Range object. These differences will be discussed below. First, let's take a look at the syntax of the Find method:

```
FindObject.(Range or Selection).Execute(FindText, MatchCase,
MatchWholeWord, MatchWildcards, MatchSoundsLike,
MatchAllWordForms, Forward, Wrap, Format, ReplaceWith, Replace)
```

Tip: There are many parameters to the Find object. The best way to find the parameter you need is to use the Macro Recorder and perform a search manually. After you've completed your search, you can view the code and obtain the proper syntax for your code.

The Find.Execute function syntax has these named arguments:

FindText	The text to be searched for. Use an empty string (" ") to search for formatting only. You can search for special characters by specifying appropriate character codes. For example, "^p" corresponds to a paragraph mark and "^t" corresponds to a tab character.
MatchCase	True to specify that the find text be case sensitive. Corresponds to the Match case check box in the Find and Replace dialog box (Edit menu).
MatchWholeWord	True to have the find operation locate only entire words, not text that is part of a larger word. Corresponds to the Find whole words only check box in the Find and Replace dialog box.
MatchWildcards	True to have the find text be a special search operator. Corresponds to the Use wildcards check box in the Find and Replace dialog box.
MatchSoundsLike	True to have the find operation locate words that sound similar to the find text. Corresponds to the Sounds like check box in the Find and Replace dialog box.
MatchAllWordForms	True to have the find operation locate all forms of the find text (for example, "sit" locates "sitting" and "sat"). Corresponds to the Find all word forms check box in the Find and Replace dialog box.
Forward	True to search forward (toward the end of the document).
Wrap	Controls what happens if the search begins at a point other than the beginning of the document and the end of the document is reached (or vice versa if Forward is set to False). This argument also controls what happens if there is a selection or range and the search text is not found in the selection or range. Can be one of the WdFindWrap constants.
Format	True to have the find operation locate formatting in addition to, or instead of, the find text.

ReplaceWith	The replacement text. To delete the text specified by the *Find* argument, use an empty string (" "). You specify special characters and advanced search criteria just as you do for the *Find* argument. To specify a graphic object or other nontext item as the replacement, move the item to the clipboard and specify "^c" for ReplaceWith.
Replace	Specifies how many replacements are to be made: one, all, or none. Can be any WdReplace constant.
MatchKashida	True if find operations match text with matching kashidas in an Arabic-language document. This argument may not be available to you, depending on the language support (U.S. English, for example) that you have selected or installed.
MatchDiacritics	True if find operations match text with matching diacritics in a right-to-left language document. This argument may not be available to you, depending on the language support (U.S. English, for example) that you have selected or installed.
MatchAlefHamza	True if find operations match text with matching alef hamzas in an Arabic-language document. This argument may not be available to you, depending on the language support (U.S. English, for example) that you have selected or installed.
MatchControl	True if find operations match text with matching bidirectional control characters in a right-to-left language document. This argument may not be available to you, depending on the language support (U.S. English, for example) that you have selected or installed.
MatchPrefix	True to match words beginning with the search string. Corresponds to the Match prefix check box in the Find and Replace dialog box.
MatchSuffix	True to match words ending with the search string. Corresponds to the Match suffix check box in the Find and Replace dialog box.
MatchPhrase	True ignores all white space and control characters between words.
IgnoreSpace	True ignores all white space between words. Corresponds to the Ignore white-space characters check box in the Find and Replace dialog box.
IgnorePunct	True ignores all punctuation characters between words. Corresponds to the Ignore punctuation check box in the Find and Replace dialog box.

As previously mentioned, there is a slight difference between returning the Find object from a Selection object and a Range object. In the event of deriving the Find object from a Selection object, when the argument *FindText* is found in the selection, the selection is then changed to *FindText*. However, when *FindText* is found when deriving the Find object from a Range object, it is the range that is redefined to reflect *FindText*.

The Dialogs Collection

The Dialogs collection represents all of the built-in dialog boxes (Dialog objects) in Word. A good understanding of the Dialogs collection will enable you to intercept Word's built-in commands and add functionality. You can display a built-in dialog box to get user input or to control Word by using Visual Basic. You'll see that you can control every aspect of the Dialogs collection that you may need. There are almost 200 built-in dialog boxes to which the Word object model gives you access.

The Show Method of the Dialogs Object

If you simply need to display a particular dialog box to the user and do not want to add any functionality, you can use the Show method of the Dialogs object. This will display the dialog according to the wdWordDialog constant that you use and execute any action taken just as if Word displayed it. The following example displays the SaveAs dialog box wdDialogFileSaveAs:

```
Dialogs(wdDialogFileSaveAs).Show
```

Once the Show method executes, the SaveAs dialog box will be displayed. If the user enters a new name and clicks OK, the file will be saved. If you need to display a particular tab to the user, you can set the Default Tab property. You can also rely on IntelliSense to display a rather lengthy list of the available options tabs. For example, if you wanted to display the

General tab of the **Tools | Options** dialog box, you could use the following code:

```
With Dialogs(wdDialogToolsOptions)
    .DefaultTab = wdDialogToolsOptionsTabGeneral
    .Show
End With
```

Note: The Show method also has an optional *TimeOut* parameter. This parameter takes a long variable type and represents the length of time the dialog box will remain displayed (in milliseconds).

The Display Method of the Dialog Object

You can use the Display method to display a dialog box without enabling the actions that are built into the dialog box. This means that any changes entered by the user will not be applied unless we use the Execute method of the dialog box. The Display method can be useful if you need to prompt the user with a built-in dialog box and return the settings. This is also the method you will be using to intercept a user's commands and carry out your own execution. For example, the following code will display the File Open dialog box and return a message box to the user with the name of the file that was selected. Remember, although the File Open dialog box is being used, the file will not actually be opened when the Display method is used.

```
With Dialogs(wdDialogFileOpen)
    .Display
    MsgBox .Name
End With
```

If you wanted to actually open the file after displaying the message box in the previous example, you can use the Execute method. The following example displays the File Open dialog box, displays a message box with the chosen file's name, and opens the file (as long as the name is not an empty string).

```
With Dialogs(wdDialogFileOpen)
    .Display
    MsgBox .Name
    If .Name <> "" Then .Execute
End With
```

Note: The Execute method will execute the appropriate actions of the dialog box based on the settings even if the dialog box is not displayed.

Dialog Box Arguments

Before we go any further in our discussion of dialog boxes, it is worthwhile to discuss arguments. You may have noticed that ".Name" did not appear in your IntelliSense options. If you rely heavily on IntelliSense, working with dialog boxes can be especially frustrating (unless you become accustomed to checking Help and finding the arguments for a specific dialog box). The actual Help topic is "Built-in dialog box argument lists," and if you start Help by pressing F1 with Dialogs selected, it's no less than four layers of Help away. This can be annoying if you're in the middle of a project and you need to find a particular argument. Figure 6-3 shows the Help dialog box with the arguments for the File Open dialog.

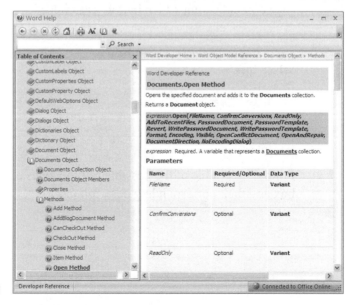

Figure 6-3

You can use arguments to set options in the dialog box once you are working with the appropriate Dialog object. In most cases the name of the argument will correspond closely to one of the options on the actual Word dialog box; checking these dialog boxes can eliminate the headaches of trying to guess the right argument in your code. You control dialog box settings in a very similar manner to the way you return them. The following example sets the Name argument of the File Open dialog box instead of returning it:

```
With Dialogs(wdDialogFileOpen)
    .Name = "Sonny Ridgeback"
    .Display
End With
```

Note: Do not use a Dialog object to change a value that you can set with a property or method.

Dialog Box Return Values

Every time a user clicks one of the buttons on a dialog box, a return value is generated. This value indicates which button was clicked to close the dialog box. The following example displays the File Open dialog box, and then displays a message box indicating which button was clicked:

```
Dim x As Integer
x = Dialogs(wdDialogFileOpen).Display
Select Case x
Case -1
    MsgBox "Open"
Case 0
    MsgBox "Cancel"
End Select
```

Following is a list of the possible return values of the dialog box and their corresponding descriptions.

Return Value	Description
−2	The Close button
−1	The OK button
0 (zero)	The Cancel button
> 0 (zero)	A command button: 1 is the first button, 2 is the second button, and so on

Other Useful Objects

The objects discussed above will probably cover 80 percent of your Word programming needs. The following objects will hopefully ratchet that number up another 10 percent. Keep in mind that there are several other objects you can use. If you need any further help, check the Object Browser in VBA. Following are brief descriptions of some other commonly used objects.

ActivePrinter

The ActivePrinter object can be used to either set or return the active printer. VBA has a few limitations in this regard, however. If you are used to programming in VB, you are aware that there is a Printers collection. This is especially helpful in an enterprise organization where there may be several printers installed on a machine. VBA does not provide this functionality.

CommandBar

In some instances you may need to work with the CommandBar object. The CommandBar object is a member of the CommandBars collection. You can access an individual CommandBar object using CommandBars(*index*), where *index* is the name or index number of a command bar. The following example steps through the collection of command bars to find the command bar named "Drawing." When this command bar is encountered, the Visible property is set to True so the command bar will be visible.

```
Dim oCmdBar As CommandBar
For Each oCmdBar In ActiveDocument.CommandBars
    If oCmdBar.Name = "Drawing" Then
        oCmdBar.Visible = True
    End If
Next oCmdBar
```

When working with the CommandBars collection, you can use a name or index number to specify a menu bar or toolbar in the list of the application's menu bars and toolbars. You will need to use the appropriate name when identifying a menu, shortcut menu, or submenu. If two or more custom menus or submenus have the same name, Command-Bars(*index*) can be used to return the appropriate one using the correct index value.

Command Bar Pop-Up Menu Project

When you right-click in a window, the resultant pop-up menu is also just a command bar. You can access it in the same way you access other command bars. Following is the code that will produce the pop-up menu shown in Figure 6-4. Use the OnAction property to set the procedure to execute when the button is chosen. For a description on how to intercept the right-click event, see the section on events in Chapter 3.

```
Public Sub AddPop-upMenu()
Dim Pop-upMenu As CommandBar
Dim myTools(1 To 3) As CommandBarPop-up
    Set Pop-upMenu = CommandBars("Text")
    Pop-upMenu.Reset
    With Pop-upMenu
        .Controls.Item("Font...").Delete
        .Controls.Item("Paragraph...").Delete
        .Controls.Item("Bullets and numbering...").Delete
        .Controls.Item("Synonyms").Delete
    End With
Set myTools(1) = Pop-upMenu.Controls.Add(Type:=msoControlPop-up)
    With myTools(1)
        .BeginGroup = True
```

```
        .Caption = "Sunny"
        .OnAction = "YourCode"
    End With
Set myTools(2) = Pop-upMenu.Controls.Add(Type:=msoControlPop-up)
    With myTools(2)
        .Caption = "Peanut"
        .Enabled = False
    End With
Set myTools(3) = Pop-upMenu.Controls.Add(Type:=msoControlPop-up)
    With myTools(3)
        .Caption = "Shani"
        .Enabled = False
    End With
End Sub
Sub YourCode()
    MsgBox "This is where you would write your code",
        vbInformation, "Pop-up"
End Sub
```

Tip: These settings will be applied to your environment. If you want to change your toolbar back to its original construction, use the Reset method.

 *Figure 6-4*

HeaderFooter

This object represents either a single header or footer. The HeaderFooter object is a member of the HeaderFooters collection. Almost all of the typical properties that pertain to collections also pertain to the HeaderFooters collection. The HeaderFooters collection contains all headers and footers within a section of the document.

Both the header and the footer use the same predefined index constants. You will use this index to return a single HeaderFooter object. The only other way of returning a HeaderFooter object is by using the HeaderFooter property with a Selection object. The proper syntax when working directly with either headers or footers is:

```
Headers(index) or Footers(index)
```

The following are the WdHeaderFooterIndex constants:

> wdHeaderFooterEvenPages
> wdHeaderFooterFirstPage
> wdHeaderFooterPrimary

Note: You cannot add HeaderFooter objects to the HeaderFooters collection.

Caution: You might encounter a potential problem when working with either headers or footers in conjunction with Word's fields.

When you are updating fields in your document you will probably use something similar to the following code:

```
ThisDocument.Fields.Update
```

The code above will not update the fields in either a footer or a header. The only way to update the fields in this case is to update the fields that pertain to that specific section's header objects. For instance, if you were to put a DocVariable field in a header in the first section of the document, the following code demonstrates how to update it:

```
ThisDocument.Variables("Test").Value = "Levi Kills Dog Toys!"
ThisDocument.Sections(1).Headers(wdHeaderFooterPrimary)
    .Range.Fields
```

Header/Footer Update

If you frequently work with Word fields and headers or footers, you will probably want to write a procedure that will update all of the fields at once. This will allow you to make a central call anytime you need to update the fields in a document. Keep in mind that you will need to enumerate through each section of the document with which you are working.

This is best accomplished using a For...Each loop using the Sections collection of the document. Here is a brief example of the necessary loop using headers (you'd want to include footers also):

```
Dim oSec As Section
For Each oSec in ThisDocument.Sections
    With oSec
    If .Headers(index).Exists Then
        .Headers(index).Range.Fields.Update
    End If
    End With
Next oSec
```

In this brief demonstration, you can see how sections work. You use the Sections property to return the Sections collection. Most frequently you'll be using either the Add method or the InsertBreak method to add a new section to a document.

Conclusion

Before jumping into document automation, it is probably a good idea to become acquainted with the Word 2007 object model. This chapter will serve as an important reference as you continue programming in Word. Document automation requires a good understanding of what Word objects you will need to use to accomplish a given task. The Word 2007 object model is the largest object model of all the Office applications.

Chapter 7

Controlling VBA Code Execution

Introduction

Once you understand the basic elements of the VBA programming language, you can create fairly rudimentary macros. When most people think of macros, they think of one completely linear task that executes lines of code sequentially before finishing. The programming involved in complex document automation requires a greater understanding of how to control the execution of the VBA code. VBA provides several conditional statements and loop functions to greatly enhance the efficiency and complexity of your code. This chapter introduces the various ways you can control program flow using VBA, and shows you how to deal with errors that you may encounter with your code.

Conditional Statements

Inevitably, you will encounter a situation that requires you to code around two or more possible situations. In other words, you will need your code to make decisions for you. This is the first step away from linear macro programming. Perhaps you need to execute different subroutines depending on whether a Boolean variable is True or False, or maybe you have numerous situations to account for. Using conditional statements enables you to implement code that will handle these situations ahead of time. Following are VBA's conditional statements and functions.

If Statements

If...Then

```
If expression Then statements
```

The simplest If statement is the use of one line of code implemented midstream to check something. When an If statement is only one line, an End If is not needed. For example:

```
If x = 10 Then MsgBox "You have reached the maximum amount."
```

The preceding example demonstrates a simple If statement that displays a message box when the variable x is equal to 10. The message box indicates that the user has reached the maximum amount of whatever the x variable is tracking. In most instances, however, you will probably handle such a situation in a more complex manner. You may want to display the message box to the user and then take a different course of action. For example:

```
If x = 10 Then
   MsgBox "You have reached the maximum amount."
   Exit Sub
End If
```

In the preceding example, the message box is displayed to the user if x = 10. Then the program automatically exits the subroutine without executing any of the code following the Exit

Sub statement. This type of statement is normally used within a loop. For example, the loop incrementally increases the variable x, but when x reaches 10, the code returns to the calling procedure in the call stack.

If...Then...Else...End If

```
If expression Then
statements
Else
[else statements]
End If
```

This type of If statement is very similar to the last, except for the ability to have a catchall that handles any situation or value other than the original If statement. Using our previous example, suppose that we want to handle x = 10 in the same manner — by displaying the message box and exiting the subroutine. The only difference is that now we want to increment x by 1 and call an external function (xManipulator) if x does not equal 10. Now, the If statement will evaluate x and if x does not equal 10, the Else branch of the statement will execute.

```
If x = 10 Then
    MsgBox "You have reached the maximum amount."
    Exit Sub
Else
    x=x+1
    Call xManipulator
End If
```

If...Then...ElseIf...End If

```
If expression Then
statements
ElseIf expression Then
[elseif statements]
Else
[elseif statements]
End If
```

This structure is very similar to the If...Then...Else...End If structure, but it involves evaluating more than one criterion before kicking into the Else branch of the logic. The following example is a subroutine that you can copy directly to the VBE to see exactly how these statements work.

```
Sub If_ElseIf_Else_EndIf()
Dim x As Integer
For x = 1 To 5
If x = 1 Then
   MsgBox x
ElseIf x = 2 Then
   MsgBox "elseif"
Else
   MsgBox "else"
End If
Next x
End Sub
```

Once you understand the basic structure of the If statement, it becomes apparent how useful it can be in programming. It is worth mentioning that there is no limitation to the number of ElseIf statements you can use in your code. You can also embed multiple If statements within an If statement.

IIf Function

IIf(*expr*, *truepart*, *falsepart*)

This is a close cousin to the regular If statement. IIf is actually a function because you pass it two sets of data, and it evaluates both and returns a value. The IIf function evaluates both *truepart* and *falsepart*, even though it returns only one of them.

Caution: Beware of undesirable results when using IIf. Because it evaluates both sets of data, when evaluating *falsepart* you may incur an error, such as a division by zero, even if *expr* is True.

Select Case

```
Select Case testexpression
[Case expressionlist-n
[statements-n]] ...
[Case Else
[elsestatements]]
End Select
```

Frequently, a programmer learns to use the If statement and figures that it can handle all of his decision logic needs. The result is that the code is filled with If...ElseIf statements that have numerous ElseIf branches, all evaluating the same variable. While If...Then...Else statements can evaluate a different expression for each ElseIf statement, a far more efficient way of controlling this code is to use the Select Case statement. The Select Case statement evaluates an expression only once, at the top of the control structure. The following example shows how Select Case statements work:

```
Select Case Number
Case 1 To 40
    MsgBox "40 or under"
Case 41, 42, 43, 44
    MsgBox "Mid 40's"
Case 45 to 100
    MsgBox "Old Geezer"
Case Else
    MsgBox "Error, greater than 100"
End Select
```

This example evaluates the value of the variable Number and matches it against the Case expressions. When it evaluates to the correct Case clause, the code following the Case clause is executed. After the code has completed, the code resumes running at the next line immediately following End Select.

Note: If Number were to match more than one Case clause, only the code following the first Case clause executes.

The Case Else clause indicates the catchall code to be executed if no match is found in the above Case clauses. Case Else is not required, but using it to pop up a message box can be useful to alert the user of an unforeseen value being evaluated. In the event that there is no match in any of the Case clauses, execution continues at the statement following End Select. Select Case statements can be nested. Each nested Select Case statement must have a matching End Select statement.

Loops

Although there are many different types of loops, their basic function is to determine how many times a block of code should be executed. The main consideration is to understand the differences in the way each looping convention acts. This will enable the programmer to use the correct loop for every convention. Even though you may have a favorite loop procedure, it is still important to understand each convention. Sometimes, trying to fit a problem into a particular loop is like trying to fit a round peg into a square hole.

The For...Next Loop

This loop repeats a block of code a specified number of times based on a counter. The counter will be incremented (or decremented) each time the loop is executed. You can also define the number by which to increment the loop. Its syntax is as follows:

```
For counter = start To end [Step step]
[statements]
[Exit For]
[statements]
Next [counter]
```

The For...Next statement syntax has these parts:

counter	The *counter* is required. It is a numeric variable that will be used as a loop counter. The variable can't be a Boolean or an array element (see the For Each...Next loop below).
start	This required value is the initial value of the *counter*.

end	This required value is the final value of the *counter*.
step	This is the optional part of the loop that is the amount *counter* is changed each time through the loop. If not specified, *step* defaults to 1.
statements	These are the statements between For and Next that are executed the number of times the loop runs.

After the code in the loop has executed, *counter* is incrementally increased by *step*. The value of *step* can be any valid incremental amount. The loop must then evaluate whether it should run the code again, or if the loop should be exited with program execution beginning immediately following the Next statement.

Tip: Do not change the value of *counter* in the code that's inside the loop. This can lead to logic errors that are very difficult to debug.

You can also place Exit For statements inside the loop to trigger an exit from the loop. Obviously, you will want to place them in some sort of conditional statement; otherwise, the Exit For will trigger every time and the code will not loop properly. Like all of the conditionals, you can also embed For...Next loops in other For...Next loops.

Caution: Remember the exponential growth you will encounter when embedding loops within other loops. Two loops that run 50 times each run 100 times total when placed in series, but when one loop is run within the other, the code effectively runs 2,500 times. This is because the second loop will run 50 times through based on each execution of the first loop.

Note: You can omit *counter* in a Next statement, and execution continues as if *counter* is included.

The For Each...Next Loop

This loop repeats a block of code by looping through each element in an array or collection. This is the correct loop to use when trying to loop through a collection of object type variables. Keep in mind that unlike For...Next loops, you can't use For Each...Next to modify the element value. The syntax is as follows:

```
For Each element In group
[statements]
[Exit For]
[statements]
Next [element]
```

The For Each...Next statement syntax has these parts:

element	This required value is the variable that will be used to iterate through the collection or array. Collections use variant variables. Arrays use either variant variables or object variables.
group	This required value is the name of an object collection or array (except an array of user-defined types).
statements	This is an optional part of the loop. These can be one or more statements that are executed on each item in group.

The code enters the For Each block for every element in the group. When the loop has cycled through every element in the group, the loop is exited and program execution continues immediately after the Next statement. You may also include Exit For statements in a For Each loop as another means of exiting the loop. Finally, just like For...Next loops, you can embed For Each...Next loops within other For Each...Next loops.

Tip: The For Each...Next loop isn't available when using an array of user-defined types. (See the "Arrays" section in Chapter 5.)

The Do...Loop Statement

The Do...Loop statement has two alternative syntaxes. It repeats a block of code while a condition is True or until a condition becomes True. In one instance of the Do...Loop, the condition is evaluated at the top of the loop (attached to the Do part). In the other instance, the condition is evaluated at the bottom of the loop (attached to the Loop part). Keep in mind that if the condition is evaluated at the bottom of the loop, the loop will always be run at least one time. The syntax is as follows:

```
Do [{While|Until} condition]
[statements]
[Exit Do]
[statements]
Loop
```

Or, you can use this syntax:

```
Do
[statements]
[Exit Do]
[statements]
Loop [{While|Until} condition]
```

The Do...Loop statement syntax has these parts:

condition	This is a numeric or string expression that is either True or False. If condition is null, it is treated as False.
statements	One or more statements that are repeated while, or until, condition is True.

Tip: You can use Exit Do statements anywhere within the Do...Loop as a means of exiting the loop.

The While...Wend Loop

This loop executes a series of statements while a condition is True. When *condition* is True, all the statements within the loop are executed until the Wend statement is encountered. Once the statements are executed, control returns to the While statement and *condition* is checked again — if *condition* is still True, the statements are executed again. If *condition* is no longer True, the program's execution will resume at the line immediately following the Wend statement. Like most loops, you can nest While...Wend loops within themselves with each Wend matching the most recent While. The syntax is as follows:

```
While condition
[statements]
Wend
```

The While…Wend statement syntax has these parts:

condition	This is a numeric or string expression that evaluates to True or False. When condition is null, it is treated as False.
statements	These are the statements that will be executed while condition is True.

Tip: The Do…Loop statement provides a more structured and flexible way to perform looping.

Alternative Flow Control

On…GoTo and On…GoSub

This is a less frequently used way to control the flow of program execution. Most programmers think only of On Error GoTo…, but you can use this to evaluate many different expressions. Programmatically, this causes execution to branch to a specified line, depending on the value of an expression. The syntax is as follows:

```
On expression GoSub destinationlist
On expression GoTo destinationlist
```

The On…GoSub and On…GoTo statement syntax has these parts:

expression	This can be any numeric expression that evaluates to a whole number between 0 and 255, inclusive. If expression is any number other than a whole number, it is rounded before it is evaluated.
destinationlist	This is a list of line numbers or line labels separated by commas.

The value of *expression* determines which line is branched to in *destinationlist*. If the value of *expression* is less than 1 or greater than the number of items in the list, one of the following results occurs:

If *expression* is	Then
Equal to 0	Control drops to the statement following On...GoSub or On...GoTo.
Greater than number of items in list	Control drops to the statement following On...GoSub or On...GoTo.
Negative	An error occurs.
Greater than 255	An error occurs.

You can mix line numbers and line labels in the same list. You can use as many line labels and line numbers as you like with On...GoSub and On...GoTo. However, if you use more labels or numbers than fit on a single line, you must use a space and the line continuation character (_) to continue the logical line onto the next physical line.

Tip: Select Case provides a more structured and flexible way to perform multiple branching.

GoSub...Return

This branches to and returns from a subroutine within a procedure. You can use any line label or line number for the *line* argument. GoSub and Return can be used to bounce anywhere within a procedure, but both GoSub and Return must be in the same procedure. You can run into some logic errors if you use multiple GoSubs in a single subroutine because the first Return statement that the execution comes across will cause the flow to branch back to the line after the most recent GoSub statement. The syntax for GoSub and Return is as follows:

```
GoSub line
line
Return
```

Note: You can't enter or exit subprocedures with GoSub...Return.

Tip: In most cases, your code will be much easier to follow if you create separate procedures. This is a more structured alternative to using GoSub...Return.

Stop

This stops execution of the code and forces the program into break mode. Stop statements can be placed anywhere in procedures to suspend execution. If you need to resume execution of the program, you can simply press F5 or the Run button on the Standard toolbar. Stop statements work exactly like setting a breakpoint in the code, but have the added advantage that they are not lost when you close out of the program. The syntax is:

```
Stop
```

Note: Make sure you know the difference between the Stop statement and the End statement: Stop doesn't clear any variables, while End does.

Choose

The Choose function selects and returns a value from a list of arguments. The Choose function's return value is determined by the index number and the possible list of choices in the function; i.e., if *index* is 1, Choose returns the first choice in the list; if *index* is 2, Choose returns the second choice, and so on. The Choose function returns a null if *index* is less than 1 or greater than the number of choices listed. The *index* value will be rounded to the nearest whole number before being evaluated if it is not an integer when passed. The syntax for Choose is:

```
Choose(index, choice-1[, choice-2, ... [, choice-n]])
```

The Choose function syntax has these parts:

index	This required numeric expression should contain a value from 1 to the number of available choices.
choice	There must be at least one occurrence of the *choice* argument. It is a variant expression that contains one of the possible choices.

Choose is most often used to look up a value in a list of possibilities. For example, if *index* evaluates to 3 and the list evaluates to choice-1 = "Shani," choice-2 = "Peanut," and choice-3 = "Debra," Choose returns "Debra." This makes the Choose function very useful if there is some correlation between the index value and the option within the choice list. There are some potential problems when using the Choose function, however. Keep in mind that like the IIf function, every choice in the list will be evaluated even though only one will be returned. You can check this using the MsgBox function in each of the choices. Every time one of the choices is evaluated, a message box will be displayed even though Choose will return only one of them.

Partition

The Partition function returns a string that indicates where a number falls within a series. If any of the parts is Null, the Partition function will return a Null. As seen in the syntax below, Partition will return a range with enough leading spaces so that there are the same number of characters to the left and right of the colon as there are characters in *stop*, plus one. This ensures that if you use Partition with other numbers, the resulting text will be handled properly during any subsequent sort operation. If *interval* is 1, the range is *number:number*, regardless of the *start* and *stop* arguments. The syntax of the Partition function is:

```
Partition(number, start, stop, interval)
```

The Partition function has these required arguments:

number	This is a whole number that you want to evaluate against the ranges.
start	This is a whole number that is the start of the overall range of numbers. The number can't be less than 0.
stop	This is a whole number that is the end of the overall range of numbers. The number can't be equal to or less than *start*.
interval	This is a whole number that is the interval spanned by each range in the series from *start* to *stop*. The number can't be less than 1.

End

The End statement ends a procedure or block of code. When the End statement is executed, all variables lose their values. If you need to preserve these variables, use the Stop statement instead. You can then resume execution while preserving the value of those variables. The End statement provides a way to force your program to halt. For normal termination of a Visual Basic program, you should unload all forms. When a program is ended, objects created from class modules are destroyed, files that were opened using the Open statement are closed, and memory used by your program is freed. The syntax is:

```
End
End Function
End If
End Property
End Select
End Sub
End Type
End With
```

The End statement has these forms:

End	This is never required but may be placed anywhere in a procedure to end code execution and clear all variables.
End Function	This is required to end a Function statement.
End If	This is required to end a block If...Then...Else statement.

End Property	This is required to end a Property Let, Property Get, or Property Set procedure.
End Select	This is required to end a Select Case statement.
End Sub	This is required to end a Sub statement.
End Type	This is required to end a user-defined type definition (Type statement).
End With	This is required to end a With statement.

Note: The End statement stops code execution without triggering the Unload, QueryUnload, or Terminate event, or any other VBA code.

Arithmetic Operators

Add (+)

This operator can be used to add numbers (expressions) together. If one or both expressions are null expressions, the result will be null. If both expressions are empty, the result is an integer. However, if only one expression is empty, the other expression is returned unchanged as *result*. When used for simple arithmetic addition using only numeric data types, the data type of *result* is usually the same as that of the most precise expression. The order of precision, from least to most precise, is byte, integer, long, single, double, currency, and decimal. For further information, please see the table below. The syntax for the Add operator is:

result = expression1+expression2

The + (Add) operator has these parts:

result	Any numeric variable
expression1	Any valid expression
expression2	Any valid expression

If at least one expression is not a variant, the following rules apply:

If	Then
Both expressions are numeric data types (byte, Boolean, integer, long, single, double, date, currency, or decimal)	Add
Both expressions are string	Concatenate
One expression is a numeric data type and the other is any variant except null	Add
One expression is a string and the other is any variant except null	Concatenate
One expression is an Empty variant	Return the remaining expression unchanged as *result*
One expression is a numeric data type and the other is a string	A type mismatch error occurs
Either expression is null	*Result* is null
Both variant expressions are numeric	Add
Both variant expressions are strings	Concatenate
One variant expression is numeric and the other is a string	Add

The following are exceptions to the order of precision described above.

If	Then *result* is
A single and a long are added	A double
The data type of *result* is a long, single, or date variant that overflows its legal range	Converted to a double variant
The data type of *result* is a byte variant that overflows its legal range	Converted to an integer variant
The data type of *result* is an integer variant that overflows its legal range	Converted to a long variant
A date is added to any data type	A date

Note: The order of precision used by addition and subtraction is not the same as the order of precision used by multiplication.

Subtract (–)

The Subtract operator can be used in two different ways: (1) to find the difference between two numbers, or (2) to indicate the negative value of a numeric expression. The first syntax example below shows the Subtract operator being used to find the difference between two numbers. The second syntax example shows the Subtract operator being used to indicate the negative value of an expression.

```
result = number1–number2
–number
```

The – (Subtract) operator has these required parts:

result	Any numeric variable
number	Any numeric expression
number1	Any numeric expression
number2	Any numeric expression

Again, the result is usually the same as that of the most precise expression with the order of precision being: byte, integer, long, single, double, and currency. The following table shows the exceptions to this order:

If	Then *result* is
Subtraction involves a single and a long	Converted to a double
The data type of *result* is a long, single, or date variant that overflows its legal range	Converted to a variant containing a double
The data type of *result* is a byte variant that overflows its legal range	Converted to an integer variant
The data type of *result* is an integer variant that overflows its legal range	Converted to a long variant
Subtraction involves a date and any other data type	A date
Subtraction involves two date expressions	A double

Note: The order of precision used by Add and Subtract is not the same as the order of precision used by Multiply.

Multiply (*)

The Multiply operator is used to multiply two numbers together. The syntax is:

```
result = number1*number2
```

The * (Multiply) operator has these required parts:

result	Any numeric variable
number1	Any numeric expression
number2	Any numeric expression

As with the previous mathematical functions, the data type of *result* is usually the same as that of the most precise expression. The order of precision, from least to most precise, is byte, integer, long, single, currency, double, and decimal. The following table shows the exceptions to this order:

If	Then *result* is
Multiplication involves a single and a long	Converted to a double
The data type of *result* is a long, single, or date variant that overflows its legal range	Converted to a variant containing a double
The data type of *result* is a byte variant that overflows its legal range	Converted to an integer variant
The data type of *result* is an integer variant that overflows its legal range	Converted to a long variant
If one or both expressions are null expressions	*Result* is null
If an expression is empty	Treated as 0

Divide Integer (\)

The Divide Integer operator is used to divide two numbers and return an integer result. The syntax is:

`result = number1\number2`

The \ (Divide Integer) operator has these required parts:

Part	Description
result	Any numeric variable
number1	Any numeric expression
number2	Any numeric expression

Numeric expressions are rounded to byte, integer, or long expressions before the division is actually performed. Usually, the data type of *result* is a byte, byte variant, integer, integer variant, long, or long variant, regardless of whether the result is a whole number. Any fractional portion is truncated. However, if any expression is null, *result* is null. Any expression that is empty is treated as 0.

Divide Floating Point (/)

The Divide Floating Point operator is used to divide two numbers and return a floating-point result. The syntax is:

`result = number1/number2`

The / (Divide Floating Point) operator has these required parts:

Part	Description
result	Any numeric variable
number1	Any numeric expression
number2	Any numeric expression

Any expression that is Empty is treated as 0. The data type of *result* is usually a double or a double variant. The following are exceptions to this rule:

If	Then *result* is
Both expressions are byte, integer, or single expressions	A single unless it overflows its legal range; in which case, an error occurs
Both expressions are byte, integer, or single variants	A single variant unless it overflows its legal range; in which case, *result* is a variant containing a double
Division involves a decimal and any other data type	A decimal data type
One or both expressions are null expressions	*Result* is null

Logical Operators

AND

The AND operator is used to perform a logical conjunction on two expressions. The syntax is:

```
result = expression1 AND expression2
```

The AND operator has these required parts:

result	Any numeric variable
expression1	Any expression
expression2	Any expression

If both expressions evaluate to True, *result* is True. If either expression evaluates to False, *result* is False. The following table illustrates how *result* is determined:

Expression1	Expression2	Result
True	True	True
True	False	False
True	Null	Null
False	True	False
False	False	False

False	Null	False
Null	True	Null
Null	False	False
Null	Null	Null

The AND operator also performs a bitwise comparison of identically positioned bits in two numeric expressions and sets the corresponding bit in *result* according to the following table:

Expression1	Expression2	Result
0	0	0
0	1	0
1	0	0
1	1	1

NOT

The NOT operator is used to perform the logical negation on an expression. The syntax is:

```
result = NOT expression
```

The NOT operator has these required parts:

result	Any numeric variable
expression	Any expression

The following table illustrates how *result* is determined:

Expression	Result
True	False
False	True
Null	Null

In addition, the NOT operator inverts the bit value of any variable and sets the corresponding bit in *result* according to the following table:

Expression	Result
0	1
1	0

OR

The OR operator is used to perform a logical disjunction on two expressions. The syntax is:

```
result = expression1 OR expression2
```

The OR operator has these required parts:

result	Any numeric variable
expression1	Any expression
expression2	Any expression

If either or both expressions evaluate to True, *result* is True. The following table illustrates how *result* is determined:

Expression1	Expression2	Result
True	True	True
True	False	True
True	Null	True
False	True	True
False	False	False
False	Null	Null
Null	True	True
Null	False	Null
Null	Null	Null

The OR operator also performs a bitwise comparison of identically positioned bits in two numeric expressions and sets the corresponding bit in *result* according to the following table:

Expression1	Expression2	Result
0	0	0
0	1	1
1	0	1
1	1	1

Comparison Operators

Following is a table that briefly describes the comparison operators you will frequently be working with in VBA. Keep in mind exactly how these operators work if you are using them in If statements — you can encounter nasty logic problems simply by having a greater than or equal to when what you really want is a greater than. You will notice that the table contains a list of the comparison operators and the conditions that determine whether *result* is True, False, or null:

Operator	True if	False if	Null if
< (Less than)	expression1 < expression2	expression1 >= expression2	expression1 or expression2 = Null
<= (Less than or equal to)	expression1 <= expression2	expression1 > expression2	expression1 or expression2 = Null
> (Greater than)	expression1 > expression2	expression1 <= expression2	expression1 or expression2 = Null
>= (Greater than or equal to)	expression1 >= expression2	expression1 < expression2	expression1 or expression2 = Null
= (Equal to)	expression1 = expression2	expression1 <> expression2	expression1 or expression2 = Null
<> (Not equal to)	expression1 <> expression2	expression1 = expression2	expression1 or expression2 = Null

When comparing two expressions, you may not be able to easily determine whether the expressions are being compared as numbers or as strings. The following table shows how the expressions are compared.

If	Then
Both expressions are numeric data types (byte, Boolean, integer, long, single, double, date, or currency)	Perform a numeric comparison.
Both expressions are strings	Perform a string comparison.
One expression is a numeric data type and the other is a variant that is, or can be, a number	Perform a numeric comparison.
One expression is a numeric data type and the other is a string variant that can't be converted to a number	A type mismatch error occurs.
One expression is a string and the other is any variant except a null	Perform a string comparison.
One expression is empty and the other is a numeric data type	Perform a numeric comparison, using 0 as the empty expression.
One expression is empty and the other is a string	Perform a string comparison, using a zero-length string ("") as the Empty expression.

If *expression1* and *expression2* are both variant expressions, their underlying type determines how they are compared. The following table shows how the expressions are compared or the result from the comparison, depending on the underlying type of the variant:

If	Then
Both variant expressions are numeric	Perform a numeric comparison.
Both variant expressions are strings	Perform a string comparison.
One variant expression is numeric and the other is a string	The numeric expression is less than the string expression.
One variant expression is empty and the other is numeric	Perform a numeric comparison using 0 as the empty expression.

If	Then
One variant expression is empty and the other is a string	Perform a string comparison using a zero-length string ("") as the empty expression.
Both variant expressions are empty	The expressions are equal.

When a single is compared to a double, the double is rounded to the precision of the single. If a currency is compared with a single or double, the single or double is converted to a currency. Similarly, when a decimal is compared with a single or double, the single or double is converted to a decimal. For currency, any fractional value less than 0.0001 may be lost; for decimal, any fractional value less than 1E–28 may be lost, or an overflow error can occur. Such fractional value loss may cause two values to compare as equal when they are not.

IS/LIKE

The IS and LIKE operators are used to compare expressions. If you are familiar with database queries, you are probably familiar with the way they work. The IS and LIKE operators have specific comparison functionality that differs from the operators in the previous tables. The behavior of the LIKE operator depends on the Option Compare statement. Briefly, Option Compare Binary results in context-sensitive string comparisons while Option Compare Text results in string comparisons that are case insensitive.

You can use LIKE in conjunction with built-in pattern matching for string comparisons. The pattern-matching features allow you to use wildcard characters, character lists, or character ranges, in any combination, to match strings. The question mark (?) is used to represent any single character, the asterisk (*) is used to represent zero or more characters, and the (#) character is used to represent any single digit (0-9). The syntax is:

```
result = expression1 comparisonoperator expression2
result = object1 IS object2
result = string LIKE pattern
```

Comparison operators have these required parts:

Part	Description
result	Any numeric variable
expression	Any expression
comparisonoperator	Any comparison operator
object	Any object name
string	Any string expression
pattern	Any string expression or range of characters

Concatenation Operators

& Operator

The & operator is used to force string concatenation of two expressions. The syntax is:

```
result = expression1 & expression2
```

The & operator has these required parts:

result	Any string or variant variable
expression1	Any expression
expression2	Any expression

If an expression is not a string, it is converted to a string variant. The data type of *result* is string if both expressions are string expressions; otherwise, *result* is a string variant. If both expressions are null, *result* is null. However, if only one expression is null, that expression is treated as a zero-length string ("") when concatenated with the other expression. Any expression that is empty is also treated as a zero-length string.

+ Operator (Visual Basic)

This operator is used to add two numbers or to return the resulting positive value of a numeric expression. This operator can also be used to concatenate two string expressions.

The syntax is:

```
result = expression1 + expression2
```

Or

```
+ expression1
```

result	Any numeric value.
expression1	Required. Any numeric or string expression.
expression2	Required unless the + operator is calculating a negative value. Any numeric or string expression.

The "+" generally performs addition when possible; however, it performs concatenation when both expressions are of type string. For example, if both *expression1* and *expression2* are numeric, the resulting value is their sum. If *expression2* is left out of the equation, the "+" operator is the unary identity operator for the unchanged value of an expression. In this case, the "+" operator retains the sign of *expression1*, so *result* is negative if *expression1* is negative. If both *expression1* and *expression2* are strings, the resulting value is a concatenation of their values. If both *expression1* and *expression2* are mixed types, different actions are performed accordingly depending on their types, their contents, and the setting of the Option Strict statement.

Call

This statement transfers control to a subprocedure, function procedure, or dynamic link library procedure (*.dll files). You are not required to use the Call keyword when calling a procedure. However, if you use the Call keyword to call a procedure that requires arguments, *argumentlist* must be enclosed in parentheses. If you omit the Call keyword, you also must omit the parentheses around *argumentlist*. If you use either Call syntax to call any intrinsic or user-defined function, the function's return value is discarded. To pass a whole array to a procedure, use the array name followed by empty parentheses. See the following syntax:

```
[Call] name [argumentlist]
```

The Call statement syntax has these parts:

Call	This is an optional keyword that may help future programmers understand that you were calling another procedure.
name	This is the required name of the procedure to call.
argumentlist	This is an optional list that includes a comma-delimited list of variables, arrays, or expressions to pass to the procedure. Components of *argumentlist* may include the keywords ByVal or ByRef to describe how the arguments are treated by the called procedure. However, ByVal and ByRef can be used with Call only when calling a DLL procedure. On the Macintosh, ByVal and ByRef can be used with Call when making a call to a Macintosh code resource.

Error Handling

In a perfect world, there wouldn't be a need for VBA error-handling code at all. The reality is that it doesn't matter how careful you are when you write your code; undoubtedly, you will have errors. If an application doesn't handle errors in a professional manner, users will become frustrated, even if the application is very refined. The Microsoft Office products provide the option to debug code on the fly. This can be either a blessing or a disaster waiting to happen. If you're in a large organization using Office 2007, you might find yourself frequently running to users' desks and debugging code right at their desktops. Obviously, this isn't the preferred manner of handling a project deployment, but if you are doing extensive Office 2007 development, you'll probably run into this.

A comprehensive error handler can provide feedback to you as a developer and help you understand where the application is breaking down. Keep in mind that any error messages displayed to an end user should be clear and concise. They should also explain exactly what steps the user should take. If they are going to lose information, let them know in the error message (this will save you from being the one to tell them).

Sometimes errors are referred to as bugs. *Bugs* can be anything from a mistake in the functionality provided (undocumented features) to a coding error that breaks execution of the program from which you cannot recover. Hopefully, you will be conscious of the possibility of bugs and code appropriately. This means that you will try to avoid losing a user's data should the program crash. There will always be instances where data cannot be recovered, but you should try to minimize both the number of these occurrences and the amount of data that is lost.

Debugging is the process of locating bugs in your application and fixing them. VBA provides several tools to help analyze how your application operates. These debugging tools are very powerful when used correctly. Frequently, a programmer finds one or two very rudimentary ways of debugging an application and tries to work them into his debugging arsenal. This is okay in the beginning, but you should always strive to find the most efficient way of debugging your code.

Error Types

Generally, there are three types of errors that you will encounter when you are writing code: syntax errors, logic errors, and run-time errors. Each type of error requires a different means of troubleshooting. Following is a brief description of each type of error.

Syntax Errors

Let's start with the easiest type of program error to deal with, the syntax error. A syntax error occurs when your code is written improperly. An example would be a misspelled or missing variable or keyword:

```
Dim strName as
```

Obviously, an essential piece of code is missing in the statement: the data type. A correct statement would read:

```
Dim strName as String
```

The key to eliminating syntax errors is to use the Option Explicit statement in every module. Option Explicit will require that all variables are explicitly declared in your project. Explicitly declaring your variables is important for several reasons. Simple misspellings in a variable name can cause unwanted behavior and data loss. When working with databases, corrupt data can be entered without any error ever being generated.

Note: VBA treats a misspelled variable as just another variable. For example:

```
lPayment = 7,224.45
Me.txtBalance.Value = lPaymint
```

The variable lPayment on the second line is misspelled. VBA won't recognize the misspelling if Option Explicit isn't turned on, and it will assume that you want it to create a new variable (variant by default). As a result, the text box will be updated with an empty value instead of the desired value of $7,224.45.

Another important reason to use explicit variable declaration is to optimize your project. By default, undeclared variables use the variant data type. This data type may use significantly more memory than you intend for the variable's purpose. For example, you may want to use a byte variable in your code. A byte occupies 1 byte of memory space. If you didn't explicitly declare the variable, it would be initialized as a variant even though it would only hold 1 byte of data. This means that you'd be using up 16 times the memory you actually need.

Remember, you can also use the VBE to force variable declaration. Simply select **Tools | Options** and go to the **Editor tab**. Once you're there you can turn Require Variable Declaration on, as shown in Figure 7-1. This will insert Option Explicit at the top of each new module; however, it will not update your existing modules. Go back into your project and insert Option Explicit in any modules you have previously created.

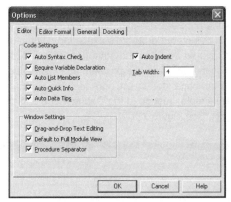

Figure 7-1: The Editor tab of the Options window

Note: VBA doesn't allow the same degree of customization as VB as far as compiler settings are concerned. However, there are still some optimizations available. In the VBE, select Tools | Options and go to the General tab. Here you will find a Compile On Demand option. If this is checked, your project should run faster because modules will not be compiled until they are loaded for execution.

Also on the General tab is a Background Compile option. This option allows the computer to compile your project in the background while the computer is idle. Selecting the Background Compile option can slightly improve the run-time speed of your project (Compile On Demand must also be enabled to use this feature). You can see both of these options in Figure 7-2.

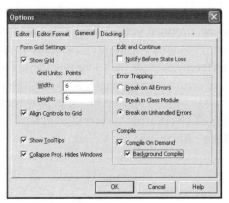

Figure 7-2: The General tab of the Options window

Caution: As a final measure of caution, you should always compile your project before it is distributed. This will ensure that all syntax errors have been found. A frequent problem is that your code will refer to a control on a form that has been deleted. If you don't compile the program ahead of time, you'll be running to desktops and moving your program's execution point to the next line of code, or worse, you'll be the author of the dreaded "All User" e-mail informing people there is a problem and instructing them to stay out of the template, document, spreadsheet, or whatever. The process is very simple: Just go to the Debug menu and choose Compile Project. See Figure 7-3.

Figure 7-3: Choose Debug | Compile Project to check for syntax errors.

Logic Errors

Logic errors occur when your code doesn't respond the way you intended. Perhaps your logic is unsound or the program flows in a different manner than you intended. The best way to check these errors is to manually step through your code using Watch windows. This can be especially tricky when using a series of UserForms — you should first make sure you understand the call stack.

Tip: If you are using a series of UserForms, do not place any code after you call the Show method of the next UserForm. Your program's execution will always resolve back through the call stack and could produce unexpected results.

Run-Time Errors

You cannot avoid run-time errors; however, you can plan for them. Planning for run-time errors involves developing an error handler. Word 2007 includes a VBA Error Handler add-in that makes working with your error handler easier. Although we'll briefly discuss this add-in toward the end of the chapter, we'll assume you are working in the normal Office environment and discuss how you can implement error handling without this add-in.

Designing an Error Handler

At this point, you should at least be familiar with VBA's debugging tools (covered in Chapter 3). An error handler is a means to trap and respond to errors that occur in your project. Error handlers can be very simple or very complex. The type of error handling you choose will depend on the complexity of your project and your time constraints.

You should implement an error handler in any procedure where you anticipate an error might possibly occur (which means just about every procedure in your application). There is usually a large amount of error-specific code in the error handler in the form of a Select Case statement. One of the best strategies is to anticipate every error you can, and use the Err.Number property in the Select Case statement to properly handle the specific error.

Note: When an error occurs in a procedure that does not have error handling enabled, VBA responds by displaying an error message. Sometimes the application will be terminated and the user won't be able to do anything or a message box is displayed. If the user selects End, he will lose what he is currently working on in most cases. Once this happens once or twice, the user will invariably hit the Debug button and then will be playing with your code. You can now see the extreme importance of utilizing proper file management and proper error handling. Hopefully, your error handler will prevent the user from ever seeing such a message box, but if it doesn't, hopefully you are utilizing some of the file management techniques covered earlier in the book so that users can't write changes to the code in your project.

Error-Handling Basics

An extremely well-written application will properly handle every error that it encounters, but having the time or the resources to write such an application is very rare. In fact, most Office projects never implement error handling. However, you will undoubtedly implement a comprehensive error-handling routine after reading this section.

Speaking more practically, it's best to devise a concise error-handling routine for your project at the outset. You can always add Case statements to handle future errors (they'll only happen once, right?). In a nutshell, your basic error handler should recover from the error quickly and transparently to the user, if possible. No developer, no matter how diligent or experienced, will anticipate every error that can occur. In the worst case, your error terminates the application, records information about the error to an error log, and perhaps records the user's input to a delimited text file of some sort.

Handling VBA errors is very straightforward; there are two basic tools you can use. One is the On Error statement, which you use to enable error handling in a procedure. The other is the Err object, which contains information about an error that has already occurred.

If execution passes over to your error handler, your code must determine which error has occurred and either fix the error or raise the error back to the calling procedure. Sometimes, errors will occur within your error handler. In this case, VBA will handle the error because error handling is no longer enabled (unless you write another procedure to handle these errors).

Note: There can only be one active error handler at any time, but there may be more than one error handler active within the current call stack.

Anticipated Errors

You will have to develop a method of dealing with errors you can anticipate. Following is a brief description of how you can handle these types of errors:

▼ Display a message box with information about the error.

▼ Display a message box with information that helps the user resolve the error (e.g., "There is no disk in the disk drive").

▼ Ignore the error and resume execution of the code.

▼ Ignore the error and exit the procedure.

▼ Use code to either correct the error or go to a "safe place" within the application.

Tip: Sketch out a brief list of common errors and make sure your error-handling routine responds to all of them.

Unanticipated Errors

Resolving unanticipated errors usually involves your catchall Case statement, Case Else. These are usually handled by saving whatever information can be reliably saved in one fashion or another and exiting the program. Make sure you let your users know what is happening throughout the process.

Caution: Watch out when saving changes to a database when an error occurs; this is potentially disastrous. It is a much better practice to save the information in a temporary file of some sort and write a routine that can update the database once the validity of the information has been checked by the user.

The Err Object

The object you will be using to obtain the necessary information about your errors is the Err object. The Err object is global, so there is no need to instantiate it. Like any other object it is comprised of properties and methods. Following is a table listing the properties of the Err object and a brief discussion of its two methods.

Err Object Properties

The Err object has the following properties:

Err.Number	This is the error number of the current error. This will be the number you use to respond to different errors.
Err.Description	This is the description of the error.
Err.Source	This is the object or application that generated the error.
Err.HelpFile	This property can be used to provide a Help button on an error message dialog box.
Err.HelpContext	This is the context ID for a topic in a Help file.
Err.LastDLLError	The last error code generated by a DLL. (This is available only on a 32-bit Windows system.)

Err Object Methods

The Err object has two methods: Err.Clear and Err.Raise.

Err.Clear

The Clear method clears the current error from memory. This removes all of the properties of the Err object. Apart from explicitly executing the Clear method, all of the following will also clear the properties of the Err object:

▼ Any type of resume statement

▼ Exiting the procedure

▼ Using the On Error statement

Err.Raise

The Raise method generates a run-time error. The Raise method has five arguments that correspond directly to the properties of the Err object: *Number*, *Source*, *Description*, *HelpFile*, and *HelpContext*. Note that these arguments are the same as those of the Err object. This can be useful when testing or debugging your application. It allows you to simulate a run-time error by passing the error code to the Raise method of the Err object. You can also use this method when you call a function in a dynamic link library (DLL), and you can pass the error value back to your application to handle the error. Finally, it allows you to generate your own user-defined errors.

Tip: Your user-defined error number must be unique. This is usually accomplished by adding your error number to the constant vbObjectError.

Enabling an Error Trap

In order to enable an error trap, the On Error statement needs to be inserted into the procedure. This line of code specifies an error handler. This error trap remains enabled as long as the procedure containing it is active. In other words, it is active until an Exit Sub, Exit Function, Exit Property, End Sub, End Function, or End Property statement is executed for that procedure (or the application encounters End). This approach allows you to create several different error traps and enable different ones at different times. Just keep in mind that only one error trap can be enabled at any one time in any given procedure.

Note: Error traps are disabled by using a special case of the On Error statement:

```
On Error GoTo 0
```

Exiting an Error-Handling Routine

There are several ways to exit an error-handling routine, as illustrated in the following table.

Resume [0]	Program execution resumes with the statement that caused the error or the most recently executed call out of the procedure containing the error-handling routine. Use it to repeat an operation after correcting the condition that caused the error.
Resume Next	Resumes program execution at the statement immediately following the one that caused the error. If the error occurred outside the procedure that contains the error handler, execution resumes at the statement immediately following the call to the procedure wherein the error occurred, if the called procedure does not have an enabled error handler.
Resume *line*	Resumes program execution at the label specified by *line*, where *line* is a line label (or non-zero line number) that must be in the same procedure as the error handler.
Err.Raise Number:= *number*	Triggers a run-time error. When this statement is executed within the error-handling routine, Visual Basic searches the calls list for another error-handling routine.

Writing an Error-Handling Routine

The first step in writing an error-handling routine is creating a label to mark the beginning of the routine. This label should have a descriptive name and must be followed by a colon. Usually, your error-handling code will be at the end of the procedure with an Exit Sub, Exit Function, or Exit Property statement immediately before the label. This method allows the procedure to avoid executing the error-handling code if no error occurs.

As we've already noted, the body of the error-handling routine contains the code that actually handles the error, usually in the form of a Select Case or, somewhat less frequently, an If…Then…Else statement. The Number property of the Err object contains a numeric code representing the most recent run-time error. By using the Err object in combination with Select Case, you can take specific action for any error that occurs.

Centralized Error Handling

You've probably already noticed that some projects generally keep raising the same errors over and over. While you could have an error handler in every procedure, it makes much more sense to centralize your error handling; this will allow you to reduce the amount of code in your project because your error-handling code can call a centralized procedure to accomplish these tasks. This also allows you to use a generic error handler in each procedure and pass the relevant information to your central error handler. There are too many errors to begin going through them one by one, and the errors you commonly encounter may not be the same as those someone else's program encounters. The example in the "Error-Handling Project" section demonstrates the insertion of a very basic error-handling routine. It will be up to you to augment the procedures for your specific project.

Collecting Additional Error Information

While the Err object provides a great deal of information, there may be additional elements you need to correctly fix these errors. You want to ensure that your error handler records all of the information you need to properly troubleshoot the error. In some cases, that may even mean prompting the user with a UserForm to fill out relevant information. The more information you gather at the error handler level, the less you'll have to gather through interaction with the user. (Remember, this is an unnecessary use of your time and the user's.) Following is a short list of considerations to keep in mind when developing your error handler:

1. In any sort of enterprise development, you'll undoubtedly want to gather the user's name. This can easily be done in Office applications by using the globally available UserName property. Otherwise, you'll need to grab the currently logged in user through an easy-to-implement Windows API call.

2. If possible, obtain the name of the UserForm or module and the procedure involved. In almost all instances, you'll

want to gather this information so you know exactly where the error occurred. As you will see, this is a simple matter of passing the UserForm and procedure to the error handler.

3. You will also want to obtain the date and time the error occurred. This can also be valuable information when trying to see how frequently particular errors occur. It can also be a means of evaluating the success of your staged deployment.

4. In some cases, you will want to know the name and value of the active control. Again, this is easily accomplished by passing the name of the active control where the error occurred.

5. If you're working with a database, you'll probably want to obtain the ID of the current record. Sometimes, particular records prove to be problematic, usually because of values that don't follow the conventions you expect them to. For example, you may have a data field formatted to receive only numerical values for a Zip code and someone enters the Zip code, a hyphen, and four additional numbers.

6. If you are using a truly centralized error handler, that is, one that is used in multiple applications, you will want to obtain the name of the application in which the error occurred.

7. Lastly, you may want to query the users to gather any notes they may have about the error. A simple, open-text UserForm can allow users to enter what they were doing when the error occurred. In order to make your application as user-friendly as possible, you should make the entry of data into this form completely optional.

Error Reporting

Now that you know what types of information you need to collect, you need to formulate a strategy to gather the information in a central location. This will allow you to receive immediate notification when an error occurs. Additionally, if you designed your error handler properly, you will have all of the information needed to identify and fix the error and you will have the data saved for historical analysis. There are several ways you can store the information. Remember, you can use automation to open just about any application where you'd want to store the information. Using only the tools available in the Microsoft Office 2007 suite, you can have the error information:

▼ E-mailed to either an individual or a shared mailbox using Outlook

▼ Saved in an Excel spreadsheet

▼ Saved in an Access database table (or a more powerful database, if necessary)

▼ Saved in a text file

▼ Added to an Outlook calendar

Error-Handling Project

We will now create a small, centralized error handler in a class module and see how it can interact with your program. To start off, we will declare three module-level variables in the class module. This project will be logging errors to an Excel spreadsheet. In this case, we are working on a local computer, but keep in mind that this spreadsheet could be located on a network drive to handle use by everyone.

The variables correspond to an instance of the Excel application, a workbook, and a worksheet. For our illustrative purposes, we will make one method publicly available from the error handler. This method is represented by the GetError function, which returns an integer to the calling procedure. As you will see, you can come up with several different return values that you can insert into your procedures. You will see how we use these return values to react appropriately.

The beginning of the procedure is relatively straightforward: The workbook ErrorSheet.xls is opened, and the arguments of the function are inserted into the spreadsheet along with the user's name and the date. Next, a row is inserted to assure that the most recent values will always be in the topmost row. See Figure 7-4.

The meat of the procedure is at the end. The Select Case statement is the code you will implement to handle each individual type of error. For this example, I've listed only two: Case 11 corresponds to a division by zero error and Case 13 corresponds to a type mismatch error.

Caution: You must carefully analyze your errors and send the appropriate return code back to the error trap in the error generating procedure. As you'll see, you will be programming at two different levels when implementing such an error handler.

```
Private oXL As New Excel.Application
Private oErrWkbk As Workbook
Private oErrSprsht As Worksheet
Function GetError(Num As Integer, Desc As String) As Integer
Set oErrWkbk = oXL.Workbooks.Open("C:\wordware\ErrorSheet.xls")
Set oErrSprsht = oErrWkbk.Sheets("ErrorSheet")
With oErrSprsht
    .Cells(2, 1) = Desc
    .Cells(2, 2) = Num
    .Cells(2, 3) = UserName
    .Cells(2, 4) = Date
    .Rows(2).Select
End With
oXL.Selection.EntireRow.Insert
oErrWkbk.Close SaveChanges:=True
Set oErrSprsht = Nothing
Set oErrWkbk = Nothing
Set oXL = Nothing
Select Case Num
'this is where all of the case statements
'go with the appropriate error handling
'code (don't forget to pass the return character)
Case 11
    Dim TryAgain As Single
    TryAgain = MsgBox("A division by zero has been attempted." & _
    vbNewLine & "Do you want to try again?", vbYesNo, "Error")
        If TryAgain = vbNo Then
            GetError = 1
        Else
            GetError = 2
        End If
```

```
Case 13
    MsgBox "A Type Mismatch error has occurred." & vbNewLine & _
    "Please make sure the form is filled out correctly", _
    vbCritical, "Error"
    GetError = 1
Case Else
    GetError = 4
End Select
End Function
```

A	B	C	D
1 Description	Number	Username	Date
2			
3 A division by zero has been attempted.	11	Scott.Driza	1/8/2009
4 A Type Mismatch error has occurred."	13	Scott.Driza	1/8/2009
5			

Figure 7-4

When the Divide button is clicked, an input box queries the user for a value. If the user enters 0, an error is generated. Similarly, if nothing is entered, a type mismatch occurs. The first thing to do in any of the modules or UserForms is to create a new instance of the ErrorHandler class. Once the ErrorHandler class exists, each procedure will turn on error trapping. As you can see, there is a Select Case statement that acts according to the return value of the global error handler.

This approach allows you to do several different things. You can implement arbitrary points in your code where you want to resume execution. This lets you fix the problem in an error handler and resume execution at different spots in the procedure based upon the return value. Essentially, this allows you to act upon your own system of return values. You can also combine several different errors by returning the same value for each one. The following code shows an example of adding resume execution points.

```
Option Explicit
Dim Handler As New ErrorHandler
Private Sub cmdDivide_Click()
On Error GoTo ErrTrap
Dim iInt As Integer
Point1:
iInt = InputBox("Divide 100 by:", "Error Example")
lblError.Caption = "100 divided by " & iInt & _
" = " & 100 / iInt
```

```
MsgBox "We are now at the next line."
Exit Sub
ErrTrap:
Dim iErr As Integer
iErr = Handler.GetError(Err.Number, Err.Description)
Select Case iErr
Case 1
    MsgBox "This form will be re-initialized", vbOKOnly, "Error"
    Unload Me
    frmError.Show
    Exit Sub
Case 2
    Resume Point1
Case 3
    Resume 0
Case 4
    Resume Next
Case 5
    MsgBox "Fatal error, all data will be lost!", vbCritical, _
    "Error"
    End
End Select
End Sub
```

Note: To extend this error handler even further, you can use Visual Basic to create a DLL (COM object) that can be used with any Component Object Model (COM)-compliant application.

Developer Error Handler Add-in

Word 2007 contains an error handler add-in that greatly simplifies the creation of standardized error handler code. This will make your code more professional and easier to debug. The VBA Error Handler add-in inserts preformatted error-handling code into whatever procedures you select in your project. The actual error handler code is based on error-handling templates that you can create (.eht files). Choose the Error Handler by selecting **Add-ins | Add-in Manager** from within the VBE.

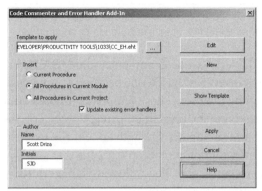

Figure 7-5: The Code Commenter and Error Handler Add-In dialog box

The dialog box shown in Figure 7-5 is the starting point of the error handler. The Insert area defines where the error-handling code will be added. You can choose to add it to the current procedure, all procedures in the current module, or all procedures in the current project. The Template to apply text box contains the path to the template file (.eht) that contains formatting instructions for the error handler. If you know the path to one of your files, you can enter the path and file name, or you can use the Browse button to search for a template file. The Update existing error handlers check box allows you to update all existing error handlers within the scope selected in the Add Error Handlers To group so they match the currently selected template. The Show Template button displays the Show Template dialog box, allowing you to view the contents of the currently selected template.

Note: The error handler will not modify any code if it finds "On Error Goto <label>" within a procedure. If the error handler finds "On Error Goto" or "On Error Resume Next," however, the code will be modified according to the specified template.

You can use the Name and Initials information to add your name and initials to the error handler. The error handler stores this information in the Registry for future use. This information appears as part of the error handler with the default template. If you leave these fields blank, the name and initials will default to the registered user.

> **Note:** The Show Template dialog box doesn't allow editing. To edit the template file, open it in Notepad or another text editor.

Both the VBA Code Commenter and VBA Error Handler add-ins insert text based on specified templates that can be created by the user. These templates follow certain conventions and may be created by using Notepad or another text editor and saving the file with an .eht file extension. These templates contain replaceable tokens that specify what will be added to your code. The following table briefly lists the tokens used by each add-in:

Token	Meaning
$$A	Author; replaced with the current author name
$$B	Procedure body
$$D	Current date; formatted as Windows short date
$$H	Header comments
$$I	Author initials
$$N	Name of procedure; replaced with the fully qualified procedure name, including the class name if it's a member of a class
$$P	Project name
$$T	Current time; formatted as Windows short time
$$V	Header variables
$$Y	Type of procedure; replaced with "Sub," "Function," or "Property" as appropriate
$$SA	Start Auto; used to flag the start of an inserted error handler
$$EA	End Auto; used to flag the end of an inserted error handler
$$SH	Start of header
$$EH	End of header

> **Note:** In order to be recognized as a valid template file, the file must contain at least the following tokens: $$B plus either $$SH and $$EH or $$SA and $$EA. If the required tokens are missing, an error will occur when attempting to load the .eht file.

Conclusion

This chapter explored some ways of controlling execution of the VBA code and also introduced you to several different ways of creating loops. VBA provides several conditional statements and loop functions to greatly enhance the efficiency and complexity of your code. Conditional statements help you control the way your code will branch. Branching techniques allow you to avoid initializing variables and performing procedures that may be unnecessary. Another important element of advanced programming is a good understanding of what operators are available and how they work. These operators allow you to use conditional statements and loops properly.

This chapter also introduced you to the concept of error handling. You will undoubtedly want to implement some error handling in your code. The type and extent of your error handling are completely at your discretion, but keep in mind that sometimes it's preferable to handle the error in code without notifying the user or to warn the user in a way that doesn't stop their workflow. If an application doesn't handle errors in a professional manner, users will become frustrated, even if the application is very refined. A comprehensive error handler can provide feedback to you as a developer and help you understand where the application is breaking down. Hopefully, you will be conscious of handling errors as you create your project. There will always be instances where data cannot be recovered, but you should try to minimize the number of these occurrences as well as the amount of data that is lost.

Chapter 8
Document Automation and Management

Introduction

At the most basic level, document creation involves two possible flows of data. Either the data exists elsewhere and needs to be used to create a document, or the first entry of the data will be done in Word and used to create a document. In the second instance, Word must interact with some external database to store the information. Word is capable of storing data from one session to the next, but there are obvious disadvantages (reporting, overall view, etc.) to storing data in Word documents. Duplicate data entry is a sure sign of inefficiency, as well as a frustration for users. Also, questions of how and where a document is stored are concerns in automating documents. This chapter will look at not only how to automate document creation but also how to manage these documents.

What Is Document Automation?

It hasn't been that long since lengthy documents were typed page by page. The typewriter was a revolutionary instrument. Early word processors were looked at as a major advance over the typewriter, and by today's standards, they both sound monotonous. Most organizations that have document preparation systems have canned (out-of-the-box) solutions. These are notoriously difficult to work with and may not even let an organization use its own documents. Some do not even provide a text editor. In other words, you're stuck with what you get.

An Automated Way to Produce Documents

The major advantage of Word-based document automation is that VBA provides a way for the user to control the creation of documents. In some offices, documents are created using the cut and paste method. This was initially looked at as a major advantage in and of itself. However, there was still a problem with matching pronouns and names throughout the document. Ideally, any document creation system should contain all the language dependencies and insert the proper pronouns depending on the names of the parties.

This is easily accomplished with Word using VBA. Further, maintaining the system doesn't require a programming genius. All users can make suggestions and, in some cases, even implement the changes themselves.

In all cases, an automated template solution will obtain the correct data to enter into the document; this data may be obtained from a database, or from a UserForm that queries a user to input relevant information. This data is used either to fill the document or to make decisions and react accordingly. The first use is simple to illustrate. Imagine having a lengthy contract that requires the names of each party in several places. You can type this into a text box and automatically insert it in appropriate places in the document. The second use of data, making decisions and reacting, is somewhat more multifaceted. Now, let's assume that there are different versions of the same document depending on whether a party is a business or individual. You could have an option button that required the user to choose either a business or individual. If "individual" was checked, you could put in different requirements, eliminate lengthy signature blocks, and use the correct terminology. If "business" was checked, the code could ask for a state of incorporation, include lines for titles in the signature block, and include wholly different provisions. This can all be done without ever manually editing the document.

Document Automation Approaches

Now that you understand what an automated template is, you have to make some decisions as to your initial approach to creating an actual system. It is unlikely that you have only one document that you would like to automate. As your organization grows, it's likely that you will need both additional templates and modifications to your existing templates.

You can create different automated templates for each document that you wish to automate. For example, you could have different fax, memo, and letter templates, or you could combine all three into one template and choose the appropriate document depending on what the user chooses.

There are advantages and disadvantages to each approach. It is easy to click on whatever template you need when you have relatively few templates. However, if you have ten completely different letters, it might be difficult to separate them in a manner that makes sense to a new user. It might be easier for you to make one "letter" template that has ten different option buttons with more lengthy explanations of the purpose for which each is intended. Remember that although the name of a file makes perfect sense to you, it might not be clear to everyone who might possibly use it.

Some generalizations apply. If you are going to be producing lengthy documents that include similar language, you may want to use a true assembly approach. This would be a single template that produces documents by retrieving paragraphs and sections depending on which choices a user makes. This allows you to keep a "language bank" that enables you to make any changes in one spot versus changing the exact same language in ten different documents.

The assembly approach requires more work at the outset, but makes the follow-up changes much simpler; that is, if the changes are to the language only. The downfall is that you can wind up with unexpected snares since your code affects the creation of all the documents. You may make a change intending to affect only one document, but in fact you may change others in unintended ways. This approach requires careful thinking at the outset.

An easier way is to create a new template as the need arises. This allows a much quicker turnaround and provides users with more "feel" for the documents because they are making a choice. The only time this becomes a problem is when there is multiple data entry. For example, a secretary creates a proposal letter including a customer's information. Later, a legal secretary retypes all the previous information to create a contract. Again, after the deal is closed, a congratulatory letter goes out. You can see the need to think through your approach at the outset.

Data Integrity

The final consideration when beginning a document assembly system is that of data integrity. Every organization keeps data in one way or another. There may be paper files hanging around, ledger sheets, or even a central database. If you are not storing your information electronically, now is your chance. The fact of the matter is that Word provides a great way to retrieve and store data at the earliest stages of any relationship.

In most organizations this is a conceptual nightmare. Central databases grow quicker than they can be changed to accommodate users and they are usually the sole province of the systems department — which may be very detached from the actual users. The aim of a Word document assembly system, whether created by a systems person or by an office user, is to put the power in the hands of the people who need it most. Secretaries routinely toil at tasks that could be made much more efficient. Their needs, however, are not a systems department's first priority.

Most often, the database is uploaded after a certain event happens: the deal closes and is on the books, a sale is made, a phone call is returned, etc. However, there may be a significant expenditure of resources before that point is ever reached. Imagine a new salesperson preparing a sales proposal. The systems department may not want to clutter the database with what, in effect, may amount to a cold call. This information may be just another stale record out there to slow the system down.

There may be several more preliminary events — letters, calls, searches for a paper record of what transpired — before the information gets entered into a database. In almost every case, the most important software has been the word processor. However, it isn't being used to store information, only to type in and create documents. Imagine the possibilities if the information was conveniently stored right from the outset. If only the potential customer's name is saved, that is one thing that will be eliminated in the next step. Information can be trapped the first time through and expanded on every time something is entered. Although this may resemble a normal database philosophy, databases have almost always disregarded the preparation of documents. Quite simply, different people are typing the same stuff at different times. Word now provides a convenient way to create single-record databases that store all of the pertinent information for reuse time and time again. When the database needs to be uploaded, Word can accomplish this as well.

The Actual Templates

It is important to do some very careful planning before you embark on any programming project. You can save yourself many headaches if you consider some basic structure issues from the beginning. Consider the flow of UserForms before you actually begin creating them. Determine what information you will require the user to input. Then determine any auxiliary information and what is going to trigger whether that information is optional or required. Finally, make a determination of what optional information you might need to include in the template.

The planning steps will allow you to create a structure for navigating through the template. You obviously do not want people wading through blank screens every time they go to create a document. Make sure you employ logic that guides the user through the entry of data.

There are several ways of triggering the optional information. You can use option buttons or check boxes, or you can toggle the Visible property of frames or even individual controls. The following sections will contain examples of each different way of triggering the optional information.

One final note: Keep in mind that up to one-third of the time that you spend working on any template project should be spent on design issues. Most programmers make the mistake of writing and rewriting code. You can alleviate some of the pressures if you carefully plan at the outset. A simple hour-long brainstorming session can often uncover some of the most frequently missed bugs and logic flaws that exist.

Document Creation

At the most basic level, document automation involves simply transferring the information a user enters into a form. This is analogous to simply filling in the blanks. The next level is a document that leverages the user input to fill in multiple blanks. For instance, the user may only enter his name once, but the template or program handles inserting the name in multiple locations. The third level involves document-level intelligence.

The third level includes many subsets. For example, there may be optional language; that is, there may be language that either appears or it doesn't. This can take the form of anything from words that are inserted if a condition is true to building and inserting completely different documents. For instance, a document may read:

Customer (and Customer's spouse) agree(s) to…

The resultant document will either read:

Customer agrees to…

Or

Customer and Customer's spouse agree to…

The next subset of document-level intelligence is dependent language. Dependent language is similar to optional language, but can have multiple combinations. These combinations may be mutually exclusive or not. The following table illustrates the difference between mutually exclusive dependent language and combination-dependent language.

Mutually exclusive dependent language	Combination-dependent language
Purchase will consist of (Wood/Nails/Paint)	Purchase will consist of [(Wood) + (Nails) + (Paint)]
The resultant document will read:	The resultant document will read:
Purchase will consist of Wood…	Purchase will consist of Wood…
Or	Or
Purchase will consist of Nails…	Purchase will consist of Wood and Nails…
Or	Or
Purchase will consist of Paint…	Purchase will consist of Wood and Paint…
	Or
	Purchase will consist of Wood, Nails, and Paint…
	Or
	Purchase will consist of Nails…
	Or
	Purchase will consist of Nails and Paint…
	Or
	Purchase will consist of Paint…

The illustration above shows how quickly the complexity level of a document can increase. You can also see that from a programming perspective, optional language and mutually exclusive dependent language are much easier to handle because you are dealing with either the absence or presence of a value, or different possible values. Combination-dependent language is where the inevitable problems will arise. Not only do you have to account for the different items (i.e., Wood, Nails, and Paint), but you also must account for the correct punctuation, line spacing, resultant page breaks, etc.

Combination-Dependent Language Possibilities

There are two diametrically opposed ways of handling combination-dependent language. The first is to have each possibility accounted for and insert the appropriate text in the proper place. In the previous example of Wood+Nails+Paint, that would involve storing each of the seven possibilities elsewhere and having a single insertion point. The next option is to build the language on the fly. It is usually better to build the language on the fly unless there are very few possibilities and those possibilities are very complex.

Tip: Obviously, there will be instances when you utilize combinations of both. You may want to store a few of the possibilities and include variables within those combinations. We will cover this possibility later.

Alternatively, you may want to include the logic in the actual Word document by using Word's If fields. It is good to attempt to maintain a consistent approach throughout, but as you will see in the following section, it is usually best to store the language in a separate area rather than building it separately in VBA (unless you build it in a reusable module!). The reason is that you may need to include the exact same language in a future variation of the document or in a completely new document.

Modularity

The final concern is that of modularity. This is a critical concern whether you are building a complete documentation system or starting with a single document. Take our previous purchase example. This purchase definition may need to appear in a proposal to the customer, the sales agreement, and a delivery acknowledgment. There may even need to be slight variations in the way it appears in each of the documents. However, if you do not take a modular approach from the beginning you are ensuring future inefficiencies.

Suppose that, sometime down the road, we want to include Glue in the list of possible purchase items. If we utilized a standard VBA on-the-fly approach, we will have to change the code in three different places. If we used document-level intelligence but didn't make that section a different document, we will have to make the change in three different documents. Neither of these may seem overly cumbersome, but think about when the organization has 30 documents instead of three.

Note: It is possible to use either VBA or document-level intelligence and still incorporate modularity. We will look at both possibilities in a bit.

Building Documents with Automated Templates

Okay, so now that you know what the concerns are, we need to discuss actually building the document. There are several ways of inserting text into a document. Some people have utilized the VBA Write function to create fairly complex text documents and then import them into Word. This book will not cover that approach for the obvious reason that Word has almost infinitely more functionality that may be accessed directly! For our working purposes, we will be using DocVariable fields and including all of the text in the templates.

As previously discussed, your ability to build optional language as well as dependent language is determined primarily by the method you use to insert text into the document. Building the actual document templates is easy once you understand that there are two different things you need to do.

1. Insert language into a specific place in the document. This is easiest to think of in terms of a fill-in-the-blank form.

2. Build intelligence into the document using conditional statements. This covers adding additional documents, if necessary, and using language dependencies.

Breaking the Project Down into Components

A common mistake in almost every type of endeavor is to jump right in without doing any planning. Think about trying to build a bridge without planning; that wouldn't be very easy. Neither is trying to create a document automation system. Your system will obviously evolve over the years, but it is best to start with a fundamentally sound approach.

Common Language

There are several things to keep in mind when planning a document automation system. First off, look for commonalities between documents in your organization. For instance, you may have a relatively standard set of definitions for each agreement or a standard introductory paragraph.

Note: The parts of the documents do not have to be identical, just close enough to make them easy to work with.

Take the following definition and representations, for instance:

Definition: "Pet" shall mean the dog, fish, or bird being sold by Seller to Buyer.
Representation: { IF { DOCVARIABLE Pet } = "dog" "The Pet has been given a rabies vaccination." ""}{ IF { DOCVARIABLE Pet } = "fish" "The Pet is guaranteed to be slime free." ""}{ IF { DOCVARIABLE Pet } = "bird" "The Pet has been fed rice before being sold to Buyer." ""}

In the above example, there is a definition of the term "Pet." This term may refer to a dog, fish, or bird. (You'd want to include the precise item here with DocVariable fields as well, but this is for illustrative purposes.) Notice that an If field is used to trigger the appropriate representation based on the actual Pet type. The actual type of Pet will not be included in this portion of the text, but the appropriate representation will.

Now, suppose there are currently separate documents, each dealing with a specific kind of pet. You can see how these documents could be consolidated to incorporate the above section.

Perhaps the remainder of each document is entirely different. In this case, the above section could be maintained as a separate document and included in each of the three templates using an IncludeText field. In either case, the focus is on language maintenance. You don't want to make the same changes in several different places. This opens the door for discrepancies between documents, inconsistent language, and frustration on your part.

Common Documents

The second thing to keep in mind is common documents. Your organization may have a specific document that is generated in connection with all transactions. For instance, there may be a memo to the accounting department every time a sale is made. Now, let's pretend that there are several different kinds of sales that can occur, each necessitating a different document. At the outset, you need to make sure that you use one of the accounting memos and programmatically include it into every other document template. If you don't, you'll have to change each document when the memo changes. Furthermore, if you develop any additional products or services that require the implementation of a document, you will have to include the accounting memo as well. You can see that planning is crucial! As an organization grows, an inefficient initial implementation can exponentially increase the amount of work required.

Locking Documents

One of the biggest advantages of using Word for your document assembly is that the finished product is a Word document. Many canned assembly systems create documents in a proprietary format. In some cases, these documents can be imported into Word. In other cases, the document may only be edited in the assembly system's editor. In still other cases, the document may not be edited at all. If your organization creates numerous identical documents, then you may want to prevent users from altering the contents of the documents.

Even if your business people scoff at using Word to automate the production of very simple, reproducible documents, using Word in conjunction with text locking offers one enormous benefit: The appropriate people in the organization can unlock the document and make changes when necessary.

As business transactions evolve, the level of customization necessary to "close the deal" inevitably increases. Document assembly systems that either prevent changes to the resultant document or require cumbersome methods to change the document can cause huge inefficiencies for the organization. Instead of modifying the appropriate document, either an entirely new document is created from scratch or a rider is attached to the agreement and sections of the original document are stricken or altered. Not only is this inefficient, but in today's marketplace this is unprofessional.

Locking the resultant Word document is easily accomplished by including the following procedure (or a slight modification of it) into your document templates:

```
Sub Protect()
    ActiveDocument.Protect Password:="test", NoReset:=False, _
        Type:=wdAllowOnlyFormFields
End Sub
```

This code locks the entire document. In some cases, you will only want to lock a portion of it. You can accomplish this by using the *Type* argument of the Protect method. A complete discussion of protecting documents, as well as your code, is included toward the end of this chapter.

Building Language in a Text Box

Finally, there may be unique circumstances where you want to provide the ability to change specific language and where locking individual sections is just too burdensome. You can still provide the user with the ability to make changes and then lock the resultant document by using dynamic language in conjunction with a UserForm.

The following project can also be found on the companion web sites for the book (www.wordVBA.com or www.wordware.com/files/word2007). The code requires three module-level variables all defined as strings. The reason these variables are declared at the module level is that they will need to be accessed from different procedures throughout the module. First, we'll discuss the Initialize event. This event calls three different procedures. The first two set the visibility settings for the label and text box corresponding to the Dog and Cat check boxes to False. This ensures that every time the form is initialized, those controls will not be visible. Lastly, the event calls the BuildLanguage procedure. Before we discuss exactly how that procedure works, let's take a look at how the UserForm looks when it is first initialized, as shown in Figure 8-1. You will notice that neither check box is checked, and the language reads "Please watch my house while I am gone."

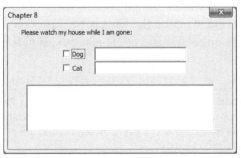

Figure 8-1

```
Option Explicit
Dim sDog As String, sCat As String, sLanguage As String
Private Sub UserForm_Initialize()
    Dog_Visible False
    Cat_Visible False
    BuildLanguage
End Sub
Sub Dog_Visible(bVis As Boolean)
    txtDog.Visible = bVis
    lblDog.Visible = bVis
End Sub
```

```
Sub Cat_Visible(bVis As Boolean)
    txtCat.Visible = bVis
    lblCat.Visible = bVis
End Sub
```

Now let's discuss what happens when either of the check boxes is checked. Initially, you should note that you could also call the BuildLanguage procedure generally in these procedures instead of just if the user deselects the option. If the user deselects the option, we need to clear the text box and change the main text box back to its correct state.

The process of building language dynamically in a TextBox can be very tricky, so examine your code carefully and see what works best for you. Similarly to the UserForm's Initialize event, these check boxes simply toggle the visibility settings for their corresponding controls.

If one of these options is checked, the corresponding label and text box become visible. At this point the user may enter information into the text box. As soon as the user begins to type in the text box, the text in the main text box will change to include the chosen option and the name of the pet will actually be included on the fly. This is because every time the text changes in either the dog or cat text box, BuildLanguage is called.

Note: Another alternative is to wait until the user exits the text box to update the language. This can be accomplished with the AfterUpdate event or the Exit event. (Keep in mind the differences between the two events!)

```
Private Sub chkCat_Click()
    If txtCat.Visible = True Then
    Cat_Visible = False
    txtCat.Value = vbNullString
        sCat = vbNullString
        BuildLanguage
    ElseIf txtCat.Visible = False Then
        Cat_Visible True
    End If
End Sub
Private Sub chkDog_Click()
    If Me.txtDog.Visible = True Then
```

```
      Dog_Visible False
      txtDog.Value = vbNullString
      sDog = vbNullString
      BuildLanguage
   ElseIf Me.txtDog.Visible = False Then
      Dog_Visible True
   End If
End Sub
```

Now, we'll discuss the BuildLanguage procedure. This procedure is called every time the form is initialized, and every time one of the two text boxes changes. It has one local string variable. The first If statement is a three-tiered conditional statement that sets the value of the local variable sOpt. This variable ensures that the appropriate language (or lack thereof) appears at the beginning of the second sentence.

The sentence pertaining to the cat will always be the second sentence. If there is no second sentence, chkCat is False and the variable will be vbNullstring. If only the cat option is chosen, chkCat is True and chkDog is False, and the beginning of the sentence will start with a capital "D." If both of the options are chosen, chkCat is True and chkDog is True, and the sentence will start with "Also, d" and the sentence will read correctly.

```
Private Sub BuildLanguage()
Dim sOpt As String
   If chkDog = True And chkCat = True Then
      sOpt = "Also, d"
   ElseIf chkCat = True And chkDog = False Then
      sOpt = "D"
   Else
      sOpt = ""
   End If
   sLanguage = "Please watch my house while I'm gone. " & _
   sDog & sOpt & sCat
   txtLanguage = sLanguage
End Sub
```

Okay, now that we've examined what is happening, we can take a look at the specific change events and the actual production of a sample document, and call the Protect procedure. You can see in each procedure that the respective variable is set when the text is changed. Again, keep in mind that you could be working with a variable that represented just the "name," and a variable containing the sentence could have been used in the chkBox events. As a name is typed into the Dog text box, the main language will change accordingly. See Figure 8-2.

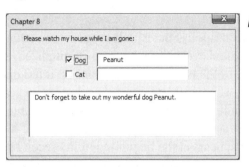

Figure 8-2

```
Private Sub txtCat_Change()
    sCat = "Don't forget to take out my special kitty " & _
    txtCat & "."
    BuildLanguage
End Sub
Private Sub txtDog_Change()
    sDog = "Don't forget to take out my wonderful dog " & _
    txtDog & ". "
    BuildLanguage
End Sub
```

The last item to take care of is to prepare a document from the information. The contents of the text box could have been inserted into one of Word's fields, but for this sample we simply select the range of the ActiveDocument and type "Note!". The selection is then collapsed to the end and a paragraph is inserted. Next, the main language will be typed into the document. Lastly, the Protect procedure described above is called. The end result is a document that appears as you see in Figure 8-3.

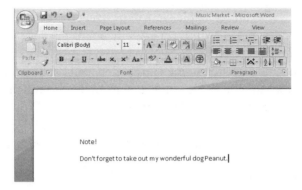

Figure 8-3

```
Private Sub cmdDocs_Click()
    ActiveDocument.Range.Select
    Selection.TypeText Text:="Note!"
    Selection.Collapse wdCollapseEnd
    Selection.TypeParagraph
    Selection.TypeText Me.txtLanguage.Value
    Protect
    End
End Sub
```

Note: This example was very simple in the fact that the resultant document incorporated only the text that was in the main text box. If you incorporate this technique, you will probably want to use it in conjunction with a template that incorporates Word fields to enter the language into the document. This way you could keep the template's boilerplate language free from modification, and allow a user to modify only the language that you give them access to in the UserForm. Once the document is created, the entire template is locked from modification.

Building Documents Dynamically

In some cases you will need to build documents on the fly. There are several ways to do this, but we will explore using our trusty friend, the document variable. You will see in this section how you can create document variables dynamically and keep track of them for your document automation purposes.

For this example we will be using the UserForm shown in Figure 8-4. This project actually builds the documents every time the Another Document button is pressed. It does this by adding a section to the current document and updating the DocVariable fields in the document that is brought in using an IncludeText field. This will give you a good idea of how to use these fields in conjunction with others for document automation. You should be able to see the advantages of this approach immediately. The biggest advantage is that you only need to house one template that contains the boilerplate language.

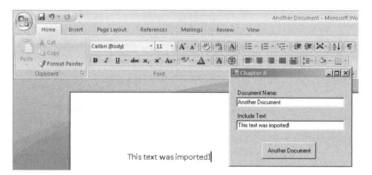

Figure 8-4

As you can see in Figure 8-4, the text from the UserForm has been included in the document. If you look closely, you will also see that there is a section break beneath the UserForm language. The following code explanation describes how to create this functionality.

Note: This example involves dynamic control creation as well as dynamic document creation. You will also find another example of dynamic control creation in Chapter 9.

The first two lines of code are general declaration statements. Obviously, Option Explicit requires explicit variable declaration. In order to make this example a little easier to understand, I've changed the standard array numbering to Option Base 1. This means that the first element of all arrays in this module will begin with the number 1 instead of the default number 0 (zero).

I've divided UserForm's code module into three different procedures. The first procedure is the Click event of the cmdAnother button. The code behind this procedure will generally deal with the dynamic creation of a new page on the MultiPage control every time the button is clicked. The Index property is available for most VB controls. VBA, however, doesn't provide an Index property for controls and thus doesn't provide for dynamic control creation in the same manner as VB. But with a little creativity, you can accomplish practically the same thing.

The next thing you will notice is that a dynamic array of the variable type Page is dimensioned. These variables will be used to assign an object variable equal to a page of the MultiPage control. (Note that the Set keyword is always used with object variables.)

Each of these pages can be individually accessed using the appropriate member of the array. However, we're still only creating blank pages, which aren't very helpful. To add functionality, we need to add controls to the new pages.

This code copies the controls from the first page and pastes them to the newly created pages. All this is done without creating object variables to represent the controls. At first glimpse, adherents of the traditional way of creating controls will most likely scoff at such a method. However, the programmer still has full control over all the properties of the control, except now none of them will show up through the IntelliSense feature. As you can see, you can access the controls through the page's Controls collection. This is how we will obtain the value of the individual text boxes. The following is the code for the Click event procedure of the cmdAnother button.

```
Option Base 1
Option Explicit
Private Sub cmdAnother_Click()
    Dim pgDog() As Page
    Static iDogCounter As Integer
    iDogCounter = iDogCounter + 1
```

```
    ReDim Preserve pgDog(iDogCounter + 1)
    Set pgDog(iDogCounter) = Me.mpgDog.Pages.Add(bstrcaption:= _
        "Dog #" & iDogCounter + 1)
    BuildDocPieceByPiece
    Me.mpgDog(0).Controls.Copy
    pgDog(iDogCounter).Paste
    pgDog(iDogCounter).Controls(2).Value = ""
    pgDog(iDogCounter).Controls(3).Value = ""
End Sub
```

Note: Remember that these run-time controls are "passive" controls. In other words, you cannot trap for their events. While this is fine for text boxes, if you are adding command buttons, you probably want to trap their events.

The subroutine below is also called every time the cmdAnother button is pressed. This is the code responsible for the actual building of the document. First, we are using a static variable as a counter. The Static keyword ensures that the variable will maintain its value once the procedure has finished executing. The next line of code initializes the value of the counter and adds the appropriate increment every time the procedure is run. The With block assigns the document variable's value to the appropriate control in the MultiPage control's collection. Finally, a section is added to the ActiveDocument. This section then incorporates an IncludeText field that will return the static document that will be used over and over to build the active document.

Note: Make sure you understand that there are only two document variables being represented by this example. The next example will show you how to build document variables dynamically.

```
Sub BuildDocPieceByPiece()
Static iSec As Integer
iSec = iSec + 1
    With ActiveDocument
        .Variables("Name").Value = Me.mpgDog(iSec - 1).Controls(2) _
            .Value
        .Variables("Description").Value = Me.mpgDog(iSec - 1) _
            .Controls(3).Value
```

```
    End With
    ActiveDocument.Sections.Add
    ActiveDocument.Sections(iSec).Range.Select
    Selection.Fields.Add Range:=Selection.Range, _
        Type:=wdFieldEmpty, _
        Text:="INCLUDETEXT ""c:\\Wordware\\Dog Description.dot""", _
        PreserveFormatting:=True
End Sub
```

The last procedure represents the code behind the cmdFinish
button. This code first calls the Click event of the cmdAnother
button to "catch up." As you can see, this code is necessary to
include the UserForm's final item in the document. The Fields
collection of the active document is then unlinked. The cursor
is positioned at the beginning of the document, the form is
unloaded, and screen updating is turned back on.

```
Private Sub cmdFinish_Click()
cmdAnother_Click
With ActiveDocument
    .Fields.Unlink
End With
Selection.HomeKey Unit:=wdStory
Unload Me
Application.ScreenUpdating = True
End Sub
```

As you've seen, using dynamic control creation in conjunction with IncludeText fields and document variables is a great
way to build documents dynamically. You'll notice that the
functionality provided here closely resembles that of a mail
merge. In both cases, a static document (main document) is
used to house the document-level logic and boilerplate text.
The above example works best when relatively simple documents are involved and maintaining the information contained
in the document isn't necessary. The obvious downfall of the
approach discussed above is that the information is lost once
the section is created. The following section will show you
how to maintain the value of document variables by creating
them dynamically.

Dynamic Document Variables

This example briefly shows you how you can create document variables dynamically. There is no document creation in this example. Instead, you will simply see how document variables are created in a document and how you can navigate through them. Before we begin discussing the actual code involved, it is probably best to discuss what is actually happening.

Once you understand the example, it will seem relatively straightforward. There are several small procedures involved because we are providing navigation techniques. These techniques involve the use of two counters. The first counter keeps the total number of records that we create, and the second counter represents the current record. These "records" are not records in the traditional sense of the term; rather, they represent a set of document variables according to the extension of the document variables. Thus, the records will be differentiated by the following convention: *variableNameX*, *variableNameY*, and so on. Figure 8-6 shows the UserForm when it contains 21 total records and is displaying the 15th record.

Figure 8-5

Sample Legal Contract

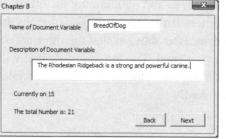

Figure 8-6

The code begins by using the Option Explicit statement. The two module-level variables are integers that will be used as counters. The Initialize event of the UserForm initializes the values of both counters (initially set at 1), and sets the Caption property of both labels. One label corresponds to the current record and the other corresponds to the total number of records.

```
Option Explicit
Dim iCnt As Integer
Dim iTotal As Integer
Sub UserForm_Initialize()
    iCnt = 1
    iTotal = iCnt
    Me.lblCurrentNumber.Caption = iCnt
    Me.lblTotal.Caption = "The total Number is: " & iTotal
End Sub
```

The next two procedures are the Click events of the Back and Next buttons. The Next button runs the CheckValues procedure. This procedure, shown below, makes sure that there are values in the text boxes. The Back button first checks to see if the user is on the first record. If so, a message box is displayed and the procedure is exited; if not, the CheckValues procedure is called. Next, both buttons call the Navigate subroutine and pass their corresponding values to the routine.

```
Private Sub cmdNext_Click()
    CheckValues
    Navigate "Next"
End Sub
Private Sub cmdBack_Click()
    If iCnt = 1 Then
        MsgBox "You are already at the first item!", vbCritical, _
        "Error"
        Exit Sub
    End If
    CheckValues
    Navigate "Back"
End Sub
Sub CheckValues()
    If Me.txtName.Value = "" Or Me.txtDescription.Value = "" Then
        MsgBox "You must enter a value in each text box!", _
            vbCritical, "Error"
```

```
    Exit Sub
  End If
End Sub
```

The Navigate procedure takes one argument and acts accordingly using an If statement. Both branches of the If statement call the WriteVars and UpdateBoxes procedures. Understanding the call stack is important for this subroutine. WriteVars is always called first because you want to write the current record using the iCnt variable. The next thing that happens in either case is the iCnt variable is changed appropriately; this ensures that the UpdateBoxes procedure will update the next appropriate record. You will notice that both segments of the If statement are identical except for the fact that the Next button increments the iCnt variable by 1, and the Back button decrements the iCnt variable by 1.

Note: This is the common format when working with counters. You can include any number of logic variations, but most other variations make your code confusing for others.

```
Sub Navigate(button As String)
If button = "Next" Then
    WriteVars
    iCnt = iCnt + 1
    UpdateBoxes
ElseIf button = "Back" Then
    WriteVars
    iCnt = iCnt - 1
    UpdateBoxes
End If
Me.lblCurrentNumber.Caption = iCnt
Me.lblTotal.Caption = "The total Number is: " & iTotal
End Sub
```

The WriteVars subroutine simply creates (or sets) the value of the document variable equal to the value of its corresponding text box's value. The document variables are enumerated by concatenating the variable name with the value of the counter. This is essentially creating an array of document variables.

The UpdateBoxes subroutine first checks to see if the current counter is greater than the total number of records. If it is, the text box values are cleared and the total counter is incremented by 1; if it is not, the text box values are set equal to the document variable represented by the current counter. This is often referred to as the document variable's extension.

```
Sub WriteVars()
    ActiveDocument.Variables("Name" & iCnt).Value = _
        Me.txtName.Value
    ActiveDocument.Variables("Description" & iCnt).Value = _
        Me.txtDescription.Value
End Sub
Sub UpdateBoxes()
    If iCnt > iTotal Then
        Me.txtName.Value = ""
        Me.txtDescription.Value = ""
        iTotal = iCnt
    Else
        Me.txtName.Value = ActiveDocument.Variables("Name" & _
            iCnt).Value
        Me.txtDescription.Value = ActiveDocument.Variables(" _
            Description" & iCnt).Value
    End If
End Sub
```

As you've seen, it is easy to create dynamic document variables. Keep in mind that the extension of these variables provides for tremendous functionality. You can iterate through the document variable collection of a document using these extensions to act appropriately. If you are using a static document, as described in the previous example, you can programmatically strip the extension off of the document variable and use it to update a constant DocVariable field in a boilerplate document.

Document Management

Another key concern when automating documents is that of document management. Basically, this is the "where" and "how" of document storage and involves the storage of the actual document file and the summary information (author, keywords, etc.) necessary to access the document. Although creating an entire document management system is beyond the scope of this book, this section discusses some of the concerns in document management. This section also demonstrates some fairly rudimentary document management approaches that can be easily implemented in Microsoft Word. In the next section, we'll address the management of document content.

Document Storage Alternatives

Normally, a document is simply stored as a file on one of the network servers. The document summary information is saved in the properties of the document file. This system has several obvious disadvantages. First, users may use different conventions when storing files and organizing folders. Second, some users may not be very familiar with navigating through the Windows directory structure. Third, there is no way to query or filter documents based on the document summary information.

As an alternative, you can also track the location of the document as well as document summary information in a SQL Server or Access database. This allows the document summary information to be queried through the database. The downfall is that a separately developed front-end application is necessary to navigate the documents. Many readily available document management solutions use this principle.

Managing Documents

In many organizations, the most important information resides in the form of documents. This information can range from internal policies and procedures to important customer or client information. If your organization has an extensive library of documentation or routinely has documents "marked up" or changed, you may want to explore document imaging. On the front end, Word provides several tools to help with the organization and storage of documents. These tools are discussed below.

File Properties

File properties are details about a file that help identify it — for example, a descriptive title, the author name, the subject, and keywords that identify topics or other information in the file. Use file properties to display information about a file or to help organize your files so that you can find them easily later.

File properties fall into these categories:

▼ Automatically updated file properties include statistics that are maintained for you, such as file size and the dates files are created and last modified. For example, you can search for all files created after March 3, 1996, or for all files last modified yesterday.

▼ Preset file properties (such as author, title, and subject) that already exist, but require that you enter a text value. For example, in Word, add the keyword "customers" to your sales files and then search for files with that keyword.

▼ Custom file properties are those to which you assign a text, date, number, or "yes" or "no" value. You can choose from a list of preset names or add your own. You can also link custom file properties to specific items in your file, such as a named cell in Excel, a selected item in PowerPoint, or a bookmark in Word. For example, in a contract form created in Word, create a custom file property that is linked to a form field containing the contract's expiration date. Then you can search for all contract files with specific expiration dates.

Note: If you want to be reminded to set file properties for every file you create, you can have Word automatically display the Properties dialog box when you save files for the first time. See Figure 8-7.

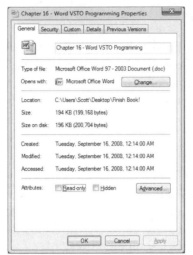

Figure 8-7

AutoSummarize

When you use the AutoSummarize feature, it automatically fills in the preset file properties for keywords and comments. If you don't want AutoSummarize to replace your existing keywords and comments, clear the Update document statistics check box in the AutoSummarize dialog box found in the Word Options area. You can also add AutoSummarize to the toolbar by clicking **Office button | Word Options | Customize**, clicking **All Commands** in the Choose commands from list, and then choosing **AutoSummary Tools**.

Searching Documents

The key to success when working with any type of document management system is providing the capability to search and retrieve documents. Users are much more likely to embrace a system that allows them several methods to find what they need. In many cases, a user may have only bits and pieces of the information necessary to retrieve a document. Documents become "lost" for many reasons in the digital world — accounts change hands, drives are backed up or remapped, employees leave, etc. The focus of this book is the actual preparation of documents; however, remember that if your automation system is successful, you will undoubtedly need to provide (or purchase) a document management tool. Let's take a look at some commonly used search techniques that may help your organization successfully employ a document management solution.

Searching By Customer or Contact Number/Database Key/Unique Identifier

The most common type of search, and often the most productive, is a search for a specific customer or contact. Take the state driver's licensing database, for example, where searching by an individual license number either provides one matching record or no records, which means that the number is not licensed by the state. This example shows top-level indexing, where the index (the individual's license number) is used to "index" the information for that record (the individual's personal information). The importance of implementing a top-level index cannot be overstated.

Top-level index numbers are easily created in the database world. When you are dealing with documents, however, this is somewhat problematic. A surefire way to know that the correct identifier is attached to a document is to force users to enter the document preparation system from within a customer or contact in the database. This method allows you to pass the correct identifier and include it in the document properties section. Once the correct identifier is stored in the document properties, you can utilize Word's search mechanism to find the appropriate documents. Further, since the documents are being started from a central database, creation of a document can be tracked there.

In theory, the above approach should work great, and it does, as long as the documents cannot be modified once they are created. In reality, most organizations are too dynamic to force such a mechanism upon their users (remember, these documents would have to be locked or the content could be manipulated at will). In short, by locking documents and forcing database control over the documents, you lose some of the functionality that makes Word-based assembly systems so powerful. The trade-off is that if the documents aren't locked, they can be cut and pasted to accommodate other customers or contacts and data integrity is lost (unless you have powerful procedures in place and a solid buy-in from management).

Searching By Document Properties (Author/Subject/Keyword, etc.)

One of the great things about Word templates is that the information stored on the Summary tab of the Document Properties dialog box is carried forward. This means that all documents prepared from a certain template will have the information from the file used to originally create the document. These built-in document properties are a great place to store information specific to the creation of a document. For instance, if you obtain a customer's name in a VBA UserForm, you could use that name to populate one of the built-in document properties. Searches will be even easier if you can use these built-in properties in combination with one another. You could include any combination of information that you choose.

Tip: You can obtain great results by using a database in conjunction with a Word template. You can require your users to choose a customer from a read-only list that is populated by a database query. You can then return the appropriate identifier and populate a document property with that information.

Contents Searching

Another method that can be used to find documents is through the use of Word's full text search capability, which we discussed in Chapter 2. Before dismissing the idea of actually managing documents based on their content, you must realize that advocates of using this simplistic method of searching point to the fact that up-front indexing and development costs are completely eliminated. In other words, this form of document management really involves no specific document file management (although imaging may be implemented and, therefore, image files may be managed).

In relatively simple organizations or organizations that seldom search or reuse documents, this may be an appropriate method of document management. Of course, this assumes that all of the other components are managed properly as well (including the actual file system, folders, archives, hardware, etc.). Word's content searching is surprisingly robust. You can search entire drives for documents containing certain text items.

Managing Content

Once you have a document assembly system in place, you will undoubtedly have the need to update the content in the individual templates. This means that you will need a mechanism in place to keep track of changes that occur in the subsidiary documents or templates upon which your business documents are based. Changes to the subsidiary templates can be broadly grouped into two different kinds: changes that affect the logic of the document and changes that only affect the language of the document.

Logic Changes

There will be instances where the logic behind the document needs to be changed to accommodate the request of a user. These changes always require contact with systems personnel. Some businesses choose to grant wide latitude to the content of their documents; frequently managers and in-house lawyers have the ability to change the actual content of the template. This is fine, as long as there is some way to keep track of the changes.

If these changes involve changes to logic, then someone with knowledge of how the document works — the built-in Word fields and the mechanism for updating those fields — must be involved to ensure that the template doesn't become corrupt. This means that the organization must also have a system in place for testing the changes before they are implemented office-wide. Even changes that appear relatively minor should be tested. Basically, any changes that aren't in the boilerplate language of the document should go through a rigorous testing process.

Language Changes

There will be times when a manager or an in-house attorney needs to make changes to the boilerplate language of the template. It is advisable to have any changes tested, but sometimes this is impractical. In this case you need to develop a way to keep track of the different versions and the dates of their implementation.

It's already been stated that all of your documents should exist in a central repository on the network. You should also have a private backup folder on that same drive that can be used to track the different versions of documents. The following section and corresponding code illustrates a simple method to allow users with certain privileges to update the content of a document. Again, use this method cautiously because, when it comes to users, what can go wrong will go wrong.

Template Change Tracking Project

First off, some fundamentals: This example assumes, and indeed works best with, a staging environment that is an identical replication of the production environment. From an administration standpoint, you never want developers playing in traffic. Even these simple changes to the content of a template are essentially development. While it may be impractical to require every insertion of a comma to go through the administrative process, it is not impractical to simply request that a template be uploaded from a staging server to a production server.

Another element of this example is that we do not want to change functionality for the user charged with modifying the template. Windows users are familiar with Save and Save As, so we want to make the tracking of their versions as simple as possible and track all changes made to the templates. A certain component of this process is training those in charge of maintaining the templates on what changes they are capable of making without the help of the systems department, and how to make changes in the staging environment. We don't want the users saving changes every two seconds, and it is important for them to know why they shouldn't make changes outside of the staging environment.

It is recommended that you create your own custom document property, as Word's internal revision number can be somewhat deceiving at times. The custom document property that you create can keep track of the exact number of times the template has been saved.

With that qualification in place, notice that we will be disabling the Save As functionality. If the user tries to save the template outside of the staging area, the message box in Figure 8-8 will be displayed.

Figure 8-8

```
Sub FileSaveAs()
    MsgBox "You are not allowed to save templates " & _
    "outside of the staging environment.", vbCritical, _
    "Error Saving Template"
End Sub
Sub FileSave()
Dim sRevNum As String
    sRevNum = ThisDocument.CustomDocumentProperties( _
    "RevisionNumber") + 1
    Do Until Len(sRevNum) = 5
    sRevNum = "0" & sRevNum
Loop
    ThisDocument.CustomDocumentProperties("RevisionNumber") = _
    sRevNum
    ThisDocument.SaveAs FileName:="C:\wordware\archive\" & _
    Left(ThisDocument.Name, Len(ThisDocument.Name) - 4) & _
    ThisDocument.CustomDocumentProperties("RevisionNumber")
```

```
    ThisDocument.SaveAs FileName:="c:\wordware\" & _
    Left(ThisDocument.Name, Len(ThisDocument.Name) - 9)
End Sub
```

Automatically Tracking Word Documents in Outlook

You've already seen that you can find out how much total time has been spent editing a document by viewing its properties. However, in some cases you may want to see how much time has been spent working on a document over the course of many days. In other cases, you may remember working on a document sometime in the past few weeks, but you now have no recollection of what document you were working with (and it's not in your history either).

Of course, you could program around all of the above situations and write the specific data to a database or create reports, but Outlook 2007 provides a much better tool: Journal tracking allows you to track your documents through Outlook's Journal feature. This makes it easy to graphically see how much time you've spent working on a document and exactly when it was edited.

The first step of the process is to start Microsoft Outlook. Once you are in Outlook, choose **Tools | Options** and choose the **Preferences** tab. See Figure 8-9. The Preferences tab is where you access many of Outlook's customization features. Next, press the **Journal Options** button in the Contacts and Notes section; this will display the Journal Options dialog box. This dialog box provides many options specific to Outlook in the list box on the upper-left side. The list box on the lower-left side lists other Microsoft Office applications. You can track Word documents by selecting the check box that corresponds to Word.

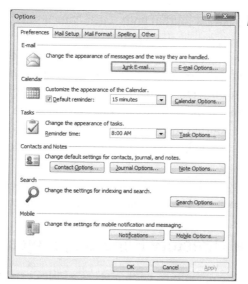

Figure 8-9

You can keep track of your documents on a daily, weekly, or monthly timeline by clicking the appropriate button in Outlook. Figure 8-10 shows the Outlook Calendar view. The standard Calendar toolbar shows the available buttons, and you can see that the daily view is selected. Each document icon in the Journal window has a duration bar on top. This indicates how long the document was open.

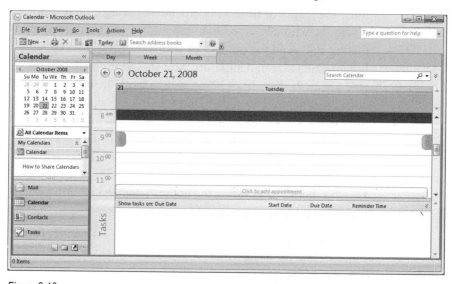

Figure 8-10

Once you have a journal entry open, you'll see that it contains information such as the duration of time the file was open and what time it was opened. If you want to assign the file to a contact, you can do so by clicking the Contacts button and choosing from your available contacts. You can also edit the information in the journal entry and save it. You can see that Outlook's Journal tracking system provides a powerful tool that can really help when trying to track Word documents.

Note: Documents that are automatically recorded in the Outlook Journal sometimes take a few minutes to appear in the Journal.

Central Directory Reporting Project

In many organizations, certain types of files exist in a central folder. Users may be able to save certain documents to their C: drives, but other documents may need to be accessible to everyone on the network. There are several advantages to saving documents in enterprise-wide folders. For example, you can break up the folders into certain types of documents, every user will be able to view the content of another user's documents, and it helps promote uniformity.

Word's built-in document properties also help you determine the length of time a document was being edited, who created it, who last saved it, number of pages, number of paragraphs, and even the number of words. Depending on your organization size and structure, you should immediately be able to see the benefit of being able to track the statistics on such documents. The added ability to track documents by date means that you should be able to extract most of the pertinent data you need and compile a report from it. The code below shows an example of extracting pertinent data. This code loops through all documents (ending with .doc) in the directory "D:\book\" and stores the author's name, creation date, and the total time spent on editing the document.

```
Sub FindFiles()
Dim sFileName As String
Dim oDoc As Document
Dim iCount As Integer
```

```
sFileName = Dir("D:\book\")
Do While sFileName <> ""
    If Right(sFileName, 3) = "doc" Then
        Set oDoc = Documents.Open("D:\book\" & sFileName, False, _
        True, False)
        iCount = iCount + 1
        ReDim Preserve Files(iCount) As File
        Files(iCount).Author = oDoc.BuiltInDocumentProperties( _
        wdPropertyAuthor)
        Files(iCount).CreateDate = oDoc.BuiltInDocumentProperties( _
        wdPropertyTimeCreated)
        Files(iCount).TotalTime = oDoc.BuiltInDocumentProperties( _
        wdPropertyVBATotalEdit) oDoc.Close SaveChanges:=False
    End If
    MsgBox sFileName
        sFileName = Dir
Loop
End Sub
```

Protecting Your Code

An aspect of programming that is often overlooked until it is too late is that of security. Security encompasses several different aspects, but there are some things to keep in mind when programming in Microsoft Word. You may want to restrict access to certain templates. This can be done either in the administrative process when giving rights to a certain network drive, or in the development process through the use of password protection. Inevitably, you will want to protect your code from prying eyes. If your error trapping routine fails, you do not want your users playing with the code in a template. Additionally, Word is the most common vehicle for macro viruses. For more macro security information, please refer to Chapter 4.

Protection Strategies

A preliminary consideration when creating a security plan is to always write your code so that controls are only visible in the appropriate situations and to authorized users. This requires that you plan around the actual process that the user is undertaking. For instance, suppose your template project will be used to create several different documents. You will want to: (1) decide which type of document the user is creating in the beginning, (2) hide any controls that are not necessary for the production of that document, and (3) employ branching logic that guides the user through the process of gathering the information. (This may require that some UserForms are never even displayed to the user. When working with the actual controls on a form, the Visible property makes a control visible or invisible.)

Another strategy is to set a control's foreground and background to the same color when the control is unnecessary or unauthorized users run the application. This hides the information from unauthorized users. The ForeColor and BackColor properties determine the foreground color and the background color. Finally, you can also disable a control when unauthorized users run the application. This allows users to see the control, but prevents them from entering information. The Enabled property determines when a control is disabled.

Note: Disabling a control is a great way to provide read-only information to a user. For instance, you may require the entry of a unique identifier. Once this identifier is chosen, you will want to disable the control for future use so that information specific to that identifier isn't changed to another record.

Passwords

In some instances, you will want to require a password for access to the application or a specific control. For those of you familiar with the old ECHO OFF method, you'll be glad to know that VBA provides the PasswordChar property to define placeholder characters. This allows you to prevent the password from being displayed. Instead, a placeholder character will be displayed as the user types each character.

Note: Using passwords or any other techniques listed can improve the security of your application, but does not guarantee the prevention of unauthorized access to your data.

Preventing User Interference

One of the most frequent problems when working with UserForms is that the user has the ability to close the UserForm by clicking the small "X" (Cancel) button located in the upper right-hand corner. This has all sorts of unwanted effects. First off, any variables in use will lose their state (value). Secondly, the user will be left staring at a blank screen, or worse the code in the underlying template. All the UserForm's controls will also lose their values.

Luckily, VBA captures this scenario in the UserForm_QueryClose event and allows you to stop the user in his or her tracks. The following procedure can be implemented globally by inserting it into a standard module. This allows you to handle the event for all forms in one place. In some instances, you may want to take a different action depending on the form. As you can see, the UserForm_QueryClose event simply calls the global procedure and passes its parameters forward. The global procedure then "intercepts" the event by setting Cancel to True and displaying a message box to the user. Once the user clicks the OK button, the UserForm resumes control.

```
Public Sub Disable_X(Cancel As Integer, CloseMode As Integer)
If CloseMode = vbFormControlMenu Then
    Cancel = True
    MsgBox "You must exit by selecting the exit button on the _
    Switchboard!", vbCritical, "Error"
End If
End Sub
Private Sub UserForm_QueryClose(Cancel As Integer, CloseMode As _
    Integer)
    Disable_X Cancel, CloseMode
End Sub
```

Document Protection Strategies

As you saw in the previous section, Word provides ways to programmatically restrict access to a document. You can do this by assigning a password to open the document, which prevents unauthorized users from opening the document. You can also assign a password to modify the document, which allows others to open the document but not to save changes without the password. If someone opens the document without the password to modify the document, that person can save the document only by giving it a different file name.

Another strategy is to only allow read-only access to the document. If someone opens the document as a read-only file and changes it, that person can only save the document by giving it a different file name. If someone opens the document as a read/write file and changes it, the document can be saved with its original file name.

If your organization takes advantage of document routing, you can assign a password when a document is routed for review. This prevents any changes except for comments or tracked changes. This is a great way to keep others from actually altering a document. You will be able to see what they propose, but they will be unable to change the actual content of the document. For lengthy legal documents, this can be a valuable asset that can save time as users look back through their completed document.

If you are using sections, you can assign a password to prevent others from changing the sections you specify. This method of protection offers the most flexibility as you can use different types of section breaks to distinguish parts of a document. In other words, you could lock individual paragraphs on a page. You can see where this could provide great flexibility when working with complex documents.

Caution: If you protect a document with a password, do not forget it. If you do, you can't open the document, remove protection from it, or recover data from it. It's a good idea to keep a list of your passwords and their corresponding document names in a safe place.

Conclusion

This chapter looked at what document automation is and various approaches to automating documents. This chapter also demonstrated some fairly rudimentary document management approaches that can be easily implemented in Microsoft Word as well as some security concerns that may arise. Although creating an entire document management system is beyond the scope of this book, this chapter discussed some of the concerns of document management including storage alternatives, file properties, and various other tools provided by Word to help manage, protect, and organize your documents.

Chapter 9

VBA Projects

Introduction

In this chapter we focus on two individual VBA projects. The first project demonstrates the use of dynamically created controls, which are frequently necessary in document automation programming. The Index property is available for most VB controls. VBA, however, doesn't provide an Index property for controls and thus doesn't provide for dynamic control creation in the same manner as VB. The second project demonstrates how Word can be used to create what is essentially a document assembly system that customizes itself for each user.

Dynamic Control Creation with VBA

Programmers familiar with Visual Basic may be surprised to find that Microsoft neglected to include control arrays in VBA 6.0. Control arrays allow the creation of run-time controls, as long as a control of the same type already exists and the existing control has an index of 0.

As previously mentioned, VBA doesn't provide an Index property for controls and thus doesn't provide for dynamic control creation in the same manner as VB. But with a little creativity, you can accomplish practically the same thing.

The Traditional Method

The main thing to remember about controls is that they are objects. As objects, they have properties and methods you can manipulate at design time or run time to achieve the desired results. This chapter presents two common ways to create controls at run time in VBA. Virtually any run-time control creation will use a variation of one of these two methods. The most common way (the traditional way) is to create a control object variable to contain the run-time control, as shown in Listing 9-1 below. Figure 9-1 shows a MultiPage control with two text boxes and a combo box.

Listing 9-1: Traditional method

```
(Please note the additional code specified in the code blocks
below)
Option Explicit
' Dimension a variable as a new instance of Form1.
Dim frmNew As New UserForm1
' Dimension specific object arrays.
Dim pg(1 To 5) As New Page
Dim txtFName(1 To 5) As New Control
Dim txtLName(1 To 5) As New Control
Dim cboTle(1 To 5) As New Control
' Dimension a counter variable so that it keeps its value.
' Note: This could also be done locally with a static
' variable that would exist for the life of the module.
Dim x As Integer, y As Integer
Private Sub cmdNewForm_Click()
' Display a dynamically-created version of the UserForm.
frmNew.Show
End Sub
Public Sub cmdNewPage_Click()
' Used to keep track of how many pages are created and
' sets the array index accordingly.
x = x + 1
' Prevent user from getting error.
If x = 6 Then
MsgBox "You can only create 6 total pages!", vbCritical
```

```
Exit Sub
End If
' Set member of page array to the newly created page.
Set pg(x) = Me.MultiPage1.Pages.Add
' Set members of the control arrays to the
' newly created controls.
Set txtFName(x) = pg(x).Controls.Add("Forms.TextBox.1")
txtFName(x).Left = 36
txtFName(x).Top = 12
txtFName(x).Width = 132
Set txtLName(x) = pg(x).Controls.Add("Forms.TextBox.1")
txtLName(x).Left = 36
txtLName(x).Top = 36
txtLName(x).Width = 132
Set cboTle(x) = pg(x).Controls.Add("Forms.ComboBox.1")
cboTle(x).Left = 36
cboTle(x).Top = 60
cboTle(x).Width = 132
End Sub
Public Sub cmdValue_Click()
Me.Hide
' Run a loop that displays the value of the text boxes.
For y = 1 To Me.MultiPage1.Pages.Count
If y = 1 Then
MsgBox "The value of the text is " & _
Me.txtFirstName.Value
Else
MsgBox "The value of the text is " & txtFName(y - 1)
End If
Next
End Sub
```

Before we begin adding run-time controls, let's take a look at the creation of a run-time form. Sometimes, all the functionality you require can be accomplished by creating another instance of the form at run time. The following lines of code (also found in UserForm1) will create a run-time instance of the form:

```
Dim frmNew As New UserForm1
Private Sub cmdNewForm_Click()
frmNew.Show
End Sub
```

Notice that in this case, the new form contains all the controls and functionality of the original form. (You can move the forms to different areas and hit the button to see that it's creating new forms.) However, there will be times when you want to see the additional sets of controls all at once. This is where the MultiPage control becomes quite useful. UserForm1 (see Figure 9-1) uses the following code to create an additional page every time the New Page command button's Click event is fired:

```
Private Sub cmdNewPage_Click()
Me.MultiPage1.Pages.Add
End Sub
```

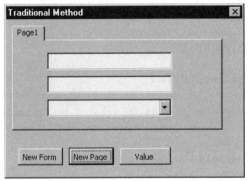

Figure 9-1:
UserForm1

This code creates a new page, but it's not assigning another object variable to the page and thus the new page's properties are difficult to work with. If, however, we set the page equal to an object variable, we gain access to some added functionality. (Note that the Set keyword is always used with object variables.) The most complete way of adding pages is to create an array of pages using the following code:

```
Dim pg(1 To 5) As New Page
Private Sub cmdNewPage_Click()
Static x As Integer
x = x + 1
Set pg(x) = Me.MultiPage1.Pages.Add
End Sub
```

This code uses pg(1 To 5) to capture each of the newly created pages. These pages can be accessed individually using the appropriate member of the array. However, we're still only creating blank pages, which aren't very helpful. To add functionality, we need to add controls to the new pages.

Again, we can accomplish this through the use of arrays and the appropriate object variables. One of the parameters of the Control.Add method is *Name*. The *Name* argument can become confusing. In most cases, it's easier to refer to the index value of the array. The code below, when added to the New Page command button, will create additional controls and the corresponding object variables:

```
Set txtFName(x) = pg(x).Controls.Add("Forms.TextBox.1")
txtFName(x).Left = 36
txtFName(x).Top = 12
txtFName(x).Width = 132
Set txtLName(x) = pg(x).Controls.Add("Forms.TextBox.1")
txtLName(x).Left = 36
txtLName(x).Top = 36
txtLName(x).Width = 132
Set cboTle(x) = pg(x).Controls.Add("Forms.ComboBox.1")
cboTle(x).Left = 36
cboTle(x).Top = 60
cboTle(x).Width = 132
```

Note that we used slightly different names for each of these controls. VBA forces you to do this because control arrays are not intrinsically allowed. If you try to set a control array with the same name as an existing control, you'll see the warning message shown in Figure 9-2.

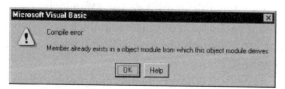

Figure 9-2: Error received when having multiple controls with the same name

The next command button, Value, runs a simple message box procedure that demonstrates how you can use the values of the dynamically created controls in any of the ways in which you could use design-time controls and their values.

Let's take a moment to carefully analyze the controls we're creating. We're dimensioning the variables as "controls," but not as actual text boxes or combo boxes. The result is that some of the properties and methods of the controls will *not* show up with the IntelliSense feature, but this doesn't mean they're not available. IntelliSense recognizes only that the variable is a "control," but it doesn't know the actual type of control. Therefore, IntelliSense lists the properties common to all controls. For example, IntelliSense won't display the BackColor property, but assigning a value to the BackColor property is still syntactically correct. When assigned to the Click event of a command button, the following code will change the background color of the text box. Note that we cannot use the New keyword when dimensioning variables to be text boxes; we get a type mismatch error if we try to create an array of specific controls. Thus, we must use the control type for our dynamically created controls:

```
txtFName(x).BackColor = vbRed
```

Note: All forms created using the traditional method are modal.

A Shortcut Method

Every programmer knows there is often more than one "correct" way of accomplishing a given task. The previous section walked through what is, essentially, an alternative means of creating dynamic control arrays. Obviously, this requires the explicit declaration of object variables to contain the run-time controls. This provides you with full access to the control's properties.

There is a quicker method that provides basically the same control over the dynamically created controls. The shortcut method is shown in Listing 9-2. The following code demonstrates a copy-and-paste method of adding a collection of controls to another MultiPage control:

```
Private Sub cmdNewPage_Click()
Static x As Integer
x = x + 1
Me.MultiPage1.Pages(0).Controls.Copy
Me.MultiPage1.Pages.Add
Me.MultiPage1.Pages(x).Paste
End Sub
```

This code copies the controls from the first page and pastes them to the newly created pages. All this is done without creating object variables to represent either the pages or the controls. At first glance, adherents of the traditional way of creating controls will most likely scoff at such a method. However, the programmer still has full control over all the properties of the control — except now none of them will show up through the IntelliSense feature.

In Listing 9-2 you'll see that a simple loop runs through the pages of the MultiPage control and displays a message box with the value of the control indexed at 0. This is somewhat trickier than setting an object variable equal to the new control. In this method, we must know the index of the control as it exists on the page. If worse comes to worse, you can set values to the controls and distinguish them by displaying message boxes corresponding to each index on the page.

Notice that we're using the SelectedItem property to identify which page is active. The Color button changes the BackColor of the text box on the selected page. This is useful to demonstrate that the controls are actually being copied and pasted every time the Click event fires. If you add a page while the first page's text box is white, the newly created page contains a white text box. If you change the first page's text box to red and add another page, its text box will be red, and the second page's text box will remain white. This demonstrates that you're really creating new objects with every Click event (see Figure 9-3).

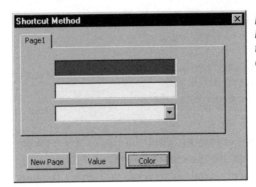

Figure 9-3: The Color button changes the text box background color to red.

Listing 9-2: The shortcut method

```
Option Explicit
Private Sub cmdColor_Click()
' If statement to change the color of the text box.
With Me.MultiPage1.SelectedItem.Controls(0)
If .BackColor = vbRed Then
.BackColor = vbWhite
Else
.BackColor = vbRed
End If
End With
End Sub
Private Sub cmdNewPage_Click()
' Counter variable used to keep track of the index.
Static x As Integer
' Adds 1 to x every time the procedure is run.
x = x + 1
' The following three lines copy the controls from the design
' time page, add one page to the multipage control, and finally
' paste the controls to the newly created page.
Me.MultiPage1.Pages(0).Controls.Copy
Me.MultiPage1.Pages.Add
Me.MultiPage1.Pages(x).Paste
End Sub
Private Sub cmdValue_Click()
Dim y As Integer
' A loop to display the values of the run-time controls.
For y = 1 To Me.MultiPage1.Pages.Count
Me.MultiPage1.Value = y - 1
MsgBox Me.MultiPage1.SelectedItem.Controls(0).Value
Next y
End Sub
```

A Final Note

Remember that these run-time controls are "passive" controls. In other words, you cannot trap for their events. While there are ways of creating active run-time controls, they are beyond the scope of this chapter. The preceding examples offer most of the functionality necessary when using dynamically created controls.

Automating Document Creation with Word Templates

With a little creativity, Word can easily be programmed to dramatically save time in document production, data gathering, and inter-Office application automation. You can use Word templates to create what is essentially a document assembly system that customizes itself for each user. Such templates can totally eliminate the weekly or, in some cases, daily cutting and pasting, and provide uniform documentation throughout any organization. Imagine the benefit if remote users need to submit information in a consistent manner; e.g., a national sales force submitting written proposals.

This section describes such a document "assembly line" by creating a template system you can easily customize and augment to fit your needs. Following is the code behind the frmInfo UserForm, shown in Figure 9-5.

Listing 9-3: frmInfo UserForm

```
Option Explicit
Dim sDesigPath As String
Dim sIniFile As String
Private Sub UserForm_Initialize()
' "Me" is always the active UserForm.
With Me
' Initialize text boxes with Word's option settings.
' Note that these can still be changed.
.txtYourname = Application.UserName
.txtInitials = Application.UserInitials
' This adds each label to the list at run time.
With cboYourtitl
```

```
.AddItem "President"
.AddItem "Vice President"
.AddItem "Assistant Vice President"
.AddItem "Senior Vice President"
.AddItem "First Vice President"
.AddItem "Administrative Assistant"
.AddItem "Secretary"
.AddItem "Treasurer"
.AddItem "Lowly Cube Grunt"
End With
With cboClosing
.AddItem "Very truly yours,"
.AddItem "Sincerely,"
.AddItem "Sincerely yours,"
.AddItem "Respectfully,"
.AddItem "Respectfully yours,"
End With
End With
End Sub
' Ends the running procedure and unloads the form.
Private Sub cmdCancel_Click()
End
End Sub
Private Sub cmdFinish_Click()
' Checks the second address text box for a null value.
' If it contains a null value, sets it equal to "x".
If Me.txtAdd2.Value = "" Then
Me.txtAdd2.Value = "x"
End If
' Create subfolder in the UserTemplates path. When
' populated with templates it will appear in the
' New dialog box.
sDesigPath = _
Options.DefaultFilePath(Path:=wdUserTemplatesPath)
MkDir (sDesigPath & "\Basic Templates")
' Save this template to the new directory under 3 names.
ActiveDocument.SaveAs FileName:=sDesigPath & _
"\Basic Templates\" & "Fax.dot"
ActiveDocument.SaveAs FileName:=sDesigPath & _
"\Basic Templates\" & "Letter.dot"
ActiveDocument.SaveAs FileName:=sDesigPath & _
"\Basic Templates\" & "Memo.dot"
' Create the initialization file and set the keys
' equal to the text box values.
sIniFile = sDesigPath & "\Basic Templates\Personal.ini"
```

```
System.PrivateProfileString( _
sIniFile, "Personal", "Name") = Me.txtYourname
System.PrivateProfileString( _
sIniFile, "Personal", "Fax") = Me.txtFax
System.PrivateProfileString( _
sIniFile, "Personal", "Phone") = Me.txtPhone
System.PrivateProfileString( _
sIniFile, "Personal", "Title") = Me.cboYourtitl
System.PrivateProfileString( _
sIniFile, "Company", "Add1") = Me.txtAdd1
System.PrivateProfileString( _
sIniFile, "Company", "Add2") = Me.txtAdd2
System.PrivateProfileString( _
sIniFile, "Company", "City") = Me.txtCity
System.PrivateProfileString( _
sIniFile, "Company", "State") = Me.txtState
System.PrivateProfileString( _
sIniFile, "Company", "Zip") = Me.txtZip
System.PrivateProfileString( _
sIniFile, "Personal", "Closing") = Me.cboClosing
System.PrivateProfileString( _
sIniFile, "Company", "Company") = Me.txtCompName
' This closes the template, unloads the form,
' and displays a message box.
ActiveDocument.Close SaveChanges:=wdDoNotSaveChanges
Unload Me
MsgBox "Select Office button | New and click Basic Templates.", _
, "Basic Template Setup"
End
End Sub
```

What It Does

The template creates three other templates, and stores information needed to complete them in an initialization (.ini) file. This is done simply by opening the file, which displays a user form requiring the user to enter basic information such as name, address, phone, and fax number (we'll discuss this more in a bit; it's shown in Figure 9-5). This information is saved in an initialization file for the new templates.

Next, a folder named \Basic Templates is created under \Program Files\Microsoft Office\Templates. This causes the folder to appear as a page on the New dialog box, which is displayed by selecting **Office button | New** in Word. This folder will be populated with three templates: Fax.dot, Letter.dot, and Memo.dot, as shown in Figure 9-4.

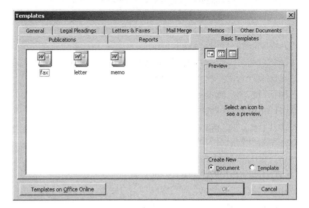

Figure 9-4: Fax.dot, Letter.dot, and Memo.dot shown in the new Basic Templates folder

At this point the original template is no longer necessary. The three new templates will run their own user forms so the user can input relevant information and use a "link" to the initialization file to finish creating the resulting documents. The finished documents will contain both the user's default information (stored in the initialization file) and the specific information entered by the user.

How It Works

Word contains "Auto" macros that run when certain events occur. The AutoOpen macro (shown below), for example, runs when a document or template is opened. The AutoNew macro runs whenever "New" is used to run a template. This file stores both of these macros in a VBA module, but note that the ThisDocument section can contain them as well.

```
Sub AutoOpen()
' Ensure the three new templates aren't opened (only Office _
' button | New).
If ActiveDocument.AttachedTemplate = "Letter.dot" Then
MsgBox "You must use these as Office button | New"
```

```
ActiveDocument.Close SaveChanges:=wdDoNotSaveChanges
End
ElseIf ActiveDocument.AttachedTemplate = "Fax.dot" Then
MsgBox "You must use these as Office button | New"
ActiveDocument.Close SaveChanges:=wdDoNotSaveChanges
End
ElseIf ActiveDocument.AttachedTemplate = "Memo.dot" Then
MsgBox "You must use these as Office button | New"
ActiveDocument.Close SaveChanges:=wdDoNotSaveChanges
End
End If
' Display Information form in the original template.
frmInfo.Show
End Sub
```

You do not want someone opening a template and overwriting fields by accident. The If...Then...ElseIf structure ensures the resulting fax, memo, and letter templates cannot be opened by mistake. Attempting to open one of these templates displays a message box. When the user clicks OK, the template will close. Setting the Close method's *SaveChanges* parameter to wdDoNotSaveChanges prevents the Save dialog box from being displayed when the template is closed. The final statement in the AutoOpen macro is:

```
frmInfo.Show
```

The set-up UserForm named frmInfo is shown in Figure 9-5. The code associated with the UserForm is shown in Listing 9-3. This UserForm is only displayed when the original template runs the AutoOpen macro. It contains labels, command buttons, combo boxes, and text boxes (all of which can be enhanced by setting the ControlTipText property to provide additional information when the user highlights one with the mouse). The combo boxes and text boxes are used to obtain information from the user that will be stored in the initialization

Figure 9-5: The frmInfo UserForm

file. As you can see, the AddItem method is used to set the list of each combo box at run time. You may also want to set the combo box's Enter event to fire its DropDown method so it will automatically display the list.

The event handler for the Cancel button simply contains the End command. A good precaution, however, would be to close the template to prevent tampering. Nevertheless, use Application.Quit with great care, as most users dislike programs that shut down without asking first.

The Finish button must accomplish three things: create a subfolder that appears in the user's Office button | New window; populate this subfolder with templates; and save the user's basic information in an initialization file. The newly created templates will use these initialization settings as well as the UserForm results to update Word fields and produce a document.

You can see in Listing 9-3 that a locally declared string variable, sDesigPath, is set equal to:

```
Options.DefaultFilePath(wdUserTemplatesPath)
```

This path corresponds to the settings in Word's Office button | Word Options | Advanced | File Locations | User Templates section. The MkDir command uses a concatenated file name consisting of the variable and a new folder name (including a backslash) to create the subfolder in the default UserTemplates path. The subfolder has been created, but it won't show up as a page in the New dialog box until it contains templates. Note that the page has the same name as the folder.

The next step is to save the template under the new template name in this folder (or to FileCopy other templates). Here, the SaveAs method of the ActiveDocument is used. The *Filename* argument is set equal to sDesigPath, representing the default UserTemplates folder, the name of the new folder, and the names of the three new templates.

The final step is creating the initialization file to store the user information so the other templates can later retrieve it. This is done using the System.PrivateProfileString property.

This property takes three arguments: *Filename*, *Section*, and *Key*. The initialization file is given the standard .ini extension.

The *Filename* argument specifies the location of the initialization file. The file can be stored anywhere, but the new Basic Templates subfolder is the most convenient place because the sDesigPath variable specifying its location already exists. Further, keeping files in a central location is a good practice and saves future programmers from unnecessary hunting.

The *Section* argument indicates the heading within the initialization file where the information is stored. The file may be broken into sections for easier reference. The code in Listing 9-3 uses Personal and Company sections. Notice that the values are stored in the correct section independent of the sequence in which they are created.

The last part of the System.PrivateProfileString is the *Key* argument. It specifies the precise location in the .ini file where the information resides. Listing 9-3 shows these keys are set equal to the value of the form's text boxes and combo boxes. The Value property for a text box or combo box is always identical to its Text property. Value is the default property of both controls, and therefore doesn't require specific identification.

Figure 9-6 shows how the *Key* values are stored in the initialization file. Keep in mind that if a user enters incorrect information in the basic setup, the initialization values are easily changed using any ASCII editor, such as Notepad.

Figure 9-6: Key values of the .ini file are easily changed using an editor such as Notepad.

Attending to the housekeeping items is the last order of business. The active document is closed without the user being prompted to save changes. Then, the UserForm is unloaded and a message box is displayed, instructing the user to view the new templates. When the user clicks OK, End is used to finish the setup.

The Newly Created Templates

Each new template produces a different document, even though they are exactly the same except for their names. The AutoNew macro runs every time the user goes to Office button | New | Basic Templates and chooses one of them. Remember that the AutoOpen macro prohibited these new templates from being opened. The original template, however, contained an AutoNew macro that has been copied to each of the three new templates. This macro controls which UserForm will be displayed. The work of creating the document is left to the UserForm. The AutoNew code is seen below:

```
Sub AutoNew()
' Turned off ScreenUpdating to save time and prevent user
' from seeing background work.
Application.ScreenUpdating = False
' Display correct UserForm depending on AttachedTemplate
' property.
If ActiveDocument.AttachedTemplate = "Letter.dot" Then
frmLetter.Show
ElseIf ActiveDocument.AttachedTemplate = "Fax.dot" Then
frmFax.Show
ElseIf ActiveDocument.AttachedTemplate = "Memo.dot" Then
frmMemo.Show
End If
End Sub
```

The first thing the AutoNew macro does is turn screen updating off. This prevents users from seeing the document's fields being updated and the sections being deleted. In larger templates this can provide a marked speed improvement as well.

The next If structure uses the AttachedTemplate property to check which template is being used. The Name property of the ActiveDocument will not work. Remember that a template is only the basis for a document. The name of the ActiveDocument would be Document*n*, with *n* being the number of newly created documents. The If statement displays the appropriate UserForm.

The three UserForms are shown in Figures 9-7 through 9-9. The code behind each new template's UserForm is generally the same, as shown in the code below each respective figure. So, rather than discuss each UserForm individually, we'll discuss the basic approach. If there are lists or default values, those are set in the form's initialization event. All variables are explicitly declared and the Cancel button fires the End command.

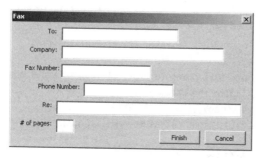

Figure 9-7: UserForm for the Fax template

Listing 9-4: The frmFax UserForm

```
Option Explicit
Dim sIniFile As String
Private Sub cmdCancel_Click()
' End running procedure and unload the form.
End
End Sub
Private Sub cmdFinish_Click()
With ActiveDocument
' Set Docvariables equal to UserForm values.
.Variables("sTowho").Value = Me.txtTowho.Value
.Variables("sRe").Value = Me.txtRe.Value
.Variables("iNopages").Value = Me.txtNopages.Value
' Set Docvariables equal to ini file keys.
sIniFile = Options.DefaultFilePath( _
Path:=wdUserTemplatesPath) & _
"\Basic Templates\Personal.ini"
.Variables("sCompName") = _
System.PrivateProfileString( _
sIniFile, "Company", "Company")
.Variables("sYourname") = _
System.PrivateProfileString( _
sIniFile, "Personal", "Name")
.Variables("sFaxno") = System.PrivateProfileString( _
sIniFile, "Personal", "Fax")
.Variables("sPhoneno") = System.PrivateProfileString( _
sIniFile, "Personal", "Phone")
```

```vba
.Variables("sAdd1") = System.PrivateProfileString( _
sIniFile, "Company", "Add1")
.Variables("sAdd2") = System.PrivateProfileString( _
sIniFile, "Company", "Add2")
.Variables("sCity") = System.PrivateProfileString( _
sIniFile, "Company", "City")
.Variables("sState") = System.PrivateProfileString( _
sIniFile, "Company", "State")
.Variables("sZip") = System.PrivateProfileString( _
sIniFile, "Company", "Zip")
' Set empty text boxes to empty strings to avoid errors
' appearing in the documents.
If Me.txtCompany.Value <> "" Then
.Variables("sCompany").Value = Me.txtCompany.Value
Else
.Variables("sCompany").Value = " "
End If
If Me.txtFaxno.Value <> "" Then
.Variables("sFax").Value = Me.txtFaxno.Value
Else
.Variables("sFax").Value = " "
End If
If Me.txtPhoneno.Value <> "" Then
.Variables("sPhone").Value = Me.txtPhoneno.Value
Else
.Variables("sPhone").Value = " "
End If
End With
' Unload the running UserForm.
Unload Me
' Update Docvariable fields and unlink them.
With ActiveDocument
.Fields.Update
.Fields.Unlink
End With
' Delete sections of template that won't be used.
ActiveDocument.Sections(1).Range.Delete
ActiveDocument.Sections(2).Range.Delete
ActiveDocument.Sections(2).Range.Delete
' Turn ScreenUpdating back on.
Application.ScreenUpdating = True
End Sub
```

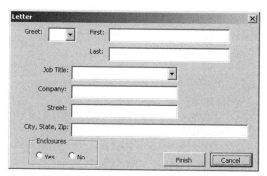

Figure 9-8: UserForm
for the Letter template

Listing 9-5: The frmLetter UserForm

```
Option Explicit
Dim sIniFile As String
' Set lists for the combo boxes
Private Sub UserForm_Initialize()
With Me
With cmbGreet
.AddItem "Mr."
.AddItem "Mrs."
.AddItem "Ms."
.AddItem "Dr."
.AddItem "Mr. & Mrs."
.AddItem "Mr. & Ms."
.AddItem "Dr. & Mrs."
.ListIndex = 0
End With
With cmbJob
.AddItem "President"
.AddItem "Vice President"
.AddItem "Executive Vice President"
.AddItem "Senior Vice President"
.AddItem "Assistant Vice President"
.AddItem "Chairman"
.AddItem "Treasurer"
.AddItem "Secretary"
.AddItem "Chief Financial Officer"
.AddItem "Attorney At Law"
.AddItem "General Counsel"
End With
' Set initialization for option buttons.
Me.optEnclosureNo = True
End With
End Sub
```

```
Private Sub cmdCancel_Click()
' End running procedure and unload form.
End
End Sub
Private Sub cmdFinish_Click()
With ActiveDocument
' Set Docvariables equal to UserForm values.
.Variables("sGreet").Value = Me.cmbGreet.Value
.Variables("sFirst").Value = Me.txtFirst.Value
.Variables("sLast").Value = Me.txtLast.Value
.Variables("sStreet").Value = Me.txtStreet.Value
.Variables("sCtyst").Value = Me.txtCtyst.Value
.Variables("sToComp").Value = Me.txtCompany.Value
.Variables("sTitle").Value = Me.cmbJob
' Set up the enclosure option.
If Me.optEnclosureYes = True Then
.Variables("bEnc").Value = "x"
End If
' Set Docvariables equal to ini file keys.
sIniFile = Options.DefaultFilePath( _
Path:=wdUserTemplatesPath) & _
"\Basic Templates\Personal.ini"
.Variables("sCompName") = _
System.PrivateProfileString( _
sIniFile, "Company", "Company")
.Variables("sYourname") = _
System.PrivateProfileString( _
sIniFile, "Personal", "Name")
.Variables("sYourfax") = System.PrivateProfileString( _
sIniFile, "Personal", "Fax")
.Variables("sYourphone") = _
System.PrivateProfileString( _
sIniFile, "Personal", "Phone")
.Variables("sAdd1") = System.PrivateProfileString( _
sIniFile, "Company", "Add1")
.Variables("sAdd2") = System.PrivateProfileString( _
sIniFile, "Company", "Add2")
.Variables("sYourtitl") = _
System.PrivateProfileString( _
sIniFile, "Personal", "Title")
.Variables("sCity") = System.PrivateProfileString( _
sIniFile, "Company", "City")
.Variables("sState") = System.PrivateProfileString( _
sIniFile, "Company", "State")
.Variables("sZip") = System.PrivateProfileString( _
```

```
sIniFile, "Company", "Zip")
.Variables("sClosing").Value = _
System.PrivateProfileString( _
sIniFile, "Personal", "Closing")
End With
' Unload the running UserForm.
Unload Me
' Update the Docvariable fields and unlink them.
With ActiveDocument
.Fields.Update
.Fields.Unlink
End With
' Delete sections of the template that won't be used.
ActiveDocument.Sections(1).Range.Delete
ActiveDocument.Sections(1).Range.Delete
ActiveDocument.Sections(2).Range.Delete
' Turn screen updating back on.
Application.ScreenUpdating = True
End Sub
```

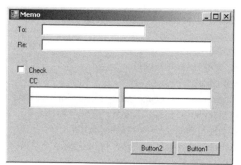

*Figure 9-9: UserForm
for the Memo template*

Listing 9-6: The frmMemo UserForm

```
Option Explicit
Dim sIniFile As String
' Keep the user from seeing the text boxes unless the user
' clicks the CC control.
Private Sub UserForm_Initialize()
With Me
.txtCc1.Visible = False
.txtCc2.Visible = False
.txtCc3.Visible = False
.txtCc4.Visible = False
End With
End Sub
```

```vba
' If the CC check box is checked make the four text boxes for
' CCs visible; otherwise invisible.
Private Sub chkCcs_Click()
If Me.chkCcs = True Then
With Me
.txtCc1.Visible = True
.txtCc2.Visible = True
.txtCc3.Visible = True
.txtCc4.Visible = True
End With
Else
With Me
.txtCc1.Visible = False
.txtCc2.Visible = False
.txtCc3.Visible = False
.txtCc4.Visible = False
End With
End If
End Sub
Private Sub cmdCancel_Click()
' End the running procedure and unload the form.
End
End Sub
Private Sub cmdFinish_Click()
With ActiveDocument
' Set the Docvariables equal to the UserForm values.
.Variables("sTowho").Value = Me.txtTowho.Value
.Variables("sRe").Value = Me.txtRe.Value
' Set Docvariables equal to .ini file keys.
sIniFile = Options.DefaultFilePath( _
Path:=wdUserTemplatesPath) & _
"\Basic Templates\Personal.ini"
.Variables("sCompName") = _
System.PrivateProfileString( _
sIniFile, "Company", "Company")
.Variables("sYourname") = _
System.PrivateProfileString( _
sIniFile, "Personal", "Name")
.Variables("sYourphone") = _
System.PrivateProfileString( _
sIniFile, "Personal", "Phone")
' Set empty text boxes to empty strings to avoid having
' errors appear in the documents.
If Me.txtCc1.Value <> "" Then
.Variables("sCc1").Value = Me.txtCc1.Value
```

```
Else
.Variables("sCc1").Value = "x"
End If
If Me.txtCc2.Value <> "" Then
.Variables("sCc2").Value = Me.txtCc2.Value
Else
.Variables("sCc2").Value = "x"
End If
If Me.txtCc3.Value <> "" Then
.Variables("sCc3").Value = Me.txtCc3.Value
Else
.Variables("sCc3").Value = "x"
End If
If Me.txtCc4.Value <> "" Then
.Variables("sCc4").Value = Me.txtCc4.Value
Else
.Variables("sCc4").Value = "x"
End If
End With
' Unload running UserForm.
Unload Me
' Update the Docvariable fields and unlink them.
With ActiveDocument
.Fields.Update
.Fields.Unlink
End With
' Delete sections of the template that won't be used.
ActiveDocument.Sections(1).Range.Delete
ActiveDocument.Sections(1).Range.Delete
ActiveDocument.Sections(1).Range.Delete
' Turn screen updating back on.
Application.ScreenUpdating = True
End Sub
```

The Finish button handles the creation of the document. Each form's Finish button does primarily the same thing. The first part of the code is a large With block that uses the ActiveDocument object. The ActiveDocument.Variables(Index) property corresponds to each DocVariable field in the template, with the index being the name of each DocVariable field (DocVariable fields are discussed below). The syntax requires the DocVariable name to be enclosed in quotation marks.

The first part of the With block sets the Value property of each DocVariable equal to its corresponding text box value. The second set of variables is set equal to the corresponding Key of the initialization file. Note the *Filename* argument of the System.PrivateProfileString that is again declared to the newly created subfolder. A variable could have been set to this path earlier. However, this code would be very important if this was actually a separate template being copied to that folder by the template setup UserForm. While copying one file three times is convenient, many programmers (myself included) don't like a file to contain forms and code that will never be used.

The next part of the With block is a set of If statements that check the value of certain text boxes. If the text box contains a value, then that value is set equal to the corresponding DocVariable field. If the text box is blank, the code automatically sets it equal to a space. Note that a space is a one-character string, and is different from a null value. If a null value is passed to a DocVariable, the resulting document will contain the message "Error, Variable not defined" in place of the DocVariable field. Inserting a blank avoids these errors.

The next step is to update the fields in the document using the ActiveDocument.Fields.Update method. This goes through every DocVariable field in the document and sets the values defined in the code preceding it. After the fields are updated, they must be unlinked.

Finally, the sections of each template that won't be used are deleted; e.g., the fax template deletes the memo and letter sections. This is accomplished by using the Delete method of each section's Range property. Note that the index value of each ActiveDocument.Section is decremented by one as they are deleted; i.e., if you delete the first section, the second section will become the first, the third will become the second, etc.

After the superfluous sections are deleted, the form is unloaded and ScreenUpdating is set to True so the user can see the finished document.

The Template

We've been focusing on the VBA aspect of this technique. However, the template itself must enable the variable values to be transferred. To create a blank template, select **Office button | New | Blank and recent | Blank document | Create** in Word. The text is divided into three sections using the **Insert | Page Break** command. Breaking the text into three sections allows the manipulation of one section without affecting the others.

There are several ways to transfer text from a VBA UserForm to the resultant document. In this chapter we use DocVariable fields. DocVariable fields have several advantages over the alternatives. One is that the DocVariable field may be formatted in the template at design time. The resulting text will appear in the same format as the DocVariable field. For example, the DocVariable sCompname is formatted using bold text, shadow, and a 14-point font. The corresponding text in the finished document will be formatted the same.

Another advantage is that the same DocVariable field may appear many times in the template. This is a distinct advantage over inserting text at bookmarks. Further, in very large documents it's faster to update and unlink DocVariable fields than to include Merge fields or Ref fields.

Another advantage is that DocVariable fields can be embedded in If fields. This opens the possibility for multiple language dependencies. An example would be an If field looking at a Boolean value and setting gender-specific pronouns throughout an entire document.

A very simple If field is used in the address portion of the Fax and Letter sections. VBA code could delete a line, but the simpler alternative is to create an If field that checks for an "x" value. If the second line of the address is omitted in the original setup template, the initialization Key is set to "x". That value is passed to the If field. If it is anything other than an "x", it is inserted in the document. If the Key's value is "x", it responds by moving the line below it up to compensate. If fields can even be embedded within other If fields.

As you can see, the setup template produces the illusion that it creates three different, customized templates. With minor changes, this provides a way to set up your own templates on individual computers by distributing a single file. You may need to include some brief instructions since many users have Word set to prompt them when a document contains macros.

Keep in mind that future templates can reference the same initialization file, modify it, or create an entirely new one. Furthermore, variable values can be stored in the Windows Registry, in the document properties, in tables, by using sequential file access, or by reinitializing DocVariable fields. For more information on the topics addressed in this chapter, see the corresponding topics in Microsoft Word and Visual Basic for Applications Help. And don't forget to set the tab order of the controls in your forms!

Conclusion

This chapter has focused on two individual VBA projects. The first project demonstrated the use of dynamically created controls, which are frequently necessary in document automation programming. We also discussed a workaround for VBA's lack of the Index property. The Index property, which is available for most VB controls, is not available in VBA. Thus, VBA doesn't provide for dynamic control creation in the same manner as VB. The second project demonstrated how Word can be used to create what is essentially a document assembly system that customizes itself for each user. The following chapters will begin introducing some of the concepts behind Word 2007 XML.

Chapter 10

Word's XML Functionality

Introduction

This chapter introduces the features of Word 2007 that are used to create and edit XML documents. Word has always had the ability to create customized Word solutions to walk users through the creation of documents. There is WordBasic and VBA, but in this chapter we will be looking at programming against the custom task pane using XML functionality. In order to understand how the functionality works, we first need to examine the XML components of Word 2007. From a functional standpoint, Word 2007 works the same as Word 2003, but Microsoft has eschewed the "smart document" terminology in favor of VSTO tools. This chapter demonstrates the backward-compatible (2003 only) features that allow you to work through very basic examples designed to give a quick but thorough introduction to these features. Custom task pane solutions utilize XSD, XML, and a *code behind* (via Visual Studio) custom task pane to interact with a user. Code behind is Microsoft's terminology to describe writing Visual Studio solutions that exist "behind" the document — as opposed to VBA solutions that reside as part of the document. As you'll see, the code-behind features are made possible via an XML manifest that describes the different components of your XML solution.

XML Basics

The real power of XML lies in using a vocabulary that describes the meaning of the document, not just the appearance. This XML document identifies the meaning of the data elements, as well as their location in the document.

The following figure shows what the raw XML looks like without any of the associated Word formatting (WordProcessingML) in it.

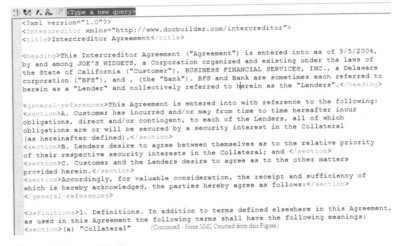

Figure 10-1: A raw XML file

The same raw XML that is displayed in Figure 10-1 can also be opened in Microsoft Word 2007, as shown in Figure 10-2.

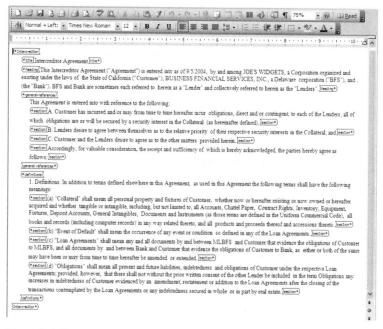

Figure 10-2: The same raw XML from Figure 10-1 opened in Word 2007

Introduction to the Word 2007 XML Toolbar

Word 2007 allows you to work with the XML representation of a document just as you would work with a regular Word document, allowing you to save, edit, and even create well-formed XML documents from scratch. In this section we introduce the Word 2007 XML toolbar features and explain how you can use them in your document automation projects.

Word 2007 XML support allows you to create meaningful tags so that you can structure and organize the text (data) within your Word document. This allows you to view your traditional Word document not only as a document but also as a repository of structured data. For our discussion we'll use an example document called "Intercreditor Agreement". This is a common form document among lenders who are loaning money to a specific business entity. This document specifically describes what each lender is entitled to in the event of default by the borrower (this is, of course, a gross generalization; the legal meaning isn't important in this context). In this chapter, we'll pretend that a user creates this document from scratch and then wants to define the elements within the document via Word 2007 XML markup. This way, the information in the document could then be sent to a database or consumed via some other external system.

One of the most important aspects of the XML features of Word is the ability to view a traditional Word document as having both a printable document aspect and a data repository aspect contained within XML. This allows previously unusable data (or, at least, unusable by conventional means) to be repurposed in ways that are meaningful to a specific organization. Further, Word 2007 allows you to associate XML schemas with a document so that its contents are clearly organized and defined. XML schemas even allow the XML document to be validated according to the data definition contained in the schema.

Note: Many of the XML features discussed in this chapter and the following chapter, except for saving documents as XML with the Word XML schema, are available only in Microsoft Office Professional Edition 2007 and stand-alone Microsoft Office Word 2007.

Microsoft designed Word 2007 to be as easy to use for as many people as possible. This means that some functionality was intentionally left out because it could be confusing to end users. The fact that you're reading this book means you are obviously a little more involved with Word than the typical business user and thus fall into the category Microsoft refers to as a "developer" of Word solutions.

The Word XML toolbar appears under the Developer tab in the XML section (see Figure 10-3).

Figure 10-3: The Word XML toolbar

Caution: This toolbar only works with Microsoft Office Word 2007 and requires that .NET Programmability Support is enabled on your development computer prior to attempting to install or run the toolbar.

Derived XML Schemas

Generating schemas is very easy using a tool provided by Microsoft called Infer.exe. It is available at Microsoft XML Downloads (http://msdn.microsoft.com/en-us/xml/bb190622.aspx). It is very easy to use — create a directory, put examples of all varieties of your XML documents to validate in the directory, CD to the directory, and run. It outputs a schema that correctly identifies attributes and/or elements. Figure 10-4 shows how to create a schema using this tool.

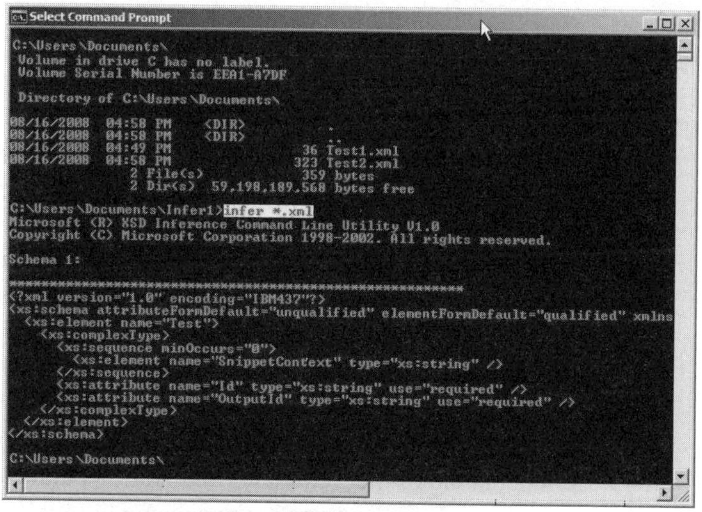

Figure 10-4: Create an XML schema by using Infer.exe.

Don't worry if the schema looks exceedingly complex at this point. You can open the schema in the editor of your choice, but Internet Explorer and Notepad are just fine. We will dive into XML schemas in more detail in the following chapter.

For our current purposes, we just want to walk through the steps so that the following sections will make more sense to you. The schema is shown in Figure 10-5.

```
<?xml version="1.0" encoding="utf-16"?>
<!--Schema generated by the Word XML Toolbox for Microsoft Office Word 2003-->
<xs:schema xmlns:tns="schemas-MSWordXmlToolbox#09052004-123413" attributeFormDefault="unq
    <xs:element name="Intercreditor">
        <xs:complexType mixed="true">
            <xs:sequence>
                <xs:element name="title" type="xs:string"/>
                <xs:element name="heading" type="xs:string"/>
                <xs:element name="general-references">
                    <xs:complexType mixed="true">
                        <xs:sequence>
                            <xs:element maxOccurs="unbounded" name="section" type="xs:str
                        </xs:sequence>
                    </xs:complexType>
                </xs:element>
                <xs:element name="definitions">
                    <xs:complexType mixed="true">
                        <xs:sequence>
                            <xs:element maxOccurs="unbounded" name="section" type="xs:str
                        </xs:sequence>
                    </xs:complexType>
                </xs:element>
            </xs:sequence>
        </xs:complexType>
    </xs:element>
</xs:schema>
```

Figure 10-5: The schema created using the XML toolbar

You may notice some other things that the Word XML toolbar does by default. If you check the Word 2007 schema library, you'll see that the associated schema has been added. The Word schema library is used to specify the namespaces that your document can access. It can also be used to configure options and associated XSLT transforms with a schema. (XSLT transforms will be covered in more detail in a later section of this chapter.) Schemas in the schema library are available to attach to a document and are listed on the XML Schema tab of the Templates and Add-ins dialog box.

If a schema appears in the schema library, it is available for the template solution you are working on. In our example, make sure the Intercreditor Agreement document is active and choose Schema from the Developer tab to see the list of schemas currently available. In this example, we'll be saving everything to the local drive on your machine. For enterprise solutions, you'd probably be creating and testing them locally and then working through your managed deployment solution to make them available to the enterprise users. This usually involves placing them on a publicly available file share or, perhaps, a Microsoft SharePoint site.

Now we want to associate the document with the schema and makes sure that it validates against the schema. (Of course, intuitively we know that it will because it is all currently being created based on the same source information, but working through this section is worth the effort.) Select the box next to the schema we just created, then in the Schema validation options section, check the box next to Validate document against attached schemas. Save the changes to the Intercreditor Agreement document.

Adding XML Markup to a Document

Now that we have an XML schema in our schema library, we can begin marking up an existing Word document to make it conform to the schema. This is actually the process of defining sections of the document according to the rules laid out in the schema. For purposes of this section, we'll take a simplified version of the Intercreditor Agreement and mark it up. The text of the Simple Intercreditor document is shown in Figure 10-6 below.

Intercreditor Agreement

This is an agreement between BANK and CUSTOMER.

This agreement contains the following provisions:

1. Texas law will govern this agreement.
2. Parties agree to arbitration.

Definitions:

"Collateral" means all personal property and fixtures of Customer.

Figure 10-6: Text of the Intercreditor Agreement document

Now, let's suppose we have an existing document that we want to attach to an XSD schema. We already have a schema in our schema library thanks to the work we did at the beginning of the chapter. Open the Simple Intercreditor document if you haven't already done so (this file is available in the companion files download). As you'll see, the document is simply a trimmed-down version of the document shown in the figures in this chapter. Now that you have the document open, please choose **Schema** from the Developer tab. This will open the Templates and Add-ins dialog box, as shown in Figure 10-7.

Once you have the dialog open, select the **XML Schema** tab. As you've already seen, this tab displays the available XML schemas. The process of associating an XML schema with an XML document is not specific to Word 2007. In general, XML documents can contain references to external sources. XML schemas are just one example of this. We are going to select the schema we created above.

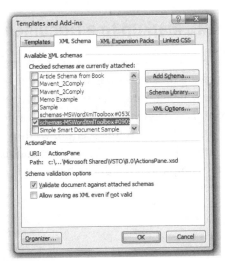

Figure 10-7: The Templates and Add-ins dialog box

You'll notice that the URI lists the information that was generated by the XML toolbar. This information is informative, but it is important to note that the XML toolbar arbitrarily assigns this information. There was nothing intrinsic to the document that caused the XML toolbar to assign the associated identifier to this namespace. The important thing, of course, is that the reference to the schema is correct. Word takes care of this for you, but you could just as easily edit the WordProcessingML in Notepad and add the reference yourself. (From a practical standpoint, you will almost never be in a position where you need to do this, but it is important to realize that you are just working with text that happens to conform to the rules of XML.)

The Schema validation options check boxes allow you to define how you want Word to validate the document according to the schema. As you'll see, we've checked Validate document against attached schemas because we want to make sure that our document is valid according to the schema we've chosen. We'll discuss validity and well-formedness in the following chapter. You'll also notice that the Allow saving as XML even if not valid option is purposely not checked. This will force the user to make the document conform to the validity rules ascribed within the XML schema; otherwise, the user will not be able to save changes to the document.

After applying the schema to the current document (the Intercreditor Agreement), you'll notice that the entire document is encapsulated between two tags. These correspond to the XML opening tag of <Intercreditor> and the XML closing tag of </Intercreditor>, but Word neatly interprets them for you and displays them to you in a user-friendly, colorful way.

Consistent with the entire Word interface, squiggly lines are displayed to indicate that there may be a problem. In this case, the maroon squiggly line running down the left side of the screen shown in Figure 10-8 indicates that the document does not conform to the associated XML schema. Even though we've added the root element (Intercreditor) to the document, there are still other elements defined in the XML schema that are not defined within our document. Fortunately, Word 2007 provides an easy-to-use interface to define such elements right within the Word application.

Figure 10-8: The maroon squiggly line on the left side indicates that the portion doesn't conform to the associated XML schema.

If your XML Structure task pane is not visible, open it by clicking on the View menu and selecting **Task Pane**. The task pane will appear, but will not appear every time you start Word unless you check the box beside Show at startup. You can then navigate to the correct task pane by selecting the drop-down at the top of the task pane and selecting **XML Structure**. You should now have the XML Structure task pane visible within your Word application. At this point, your task pane should look identical to the one shown in Figure 10-9. The main portion of the task pane is dedicated to a tree view control that shows the elements as they have been currently defined in the existing document. This task pane is "intelligent" in that it also displays problems with your markup via question marks and check box prompts.

Figure 10-9: XML Structure task pane showing the child elements of the root node

---

Note: The Show XML tags in the document check box merely toggles the visibility of the maroon placeholders within the UI. This is a convenient feature to use when editing at the same time you are marking up a document. Many times you may inadvertently move or delete text. It may be difficult to see exactly what it will look like when the tags are displayed, so Microsoft has provided an easy mechanism to toggle the visibility back and forth.

At the bottom of the task pane you can see the elements that you can apply to the current selection. Some people find the process of assigning element names to "chunks" of text (selections) counterintuitive. Once you get the hang of it, you'll find that assigning markup is actually fun! The list box at the bottom of the task pane displays only the available elements for the context you are currently working in. For instance, Figure 10-9 shows all of the child elements of the root node. This is because we currently have the cursor positioned within the beginning and ending tags for Intercreditor. If you have the List only child elements of current element check box selected (as shown), once you begin adding markup the window will only display elements relevant to where your cursor position resides. This assistance does not mean the interface is entirely foolproof. You can still add elements that break the rules of the schema. These will be displayed in the top tree view window with a yellow caution marker with a black "X" inside.

Please continue marking up your text until it resembles the text shown in Figure 10-10. Keep in mind the hierarchical nature of the XML schema we are working with when assigning your markup. This means that all of the elements need to be properly nested. Intercreditor is the root element, which should surround every other element in the document. The following elements should appear within the Intercreditor element in the following order with no overlap: title, heading, general-references, definitions. In addition, general-references can have multiple elements named "section."

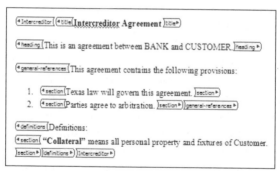

Figure 10-10: Make sure Increditor is the root element that surrounds all other elements.

Once your text is properly marked up, you'll notice that the view in the task pane has changed dramatically. If you've done everything correctly, your task pane should resemble the one displayed in Figure 10-11. If you take a closer look, you will be able to see that XML documents are always hierarchical in nature, which means they always have a top-level or root element and then child elements. This is displayed in the task pane via the collapsible plus (+) and minus (–) signs. If you're familiar with Windows, then you're familiar with how these options work. You can navigate through long documents using these features as well. You can see how the XML serves not only as a view to the structure of the data, but as a shortcut to the various areas within the XML file as well.

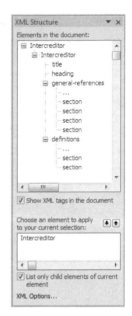

The next thing we want to do is to save out the data from our example. This may sound easy, but there are important implications involved with what we are actually doing. Normally we would just save the document and you'd be done with it. We can do exactly the same thing here, but we can also save it as an XML document. What we're really doing when we save as XML is saving it as WordProcessingML, which contains all of the pertinent Word information (and as you'll see, there is a lot of information in addition to the text of a Word document) as well as our given text.

Figure 10-11: The tree list after marking up the Increditor document

Secondly, by assigning XML tags to a document you've defined those selections as actual data elements. From an IT perspective, there is a big difference in having a DOC file that has a customer's name in it and having an XML file that has a CustomerName element. Regular Word documents are notoriously hard to work with from a data perspective.

Lastly, we have the ability to eliminate all of the proprietary WordProcessingML information from the XML file and save it strictly as XML. For now, choose **Office button | Save As** to display the Save As dialog box shown in Figure 10-12. In the bottom right-hand corner, you'll notice that the Save data only check box is selected. This option tells Word to exclude all of the WordProcessingML elements from the resultant XML file. As you'll see, this means that all of the formatting, styles, document properties, etc., will not be stored with the XML. Word is saving the document as a raw XML file. This doesn't mean Word can't open it right back up. It just means that the other information contained within the document is eliminated.

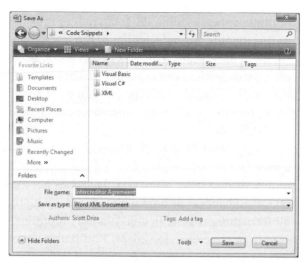

Figure 10-12

XML data is saved as data only by default based on the Save data only option in the XML Options dialog (Developer tab | Schema | XML Schema | XML Options).

After we save the document as XML, we can open it up via Internet Explorer. Figure 10-13 shows what the XML representation of the file looks like when displayed in IE. You'll notice an XML declaration at the top of the file that appears in blue. The color blue indicates that the line is informational only and does not affect the structure of the XML. This is important because, as you'll see, every XML document needs one — and only one — root element. For instance, if the declaration at the top were not interpreted as XML, the document would not adhere to the well-formedness structure set out for XML documents.

Next, you'll notice that the root element Intercreditor appears on the second line much as you'd expect. In addition, there is an XML attribute (covered in detail in the next chapter) that defines the associated schema. This section appears in bright red. This is the same schema that was associated with the document via the Word interface. At the time, we noted that we could add the same association simply by typing it in correctly via Notepad. You can now see exactly how that association would be accomplished. Further, the fact that this attribute appears within the Intercreditor opening bracket means that the attribute applies to the Intercreditor element, which in turn means it applies to this entire document. Attributes, by definition, can contain metadata about the element they appear within. Attributes cannot exist apart from an element. Finally, you'll notice that there are no other attributes in our XML file.

In the rest of the XML file, you'll notice that the elements appear in normal weight, blue and maroon text. The data is represented in bold, black text. This does not mean that the text would appear as bold within Word. Quite the contrary; all formatting is gone in this data-only representation of our simple Intercreditor document. You'll also notice that the tags appear in the exact sequence that was laid out in the Word interface. Internet Explorer only displays well-formed XML. Because of the XML standards, IE doesn't know how to display malformed XML and will not display it at all but will instead display a descriptive error message.

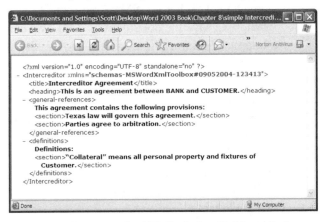

Figure 10-13: The Intercreditor XML file displayed in Internet Explorer

If we switch back to Word, we can open up the data-only XML file we saved and see how the result appears (shown in Figure 10-14). The first thing you'll notice is that all of the formatting has disappeared. Next, you will see that all of the elements appear nested with no semblance of the indentation applied to the earlier document. This information is also not stored in data-only mode. The most important thing to recognize about data-only mode is that you are saving only the XML information and not the peripheral information.

You can also toggle between viewing and hiding the XML markup. You can do this via the XML Structure task pane by checking or unchecking the Show XML tags in the document check box. Figure 10-14 shows how Word displays the XML document when Show XML tags in the document is turned on, while Figure 10-15 shows how the XML is displayed with the Show XML tags in the document turned off.

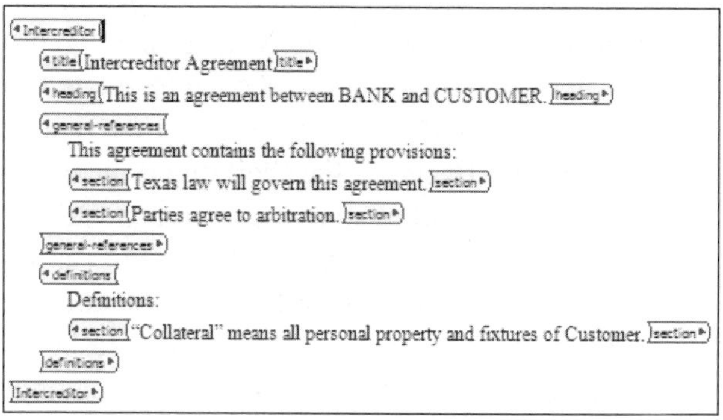

Figure 10-14: Word displaying the XML tags of the Intercreditor Agreement file

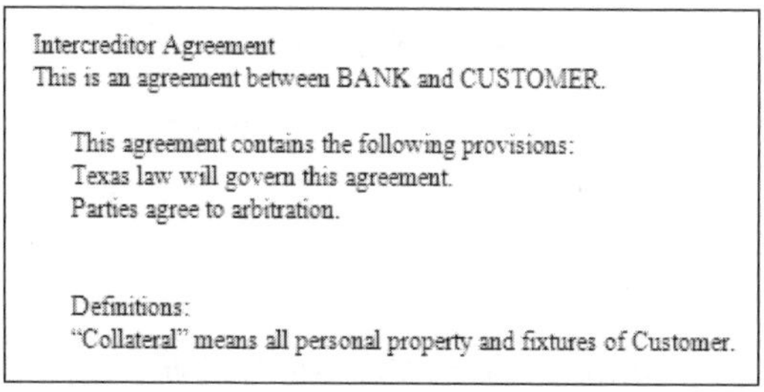

Figure 10-15: The same file without markups

Transforming the XML via XSLT

So now we have this XML data that we know is valid according to our XSD schema. We also know that XML provides powerful ways to repurpose data so that it can do different things or look different ways. The mechanism for controlling the display of this data is called an Extensible Stylesheet

Language Transformation (XSLT), or simply a *transform*. Transforms can be amazingly complex or incredibly simple. For example, after you validate an XML data file against a schema, you can apply a transform that turns the data into a very complex report for management purposes. This same data file can be transformed into an HTML page on your corporate web site. The data file could even be transformed into a PowerPoint presentation or be facilitated for the exchange of data between back-end systems such as databases. The combination of an XML data file, an XSD schema, and an XSLT transform constitutes a basic XML system. Word 2007 provides all of the tools that are needed to create such a system. In fact, we are in the process of doing just that right now.

Figure 10-16 shows the shell of a typical transform. Again, this is merely text that conforms to XML's rules. You can create XSLT transforms via something as simple as Notepad. The top line is a declaration that the document conforms to XML. The root element is then xsl:stylesheet with two attributes: (1) the version number corresponding to the version of stylesheet, and (2) a namespace declaration that declares the stylesheet as an XSLT transform.

```
<?xml version='1.0'?>
<xsl:stylesheet version="1.0"
xmlns:xsl="http://www.w3.org/1999/XSL/Transform">

<xsl:template match="/">

</xsl:template>

</xsl:stylesheet>
```

Figure 10-16: A typical transform shell used to edit an XSLT file

Now that we've introduced the bare minimum of how an XSLT transform works, let's take a quick look at a couple of examples. Figure 10-17 shows a complete XSLT transform based on the XML data we've saved out in the Intercreditor.xml file. The first thing you will notice is the namespace declaration section near the top of the file. In addition to the standard declaration referencing the w3.org standard Transform namespace, there is a declaration associating the WordProcessingML namespace with the "w" prefix. There is also an "ns6" declaration referencing the schema we created earlier in the chapter.

The XSLT processing begins with the xsl:template match tag found on the sixth line from the top. This is simply telling the XSLT interpreter to match against the root node of the XML file it is attempting to transform. After this tag, the direct use of WordProcessingML begins. The first tag declares that we are working with the "w" (WordProcessingML namespace) and it is a Word document. The xml:space attribute simply declares that the spacing will be preserved. This will affect the look of the resultant Word document. The body section is where the text will be displayed. You will see that the text is nested beneath <w:p>, <w:r>, and <w:t> tags. Within this structure is the predefined text of "this is an," which will simply appear in the resultant Word document. Finally, you'll see the xsl:value-of tag, which is a processing instruction that tells the XSLT processor to go out and grab a piece of data and insert it at a specific place.

```
<?xml version='1.0'?>
<xsl:stylesheet version="1.0"
xmlns:xsl="http://www.w3.org/1999/XSL/Transform"
xmlns:w="http://schemas.microsoft.com/office/word/2003/wordml"
xmlns:ns6="schemas-MSWordXmlToolbox#09052004-123413" >

<xsl:template match="/">
<w:wordDocument xml:space="preserve">
   <w:body>
      <w:p>
    <w:r>
      <w:t>this is an
        <xsl:value-of select="ns6:Intercreditor/ns6:title"/>
      </w:t>
    </w:r>
   </w:p>
  </w:body>
</w:wordDocument>
</xsl:template>

</xsl:stylesheet>
```

Figure 10-17: XSLT transform for the Simple Intercreditor.xml file

Before we look at what the resultant Word document looks like when the XSLT transform is applied, let's take another look at what the XML file looks like in Internet Explorer, as shown in Figure 10-18. Again, you can see all the sections in XML exactly as they are interpreted by IE. Notice how the same file is displayed differently from the way it appears in Word, despite it having the same underlying data. In addition, you'll see the attribute declaration referencing the XML schema we created above.

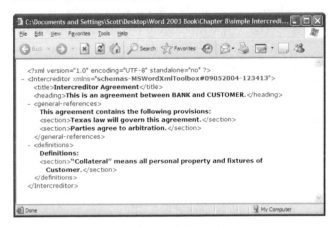

Figure 10-18: The same file displayed in Internet Explorer

Now let's step through the process of associating the transform with the XSD file created above and then viewing the transformed XML we just viewed in Internet Explorer. First we need to open the XML file in Microsoft Word. Stylesheets are associated with schemas in Word's Schema Library. In Microsoft terminology, these are "solutions." In order to associate the XSLT file with the XSD file via Word, select the **Developer** tab and click on **Schema**. Once the Templates and Add-ins dialog appears, choose the **XML Schema** tab, click on **Schema Library**, and select the schema created by the XML toolbar earlier. Now, it's just a matter of clicking **Add Solution** and browsing to the location of the XSLT transform. In this instance, you will use the default type, which is XSLT Transformation. You can enter an alias in the Alias box so that there is a more meaningful name associated with the solution. In this case, I've merely used the name Intercreditor 01 to reference the first XSLT transform we will look at.

Note: You can associate multiple stylesheets with the same schema. This is because a single stylesheet may only transform a certain piece of the document.

Figure 10-19: Give a meaningful name to your solutions for easy reference.

Now the task pane should appear similar to the one shown in Figure 10-19. This displays the different data views available to a particular XML document. In this case there are two views currently available. The first view is the Intercreditor 01 solution view, which applies the XSLT transform to our XML file (as long as the XML file is valid according to the associated schema as well). Selecting this choice in the list box displays a simple Word document, as shown in Figure 10-20.

Figure 10-20: Intercreditor 01 view of Simple Intercreditor.xml

You can also select the "data only" view, which displays the XML file as it appears in Figure 10-21. This shows the XML tags according to Word's XML representation. Word allows you to toggle back and forth between the two views instantaneously and also allows you to choose a different XSLT solution altogether with the **Browse...** option. Selecting this option opens a dialog that allows you to associate a different XSLT altogether.

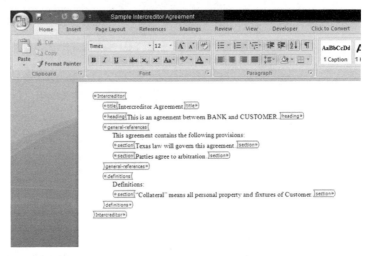

Figure 10-21: Data only view of Simple Intercreditor.xml

We're almost finished with the introduction to the XML features of Word 2007. As you can see, things have gotten very complex behind a seemingly normal Word document. There is one more XSLT solution (Intercreditor 02) that we will briefly examine to cover a specific point. In the Intercreditor 01 solution, we simply grabbed one piece of data (the "title" tagged data) from the XML file and displayed it via WordProcessingML with some associated text.

Please select **Browse…** from the task pane and navigate to the directory where you placed the companion files for this chapter (available for download at www.wordware.com/files/word2007 or www.docbuilder.com). Once you've found the Chapter 10 directory, choose the Intercreditor 02.xslt file. This is dynamically applying the transform to the XML data so that Word will display the result in the standard Word document window. After selecting the Intercreditor 02 solution, the Word task pane should look similar to Figure 10-22 and the resulting document should look like Figure 10-23.

Figure 10-22: Add the Intercreditor 02.xsl file to the task pane.

As you can see in Figure 10-23, the XSLT solution "looped" through the nested <section> elements in the <general-references> section to create a Word table containing a row for each entry. This example shows a slightly more complex use of XSLT and WordProcessingML. The accompanying XSLT file in Figure 10-24 shows how it appears when opened via Internet Explorer.

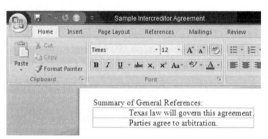

Figure 10-23: Simple Intercreditor.xml displayed through the Intercreditor 02 solution

Figure 10-24

The XSLT shown in Figure 10-25 is only the relevant WordProcessingML piece of the file. In all other respects, the file is identical to the solution displayed in Figure 10-21 using Intercreditor 01. This section shows a normal text run (static text) for the line, "Summary of General References:" and then introduces the xsl:for-each processing command. This command is what allows Word to loop through the sections and display them appropriately in the table. The table is created by the <w:tbl>, <w:tblPr>, <w:tr>, and <w:tc> WordProcessingML tags. It isn't important at this stage to know exactly how to use the tags or what the tags mean, but it is important to grasp the tremendous power available when using XSLT to transform XML data into what essentially looks exactly like a normal Word document.

```
<w:wordDocument xml:space="preserve">
  <w:body>
    <w:p>
      <w:r>
        <w:t>Summary of General References:</w:t>
      </w:r>
    </w:p>
    <xsl:for-each select="ns6:general-references/ns6:section">
      <w:tbl>
        <w:tblPr>
          <w:tr>
            <w:tc>
              <w:p>
                <w:r>
                  <w:t>
                    <xsl:value-of select="."/>
                  </w:t>
                </w:r>
              </w:p>
            </w:tc>
          </w:tr>
        </w:tblPr>
      </w:tbl>
    </xsl:for-each>
  </w:body>
</w:wordDocument>
```

Figure 10-25: Section of the Intercreditor 02 XSLT transform

Conclusion

As you've seen, this chapter introduced some XML features of Word 2007 that allow you to create and edit XML documents. Although Word has always had the ability to create customized Word solutions, the custom task pane offers a way to walk users through the creation of documents. Interactive task pane solutions are dependent upon all of the XML features in Word 2007; understanding the XML components in Word 2007 is vital to creating a good user experience. This chapter allowed you to work through some very basic examples designed to give a quick but thorough introduction to these features. Custom task pane solutions utilize XSD, XML, and a code behind (via Visual Studio) to interact with users.

Chapter 11
XML Introduction

Introduction

The last chapter was an introduction by fire to the XML features of Word 2007. This chapter is meant to slow things
down a bit and introduce not only some XML fundamentals,
but also some of the possibilities that XML has provided to
Word 2007. If you are unfamiliar with XML, it is highly recommended that you read through this chapter in its entirety. If
you are comfortable with your knowledge of XML, you may
wish to read it purely for its supplemental value. In general, a
good understanding of XML is necessary to utilize the
XML-related functionality provided in Word 2007. In general, the reader should be able to grasp most of what is
necessary by working through the projects in this chapter.

A Brief Look at Word 2007 and XML

The DOC file has been Word's faithful companion since its
inception, and the DOC file format has obviously served users
well. The problem with the DOC format is that it is a proprietary binary format and it isn't easy to access data from within
these files. (Although I've seen numerous instances of a large
directory housing Word documents that acted as a database,

this is not good architecture.) Fortunately, Word 2007 offers several options including the use of XML as a native Word format. The upside of this is that by saving documents in an XML format, information can be retrieved easily via standard XML tools (XPath queries).

There are several intriguing uses of XML with Word 2007. One possibility is to transform XML documents into other types of documents with Word 2007. Microsoft has released an XSLT processor that takes a Word 2007 XML document and transforms it into an HTML document. The resultant document can be viewed via a web browser. The implication is not merely that a document can be saved as HTML; we've been able to do that since Word 2000. The real power lies in the ability to transform the data within the Word document and make it available via the web.

Word 2007 also includes features to force the entry of data into an XML document. All of this is done behind the scenes, transparent to the user. One particular frustration of IT departments everywhere has been the inability to use data housed within Word documents. Word 2007 changes all of that. It will obviously take some time for the IT community to embrace this functionality, but Microsoft has made it available nonetheless. Essentially, a document can be annotated via an XML schema and then protected. This will allow users to only add or edit information in specific locations throughout the document. When the user saves the document, the data is written directly to an XML document. This allows the data specific to the XML document to be easily consumed by another application or a database.

What Is XML?

XML is a markup language for documents containing structured information. Structured information contains both content (words, pictures, etc.) and metadata. Metadata provides some indication of what role that content plays (for example, content in a section heading has a different meaning than content in a footnote, which means something different than content in a figure caption or content in a database table, etc.). A markup language is a mechanism to identify structure within a document. The XML specification defines a standard way to add markup to plain text documents via opening and closing tags.

In order to fully understand XML, it is important to understand the needs that gave rise to it and the reason why it was created. XML was created primarily so that richly structured data could be exchanged over the Internet. The readily available alternatives were HTML and SGML, neither of which was ideal for this purpose. HTML does not provide for a completely arbitrary structure; SGML provides arbitrary structure, but is too complex to implement for the vast majority of purposes that gave rise to XML.

A Note on the Word "Document"

XML has emerged as a standard mechanism for transferring data between applications. For the purpose of this book, the word "document" refers not only to traditional Word documents, but also to the more specific Word XML document. An attempt will be made to differentiate the types, but keep in mind that the terminology is the same.

How XML Compares to HTML

Initially, many people are apt to lump XML and HTML together conceptually. This is most likely because of the similarity of the syntax, as both use opening and closing tags. However, in HTML, both the tag semantics and the tag set are fixed because they must be interpreted by a browser. An <h1> is always a first-level heading and the tag <BorrowerFirst-Name> is meaningless. A browser interprets HTML tags to determine how to format what is in between the opening and closing tags. With XML, a browser such as Internet Explorer makes sure the XML document adheres to the rules of XML.

The W3C (World Wide Web Consortium), in conjunction with browser vendors and the WWW community, is constantly working to extend the definition of HTML to allow new tags to keep pace with changing technology and to bring variations in presentation (stylesheets) to the web.

In contrast to HTML, XML does not have a prescribed tag set or semantics of its use. XML is really a metalanguage for describing markup languages in general. XML facilitates the definition of structural relationships between data and allows for those relationships to be represented via the use of tags. The metadata concerning the structural relationship of the data can be accomplished via the use of attributes, which are also defined by the XML specification.

Note: XHMTL is starting to gain ground industry wide. XHTML can be thought of as HTML documents that also adhere to XML's rules. For instance, all tags use lowercase element and attribute names. <h1> is a valid XHTML element, while <H1> is not.

XML Compared to SGML

Roughly speaking, XML is a restricted form of SGML. SGML stands for the Standard Generalized Markup Language defined by ISO 8879. SGML has been the standard, vendor-independent way to maintain repositories of structured documentation for a long, long time. One of the downfalls of SGML is that it is not well suited to serving documents over the web. SGML is too unstructured to be of much use in the lightweight world of the web. Defining XML as a restricted form of SGML does not mean that one needs to understand SGML, but rather implies that a completely SGML-compatible system would inherently be able to utilize XML. However, such a discussion is largely theoretical in the context of this book.

XML Development Goals

The XML specification sets out specific goals for XML. If you are interested in more technical detail about a particular topic, please consult the specification. Following is a brief overview of the goals XML hopes to address. For more information, please consult the World Wide Web Consortium web site at www.w3.org.

XML should be Internet friendly. XML documents must be as accessible as HTML documents, and users should be able to view XML documents as easily as they can view HTML documents.

XML needs to support a wide variety of applications. XML should be flexible enough to be beneficial to a wide variety of diverse applications: authoring, browsing, content analysis, etc. Although the initial focus is on serving structured documents over the web, it is not meant to narrowly define XML.

Every effort should be made to keep XML a clean and "tight" specification — free from superfluous options. This translates into keeping the number of optional features in XML to an absolute minimum. Neat-to-have features inevitably create compatibility problems when users want to share documents.

XML documents need to be human-legible and reasonably clear of confusion. The idea here is that if you don't have an XML browser and you are attempting to decipher a block of XML, you should be able to look at it in the text editor of your choice and be able to ascertain what the data is, what the elements are, and how it is structured.

There has been a conscious effort throughout the growth of XML that the XML design should be prepared quickly. From a historical standpoint, information technology standards efforts are notoriously slow. The original need for XML was immediate, and XML as a concept was to progress as quickly as possible.

There has always been a focus toward accessibility. The standard promulgated a vision that XML documents shall be easy to create. Obviously, there are some extremely complicated XML documents in existence. However, it is still relatively easy to whip up a valid XML document with Notepad.

XML Basics

The following sections discuss some of the concepts necessary for understanding XML.

Well-Formedness Rules

XML elements and attributes must follow certain rules in order for the document to qualify as being "well formed." If a document is not well formed, the document is technically not XML — even if it has an .xml extension. Most programs that deal with XML will not work if a document is not well formed.

The XML specification prohibits XML parsers from trying to fix or even understand malformed documents. If the parser or browser conforms to the XML specification, all it can do is issue a message that substantively reports the error. In other words, the industry standard when encountering malformed XML is to report the error and abort the program. There are more than 100 different rules an XML document must follow in order to be considered "well formed." Don't let that statistic scare you; most of these rules prohibit things that are counterintuitive anyway.

XML Declaration

XML declarations are used to describe the various types of XML authoring. The Standalone Document Declaration allows the document author to specify whether external markup declarations may exist. This attribute can be equal to yes or no and is always the former in well-formed documents. The encoding declaration allows authors to specify the character encoding that they are using. This declaration only needs to be used by authors that are using a character encoding other than US-ASCII, the most common, or UTF-8.

There are three basic XML declarations listed below. The first two declarations can be used to describe well-formed and valid XML documents, respectively. The third declaration can be considered the default XML declaration, stating that it is an

XML version 1.0 document, that it cannot stand alone from external markup declarations, and that it is encoded in UTF-8, an 8-bit Unicode character encoding. Use the first XML declaration when creating your own well-formed XML documents.

```
<?xml version="1.0" standalone="yes"?>
<?xml version="1.0" standalone="no"?>
<?xml version="1.0" standalone="no" encoding="UTF-8"?>
```

Naming Conventions

The following rules apply to names for elements, attributes, and entities within XML.

▼ Names should only use a colon if they use namespaces, which are a way of indicating the markup language that a particular element or attribute is utilizing. Namespaces will be discussed in more detail later.

▼ Names can contain letters (a-Z), periods (.), colons (:), underscores (_), and numbers (0-9). In all cases, the name *must* start with a letter, colon, or underscore.

▼ Names cannot start with the characters "XML" in either lowercase, uppercase, or mixed. These characters are considered to be reserved according to the standards from the W3C.

Below are examples of valid and invalid naming conventions for XML:

Valid	Invalid
<fourth> </fourth>	<4th> </4th>
<borrower.name>	<borrower:name> *
<member>	<xmlMember>

* If there is no "borrower" namespace.

Caution: Remember that in all instances XML is case sensitive.

XML Elements

Every XML document has *elements*, which can simply be thought of as the tags in the XML document. In addition to the naming conventions described above, there are some basic rules that apply to elements. This section discusses those rules.

Top-Level Element (Document Element)

XML requires that there be a single top-level element that contains everything within the XML document. This is sometimes referred to as the "document element." In XHTML, the top-level element is <html> (lowercase, of course). This is one of the rules of well-formedness of XML.

Well Formed	Not Well Formed
<?xml version="1.0" standalone="yes"?>	<?xml version="1.0" standalone="yes"?>
<borrower>	<borrower>
< first.name >Scott</first.name>	</borrower>
</borrower>	<first.name>
	</first.name>

End Tags

Well-formed XML must always have starting and ending tags unless they are considered "empty elements," which use a special syntax. The closing tag must always have the element name prefixed with the forward slash character (/). The data will appear between the beginning and ending tags.

Empty elements are elements that do not utilize two tags. In this case there is simply one tag that has a forward slash before the closing angle bracket rather than a starting and ending tag combination. Keep in mind that these elements are described as "empty" because they cannot contain data between the opening and closing tag. However, some XML documents use a data attribute within the tag to identify the data.

Well Formed	Not Well Formed
<?xml version="1.0" standalone="yes"?>	<?xml version="1.0" standalone="yes"?>
<borrower>	<borrower>
<first.name>Scott</first.name>	<first.name>Scott<first.name>
</borrower>	<borrower>
<?xml version="1.0" standalone="yes"?>	<?xml version="1.0" standalone="yes"?>
<borrower>	<borrower>
<first.name data="Scott"/>	<first.name data="Scott"">
</borrower>	</borrower>

Nested Elements

Elements in XML must be properly nested. As we've seen with the top-level element, everything must reside appropriately within the element that houses it. Technically speaking, this is a requirement of HTML as well, but browsers have been very liberal when interpreting HTML. Properly nested elements will form a hierarchy within the document with the top-level element as the root of the hierarchy.

In HTML, many people become sloppy and do something like the following:

```
<b><p>Rob Mathews</b> is a good guy.</p>
```

This will appear properly in almost all browsers but is not technically correct. Instead, it should appear properly nested as:

```
<p><b>Rob Mathews</b> is a good guy.</p>
```

XML Attributes

There is no requirement that an XML document utilize attributes. Conceptually, attributes are used as metadata within the XML document to provide additional information regarding the element. In some cases, authors use attributes to contain data as seen in the above example of empty elements. In most instances, this is done merely to save space.

Attributes are name-value pairs that appear within the element's opening tag. The value must be enclosed in either single or double quotes. There must be an equal sign (assignment operator) between the name and value, indicating that the value is assigned to that particular attribute.

Note: Single and double quotes cannot be used interchangeably within the same element.

Well Formed	Not Well Formed
<?xml version="1.0" standalone="yes"?>	<?xml version="1.0" standalone="yes"?>
<borrower>	<borrower>
<first.name data="Scott"/>	<first.name data=Scott/>
</borrower>	</borrower>

Entity References

You're probably familiar with a number of entity references from HTML. For example, © inserts the copyright symbol and ® inserts the registered trademark symbol. XML predefines the five entity references listed in Table 11-1. These predefined entity references are used in XML documents in place of specific characters that would otherwise be interpreted as part of the markup. For instance, the entity reference < stands for the less than sign (<), which would otherwise be interpreted as beginning a tag.

Table 11-1

Entity Reference	Character
&amp;	&
&lt;	<
&gt;	>
&quot;	"
&apos;	'

Caution: In XML, unlike HTML, entity references must end with a semicolon. For example, > is a correct entity reference; &gt is not.

Standard less than signs and ampersands in normal XML text are always interpreted as starting tags and entity references, respectively. Therefore, less than signs and ampersands that are text rather than markup must always be encoded as < and &, respectively. Attribute values are text, too, and as you already saw, entity references may be used inside attribute values.

Other than the five entity references already discussed, you can only use an entity reference if you define it in a DTD first. For those unfamiliar with DTDs, if the ampersand character appears anywhere in your document it must be immediately followed by amp;, lt;, gt;, apos;, or quot;. All other uses violate well-formedness rules.

Comments

XML comments are almost exactly like HTML comments. They begin with <!-- and end with --> . All data between the <!-- and --> is ignored by the XML processor. It's as if it weren't there. Comments can be used to include notes to yourself or your coauthors, or to temporarily comment out sections of the document if necessary.

Since comments aren't elements, they may be placed before or after the root element. However, comments may not come before the XML declaration, which must be the very first thing in the document. Comments may surround and hide tags.

There is one final constraint on comments. The two-hyphen string (--) may not occur inside a comment except as part of its opening or closing tag. This also means that you may run into trouble if you're commenting out a lot of C, Java, or JavaScript source code that's full of expressions such as i-- or numberLeft--. Generally, it's not too hard to work around this problem once you recognize it.

Processing Instructions

Processing instructions are like comments that are intended for computer programs reading the document rather than people reading the document. However, XML parsers are required to pass along the contents of processing instructions to the application on whose behalf they're parsing, unlike comments, which a parser is allowed to silently discard. The application that receives the information is free to ignore any processing instruction it doesn't understand.

Processing instructions begin with <? and end with ?>. The starting <? is followed by an XML name called the target, which identifies the program that the instruction is intended for, followed by data for that program. For instance, let's pretend that the following instruction occurs in a file:

```
<?xml-stylesheet type="text/xml" href="Intercreditor01.xsl"?>
```

The target of this processing instruction is xml-stylesheet, a standard name that means the data in this processing instruction is intended for any web browser that can apply a style sheet to the document. type="text/xml" href="Intercreditor01.xsl" is the processing instruction data that will be passed to the application reading the document. If that application happens to be a web browser that understands XSLT, then it will apply the style sheet Intercreditor01.xsl to the document and render the result. If that application is anything other than a web browser, it will simply ignore the processing instruction.

Note: The XML declaration is technically not a processing instruction. The difference is academic unless you're writing a program to read an XML document using an XML parser. In that case, the parser's API will provide different methods to get the contents of processing instructions and the contents of the XML declaration.

Finally, xml-stylesheet processing instructions are always placed at the beginning of the document between the XML declaration and the root element start tag. Other processing instructions may also be placed in this area (sometimes called the "prolog"), or at almost any other convenient location in the XML document before, after, or inside the root element. For example, PHP processing instructions generally appear wherever you want the PHP processor to place its output. The only place a processing instruction may not appear is inside a tag or before the XML declaration.

The target of a processing instruction may be the name of the program it is intended for or it may be a generic identifier such as xml-stylesheet that many different programs recognize. The target name xml (or XML, Xml, xMl, or any other variation) is reserved for use by the W3C. However, you're free to use any other convenient name for processing instruction targets. Different applications support different processing instructions. Most applications simply ignore any processing instruction whose target they don't recognize.

The xml-stylesheet processing instruction uses a very common format for processing instructions in which the data is divided into pseudo-attributes; that is, the data is passed as name-value pairs, and the values are delimited by quotes. However, as with the XML declaration, these are not true attributes because a processing instruction is not a tag. Furthermore, this format is optional. Some processing instructions will use this style; others won't. The only limit on the content of processing instruction data is that it may not contain the two-character sequence of a question mark and greater than (?>), which signals the end of a processing instruction. Otherwise, it's free to contain any legal characters that may appear in XML documents.

Adding XML Tags in Word 2007

Okay, so you're probably asking yourself, "What does all of this have to do with Word 2007?" Let's take a baby step and add XML tags to a document in Word 2007. To get started, just start typing some XML tags in a Word document (we can save it as a template later) and arrange them in the order that you want. Be sure to terminate them by using the forward slash character, as shown in Figure 11-1 below. Figure 11-1 shows the document and one way to order the XML tags.

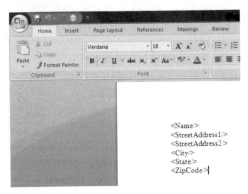

Figure 11-1: Typing XML tags directly in a document

Remember, we are still working simply. At this point, the XML tags may look like XML to you, but Word thinks of them as regular text. They are not yet identified as real XML tags so that Word responds to them as full-fledged XML in a structured document rather than just ad hoc textual input. To convert the text to true XML, you must save the document as an XML file using the Save As dialog box.

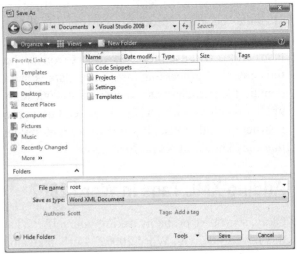

Figure 11-2: Converting ad hoc text into true XML nodes

Word will handle the conversion for you and display the previously marked-up text as valid XML interpreted by Word. The result is shown in Figure 11-3. Notice that Word created beginning and ending brackets so that the text can be typed in between them. This text is actually the data that will be represented in an XML file.

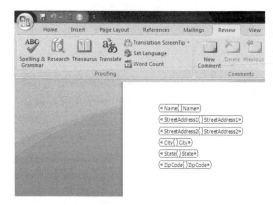

Figure 11-3: The result of converting to XML nodes

As you can see, Word 2007 is pretty smart when working with XML. The tags are named appropriately and arranged as previously defined. In addition, this document is already well formed, as Word will not create anything but a well-formed XML document when using the XML toolbox.

Adding Placeholder Text

Our XML template now has some fundamental XML elements defined. However, as it stands, it is not very user-friendly or informative as to how it should be used. There are very few instances where an end user should actually see the XML tags in the document. Word 2007 provides a convenient mechanism for changing the way the user works with marked-up XML documents. This mechanism is the addition of designated placeholder text for each of the XML tags in the document. This allows you as the document author to define the appropriate placeholder text and set the precise location where you want the text to be displayed. The Word XML toolbox includes a tool to change XML attributes for the tags in the document and add placeholder text quickly and easily. First, position your cursor over the Address tags in the newly created document, then right-click and select **Attributes** to bring up the Attributes dialog shown in Figure 11-4.

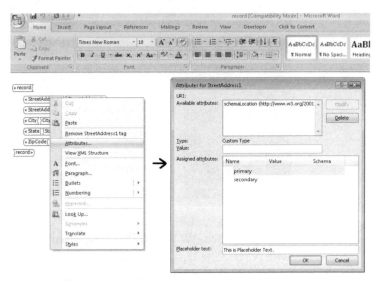

Figure 11-4: The Attributes dialog

The Attributes dialog allows you to view or change the attributes of the corresponding element. Figure 11-5 shows the highlighted Name XML element and its properties in the viewer. Type the placeholder text as shown ("This is placeholder text") and click **OK** to apply the placeholder text to the node in the document. You can work with each node so that the elements will appear with the placeholder text instead of the element name as shown for the Name element in Figure 11-5. After making changes to the nodes, close the dialog and toggle visibility to see the result.

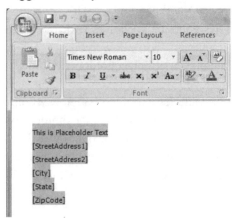

Figure 11-5: Type text into the Placeholder Text field for the current XML element.

The most convenient mechanism to do this is via the Word XML Options dialog. You can switch between viewing the documents with the tags displayed and without them displayed. Select **Show placeholder text for all empty elements** as shown in Figure 11-6.

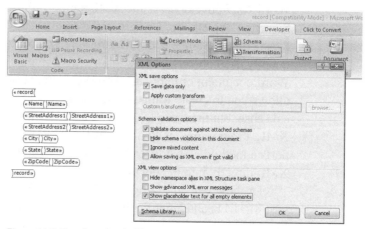

Figure 11-6: Toggling placeholder text visibility

The document with placeholder text showing should appear as shown in Figure 11-7. If you've been around Word development for awhile, this should look similar to a frequently used workaround in document templates. People have been using the MacroButton field for years as a placeholder in document templates because of its particular behavior. Microsoft intended for the MacroButton field to be an interactive tool for launching macros within the context of a document. However, more frequently, people choose to use the field simply as a placeholder for text because it displays a user prompt that disappears when the user begins typing in the field.

Enter a Name Here:
Enter a Street Address 1:
Enter a Street Address 2:
Enter a City:
Enter a State:
Enter a ZipCode:

Figure 11-7: Document showing placeholder text and XML tags turned off

Inserting XML

The template is now ready to apply formatting and set up styles so that the user has an easier time working with the resultant document. One of the most important features for Word 2007 developers is the XML support for the Range and Selection objects. As you saw in the chapters covering VBA, these objects (Range and Selection) are two of the most frequently used objects when working programmatically with a Word document or template. The Word 2007 object model allows you to create Range or Selection objects in the classical sense, but then also allows you to work with them as true XML. Programmatically, the Word 2007 Range object supports a method called InsertXML that lets you insert arbitrary XML directly into the document.

To show you an example, let's open the Visual Basic Editor (Alt+F11) and enter the InsertSomeXML macro shown in Figure 11-8. This macro is meant to show a simple example of how we can insert XML programmatically into our document. First, we'll declare a line to select the entire ActiveDocument. This allows us to then use the HomeKey method of the Selection object to position the cursor (the active Selection object) directly at the beginning of the document. The next line then uses the Selection object (the selection is the first line of the ActiveDocument) to insert beginning and ending tags (called Example) with the associated "This is an Address example" text. Also, notice that we are using a Chr(13) value at the end of the line to force a hard return to keep everything looking pretty in the actual document.

```
(General)                                          InsertSomeXML

    Option Explicit

    Sub InsertSomeXML()

    ActiveDocument.Select
    Selection.HomeKey
    Selection.InsertXML XML:="<example>This is an Address example.</example>" & Chr(13)

    End Sub
```

Figure 11-8: The InsertSomeXML macro

In order to run the macro, simply position the cursor between the Sub and the End Sub lines and press F8. This will start the code execution at the first line as indicated by the yellow highlighting that will appear on the screen. You can then step through the code by continuing to press F8 until code execution stops. You will see which line is being executed as the yellow highlighting moves from line to line.

Figure 11-9 shows how the XML looks after the line has been programmatically inserted and the XML viewing has been toggled off.

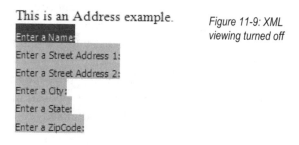

Figure 11-9: XML viewing turned off

Figure 11-10 shows how the XML looks after the line has been programmatically inserted and the XML viewing has been toggled on.

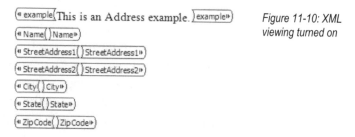

Figure 11-10: XML viewing turned on

If the specified XML text cannot be inserted into the specified range or selection, an error message is displayed. Use the InsertXML method to insert text marked up with either arbitrary XML or Word XML. The XML must be well formed. If the method uses Word XML, then it must also be valid according to the Word XML schema. For more information on the Word XML schema, please refer to the Word XML Content Development Kit, which you can find on the Microsoft Developer Network (MSDN) web site. If the specified XML text cannot be inserted into the specified range or selection, an error message is displayed.

Word 2007 XML Events

One of the most difficult aspects of working with Word-based solutions has been responding via the appropriate VBA code when a user is accessing a particular section of a template. Word 2007 contains a series of events that fire when XML-related things happen. For example, if an XML node is added that is in the wrong place, an event fires. When a user navigates among nodes, events fire as each node is entered and exited. When a user enters text into specific nodes of the XML document, events are also triggered. This has large implications because there is now the ability to trigger specific actions in exact relation to a user navigating through the document. This, in turn, also leads ultimately to a better user experience.

The following two events pertain to the Document object:

▼ The XMLAfterInsert event fires just after a new element has been inserted.

▼ The XMLBeforeDelete event fires just before an element is deleted.

These events pertain to the Application object:

▼ The XMLValidationError event fires when a validation error occurs in the document and receives a single parameter: a reference to the node with the error.

▼ The XMLSelectionChange event fires when you select a new node. This event receives parameters: the WordSelection object for the newly selected material, references to both the node that lost focus and the node that gained focus, and a reason code.

We can see how one of the preceding events is triggered programmatically by quickly adding a new subroutine to our existing example. Insert the subroutine shown in Figure 11-11 into your project and begin stepping through the code. You'll see that the code execution jumps to the Document_XMLAfterInsert subroutine following the insertion of the XML in the first subroutine.

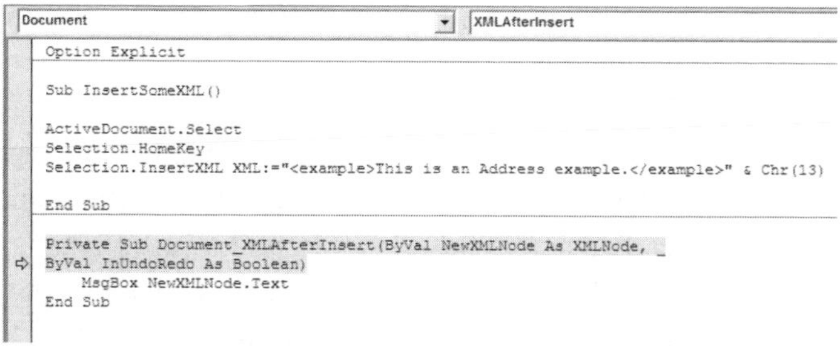

```
Document                              ▼  XMLAfterInsert

  Option Explicit

  Sub InsertSomeXML()

  ActiveDocument.Select
  Selection.HomeKey
  Selection.InsertXML XML:="<example>This is an Address example.</example>" & Chr(13)

  End Sub

  Private Sub Document_XMLAfterInsert(ByVal NewXMLNode As XMLNode, _
⇨ ByVal InUndoRedo As Boolean)
      MsgBox NewXMLNode.Text
  End Sub
```

Figure 11-11: The XMLAfterInsert subroutine

A Quick Introduction to XSD Schemas

There is something about the term "schema" that intimidates some people. Don't be one of those people. For the purpose of this book, a schema is just an ordinary XML file that lists the rules for what can and cannot appear in another XML file. Put more simply, schemas allow programs to validate data. You will see how XSD (XML Schema Definition) language schemas work through a number of examples in this book.

Schemas provide the framework for structuring data and ensuring that it follows a certain format. Schemas can provide an additional check on the content and structure of an XML document. For many programs, it isn't enough that an XML file is well formed. In many cases, an XML file must be "valid" according to a given schema.

When the data in an XML file conforms to the rules provided by a schema, that data is said to be valid. The process of checking an XML data file against a schema is called (logically enough) validation. The big advantage to using schemas is that they can help prevent corrupted data. They also make it easy to find corrupted data because XML simply stops when it encounters a problem.

Office 2007 Generalizations

The first thing to note is that Word 2007 (and the Office 2007 suite in general) does not provide a schema editor. There are several outstanding editors now available, but you'll have to obtain them in addition to Office. Of course, you can always do it the old-fashioned way and use Notepad until it no longer suits your needs.

In general, an XML schema specifies the order of tags in the XML document, indicates mandatory and optional fields, specifies data types of fields, and so on. Perhaps most importantly, the schema ensures that data values in the XML file are valid as they pertain to the parent application. The XML Schema Definition (XSD) language enables you to define the structure (elements and attributes) and data types for XML documents. It enables this in a way that conforms to the relevant W3C recommendations for XML schema. XSD is the primary schema definition language, although the DTD (Document Type Definition) standard is still in use.

Note: The XML schema specification is much longer than the XML specification. This chapter will only serve as a general introduction.

Validity — Beyond Well Formed

The first threshold an XML document must meet is that it must be well formed. This simply means that the document meets the requirements to be an XML document. A well-formed XML document is one that satisfies the usual rules of XML. For example, in a well-formed document there is exactly one data root node, all opening tags have corresponding closing tags, tag names do not contain spaces, the names in opening and closing tags are spelled in exactly the same way, tags are properly nested, etc.

The next threshold is that of validity, which means that the document passes the tests set forth in the schema. It is important to note that a valid document is also one that is well formed. In this sense the schema acts as a contract, specifying exactly what one application or part of an application must write into an XML file and another program can expect to be there. The schema unambiguously states the correct format for the shared XML.

DTD and XSD — A Little History

The first schema standard, developed alongside XML v1.0, was the DTD (Document Type Definition) schema. This, many believed, was not an ideal solution as a schema definition language, which is why Microsoft came up with XSD as its own suggested replacement and submitted this to the W3C for consideration. One of the problems was, and is, that DTDs are not XML-based, so you have yet another language to learn to go with the proliferation that comes with XML (XPath and XSL, for example). Further, developers also found that DTD lacked the power and flexibility they needed to completely define all of the data types they wanted to represent in XML. A schema that can't validate all of the data's requirements is of limited use.

Types and Elements

First off, let's take a look at the same schema we used in Chapter 10 for the Intercreditor Agreement. This schema is shown in Figure 11-12 on the following page. There are several basic things to observe. The first is that the schema definition is represented as a well-formed XML document. You will also note that schemas have a strong interrelation with namespaces. This is common to schemas in general, so a good understanding of namespaces is vitally important to understanding how XSD schemas operate. Finally, there is a built-in syntax to declare data types within the schema. You will see the type attribute used throughout all XSD files.

XSD schemas contain type definitions and elements. A type definition defines an allowed XML data type. An address might be an example of a type you might want to define. An element represents an item created in the XML file. If the XML file contains an Address tag, then the XSD file will contain a corresponding element named Address. The data type of the Address element indicates the type of data allowed in the XML file's Address tag.

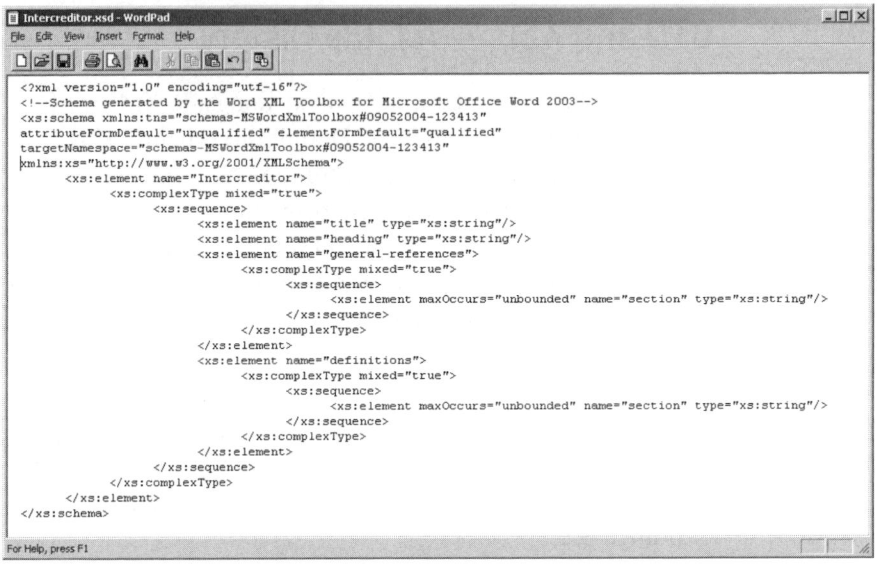

```
Intercreditor.xsd - WordPad                                                    _ | □ | x |
File  Edit  View  Insert  Format  Help

D  ☞ 🖫  ⊜ 🔍  🗛  ✂ 🖺 🖺 ⌒  🖳

<?xml version="1.0" encoding="utf-16"?>
<!--Schema generated by the Word XML Toolbox for Microsoft Office Word 2003-->
<xs:schema xmlns:tns="schemas-MSWordXmlToolbox#09052004-123413"
attributeFormDefault="unqualified" elementFormDefault="qualified"
targetNamespace="schemas-MSWordXmlToolbox#09052004-123413"
xmlns:xs="http://www.w3.org/2001/XMLSchema">
        <xs:element name="Intercreditor">
            <xs:complexType mixed="true">
                <xs:sequence>
                    <xs:element name="title" type="xs:string"/>
                    <xs:element name="heading" type="xs:string"/>
                    <xs:element name="general-references">
                        <xs:complexType mixed="true">
                            <xs:sequence>
                                <xs:element maxOccurs="unbounded" name="section" type="xs:string"/>
                            </xs:sequence>
                        </xs:complexType>
                    </xs:element>
                    <xs:element name="definitions">
                        <xs:complexType mixed="true">
                            <xs:sequence>
                                <xs:element maxOccurs="unbounded" name="section" type="xs:string"/>
                            </xs:sequence>
                        </xs:complexType>
                    </xs:element>
                </xs:sequence>
            </xs:complexType>
        </xs:element>
</xs:schema>

For Help, press F1
```

Figure 11-12: XML schema for the Intercreditor Agreement

Type definitions may be simple or complex. Simple and complex types allow definition of new data types in addition to the 19 built-in primitive data types, which include string, Boolean, decimal, date, etc.

▼ A simple type allows a type definition for a value that can be used as the content of an element or attribute. This data type cannot contain elements or have attributes.

▼ A complex type allows a type definition for elements that can contain attributes and elements.

Structure of an XSD

An XML schema is an XML document with the top-level schema element. The first requirement is that the schema element definition must include the following namespace:

http://www.w3.org/2001/XMLSchema

It could either assign a prefix such as xsd or xs, or it could make XMLSchema the default namespace. The prefix (if any) is used both for the schema component elements and in references to built-in data types.

To validate documents that use namespaces, you can specify a target namespace for the schema. Children of the schema element are called global schema components and are used to define items in the schema's target namespace.

Different kinds of components can have the same name within a given schema with one exception: simple and complex types cannot share the same name (there would be no way to distinguish between them). Elements are not types, so element names may be the same as a complex or simple type. There is no logical relationship between them, so anything that interprets the schema can distinguish between them.

XSD schemas are self documenting and can be processed by more than the intended schema validator. This is accomplished via three mechanisms that all work together: unique identifiers, extension attributes, and annotation elements.

Unique Identifiers

Schema components (such as element and simpleType) are all defined with an optional id attribute. Every value that gets assigned to an id attribute must be unique from any other appearing anywhere within the schema document. This makes the use of tools such as XPath easier when trying to find the precise location of a given component. You can think of the id attribute as a key to each particular component.

Extension Attributes

Schema components can also contain arbitrary attributes (you can name them anything you want that is within the rules). This, of course, applies to anything other than the default (think "predefined") XML schema namespace. These can be used for any number of things. They could contain metadata for use in describing the contents or provide guideposts to describe how different elements should be processed. They could even be used to describe relationships between the various elements themselves.

Annotation Elements

XSD components can have annotation elements as their first sub-element. Annotation elements are just what they sound like: English-language annotations for ease of use. In fact, you can have as many annotation elements as you want. This is what provides the ultimate flexibility in XSD. You can essentially write notes as to the intended use within the XSD itself.

Each annotation element may contain as many "documentation" and "appinfo" children as you want. (You do not need to have any at all.) The documentation element is used to provide the type of user narrative descriptions we described above. They don't have to be used strictly to describe the schema. In fact, most times they are used as plain English instructions. In some cases, these values are extracted via programs and used to provide documentation about a given schema. The appinfo element adds some specific information for a particular application. These are supplemental elements and can provide further direction for processing a given XSD.

Types

In general, types are capable of being defined independent of the elements that use them. In addition, a given type may be utilized by one or more elements. You can think of types as reusable components within the schema that make up the base for an element. Types themselves do not contain any information about a given element. Rather, they provide the framework upon which elements will be built. In addition, the framework they provide can also be used by other types. Finally, if you only intend to use a certain type once within the schema, you could (but may not want to for future use) put the definition right into the given element.

Attributes

Just as you use an XSD schema's element entities to define the data that can be contained in the corresponding XML data elements, you can use attribute entities to define the attributes the XML element can have.

Why use attributes rather than elements (referred to as attribute-centric and element-centric XML)? Well, they are often interchangeable and it is largely a matter of taste. Generally, however, elements should contain data and attributes should contain information that describes the data.

Conclusion

In this chapter, you learned about XML's well-formedness rules. In particular, you learned that XML documents are sequences of characters that meet certain well-formedness criteria. The text of an XML document is divided into character data and markup. An XML document is a tree structure made up of elements. Start tags and empty tags may contain attributes, which describe elements. Entity references allow you to include <, >, &, ", and ' characters in your document. Comments document your code for other people who read it, and parsers ignore them. Comments can also hide sections of the document that aren't ready for use. Processing instructions allow you to pass application-specific information to particular applications. In addition, you've seen some simple ways that Word 2007 uses XML and how VBA can be used to access the new XML objects.

Chapter 12

Introduction to VSTO and Visual Studio 2008

Introduction

In this chapter we change our focus and introduce Visual Studio Tools for Office (VSTO) and the Visual Studio 2008 application. By using these tools, you can go beyond the limitations of VBA offered in the Office 2007 suite. Over the years, Office has evolved from a suite of applications to a full-fledged development platform. Obviously, this created a demand for a robust, professional set of development tools. This is the primary reason Microsoft developed VSTO. While VBA may be adequate for many purposes, its main strength was in recording macros; it was never meant to be a full-fledged development environment. This lack of functionality combined with Visual Studio's overwhelming success is the reason Microsoft now includes VSTO as part of Visual Studio. In this chapter, we look at the various components of VSTO and Visual Studio and how they relate to Office application development.

Office Development History

To get a better understanding of the roles VSTO and Visual Studio 2008 play, let's take a look at how Office development has evolved. Microsoft Office was created as a set of discrete client applications, each aimed at a specific purpose, including spreadsheets, documents, slide shows, e-mail, diagrams, and so forth. Since then, Office has grown into a framework for developing applications. As an example of this, developers routinely embed Excel spreadsheet functionality into their existing Word-based applications. In other cases, Word's spell checker has been used behind the scenes to add functionality that would otherwise be nearly impossible for routine departmental business applications. This functionality is available because all of the Office applications have been designed as consumable COM servers.

Visual Basic for Applications (VBA)

Although VSTO is a powerful tool, there are still many instances when VBA still might be the ideal (or even preferred) tool. For example, VSTO only supports Office 2003 and Office 2007, so obviously any application development based on older versions of Office should take VBA into consideration. Simple macros are still best created using VBA.

With that said, VBA does have some shortcomings, especially when it comes to security. Macro viruses spread in epidemic proportions in the late '90s due to the security problems behind Office. Also, debugging and version control was difficult because VBA embeds the code directly behind an individual document or template. Finally, VBA relies purely on Visual Basic syntax. Developers skilled in different languages do not have the option of transferring that knowledge to VBA/Office development.

VSTO, VSTO 2005, and VSTO SE

VSTO relies on the .NET Framework and all the advantages associated with .NET development. The first version of VSTO allowed developers to create custom solutions in VB.NET or C# and aim them at Word using code-behind technology. This model separated the code from the document by relying on a linked .NET assembly and took full advantage of the .NET code-access security model.

While this was the beginning of true Visual Studio Office development, it didn't gather much business community support. In most cases, Visual Studio development relied on accessing the COM objects made available through the Office suite.

In the later VSTO 2005 version, coverage expanded from just Word and Excel to include Outlook and InfoPath. This version introduced tools such as data binding, data/view separation, design-time views of Word documents within the Visual Studio IDE, Windows Forms development and all of the associated controls, custom task panes, and server-side Office programming. In addition to these developments, Office 2003 offered great advancements from previous versions of Office.

On the downside, although using VSTO meant that you were truly developing in .NET, the object models exposed through the Primary Interop Assemblies (PIAs) were not friendly to Visual Studio developers. To look at it another way, programming VSTO became more of an art than a science. The available deployment options were limited and the security model, while robust, was confusing to many developers.

Office 2007 and Visual Studio 2008

VSTO has now been fully integrated into Visual Studio Professional Edition. Previously, VSTO was a separate downloaded application. In some cases, only Microsoft Developer Network (MSDN) subscribers had access to the tools. Now, the Visual Studio community is able to develop applications for Office 2007 by way of Visual Studio 2008, letting programmers target the more than 500 million users of Microsoft Office.

Developers using Visual Studio 2008 can customize Word, Excel, PowerPoint, Outlook, Visio, InfoPath, and Project to improve end-user productivity. In addition, Office 2007 developers not only have a greatly improved development environment, but they also have a much-improved Office suite with the Office 2007 system. Developers can use the new Visual Studio Office tools to create both application-level and document-level managed code customizations behind Office 2007 system applications easily and quickly. Developers can also use built-in visual designers to access the Office 2007 user interface features that ultimately lead to a greatly improved user experience.

One of the largest and most noticeable improvements in Office 2007 is the user interface. In this release Microsoft introduced the Fluent RibbonI, which replaces the previous system of layered menus, toolbars, and task panes. This new Fluent RibbonI user interface is the result of extensive usability research and testing, and is intended to be a simpler interface that maximizes efficiency. The new UI provides improved context menus, enhanced screen tips, a mini toolbar, and keyboard shortcuts that help to improve productivity.

Among other improvements, support is now available to integrate SharePoint Services into Visual Studio Tools for Office solutions. Microsoft SharePoint Services is a technology that enables businesses to improve business processes and team productivity by providing things such as collaboration tools to help people stay connected across organizational and geographic boundaries and lets users access information whenever and wherever they need.

Note: For more information, go to http://www.microsoft.com/ technet/windowsserver/sharepoint/techinfo/overview.mspx.

This means that through SharePoint Services, developers can bring collaboration services to end users, and their applications can utilize Office 2007 to manage workflow and navigation.

In addition, developers can utilize a more robust security model for their applications. The Office 2007 security model is extensible, so a framework is in place that will exist for future versions of Visual Studio and Office. But perhaps the most compelling feature of all is the full support for ClickOnce deployment of all Office customizations and applications. ClickOnce is a technology to create self-updating Windows-based applications. These applications can be installed with one click and run with minimal user interaction and can be distributed in three different ways: from a web page, from a network file share, or from media such as a CD-ROM. Developers and administrators now have access to the tools and framework for easy deployment and maintenance of their Office 2007 solutions.

What's New in Visual Studio?

Visual Studio has been the de facto standard for Windows application development since its inception and is now the preferred environment for web development as well. Visual Studio is constantly being developed and it's worth noting that Microsoft Visual Studio 2008 has improved significantly in the following five areas.

Windows Vista and .NET 3.0/3.5 Development

Developers can leverage new platform technologies and deliver more robust applications to their customers by incorporating new Windows Presentation Foundation features into both existing Windows Forms applications and new applications.

Microsoft Office Applications

As mentioned previously, prior to Visual Studio 2008, VSTO was a completely separate download and installation. However, there is no longer any need to run a separate installation. VSTO is now fully integrated into Visual Studio Professional Edition. All of the VSTO functionality is available to every developer with Visual Studio 2008 Professional and higher. VSTO enables developers to customize various Office applications, such as Outlook and PowerPoint, to improve end-user productivity and to significantly improve deployment.

Data Handling

With the introduction of Language Integrated Query (LINQ), developers can now utilize a consistent approach when working with data. LINQ can be used to perform data access with new data design surfaces and use pre-built classes for the occasionally connected design pattern.

New Web Experiences

Using Visual Studio 2008, developers can easily create web applications with more interactive, responsive, and efficient client-side execution using the seamless integration and familiar programming model of ASP.NET AJAX and other extensions and enhancements.

Application Life-cycle Management (ALM)

ALM provides great support not only for managing the entire software development life cycle, but also for the critical interaction with the final end users and managers of an enterprise application.

Note: You can obtain the latest information (as well as a continually expanding body of tips and sample code) at the Visual Studio home page located at http://msdn.microsoft.com/vstudio/.

For information specific to Office 2007 development including VSTO, refer to http://msdn.microsoft.com/office/.

New Features of Visual Basic 9.0

With the introduction of .NET, Visual Basic programmers have a more professional set of tools, including a unified framework and a managed platform. Visual Basic introduces these new tools, which were specifically designed to increase developer productivity, with the release of Visual Studio 2008. Although the greatest gains are found when developing data-oriented applications, long-time Visual Basic developers will be pleased with several new features. The new Visual Basic language extensions now include general-purpose query facilities that apply to all sources of data such as relational, hierarchical object graphs, and XML documents. Let's look at these newly introduced features in more detail.

Multi-Targeting

Previously, the .NET Framework version being targeted could often be the primary reason behind using a particular version of Visual Studio. However, Visual Studio 2008 is the first version that enables developers to target a specific version of the .NET Framework. With Visual Studio 2008, developers can open or create a project that targets the 2.0, 3.0, or 3.5 versions of the .NET Framework. In addition, the structure is in place to support multiple versions of the .NET Framework going forward. Figure 12-1 shows how to target a specific version of the .NET Framework using the New Project dialog box.

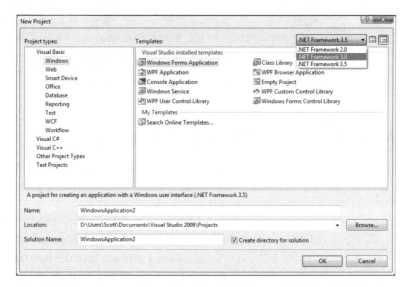

Figure 12-1: Targeting a specific version of the .NET Framework with the New Project dialog box

Visual Studio filters IntelliSense, toolbox controls, and add reference dialog items specifically based on the version of the .NET Framework that you choose at the outset. Keep in mind that you cannot target multiple versions of the .NET Framework in a single application. IntelliSense only displays features supported within the chosen version of the .NET Framework. It is also possible for you to individually compile against each .NET Framework release and debug on a version-by-version basis.

Object Initializers

Visual Basic 9.0 offers a new way of initializing complex objects. Although this feature figures squarely into other new options of Visual Basic, it is worth a quick look at just the new syntax so that you will understand the other new options available.

To illustrate the new object initializers, let's quickly cover the act of creating a new Visual Basic console project in a mini project. Begin by starting Visual Studio and creating a new project as shown in Figure 12-2. I've used the default name of Console1, but feel free to name the project anything you'd like.

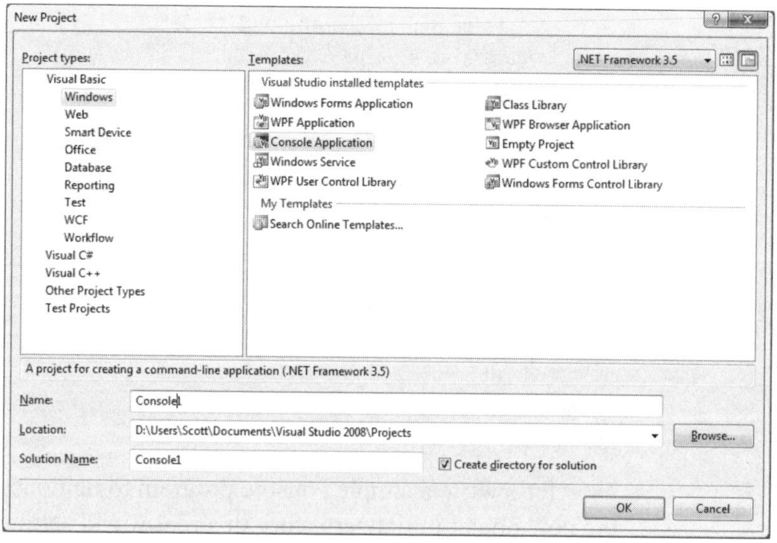

Figure 12-2: Creating a new project to illustrate object initializers

The new object initializers are an expression-based form of the With statement. Basically, these initializers allow you to create a complex object using only a single line of code. Our project will demonstrate how they work. Let's create a fictitious dog data structure, as shown in Listing 12-1, that contains a dog's name and weight. Let's represent that data structure using a Visual Basic class.

Listing 12-1: Dog class to illustrate object initializers

```
Public Class Dog
    Private nameValue As String
    Private weightValue As Integer

    Public Property Name() As String
        Get
            ' The Get property procedure is called when the value
            ' of a property is retrieved.
            Return nameValue
        End Get
```

```
        Set(ByVal value As String)
            ' The Set property procedure is called when the value
            ' of a property is modified. The value to be assigned
            ' is passed in the argument to Set.
            nameValue = value
        End Set
    End Property

    Public Property Weight() As Integer
        Get
            Return weightValue
        End Get
        Set(ByVal value As Integer)
            weightValue = value
        End Set
    End Property
End Class
```

Now let's write a simple console program to demonstrate how the new object initializers work in a real-world setting. First of all, to create an instance of the complex object and to simultaneously populate certain properties of the object, we use the new object initializer syntax New Dog With {.Name, .Weight...} for the declaration of each dog object. When we compare and contrast the declarations required in previous versions of Visual Basic, you'll notice that each property assignment requires its own line of code, as Listing 12-2 shows.

Listing 12-2: Sample project to illustrate object initializers

```
With Dog
    .Name = "Fergielicious"
    .Weight = 132
End With
Module Module1

    Sub Main()
        Dim Dogs() = {New Dog With {.Name = "Seger", _
        .Weight = 115}, _
        New Dog With {.Name = "Suni", .Weight = 94}, _
        New Dog With {.Name = "Shani", .Weight = 85}, _
        New Dog With {.Name = "Fergie", .Weight = 50}}
```

```
    For i = 0 To Dogs.Count - 1
        Console.WriteLine(Dogs(i).Weight())
    Next i
End Sub

End Module
```

Implicitly Typed Local Variables

Writing code has never been easier than it is in Visual Basic 9.0. In this new version, Visual Basic now determines the appropriate type of variable based on the value assigned to it. In other words, when using a local variable declaration, the type of the local variable is determined from the initializer expression on the right-hand side of the declaration statement. The following table shows the difference between the new variable declaration format and the traditional long form.

Variable Declaration	Equivalent Long Form
Dim *startIQ* = 100	Dim *startIQ* As Integer = 100
Dim *food* = "Peanut"	Dim *food* As String = "Peanut"
Dim *distance* = 13.1	Dim *distance* As Float = 13.1
Dim *dog* = New *Dog* With { .Name = "Fergie", ...}	Dim *dog* As Dog = New *Dog* With { .Name = "Fergie", ...}

Local variable declarations are inferred using the new Option Infer On syntax, which is the default setting for all new projects. Constantly using this new syntax for a while is a good approach to becoming familiar with it. After you get accustomed to new syntax, you'll find implicit declaration will become second nature when you are writing code. Implicitly declared variables are always early bound (you'll need to explicitly specify late binding in Visual Basic) and offer all the associated advantages, including IntelliSense, design-time syntax checking, access to built-in constants, and so forth. Inferring types prevents accidentally using late binding and, more importantly, it allows powerful extensions to binding for new data types such as XML.

LINQ

Another great feature of Visual Basic is the ability to specify Standard Query Language (SQL) such as constructs in the course of declaring a variable. With LINQ, the language integrated query framework for .NET, Microsoft intentionally utilized something close to general SQL so that programmers with existing SQL knowledge could quickly get up to speed with the query syntax.

Visual Basic also utilizes IEnumerable in the SQL construct even though the language uses implicit typing. IEnumerable allows you to loop directly against arrays and objects and access their properties directly. The compiler translates the query expression into calls to the LINQ-enabled API. This new LINQ feature implements the query operators for all types that implement IEnumerable, such as:

```
Dim bigDogs = From Dog In Dogs Where dog.weight > 85 Select dog
```

Visual Studio 2008 greatly enhances the way developers view and interact with data. Until now, programmers had to utilize different skill sets depending on the location and underlying database. With the myriad of different connection mechanisms, there have been numerous attempts to standardize data interaction, but for the first time there is a legitimate data utility that provides true data agnostic operations. The following table shows the available LINQ query operators. These operators are all conceptually similar to standard SQL operators.

Standard Query Operation	Description
OfType	Filter based on type affiliation
Select/SelectMany	Project based on transform function
Where	Filter based on predicate function
Count	Count based on optional predicate function
All/Any	Universal/existential quantification based on predicate function
First/FirstOrDefault	Access initial member based on optional predicate function
ElementAt	Access member at specified position

Standard Query Operation	Description
Take/Skip	Access members before/after specified position
TakeWhile/SkipUntil	Access members before/after predicate function is satisfied
GroupBy	Partition based on key extraction function
ToDictionary	Create key/value dictionary based on key extraction function
OrderBy/ThenBy	Sort in ascending order based on key extraction function and optional comparison function
OrderByDescending/ThenByDescending	Sort in descending order based on key extraction function and optional comparison function
Reverse	Reverse the order of a sequence
Fold	Aggregate value over multiple values based on aggregation function
Min/Max/Sum/Average	Numeric aggregation functions
Distinct	Filter duplicate members
Except	Filter elements that are members of specified set
Intersect	Filter elements that are not members of specified set
Union	Combine distinct members from two sets
Concat	Concatenate the values of two sequences
ToArray/ToList	Buffer results of query in array or list
Range	Create a sequence of numbers in a range
Repeat	Create a sequence of multiple copies of a given value

The introduction of LINQ means that developers can now deal with data using a consistent programmatic approach. This allows development efforts to integrate data access with new data design surfaces. ADO.NET utilizes LINQ and supports an occasionally connected design pattern. LINQ offers the following new capabilities for Office 2007 developers:

Language/Data Access Unification

LINQ effectively reduces complexity and boosts productivity through a set of language extensions. LINQ also augments the underlying .NET Framework to provide integrated querying for objects, databases, and XML data. Using LINQ, developers can use their native languages (C# or Visual Basic) to access data without having to use specialized languages such as SQL and XPath.

Occasionally Connected Data Access

This LINQ feature has great promise for Office 2007 developers. LINQ introduces Microsoft Synchronization Services for ADO.NET. These services provide an application programming interface (API) to synchronize data between remote services and a local store. The Synchronization Services API is modeled after the ADO.NET data access APIs.

Inside VSTO

Now let's take a look at the inner workings of VSTO (Visual Studio Tools for Office). The Visual Studio IDE is where you'll create your VSTO solutions. These solutions might be either document or application customizations. An example of an application customization is a Word application add-in that is available whenever Word is opened — even if a document isn't open. In contrast, document customizations are only available when the individual document is open. If the customization is associated with a template, then the code is only available when the template is open.

When dealing with document-level add-ins, the actual code that you write within Visual Studio is stored in a separate file associated with the document or template. Instead of being embedded directly into the document or template as a VBA solution, the code exists as a managed .NET assembly that is eventually compiled into a DLL. This originated with the first VSTO code-behind model.

Application-level solutions are created as add-ins that are automatically loaded upon instantiation of the pertinent application. What this essentially means is that (provided correct coding) application add-ins can also be shared among different Office 2007 applications. Users also have access to manually load and unload the add-in. The add-in might also be prevented from loading based on security measures.

Application add-ins typically customize the user interface by manipulating the Office 2007 Ribbon. In some cases, existing Ribbon events can be intercepted and specific code can be written to intervene in their execution.

VSTO relies on a host model. This means that the underlying Office 2007 applications are actually the hosts that support the customization. In this case, the particular Office 2007 application is implemented by its own class. This exposes the methods, properties, and events of the application as class members and makes them available with IntelliSense, which makes using the application in development easier.

VSTO Feature Set

Now that you have an understanding of how VSTO works, it's time to get a more thorough understanding of the underlying features. Keep in mind that one of the goals of VSTO (which is a common goal in current programming environments) is to separate the presentation of data from the underlying program. In the following sections, we'll be discussing various features of VSTO.

Host Items and Host Controls

Host items are the mechanisms that actually let you work with the Office 2007 applications as discrete, early-bound objects in the Visual Studio IDE. The main difference is that some dynamically created objects (for example, an Excel worksheet created at run time) do not expose the VSTO extended properties. Because the compiler doesn't know about it ahead of time, it invokes it as merely another Excel worksheet. This means that you cannot take advantage of the extended VSTO functionality as you would with a normal host item. For instance, you cannot dynamically add Windows Forms controls to the worksheet.

VSTO provides a controls collection for the controls that are added to a document or workbook. In VBA programming, you were limited to the MSForms 2 collection of controls, which did not expose a great deal of functionality. One of the best things about VSTO is that you can now use Windows Forms controls as well as traditional MSForms 2 controls. You can then iterate through the controls collection and access both the MSForms and Windows Forms controls. VSTO provides a great mechanism to add Windows Forms controls directly to a document or a worksheet. These controls are true Windows Forms controls in that they have all the properties, methods, and events associated with them. There might be some differences in how they act though. The controls were originally designed to exist on the Windows form. A document or worksheet might not have the same options available as a container that you have come to expect when working with them as Windows forms. The commonly used example is that you cannot control tab order using a document as the container.

Another difference is that the Windows Forms controls are not embedded directly into the worksheet or document. They are contained within an ActiveX control that is embedded within the document. This means that you cannot programmatically create controls the same way you would in a Windows Forms application.

In VSTO, you must use specifically designed helper methods to programmatically create dynamic controls. In addition, there is even a generic AddControl method to help facilitate the creation of dynamic controls within a VSTO project.

One thing you might notice is that certain controls are unavailable at design time on the Visual Studio Control toolbox. VSTO filters the available controls so that controls that do not work well or are unsupported are not available in the toolbox.

Smart Tags

Previous versions of Office introduced Smart Tags, which trigger events based on their property setting. VSTO has made utilizing Smart Tags easier than ever by introducing a SmartTags class that allows you to add Smart Tags to the document or worksheet by utilizing events and programming specific actions to take when that event occurs. Keep in mind that Smart Tags exist at the document level and are not available to load against application-level projects. In Figure 12-3 we see Word's formatting Smart Tag.

Figure 12-3: Word's formatting Smart Tag

The Custom Task Pane

The idea of a custom task pane was introduced with Office 2003. This task pane provided a modeless way to interact with the user. Although VBA forms could be made modeless, the user experience was not quite up to par, and therefore Microsoft wanted to give developers a better way to interact with the user. They provided a method to create custom panes that imitated the functionality of the newly created Microsoft task panes. With VSTO you can create custom task panes easily by using Smart Tags and creating expansion packs. This is another advantage over VBA. Currently, there is no way to create custom task panes utilizing VBA alone.

VSTO provides an ActionsPane object that lets you add Windows Forms controls or even custom controls with little coding. The VSTO task pane relies on the existing ISmartDocument class, but unlike the old days of creating an entire application manifest and accompanying XML and DLLs, you can now create just the code and let VSTO manage the details.

In addition, the Application objects of each Office application let you create custom task panes that are available at the application level so that an individual task pane can be available anytime you open the application. This allows you to write high-level code that can direct a user where to perform certain actions or find organization-specific help. Figure 12-4 shows the

Figure 12-4: The Research task pane

Research task pane that appears when trying to translate a portion of a document to a different language.

Data Caching

VBA developers (Word VBA particularly) have always searched for a way to persist variable data across instances of a user interaction with a document or spreadsheet. In Excel, sheets were often created specifically to act as databases. In Word, creative developers used Word's document variables to store enormous amounts of data even though that was clearly not why document variables existed to begin with. VSTO offers a much better way to persist data.

VSTO has a feature known as a data island, which allows the storage of data inside the document. This gives developers a mechanism to cache data and associate it with a specific instance of a document or spreadsheet. The primary function of data islands is to provide a disconnected mechanism that can be synced up with a back-end database in case a user is working remotely and cannot access a particular data storage device. However, this capability is also available even if the document or spreadsheet is located on a server. Server-side Office programming has always been a bad practice for obvious reasons, such as Office applications requiring a large memory footprint, and the fact that it's just not practical to instantiate numerous instances on a server. When done correctly, data caching in VSTO provides a way to get around this.

Managed Add-ins

One of the premier features of VSTO, introduced with VSTO SE, is the ability to create managed add-ins. Simply put, managed add-ins are much more stable and have a clear, concise event model. For example, instead of worrying about Word's AutoEvents (such as AutoOpen, AutoClose, AutoExit, AutoNew, and so forth), developers now just contend with a Startup event and a Shutdown event. These events are consistent across all applications that support the document-level add-ins.

In addition, add-ins are loaded into their own discrete process space. This allows them to run physically outside of the application. This means that the application cannot become corrupted in the event an add-in fails somehow.

Security and Deployment

Security and deployment have long been problems for Office developers. The VBA security model was inadequate to handle all the various options necessary. When macro viruses began spreading rampantly, many users set their macro security settings so high that they could no longer run their own internally created macro projects, defeating their purpose altogether.

Although VSTO relied on a much more robust security platform, it originally suffered from many confusing deployment issues and concerns. VSTO applications have been notoriously difficult to deploy correctly and oftentimes mandated organizational requirements that were not available. Fortunately, in later developments of VSTO, these issues have been addressed. Now, you can almost universally expect a version of the .NET Framework to be available for the targeted machines you're working with. Furthermore, Visual Studio 2008 introduces ClickOnce deployment to make deploying your solution much easier.

VSTO solutions rely on Code Access Security (CAS), which is an integral part of the .NET Framework. This takes the decision out of the hands of the user and lets the OS determine whether code is safe or not based on a set of objective criteria. This set of criteria includes the location of the customization, whether or not the code is signed, and the administrative permissions for the organization.

Enhanced Ribbon Support

As mentioned before, Office 2007 includes a dramatically new UI. Command bars and custom macro buttons are now things of the past. Office 2007 introduces a new interface called the Ribbon, which is customizable in much the same way as traditional command bars. With this new interface, you can create new tabs, groups, and buttons, and even pro-grammatically hide UI elements.

Visual Studio VSTO Integration

Most of the applications in Office only offer add-in capability. However, Word (and Excel) offers three different project types when you create a new Visual Studio project, namely document/workbook code behind, template code behind, and application-level add-ins. After you've created a new project for either of these applications, you can actually open the entire application from within Visual Studio. This concept is called the designer approach to application development.

In short, a *designer* is a container for the user interface of the actual application that you are building. This allows you to finely control the user experience by working with the same physical structure that the end user will be interacting with. You can think of this as being analogous to form development. When creating new forms, you typically add controls directly to the form via the IDE. This same application design concept is now available when using Word or Excel VSTO applications. This means that you can add controls directly to the Word or Excel solution.

Once you can actually see the visual representation of the application, you can add the controls as you choose via either Windows Forms controls or host controls. The application customization has a code file associated with it. Typically, this was referred to as the code behind file, but in today's terminology, it is referred to as just the code file.

There are numerous ways to switch to designer mode. One method is to right-click inside the code window and select View Designer. Another method is to access it from inside the Solution Explorer.

VSTO Projects

VSTO projects are created in much the same manner as any other Visual Studio project. Launch the New Project dialog from the first page of the IDE, or select the **File | Create Project** menu option. Note that there are different projects available depending on whether the targeted application is part of Office 2003 or Office 2007. The following table describes the project types available for Office 2003 and Office 2007.

Project Type	Description	Office Version
Excel workbook	Code behind an individual workbook	2003, 2007
Excel template	Code behind an Excel template that is the foundation for creating many workbooks, perhaps to create a consistent look and feel or easily reuse a predefined set of information	2003, 2007
Excel add-in	Code behind the Excel Application object for use in any subsequently opened workbooks or templates	2003, 2007
Word document	Code behind an individual document	2003, 2007
Word template	Code behind a Word template that is the foundation for creating many documents, perhaps to create a consistent look and feel or easily reuse a predefined set of language	2003, 2007
Word add-in	Code behind the Word Application object for use in any subsequently opened documents or templates	2003, 2007
PowerPoint add-in	Code behind the PowerPoint Application object for use in any subsequently opened presentations	2003, 2007
Outlook add-in	Code behind the Outlook Application object	2003, 2007
Visio add-in	Code behind the Visio Application object for use in any subsequently opened diagrams	2007
InfoPath add-in	Code behind the InfoPath Application object for use in any subsequently opened forms	2007
SharePoint sequential workflow	Used for developing a SharePoint workflow (workflow as a procession of steps)	2007
SharePoint state machine workflow	Used for developing a SharePoint workflow (workflow as a set of states, transitions, and actions)	2007

Since Visual Studio needs programmatic access to the VBA object model, the first time that you create a VSTO solution, you'll be prompted with the message shown in Figure 12-5.

Figure 12-5: Microsoft Visual Studio message

One important thing to note is that most Office 2007 object models do not include many objects that can be created with the New keyword. This is somewhat different from traditional .NET classes. In a typical VSTO solution, the Office 2007 object is created by Visual Studio when the project is created. Most of the time, the root application is passed into the solution and is exposed as an object.

The most important implication of this is that most of the properties and methods are accessed through the fully qualified hierarchy of the object model. For instance, instead of iterating through the Field object within a document by creating a new Field object, you would have to type out the full path including Word.Document.Fields instead of just typing Fields. Although this convention maybe somewhat tedious at first, you will quickly grow accustomed to it.

The following sections discuss the various parts of VSTO.

Collections

Collections generally follow a naming convention whereby the collection is the plural form of the object type that it contains. A few examples would be the Fields collection for Field objects, Paragraphs collection for Paragraph objects, or Bookmarks collection for Bookmark objects. In addition to having the normal properties of the singular object, the collection usually has items that allow for iterating through the entire collection. Most collections have a .count method that allows a for loop to iterate through the collection (e.g., for i = 1 to collection.count). You can also iterate through a collection using a for-each loop.

Enumerations

Office 2007 Application objects each contain numerous enumerations that follow an application-specific prefix model in IntelliSense. For example, Word enumerations begin with "wd" and Excel enumerations begin with "xl". These enumerations actually correspond to numeric values that can be read (using MsgBox, for example). Keep in mind that you can access IntelliSense by using the Ctrl+J shortcut key combination. Enumerations are differentiated visually from properties and methods in IntelliSense.

Properties

As illustrated previously in this book, *properties* are best thought of as the adjectives associated with an object. These are the descriptive elements of an object. Properties can generally be set at design time or during run time (with some limited exceptions). One special note is that properties might expose other objects. For example, the Excel Application object contains a property called Workbooks that actually returns a Workbook object that will have its own set of properties, methods, and events.

Some of the properties exposed by certain objects may take one or many parameter arguments (optional or required) when they are instantiated. It's important to understand that from the object's perspective, parameters are always required. From the programming perspective, an optional parameter merely means that it will be defaulted by the object in the event it is not passed in from the code.

Methods

Again, if properties are the adjectives of an object, methods are the verbs. Methods cause an action to take place. In some cases, methods return values; in other cases, the method might cause an action to occur (the Application.Close method, for example). Methods are similar to properties in that they might have associated parameters. One of the nice things about using Visual Basic is that optional arguments are handled implicitly.

Events

Events are the driving force behind the execution of your code. In essence, these are the launching points where you can begin controlling the execution of code. In most Office 2007 applications, there are few objects that trigger their own events. In order to handle events raised by the Office 2007 object models, there must be a callback method that contains the appropriate signature expected by the event. Visual Studio ensures the correct syntax by automatically generating the event code.

Programming Against the Office 2007 Object Model

At their most elemental level, Office 2007 applications are programmed as traditional COM servers and expose COM interfaces. For example, you can program directly against a Word Document object and instantiate it by using the New keyword. The Word Document object logically includes all features and functionality of the Word application. This seemingly small detail is what makes Office 2007 a true development platform. The Word Document object obviously can make use of all subsidiary objects in the object hierarchy, but it can also go *up* the chain to make use of application features as well as other higher level objects.

When programming in Visual Studio, you'll actually be opening an instance of the application directly in the development environment. This means that you can add controls directly to the template or document (or your applicable Office project). For instance, Figure 12-6 shows the Visual Studio IDE with the Word application visible.

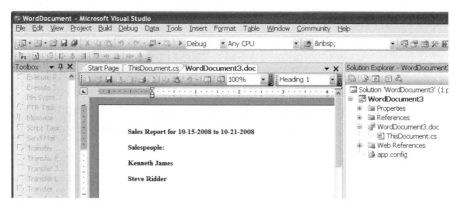

Figure 12-6: Visual Studio Word document project

This brings up a conceptual question when developing Office 2007 based solutions: What is the correct architecture for the solution? There are the following numerous options to answer this question:

▼ A simple VBA solution

▼ An add-in that is utilized within the Office application

▼ An out-of-process application that instantiates the Office application or component

▼ A .NET managed code application that works with the native Office COM object

▼ A VSTO-based solution that relies on managed code extensions and the Office PIAs

Further, there might be other business domain concerns such as targeting a specific version of Office or developing a generic solution that can make use of multiple versions of Office.

Office applications have grown and morphed through time to include their present functionality. Although the applications are all different from one another in terms of the functionality they offer, there are some consistent features among the applications and their object models. In general, the object models are all hierarchical in nature and have some sort of Document object (spreadsheets, presentations, databases, and so forth). At the root of each Office application is an Application object.

Visual Studio 2008 augments the Office programming model by adding a professional development toolset and the newly incorporated VSTO. VSTO brings a consistent approach to Office development and offers predefined project types that shortcut some of the decision making and code writing necessary to develop traditional Office solutions. As you'll see, VSTO allows the development of application customizations, document or template customizations, and the development of add-ins as well.

Types of Office Solutions

Because of the COM architecture, it has always been easy to program against Office applications and extend the functionality of the applications. VBA allows for in-process automation that runs inside the process space of the host application. The following table shows the different types of Office solutions and the various implementation features that can be accessed by each.

Type of Solution	Description
External automation	Any out-of-process use of the COM object models exposed by Office applications, including Windows Forms and console applications
In-process automation (VBA)	In-process use of the COM object models exposed by Office applications through VBA
VSTO add-in (application level)	In-process use of the COM object models exposed by Office applications, using .NET code
VSTO document-level customization	In-process use of the COM object models exposed by Office applications, using .NET code
COM add-ins	In-process DLLs generally created with Visual Studio (Office 2000 and later)
Smart Tags	Elements of text in an Office document that are recognized as having associated custom actions (Excel and Word in Office XP; Access, Excel, PowerPoint, and Word in Office 2003 and later)
Web services	Web services using either the SOAP toolkit (VBA) or .NET web service proxies

Type of Solution	Description
Custom task panes	Application-level task panes that support any ActiveX control or Windows Forms UserControl (Access, Excel, InfoPath, Outlook, PowerPoint, and Word in Office 2007)
Custom Ribbons	Document-level and application-level custom Ribbons (Access, Excel, Outlook, PowerPoint, and Word in Office 2007)

Conclusion

In this chapter we introduced the Visual Studio Tools for Office (VSTO) and Visual Studio 2008 VSTO, once a more elusive tool, is now fully integrated into the Visual Studio application. Developers using Visual Studio can now customize all applications found in the Office suite. The chapter took a look at the new offerings of Visual Basic 9.0 such as multi-targeting and the ability to target a specific .NET environment. We then looked at the inner workings of VSTO and its various features, including the support for the Ribbon UI offered in Office 2007. In the next chapter we will continue our efforts to expand our code development skills by going beyond VBA and into the full-fledged development environment of Visual Studio 2008.

Chapter 13

Moving to Visual Studio 2008 from VBA

Introduction

In this chapter we expand our programming knowledge by moving beyond VBA and into Visual Studio. If you've been developing in VBA for a while, you'll find some nice features in Visual Studio. As you'll see, the environments have many of the same features and functionality (they are, after all, both Microsoft development environments); however, Visual Studio provides features to easily accomplish things that are very difficult in VBA. Throughout this chapter, we will be comparing and contrasting everything from syntax and menu options to UserForms of VBA and Visual Studio.

VBA in Comparison to Visual Studio

As previously mentioned, the VBA integrated development environment (IDE) is essentially the same now as it was in Word 95. Visual Studio, on the other hand, has undergone tremendous change over that same time period and now offers many state-of-the-art development features. Conveniently, since many of the VBA features have an equivalent feature in

Visual Studio, VBA programmers can quickly pick up Visual Studio techniques. The look and feel of both environments are generally similar, but there are subtle differences. Let's take a look at these differences in the following sections.

VBA's Solution Explorer and Visual Studio's Project Explorer

Organization is represented using an explorer in both Visual Studio and VBA. Both of these explorers utilize a TreeView control to display the hierarchical set of objects associated with a project or solution. One of the key differences is that Visual Studio's Solution Explorer can contain multiple projects all related to a single solution. In VBA, each project is essentially a solution as well, but the idea of a "solution" does not exist in the context of VBA. Both environments contain the elements of the project, which can include code files, modules, class modules, UserForms or Windows forms, and various other resources.

When you create an Office project in Visual Studio, there are several things that are created automatically. This not only saves you time when developing, but it also creates the proper foundation upon which you can begin writing code. Based upon the New Project dialog, Visual Studio automatically creates the appropriate references and namespaces for the respective Office application(s).

The Solution Explorer windows are designed to make navigating among the objects in your project as easy as possible. You can simply click on the items in the Solution Explorer to quickly open them in the main code window. You can also quickly toggle between designer view and code view using the Solution Explorer toolbar. In most cases, you can right-click inside the Solution Explorer to bring up other menu options. In both environments, you can control the display of the window and/or control whether or not the window is dockable by using the View menu on the Standard toolbar. A comparison of the Project Explorer and the Solution Explorer is shown in Figure 13-1.

Figure 13-1:
Project Explorer
and Solution
Explorer

Visual Studio's IDE has other improvements related to Solution Explorer. Just as IE 7.0 brought tabbed browsing to the masses, Visual Studio offers VBA developers a tabbed code window to switch among the different code files in a project. This added functionality allows you to switch between files and close the various windows quickly and easily.

Another key point that differentiates VBA from Visual Studio is that VBA code runs on top of a framework that cannot be manipulated. The VBA language features are not exposed to the end developer, while Visual Studio exposes the auto-generated code via hidden files in the environment. For the most part, you do not need to concern yourself with these auto-generated files. They are hidden for a reason and that reason is to shield you from the underlying mechanics such as low-level object initialization code. This approach separates the developer code from the underlying, auto-generated code that you otherwise wouldn't see in VBA.

Although you can look at these hidden files to attain a deeper understanding of the mechanics involved, these files should not be altered. Any changes to these files will be over-written when the project is built or reopened. Either of these methods causes the automatic regeneration process to fire again and your changes will be discarded.

The Properties Windows

You'll also notice that the Properties windows appear strikingly similar in both environments. In each case, this window displays the properties of the selected object in either an alphabetic or categorized manner. Both windows have a drop-down that allows you choose the object you wish to see. Visual Studio also has a "lightning bolt" that allows you to see the events associated with a given object. VBA does not have such a mechanism, but it does allow you to see the events via the main code window. A comparison of the Properties windows is shown in Figure 13-2.

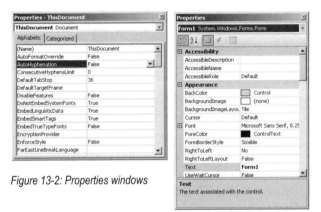

Figure 13-2: Properties windows

In both IDEs, properties can be set at design time but may not be displayed until run time. For instance, a UserForm may have child controls with the Visible property set to False, but they will still be displayed in the IDE. In other cases, such as setting scroll bars or background colors, these properties are displayed with the updated properties in the IDE as they are changed. There are other properties that can only be changed at run time. These properties, as well as read-only properties, will be disabled in the Properties window.

Although you can see the properties of high-level objects such as documents and workbooks in Visual Studio much the same way you can in VBA, there are important differences to note. In VBA, the properties of the actual workbook or document are being displayed. In Visual Studio, the Properties window is actually displaying the properties related to a Microsoft.Office.Tools.[Application].[Object] instead of the native object. The VSTO version is actually a wrapper around the native COM object and it includes many important additional properties. These properties expose functionality that simply isn't available in VBA.

The Code Windows

The Code window is the main window in both IDEs and is the primary method by which you type code. You can always get to the Code window via the View menu. The Code window is also displayed upon double-clicking items on a Windows form or MS Form 2.0. In this case, the IDE generates a stub of the Click event (or whatever event is relevant for the control you are selecting). You can also get to the Code window by right-clicking the object in the Explorer window and selecting View Code.

At the top of the Code window in each environment are two drop-down menus. The drop-down menu on the left is called the Object List. It contains a list of all objects in the active module. For instance, when the active module is a UserForm, all of the controls on the UserForm will appear in the drop-down. The drop-down list on the right is the Procedure and Event List. This list contains all of the available events for the current object. Finally, most modules also contain a General section. The General section is a place where general declarations can be typed. These include any option statements, such as Option Explicit (to force variable declaration) or Option Compare Text (to compare text rather than ASCII character values). Figure 13-3 shows a comparison of the Code windows.

Figure 13-3: Code windows

The IDE Toolbars

VBA developers should be familiar with all the typical functionality available via the Visual Studio Standard toolbar. Both applications use the Standard toolbar for typical file operations such as Save, SaveAs, Close, Open, etc. The key difference is that VBA is always operating in a single document that corresponds to a particular Office application. In other words, the document will always be a PowerPoint presentation, a Word document or template, an Excel spreadsheet, etc. In Visual Studio, there is a collection of files that comprise the overall solution. Another major difference is that Visual Studio is also capable of creating stand-alone applications.

The Standard toolbars of both environments offer functionalities such as Cut, Copy, Paste, Redo, and Undo that are nearly identical. Both have shortcuts to open other windows such as the Object Browser and the Toolbox (provided a form is active in the Code window). Both IDEs also feature shortcuts so that you can quickly search a project for a given string. You can see both toolbars in Figure 13-4.

Figure 13-4: The Standard toolbars in VBA and Visual Studio

VBA developers will note that projects are run differently in Visual Studio than they are in VBA. In VBA, the options are simply to run a project, to pause at a certain point, or to stop the code from executing entirely. The Visual Studio toolbar has a similar Run button, but the Stop and Pause buttons are not there. In addition, the project can be run in modes such as debug mode, release mode, and configuration manager mode. Furthermore, you can actually target the CPU platform that you want to simulate for your project.

The File Menus

In any solution, you'll need to understand the basic file options available to interact with your project. VBA is straightforward in this manner. You'll notice in Figure 13-5 that the VBA File menu has fewer options than the Visual Studio File menu. The primary reason for this is that when working with Visual Studio solutions you are actually working with several files at once. In Visual Studio, the Add menu option allows you to add new projects to the solution, new web sites, or new diagrams (or existing versions of each). Visual Studio also allows you to close individual files or the entire solution.

One of the main advantages that Visual Studio has over VBA is the reusability of code. Visual Studio allows you to export a given file as a template so that you can reuse it in other files as a basis for development. The other notable difference is the Source Control option. VBA was designed as a single developer environment. While it is possible to version control and source control VBA projects, you cannot do this from within the Visual Basic editor itself. In any of the Visual Studio Team editions, the File menu provides a quick shortcut to do basic source control tasks such as checking files in or out, managing workspaces, and applying labels.

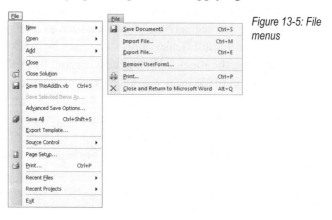

Figure 13-5: File menus

The Edit Menus

There isn't much difference to be noticed between the Edit menu of VBA and the Edit menu of Visual Studio. However, keep in mind that some menus are actually dynamic and the choices that appear depend on the context in which you are accessing the menu. The Edit menu is one of these dynamic menus. In fact, you may not see all the options shown in Figure 13-6 unless you are using the highest level access.

Most of the VBA functionality is encompassed in the Visual Studio version as well. All of the following actions are shared between Visual and VBA: Redo, Undo, Cut, Copy, Paste, Select All, Find, and Replace. At first glance it may appear that List Properties/Methods, List Constants, Parameter Info, Quick Info, and Complete Word are no longer available in Visual Studio; however, this is not the case. Visual Studio has a greatly expanded version of IntelliSense that handles these options for you. Developers that used these menu options in VBA will find that Visual Studio encompasses the same functionality while typing via IntelliSense options. If you wish, you can fine-tune these options using the IntelliSense configuration option. These features can also be accessed via the Edit menu.

Visual Studio offers a few additional options under the Edit menu. For example, you can quickly insert a file as a text file. You can use advanced options such as Bookmarks, Outlining, and IntelliSense options that can be quickly set by launching the menus. We suggest leaving the Visual Studio defaults in place until you become comfortable working in the new environment. Visual Studio also allows you to navigate among the methods of your solution by jumping to either the previous method or the next method with the click of a button. Figure 13-6 shows a comparison of the Edit menus.

Figure 13-6: Edit menus

The View Menus

The View menu provides a straightforward list of options for controlling the display of features inside the IDE. You'll immediately notice that there are many more features listed in Visual Studio's View menu than the View menu in VBA. There are, however, several commonalities between the two. The most common use for the View menu is the Toolbars menu item, which controls the visibility of the various toolbars within the IDE. VBA has four available toolbars, while Visual Studio provides over 20 toolbars.

The shared functionality of both toolbars also includes shortcuts to open the Code window, the Object Browser, and the Properties window, as well as shortcuts to the relative Explorer windows (Solution Explorer in Visual Studio and Project Explorer in VBA). The View menu in VBA provides quick access to project monitoring features such as the Immediate window, Locals window, and Watch window.

The View menu in Visual Studio also includes the Server Explorer and Team Explorer features, which are not found in the VBA View menu. Additionally, Visual Studio provides access to an Error List that checks the current syntax of all the typed code in the solution. The Visual Studio version of the View menu also includes options to navigate through the project as well as Team items such as Next Task and Previous

Task. Furthermore, Visual Studio also provides a Refresh shortcut as well as shortcuts to Property Pages when relevant. We can see a comparison of both View menus in Figure 13-7.

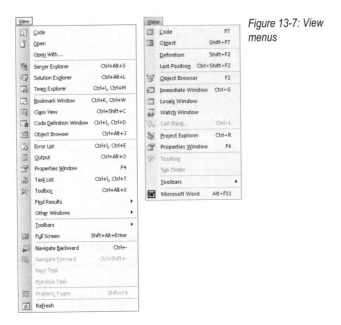

Figure 13-7: View menus

VBA Insert Menu Compared to Visual Studio Project Menu

Both development environments provide menus that allow you to add items to the current project. VBA works only in the context of a project, so the menu is titled "Insert" and provides five possible options: Procedure, UserForm, Module, Class Module, and File. This Insert menu structure has been in place since Office 97.

In contrast, Visual Studio provides a Project menu that is conceptually similar to the VBA Insert menu. This menu provides a convenient mechanism to add components to the currently selected project within a solution. The top portion of the menu provides quick access to add Windows Forms, User Controls, Components, Modules, or Classes, and is roughly equivalent (although more verbose) to the VBA menu.

In addition, Visual Studio's Project menu lets you add new or existing items to the current project and provides the Add New Distributed System Diagram and the Show All Files options. The Add New Distributed System Diagram option provides a mechanism to add supplemental metadata to your project, and the Show All Files option provides a mechanism to force the IDE to display all the files associated with a project.

The Project menu of Visual Studio provides some new functionality and encompasses some functionality that exists in other places in VBA. The most common mistake among VBA developers making the switch to VB is locating the Add Reference shortcut. In the VBA IDE, this menu option is located under the Tools menu. In Visual Studio, it exists as a child of the Project menu but it works pretty much the same as its VBA counterpart. Other options available via the Project menu allow you to do such things as add a web reference to the current project, define a launching point for the solution with the Set as StartUp Project option, list the project dependencies, and specify the order in which to build the project or solution. Finally, it adds a shortcut to view the properties of the currently selected project. The Project and Insert menus are shown in Figure 13-8.

Figure 13-8: The Project and Insert menus

The Format Menus

Almost all of the Format menu functionality is identical in both Visual Studio and VBA. Keep in mind that the Format menu is only visible in either environment when a form is active in the IDE. The Format menu allows you to align controls, make controls the same size, and space controls. You can also center controls and control the visibility layering. In addition, Visual Studio provides options to Size to Fit controls into a particular space as well as Size to Grid to provide uniformity. A comparison of the Format menus is seen in Figure 13-9.

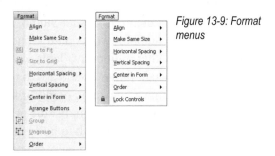

Figure 13-9: Format menus

The Debug Menus

Although the process of debugging is somewhat different between Visual Studio and VBA, the Debug menus are strikingly similar. When you create a new project with Visual Studio, you'll find the IDE creates two build configurations for your application (unless your project is a web project). You can see these configurations under the Configuration Manager option of the Build menu. The first is a Release configuration, which compiles your application so that the application will run as efficiently as possible. The second is a Debug configuration, which compiles your application for the best debugging experience. A debug build will disable optimizations as well as create portable database (PDB) files. Compiler optimizations will often rearrange instructions to increase performance or reduce memory consumption; however, these rearrangements can confuse the debugger.

Both IDEs use the Debug menu to provide quick access to the Immediate window. In addition, both IDEs use the Debug menu to Toggle Breakpoints and Step Into and Step Over code. You may notice, however, that there are a few things missing from Visual Studio that are found in VBA. The Run to Cursor and Step Out methods have been removed in Visual Studio as well as the Add Watch, Edit Watch and Quick Watch options. Visual Studio does, however, provide quick access to the Output window as well as a list of current exceptions. A comparison of the Debug menus is shown in Figure 13-10.

Figure 13-10: Debug menus

The Run and Build Menus

When you create a project in Visual Studio, you'll see a solution (.sln) file that contains information about the projects and configurations in the solution. Visual Studio will also create a solution user options (.suo) file, which contains your user options. VB.NET also creates a .vbproj file. These files are XML files that contain the build and dependency information for the current project. Visual Studio may create a .user file for user settings or a .ncb file for information about statement completion.

The Visual Studio Build menu offers some functionality that you may not be familiar with if you are coming from a VBA environment. The Clean Solution menu option will remove all the intermediate files and output directories from your solution. A comparison of the Run and Build menus is shown in Figure 13-11.

Figure 13-11: The Run and Build menus

Language Differences between Visual Studio and VBA

Before looking at the differences between the two development environments, let's first take a look at what has changed in the Visual Basic language syntax. The current version of Visual Basic, included with Visual Studio 2008, is version 9.0. VBA has been the language behind Microsoft Office for over 12 years. Throughout this time the language and IDE have not changed much. In fact, the language is still pretty much identical to the way it was in 1997. The syntax and language features have not been updated and are roughly on par with Visual Basic 6.0. Let's take a look at some of the intrinsic data types supported in Visual Studio 2008.

Data Types

There are certain data types in VBA that have been deleted or substantially changed in Visual Basic 9.0 for .NET. These variable types include variant, integer, long, currency, and some other minor variables. Since variants can be implicitly cast to other variable types, variants have always been problematic and have actually been responsible for numerous people writing poor-quality code. A VBA integer is equivalent to a Visual Basic short and a VBA long is equivalent to an integer in Visual Basic.

Fixed-Length Strings

One of the concepts behind Visual Studio is the interoperability of languages. This advancement necessitated changes to VBA's fixed-length string. In order for these variables to be fully compatible with other Visual Studio languages, support for fixed-length strings is no longer support as such, but instead has two options to evaluate depending on your needs. The first step is to determine if your fixed-length string needs to be a specific length. If it does not need to be a specific length, you can simply declare it as a regular Visual Basic string. If you do require a specific length, then the mechanism is to declare it as an array of bytes as shown below:

```
Dim ConvertedFixedLengthString(100) As Byte
```

Literal Values Instead of Windows Constants

Each Office application, including Windows and VBA, provides specific constants that generally have an integer value. In using Visual Studio 2008 Tools for Office, you must convert to the Microsoft Windows-based defined constant value when you use the mathematic literal value. In the situation where literal values are used, you must determine the constant based on Windows, and then use the equivalent constant based on Visual Studio 2008 Tools for Office. The following lines distinguish between the two languages' use of built-in constants.

```
[VBA]
.MousePointer = 10 'literal constant for vbUpArrow

[Visual Basic]
.Cursor = System.Windows.Forms.Cursors.UpArrow
```

Enumerations

Enumeration is a fundamental aspect of programming in Visual Studio/Visual Basic 9.0, but it is also one of the biggest stumbling blocks for VBA developers who are making the switch. Unlike VBA, in Visual Basic 9.0 you must fully qualify enumeration constants. If you are looking to convert specific VBA code, then you will need to change the statements to add the fully qualified enumeration name, as shown below:

```
[VBA]
ActiveDocument.Paragraphs.Count
```

```
[Visual Basic]
ThisApplication.ActiveDocument.Paragraphs.Count
```

Arrays

VBA users are familiar with using the Option Base statement to change the lower bound of an array to 1. This is helpful when iterating through something like the Paragraphs collection in Word and assigning values to an array. You could use an incremental counter to iterate up to Paragraphs.Count and your array numbering would be in sync with the Paragraphs collection numbering — and you wouldn't waste any memory by having a null (0) array item. Visual Basic does not support the Option Base statement. The only real way to migrate arrays with an Option Base 1 is to add 1 to the dimension of the array and simply have an extra slot at index 0. Obviously, the .NET Framework-based code causes some minor memory waste but continues to work. The following example shows a sample VBA Option Base 1 array and a potential workaround for Visual Basic 9.0.

```
[VBA]
Option Base 1
' a list of 10 names
Dim firstNames(10) as String
Dim i as Integer

For i = 1 to ActiveDocument.Paragraphs.Count
    FirstNames(i) = ActiveDocument.Paragraphs(i).Range.Text
Next i

[Visual Basic]
' there will be an array member, FirstNames(0), that is blank
For i = 1 to Application.ActiveDocument.Paragraphs.Count
```

```
FirstNames(i) = Application.ActiveDocument.Paragraphs(i) _
    .Range.Text
Next i
```

The numbers are logically synchronized in the above code because you have the option of declaring Option Base 1. In addition, we do not have a null placeholder in the 0 element of the array. This same code can easily be written in Visual Basic, but it is one of the rare areas that doesn't appear as elegant as the VBA method.

There is, however, one situation where this does not work. If you typically write your code to depend on the lower bound of an array being 1 instead of 0, you will need to adjust your coding style. This is typically done with an LBound function in a looping convention. For example, the code may use LBound to determine the first index of the array or may use a combination of the LBound and UBound functions to determine the size of the array.

If you are switching to Visual Basic from VBA, you'll need to keep this change in the back of your head while you're writing code. If you are migrating VBA code, the only "true" method is to change your Option Base arrays so that the array indexing values are zero-based. This leads to the most efficient use of memory, but undoubtedly requires more work during the migration.

A potentially larger problem is that Visual Basic 9.0 does not support ReDim or ReDim Preserve when working with arrays. In Visual Basic, you cannot "ReDimension" an array and declare a new upper boundary. For example, the following code works in VBA, but it is not easily migrated to Visual Basic:

```
[VBA]
Private Sub AssignNames()
Dim Names(1) as String
Dim i as Integer
Names(i) = "Peanut"
For i = 2 to Paragraphs.Count
    ReDim Preserve names(i) as String
    Names(i) = Paragraphs(i).Range.Text
Next i
```

```
End Sub

[Visual Basic]
Dim Names(100) as String 'assign arbitrarily large value and
        'risk an overflow
```

This would obviously not be the preferred method to write the code, but it is a great way to illustrate how ReDim can be used. There is no elegant means to migrate this type of code. The only possible way to migrate this code is to declare a new array and then copy the contents of the old array to the new array. Your best solution is to rethink the design from scratch and work within the confines of Visual Basic.

Dates

A feature about dates in VBA is that they can be used as integers for mathematical calculations and comparisons. This means that they can be seamlessly combined with other numbers and numerical operators. It's also possible to perform calculations using add or subtract with a date integer, resulting in another date variable. When dealing with dates, other types of mathematical operators produce numerical values.

Scope of Variables

In VBA, any variable declared in a procedure is instantiated at the beginning of the procedure no matter where the variable was actually declared. Because of this, that variable is accessible from anywhere in the procedure, regardless of its position. What this means in regard to VBA variables is that all local variables have procedure-level scope. However, in Visual Basic 9.0, you can minimize the scope of a variable to a procedure by embedding it inside a control structure such as a loop. That way, the variable is only accessible inside the given control structure. In the following example of VBA code, the variable Total is being declared within the loop; however, in the Visual Basic code example, we see that the equivalent NumPayments variable is declared before the loop. Declaring the NumPayments within the loop will cause an error when coding for Visual Basic.

```
[VBA]
Public Function GetNumPayments(ByVal LoanAmount As Integer)
Dim X As Integer
For X = 1 To LoanAmount 'instantiated when the function is called
Dim Total As Integer
Total = Total + X
Next X ' This will not generate an error because in scope
GetNumPayments = NumPayments
End Function

[Visual Basic]
Public Function GetNumPayments(ByVal LoanAmount As Integer)
Dim X As Integer 'The NumPayments declaration has been moved to
       'function scope
Dim NumPayments As Integer
For X = 1 To LoanAmount
NumPayments = NumPayments + X
Next X
GetNumPayments = NumPayments
End Function
```

Use of Parentheses in Procedure Calls

Subroutines or functions that are not passed arguments do not require parentheses in VBA. Furthermore, a function that is not assigning a value to a variable or object also does not require parentheses. In the following example, both forms of the MsgBox function work fine:

```
MsgBox "The Dog Ran up the Hill", vbOkOnly, "Error"
iResponse = MsgBox("The Dog Ran up the Hill", vbYesNo, "Error")
```

In VBA, you can call the subroutine either directly by name or by using the Call statement. When calling a subroutine directly, you never use parentheses; however, you must use parentheses if you use the Call statement and pass arguments. Confusingly enough, you do not use parentheses if you use the Call statement to call a function that does not take arguments.

Visual Basic 9.0 greatly simplifies function calling. Parentheses are always required when passing parameters in a subroutine call. In addition, the biggest difference in Visual Basic is that statements containing function calls with parentheses are evaluated differently from statements containing function calls without parentheses. The reasoning behind this is that function parameters are evaluated differently, and because the use of parentheses also determines whether or not the function returns a value. The following table shows examples of calling subroutines or functions with and without arguments.

Description	VBA Code	Visual Basic 9.0 Code
Subroutine call: no parameters	`getCustomerID`	`getCustomerID ()`
Subroutine call: no parameters, call statement	`Call getCustomerID`	`Call getCustomerID ()`
Subroutine call: with parameters	`getCustomerID "Acme Corporation"`	`ProcessClient("Acme Corporation")`
Subroutine call: with parameters and call statement	`Call getCustomerID ("Acme Corporation")`	`Call getCustomerID ("Acme Corporation")`
Function call: with parameters and assignment	`iCust = getCustomerID ("Acme Corporation")`	`Cust = getCustomerID ("Acme Corporation")`
Function call: with parameters, without assignment	`getCustomerID "Acme Corporation"` OR `getCustomerID ("Acme Corporation")`	`getCustomerID ("Acme Corporation")`

Argument Passing

Passing arguments to function parameters is one of the least understood concepts in the VBA language. Parameter arguments can be passed by reference or by value. By default, VBA passes parameter arguments by reference. In Visual Basic, the default method is to pass parameters by value.

The following code illustrates functions with ByRef and ByVal parameters:

```
[VBA]
Sub exampleByRef1(name)          ' passed by reference
name = "exampleByRef1"           ' original argument changed
End Sub


Sub exampleByRef2(ByRef name)    ' passed by reference
name = "exampleByRef2"           ' original argument changed
End Sub


Sub exampleByVal(ByVal name)     ' passed by value
name = "exampleByVal"            ' doesn't affect original argument
End Sub


Private Sub Button_Click()
Dim testName
testName = "Scott"
exampleByRef1 testName
MsgBox (testName)                ' Displays "exampleByRef1"


exampleByRef2 testName
MsgBox (testName)                ' Displays "exampleByRef2"


exampleByVal testName
MsgBox (testName)                ' Displays "exampleByVal"
End Sub
```

You can create the above code in Visual Basic by qualifying the parameters with the appropriate keyword, as shown here:

```
[Visual Basic]
Sub exampleByRef1(ByRef name_parameter As String)
' parameter passed by reference
name_parameter = "exampleByRef1" ' original argument changed
End Sub


Sub exampleByRef2(ByRef name_parameter As String)
' parameter passed by reference
name_parameter = "exampleByRef2" ' original argument changed
End Sub


Sub exampleByVal(ByVal name_parameter As String)
' parameter passed by value
name_parameter = "exampleByVal"
' change has no effect on original argument
```

```
End Sub

Private Sub Button_Click()
Dim testName As String
testName = "Scott"

exampleByRef1(testName)
MsgBox(testName) ' Displays "exampleByRef1"

exampleByRef2(testName)
MsgBox(testName) ' Displays "exampleByRef2"

exampleByVal(testName)
MsgBox(testName)
' Displays "exampleByVal", argument will not be changed
End Sub
```

Default Properties

When typing code in VBA, you can use the shortcut of eliminating the default properties. In Visual Basic 9.0, default properties are not supported. The only exception is if the properties take arguments. This is an easy migration problem to solve. You can simply expand the default property as needed whenever you use early binding and you know the type of the object. Late binding determines the resolution of the type of an identifier based on its use in the code. After you know the type, you can determine its default property.

Assignments

To distinguish between assignment of an object and assignment of the default property of the object, VBA utilizes the Set keyword. You do not need the Set keyword in Visual Basic since Visual Basic does not support default properties. In most cases, when migrating code, you can easily solve this problem by running a quick search and replace and monitor the values as you are replacing. It's also worth noting that Visual Basic no longer requires the Let keyword. The following example demonstrates VBA set assignment and Visual Basic assignment.

```
[VBA]
Dim oPara as Paragraph
Set oPara = ActiveDocument.Paragraphs(1)
```

```
[Visual Basic]
Dim oPara As New Microsoft.Office.Interop.Word.Paragraph
oPara = ThisApplication.ActiveDocument.Paragraphs(1)
```

The TypeOf and TypeName Functions

By using the TypeOf function in VBA, you can quickly determine the type of an object variable. This was typically used in
If..Then..Else statements to determine whether an object reference is of a specified object type. The basic functionality
continues to work in Visual Basic 9.0, but user-defined types,
which are now called structures, are not object types and cannot be evaluated by the TypeOf function. For example:

```
[VBA]
Type Loan
balance As Integer
End Type
Dim custLoan As Loan
If TypeOf custLoan Is Loan Then
ProcessAccount(custLoan)
End If
```

```
[Visual Basic]
Public Structure Loan
Dim balance As Integer
End Structure
Dim custLoan As Account ' For structure type checking the
    ' following syntax can be used
If custLoan.GetType Is GetType(Loan) Then ProcessAccount(custLoan)
End If
```

The TypeName function is similar in functionality, but it
evaluates strings instead of object types. The basic string
functionality has been altered a little in Visual Studio and you
may not get the anticipated results when working with
TypeName. As some basic naming conventions have changed
in Visual Basic, if you are using TypeName to trigger comparisons or in conditional statements, you could quickly find

that your code no longer appears to work. You can find a comprehensive list of the changes by visiting Microsoft's Visual Basic web site: http://msdn2.microsoft.com/en-us/vbasic/default.aspx.

Control Structures

All control structures, with the exception of the While statement, have remained unchanged from VBA to Visual Basic. A While statement in VBA ends with the WEnd keyword; however, in Visual Basic, a While statement ends with an End While statement. Another control structure difference to note is that Visual Basic no longer supports the GoSub..Return and On..GoSub statements. Traditionally, these statements were almost always indicative of sloppy coding and were rarely used in practice.

Exception Handling

Oftentimes, VBA projects were plagued with On Error Resume Next statements that could cause disastrous results. Almost all languages support some version of a try-catch structure. Java, for example, has had try-catch in place since its inception. Visual Basic .NET implements this structure with the Try, Catch, and Finally keywords. Utilizing these keywords is the preferred way to handle almost all errors in Visual Basic.

Late Binding and Early Binding

As previously mentioned, since the variant type of variable is no longer supported in Visual Basic, there is no such thing as late binding. You'll need to specifically declare your variables in Visual Basic. This can also improve your execution times as the compiler does not need to expend clock cycles trying to determine the type of variable you are working with during program execution. This also helps during development as early binding allows you to make full use of the IntelliSense features offered by the IDE.

Multiple Variable Declarations

In VBA, you can declare variables of different types in the same declaration statement, although they will default to a variant type unless you specify the data type of each one. The following example shows multiple declarations and their resulting data types:

```
[VBA]
Dim A, B As Integer ' A is Variant, B is Integer.
Dim C As Integer, D As Integer ' C is Integer, D is Integer.
```

Notice that "A" is a variant even though it is declared on the same line as the specifically declared integer variable type. In Visual Basic, you can declare multiple variables of the same data type without having to repeat the type keyword. You could migrate the previous code like this:

```
[Visual Basic]
Dim A As Object
Dim B As Short ' B is Short.
Dim C, D As Short ' C is Short, D is Short.
```

The VBA Object Model

The VBA object model contains over 350 functions, none of which have primary interop assemblies. Although you can migrate most elements of the VBA object model to a Visual Basic equivalent, there are exceptions, as shown in the following table.

VBA Object Model Function	Description
vba._HiddenModule.InputB vba._HiddenModule.InputB$	For accessing files at binary level
vba._HiddenModule.ObjPtr vba._HiddenModule.StrPtr vba._HiddenModule.VarPtr	Undocumented functions for working with pointers
vba.Conversion.CVErr	Create user-defined errors
vba.Conversion.MacID	Used on Macintosh computers in place of wildcards

VBA Object Model Function	Description
vba.DateTime.Calendar VBA.VbCalendar.vbCalGreg VBA.VbCalendar.vbCalHijri	For working with non-Gregorian calendars
vba.Strings.AscB vba.Strings.ChrB vba.Strings.ChrB$ vba.Strings.InStrB vba.Strings.LeftB vba.Strings.LeftB$ vba.Strings.LenB vba.Strings.MidB vba.Strings.MidB$ vba.Strings.RightB vba.Strings.RightB$	For manipulating non-Unicode strings
VBA.VbCompareMethod.vbDatabaseCompare	Enum, string compare, string functions
VBA.VbFileAttribute.vbAlias	Dir, Get, Set attributes
VBA.VbMsgBoxStyle.vbDefaultButton4	Used to specify that the fourth button in a dialog box is default
VBA.VbStrConv.vbFromUnicode VBA.VbStrConv.vbUnicode	Used with the StrConv function to convert to and from Unicode
VBA.VbVarType.vbDataObject	Objects that do not support the IDispatch interface

App Object

Another element of VBA that has no direct equivalent in Visual Basic is the App object. You may, however, be able to find similar functionality in Visual Basic. For example, you can map the App.LogEvent of VBA to the My.Application.Log.WriteEntry method found in Visual Basic. This is shown in the following code:

```
[VBA]
App.LogEvent "Error", vbLogEventTypeError
App.LogEvent "Warning", vbLogEventTypeWarning
App.LogEvent "Information", vbLogEventTypeInformation

[Visual Basic]
My.Application.Log.WriteEntry("Error", _
System.Diagnostics.TraceEventType.Error)
```

```
My.Application.Log.WriteEntry("Warning", _
System.Diagnostics.TraceEventType.Warning)
My.Application.Log.WriteEntry("Information", _
System.Diagnostics.TraceEventType.Information)
```

Forms and Controls in Visual Basic

Windows Forms and the associated controls are one of the areas of greatest improvement from VBA to Visual Basic. VBA utilized the MSForms 2.0 collection, and the controls offered in VBA have remained more or less the same throughout the years. In contrast, Visual Studio offers the latest controls and all the associated functionality. Before looking at the individual controls offered in Visual Studio, let's compare and contrast Visual Studio's Windows Forms and VBA UserForms.

Windows Forms

The Forms collection object in VBA has no direct equivalent in Visual Basic; however, you can utilize Visual Basic's My.Application.Forms object in much the same manner. Although the Forms collection made it easy to iterate through the existing forms in a project (even dynamically created ones) and query their associated controls or properties, you can use the My.Application.Forms object to do this same type of coding.

VBA UserForms

The core of a VBA form is the MSForms 2.0 type library, while the core of a Visual Basic Form is the Visual Basic type library. Both cores are very similar and contain a Control coclass and IControl interface. Furthermore, Label controls, TextBox controls, and events are the same for most of the controls in VBA and Visual Studio 2008 Tools for Office. Although the names for some controls change from VBA to Visual Studio 2008 Tools for Office, the functionality should remain almost exactly the same. With that said, it is advisable to migrate all VBA UserForms to Windows Forms. The following table shows the controls of the VBA UserForms and their corresponding Visual Studio counterparts. You can use this table to aid you in migration.

MSForms Controls	System.Windows.Forms Controls	Notes
Label	Label	Equivalent functionality
TextBox	TextBox	Equivalent functionality
Frame	GroupBox	Similar; see below
ComboBox	ComboBox	Equivalent functionality
ListBox	ListBox	Equivalent functionality
CheckBox	CheckBox	Equivalent functionality
OptionButton	RadioButton	Equivalent functionality
ToggleButton	CheckBox	Deprecated; use CheckBox
CommandButton	Button	Equivalent functionality
TabStrip	TabControl	Equivalent functionality
MultiPage	TabControl	Equivalent functionality
ScrollBar (Horizontal)	HscrollBar	Equivalent functionality
ScrollBar (Vertical)	VscrollBar	Equivalent functionality
SpinButton	DomainUpDown	Similar; see below
Image	PictureBox	Equivalent functionality

For the most part, the functionality and behavior of most controls remain the same. However, if you make frequent use of VBA's Frame and SpinButton controls, you may need to either create compatibility classes or re-evaluate your solutions to achieve the same functionality in Visual Studio. Visual Basic no longer supports some events that were found in VBA Forms. In other words, in a Visual Basic scenario there may be no VBA equivalent event to run. In this case, you'll want to determine how to initiate the execution of your code based upon another event. For instance, the VBA Error event cannot be trapped in Visual Basic, but you could achieve equivalent functionality by properly utilizing another error-handling mechanism such as Visual Basic exception handling.

Generally, Windows Forms are much more robust than VBA UserForms. In addition, Visual Basic offers many more controls than the controls found in VBA. If you are starting a new project from scratch, it is a good idea to familiarize yourself with the many new controls offered by Visual Studio. The following table lists the Windows Forms controls and components and summarizes their functionality.

Control or Component	Description
BackgroundWorker	Enables a form or control to run an operation in the background.
BindingNavigator control	Provides control to the user to navigate to and/or change data on a Windows form.
BindingSource	Defines data to bind to a control.
Button control	A standard button a user can click to perform an action.
CheckBox control	Indicates whether a condition is checked or not.
CheckedListBox control	Displays a list of checkable items.
ColorDialog	Allows user to select a preloaded or customized color from a displayed color palette.
ComboBox control	Displays data in a drop-down list.
ContextMenu	Displays frequently used commands to the user that are associated with the selected object.
ContextMenuStrip control	Represents a shortcut menu.
DataGrid control	Displays data in tab form from a dataset that allows changes to the data source.
DataGridView control	Provides a system for displaying and editing tabular data.
DateTimePicker control	Displays a list of dates or times from which the user can select an item.
Dialog-Box controls	Describes a set of controls that allow users to perform standard interactions with the application or system.
DomainUpDown control	Displays text strings that a user can browse through and select from.
ErrorProvider	Displays error information to the user in a nonintrusive way.

Control or Component	Description
FlowLayoutPanel control	Represents a panel that dynamically lays out its contents horizontally or vertically.
FolderBrowserDialog	Displays an interface with which users can browse and select a directory or create a new one.
FontDialog	Exposes the fonts that are currently installed on the system.
GroupBox control	Provides an identifiable grouping for other controls.
HelpProvider	Associates an HTML Help file with a Windows-based application.
HScrollBar and VScrollBar controls	Provides navigation through a list of items or a large amount of information by scrolling either horizontally or vertically within an application or control.
ImageList	Displays images on other controls.
Label control	Displays text that cannot be edited by the user.
LinkLabel control	Allows you to add web-style links to Windows Forms applications.
ListBox control	Allows the user to select one or more items from a predefined list.
ListView control	Displays a list of items with icons, in the manner of Windows Explorer.
MainMenu	Displays a menu at run time.
MaskedTextBox control	Constrains the format of user input in a form.
MenuStrip control	Provides a menu system for a form.
MonthCalendar control	Presents an intuitive graphical interface for users to view and set date information.
NotifyIcon	Displays icons for processes that run in the background and would not otherwise have user interfaces.
NumericUpDown control	Displays numerals that a user can browse through and select from.
OpenFileDialog	Allows users to open files by using a preconfigured dialog box.
PageSetupDialog	Sets page details for printing through a preconfigured dialog box.
Panel control	Provide an identifiable grouping for other controls, and allows for scrolling.

Control or Component	Description
PictureBox control	Displays graphics in bitmap, GIF, JPEG, metafile, or icon format.
PrintDialog	Selects a printer, chooses the pages to print, and determines other print-related settings.
PrintDocument	Sets the properties that describe what to print, and prints the document in Windows-based applications.
PrintPreviewControl control	Allows you to create your own PrintPreview component or dialog box instead of using the preconfigured version.
PrintPreviewDialog control	Displays a document as it will appear when it is printed.
ProgressBar control	Graphically indicates the progress of an action toward completion.
RadioButton control	Presents a set of two or more mutually exclusive options to the user.
RichTextBox control	Allows users to enter, display, and manipulate text with formatting.
SaveFileDialog	Selects files to save and where to save them.
SoundPlayer Class	Enables you to easily include sounds in your applications.
SplitContainer control	Allows the user to resize a docked control.
Splitter control	Allows the user to resize a docked control (.NET Framework version 1.x).
StatusBar control	Displays status information related to the control that has focus.
StatusStrip control	Represents a Windows status bar control.
TabControl control	Displays multiple tabs that can contain pictures or other controls.
TableLayoutPanel control	Represents a panel that dynamically lays out its contents in a grid composed of rows and columns.
TextBox control	Allows editable, multiline input from the user.
Timer	Raises an event at regular intervals.
ToolBar control	Displays menus and bitmapped buttons that activate commands.
ToolStrip control	Creates custom toolbars and menus in your Windows Forms applications.

Control or Component	Description
ToolStripContainer control	Provides panels on each side of a form for docking, rafting, and arranging ToolStrip controls, and a central ToolStripContentPanel for traditional controls.
ToolStripPanel control	Provides one panel for docking, rafting, and arranging ToolStrip controls.
ToolStripProgressBar control overview	Graphically indicates the completion progress of an action. The ToolStripProgressBar is typically contained in a StatusStrip.
ToolStripStatusLabel control	Represents a panel in a StatusStrip control.
ToolTip	Displays text when the user points at other controls.
TrackBar control	Allows navigation through a large amount of information or visually adjusting a numeric setting.
TreeView control	Displays a hierarchy of nodes that can be expanded or collapsed.
WebBrowser control	Hosts web pages and provides Internet web browsing capabilities to your application.
Windows Forms controls used to list options	Describes a set of controls used to provide users with a list of options to choose from.

Using Windows Forms Controls

In general, the best way to know and understand a function is to use it. Having said that, this section is not intended to provide a thorough description of each control; rather, it is meant to give a concise description of the Microsoft Windows Forms controls and their commonly used properties, methods, and events.

The Button Control

The Button control (shown in Figure 13-12) of the Windows form is very similar to the VBA CommandButton. This control allows the user to click it to perform an action. The button seamlessly keeps the visual aspect intact by appearing depressed when clicked on and popping back out

Button1

Figure 13-12:
The Button
control

when let go. The primary event behind the Button control is the Click event.

You can set the appropriate text to be displayed by setting the Text property of the button. The Text property can also contain an access key, which allows a user to activate the button without the mouse by pressing Alt+access key. Both the Font property and the TextAlign property control the appearance of the text. The Button control can also display images by setting the Image and ImageList properties.

The CheckBox Control

The CheckBox control (shown in Figure 13-13) is the functional equivalent of check boxes found in VBA. It is used to indicate whether a particular condition is on or off. The CheckBox is most frequently used to present a Yes/No, True/False, or multiple-choice selection to the user. CheckBox controls can be grouped together with control groups. When dealing with MSForms in VBA, check boxes were frequently grouped together using Frames. In Visual Studio, multiple check boxes may be grouped using the GroupBox control.

Figure 13-13:
The CheckBox
control

CheckBox controls are conceptually similar to radio buttons in that they give the user the option of either checking or not checking the selection. The important distinction between the two is that while multiple CheckBoxes can be selected in a given control group, the radio button selection is exclusive (only one radio button can be selected within that group).

The CheckBox control utilizes two primary properties: the Checked property and the CheckState property. The Checked property returns either True or False according to whether or not the check box was selected. The CheckState property works with the ThreeState property. If the ThreeState property is set to True, then the CheckState property may return CheckState.Indeterminate. Otherwise, if the ThreeState property is set to False, it returns either CheckState.Checked or CheckState.Unchecked. When the indeterminate state is

True, the box is grayed out to indicate the option is unavailable.

The ColorDialog Component

The Windows Forms ColorDialog component (shown in Figure 13-14) is the
commonly used dialog box that lets a user
choose a color from a palette. The user
also has the option of adding custom
colors to that palette. In the VBA environment, if you wanted to work with the
Windows Dialog components, you could
add a reference to the Common Dialog
control. These components are native to
Visual Studio.

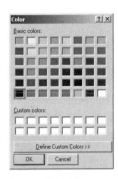

Figure 13-14: The
ColorDialog component

This exact dialog box appears in
many other applications and these types of components are
common to all Windows applications, so users should be
familiar with their use. The Color property of the ColorDialog
component returns the color selected in the dialog box. The
AllowFullOpen property is used to toggle the Define Custom
Colors button from enabled to disabled. When disabled, the
user is restricted to the predefined colors in the palette. The
SolidColorOnly property is used to enable or disable the
selection of dithered colors.

The ComboBox Control

Whether working with UserForms or
Windows Forms, one of the most frequently used controls is the ComboBox
(shown in Figure 13-15). This control is
used to display a drop-down menu that contains a list of
selectable items, but at the same time conserves space on the
form. By default, the top part of a ComboBox control resembles a text box and the bottom expandable part displays a
ListBox of items from which the user can select.

Figure 13-15: The
ComboBox control

You can programmatically add items to or delete items from a ComboBox control using the Items.Add, Items.Insert, Items.Clear, or Items.Remove methods of the ComboBox control. At design time, you can add items by using the Items property in the designer.

The key property of the ComboBox control is the SelectedIndex property. This property returns an integer value that corresponds to the position of the selected list item. You can programmatically change or set the selected item by changing the SelectedIndex value in code. Changing this property in code will cause the corresponding item in the list to appear in the text box part of the control. The control is similar to an array in that the first item in the list has a SelectedIndex value of 0. If no item is selected, the SelectedIndex value is –1.

The SelectedItem property is similar to SelectedIndex, with the difference being that the SelectedItem property returns the string value of the currently selected item. The Items.Count property displays the total number of items in the list. Keep in mind that the value of the Items.Count property is always one more than the largest possible SelectedIndex value because SelectedIndex is zero-based.

The DataGrid Control

Another one of the most frequently used data controls is the DataGrid control (shown in Figure 13-16). This control displays data in a series of rows and columns similar to a spreadsheet. Once bound to a table,

Figure 13-16: The DataGrid control

the DataGrid can control all associated data functionality with minimal programming. The DataGrid control provides a conceptual user interface for a .NET dataset, which allows navigation among related tables. The DataGrid can also be bound to multidimensional data using queries that can return multiple related tables. In doing so, navigation can be enabled to provide expanders (navigation from a parent table to a child table) in each row so that a user can traverse the data in a relational manner. When the user clicks an expandable node, it will display its child table. The user can then click the Back button to navigate back to the original parent table.

If a DataGrid is bound to a DataSet object, the columns and rows are automatically created, formatted, and filled. Columns then can be added, deleted, rearranged, and formatted as needed. The manipulation of data and data updating is handled by the Windows Forms data-binding architecture and by .NET Framework data providers, and therefore, multiple controls bound to the same data source will stay in sync.

The DateTimePicker Control

In VBA UserForms, one of the disadvantages was that MSForms did not provide a simple date control. In Windows Forms, the DateTimePicker control (shown in Figure 13-17) gives the user the ability to select a single item from a list of dates or times. If the control is used to represent a date, it appears in a

Figure 13-17: The DateTimePicker control

drop-down list as text. When a control with a down arrow is selected, a grid that looks like the MonthCalendar control drops down, which can be used for selecting multiple dates. An alternative to the grid is the up and down buttons that appear when the ShowUpDown property is set to True. This is particularly useful for editing times instead of dates.

The MaxDate and MinDate properties of DateTimePicker can control the range of dates and times that are available to the end user. The Value property contains the currently selected date and time. This value can be displayed in four formats as defined by the Format property: Long, Short, Time, or Custom. When using a custom format, you must set the CustomFormat property to utilize an appropriate string format.

The DomainUpDown Control

The DomainUpDown control (shown in Figure 13-18) appears as a text box with a pair of navigation buttons for moving up or down through a list. The control displays a text string from a predefined list of choices. The user can navigate among the strings by clicking the up and down buttons to move through a list or by using the Up and Down Arrow keys. The user can also shortcut the selection process by beginning to type an item that matches an item in the list. Note that DomainUpDown controls display only text strings. Use the NumericUpDown control to display numeric values.

Figure 13-18: The DomainUpDown control

The most frequently used properties of the DomainUpDown control are the Items, ReadOnly, and Wrap properties. The Items property contains the list of the objects whose text values are displayed in the control. The control auto-completes text that the user begins typing and matches it to a value in the list. You can let users scroll past the last item in the list by using the Wrap property. This will take the user forward to the first item in the list or back to the last item in the list.

The ErrorProvider Component

Data validation for a VBA UserForm was often a tedious process with the very real potential for error. Thankfully, Visual Studio alleviates this problem by offering the ErrorProvider component. The ErrorProvider component can be used to validate user input on a form or a specific control.

The ErrorProvider component is a much better solution than using MsgBoxes, a method frequently used when developing in VBA. With the ErrorProvider component, once a message box is dismissed, the error message falls out of scope and is no longer retrievable. The ErrorProvider component then displays an error icon next to the associated control so that when the user positions the mouse pointer over the error icon, a ToolTip appears, showing the pertinent error message.

The Icon property can be set to a custom error icon instead of the default icon. When the DataSource property is set, the ErrorProvider component can display error messages for a dataset. The key method of the ErrorProvider component is the SetError method, which specifies the error message string and where the error icon should appear.

The ErrorProvider component's key properties are Data-Source, ContainerControl, and Icon. The ContainerControl property must be set to the Windows Form in order for the ErrorProvider component to display an error icon on the form. When the component is added in the designer, the ContainerControl property is set to the containing form.

The FolderBrowserDialog Component

When adding folder browsing and selection capability to a Windows Form, the FolderBrowserDialog component is the appropriate tool. This component (shown in Figure 13-19) displays a modal dialog box that allows a user to browse and select folders. It also allows users to create new folders from within the FolderBrowserDialog component. If you want to enable file selection instead of folders, use the OpenFile-Dialog component. When the FolderBrowserDialog is added to a Windows Form, it appears in the tray at the bottom of the Windows Forms Designer.

Figure 13-19: The FolderBrowserDialog component

As with most dialog components, the FolderBrowserDialog component is displayed at run time using the ShowDialog method. You can set the RootFolder property of the FolderBrowserDialog component to start navigation in a pre-defined folder upon opening the dialog box. You can retrieve the user-selected path as a string using the SelectedPath property.

The FontDialog Component

The FontDialog component (shown in Figure 13-20) is the standard dialog box used to display the installed fonts for a given system. You can use this control with other controls to allow the selection of user-defined fonts.

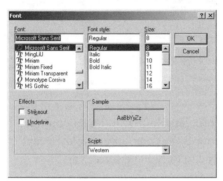

Figure 13-20: The FontDialog component

You can change the appearance of the FontDialog component through a number of properties. The Font and Color properties are what set the selections of the dialog box. The Font property sets the font, style, size, script, and effects. By default, the dialog box shows list boxes for font, font style, and size; check boxes for effects like strikeout and underline; a drop-down list for script; and a sample of how the font will appear.

The GroupBox Control

Unlike the Frame control utilized by VBA, Windows Forms use a GroupBox control (shown in Figure 13-21) to identify control groups. Typically, group boxes are used to divide a Windows Form into discrete areas of functionality, and provide a visual cue to the user to indicate a discrete set of choices. The caption of a group box is defined by its Text property. This GroupBox control is also a convenient mechanism to use at design time to set up groups or to add controls to a group.

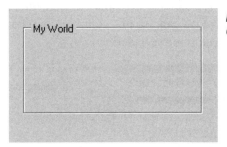

Figure 13-21: The GroupBox control

GroupBoxes are very similar to Panel controls, the difference being that GroupBoxes can only display a caption, while Panel controls can only have scroll bars.

The HelpProvider Component

The HelpProvider component of Windows Forms associates an HTML Help 1.x Help file of type .chm or .htm with your Windows application. The HelpProvider component allows the other controls to expose the Help properties of the HelpProvider component. This allows you to provide context-sensitive help for specific controls on your Windows Form, a particular dialog box, or even a specific control on a dialog box. You can even open a help file to a specific area, such as the main page of a table of contents, an index, or a search function.

The ImageList Component

The ImageList component (shown in Figure 13-22) is used to store multiple images. These images can then be utilized and displayed by other controls on the container. The ImageList control works with any control that has an ImageList property, including ListView, TreeView, ToolBar, TabControl, Button, CheckBox, RadioButton, and Label controls. It also works with the ListView control, which has both SmallImageList and LargeImageList properties.

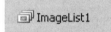

Figure 13-22: The ImageList component

The key property is the Images property. This property contains the catalog of pictures to be used by the associated control. Each individual image can be accessed by its associated index value. The ColorDepth property determines the number of colors for the associated images. All images for a given ImageList will be displayed at the same size, which is set by the ImageSize property. If any image in the collection is larger than the predefined size, it will be scaled to fit.

The Label Control

Label controls are used to display text or images that cannot be edited by the user. They are used to provide a description next to another control. You can also write code that changes the caption displayed by a label in response to events at run time. Labels cannot receive focus, so they can be used to display access keys for other controls. An access key allows a user to select a control by pressing the Alt+access key combination. The Alignment property of the Label control determines the alignment of the text within the label.

The ListBox Control

The ListBox control (shown in Figure 13-23) displays a list of selectable items, and is similar to the ListBox in VBA. Scroll bars are automatically added if the total number of items exceeds the number that can be displayed. The control also supports multiple columns that can utilize horizontal scroll bars.

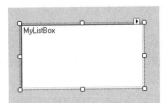

Figure 13-23: The ListBox control

Developers can control scroll appearance manually using the ScrollAlwaysVisible property of the ListBox control. When set to True, this property makes the scroll bar appear even if the number of items doesn't exceed the amount that can be displayed. The SelectionMode property determines the number of list items that can be selected at one time.

The ListView Control

The ListView control (shown in Figure 13-24) display lists of items with associated icons. The control has four view modes: LargeIcon, SmallIcon, List, and Details. LargeIcon mode displays large icons next to the item text; the items appear in multiple columns if the control is large enough. SmallIcon mode is the same except that it displays small icons. List mode displays small icons but is always in a single column. Details mode displays items in multiple columns.

Figure 13-24: The ListView control

The key property of the ListView control is the Items property, which contains the items displayed by the control. The SelectedItems property contains a collection of the items currently selected in the control. If the MultiSelect property is set to True, the user can select multiple items (to drag and drop several items at a time to another control, for example). If the CheckBoxes property is set to

True, the ListView control can display check boxes next to the items.

The MonthCalendar Control

The MonthCalender control (shown in Figure 13-25) allows you to select more than one date or even specify a range of dates. This control presents an intuitive graphical interface for users to view and set basic date information, displaying a calendar as a grid containing the numbered days of the month. The dates of this calendar are arranged in columns underneath the days of the week. You can navigate to different months by clicking the forward or back arrow buttons on either side of the month caption.

Figure 13-25: The MonthCalendar control

In addition, the MonthCalendar control's appearance is highly configurable and is very similar in look and feel to the Date controls used by Outlook. The control defaults to today's date, which is shown with a circle around it. The currently selected date is also noted at the bottom of the grid. Week numbers can be added to the calendar by setting the ShowWeekNumbers property to True. Sunday is shown as the first day of the week by default, but the FirstDayOfWeek property allows you to specify any date.

To get the control's selected values you can use the SelectionRange property of the MonthCalendar control. This returns the range of dates selected in the control. The maximum number of days that can be selected is set in the MaxSelectionCount property. The earliest and latest dates are set with the MinDate and MaxDate properties.

The NotifyIcon Component

The NotifyIcon component is used to display information to a user about what processes are running in the background. Each NotifyIcon component displays a single icon in the status area at the bottom of the screen. If you have three background processes and wish to display an icon for each, you must add three NotifyIcon components to the form. The primary properties used when working with the NotifyIcon component are the Icon and Visible properties. The Icon property specifies the icon that appears in the status area, while the Visible property controls whether or not the icon is displayed.

The NumericUpDown Control

As previously mentioned, the NumericUpDown control (shown in Figure 13-26) is essentially a text box with a pair of up and down arrows. This control displays and sets a single numeric value from a predefined list

Figure 13-26: The NumericUpDown control

of choices. The user can increment and decrement the number by clicking up and down arrows, by pressing the Up and Down Arrow keys, or by typing a number.

The Value property of the NumericUpDown control defines the current number selected in the control. The Increment property sets the amount that the value is adjusted by when the user clicks an up or down button. When the user moves the focus away from the control, the value will be validated against the minimum and maximum values.

The Panel Control

The Panel control is conceptually similar to the previously mentioned GroupBox control and is used to group other controls together. It is somewhat more limited in that a Panel control can only have scroll bars, while a GroupBox control can display a caption.

To display scroll bars, set the AutoScroll property to True. You can also customize the appearance of the panel by setting the BackColor, BackgroundImage, and BorderStyle properties of the Panel control. The BorderStyle property determines if the panel is outlined with no visible border (None), a plain line (FixedSingle), or a shadowed line (Fixed3d).

The PictureBox Control

The PictureBox control is somewhat similar to the classic VBA Picture control. This control is used to display graphics in bitmap, GIF, JPEG, metafile, or icon format. The Image property of the PictureBox control determines the picture type to be displayed. This property can be set at run time or at design time. The SizeMode property determines whether or not the control automatically resizes to fit the image.

The PrintDialog Component

The PrintDialog component doesn't have much application in the context of VSTO or VBA programming as we are usually interacting with a document whose parent application provides the print capability. The PrintDialog component is a preconfigured dialog box commonly seen in many Windows applications and is used to select a printer, choose the pages to print, and determine other print-related settings in Windows applications. This dialog can be used as an easy solution to enable printer and print-related settings selection without the necessity of creating your own custom print dialog box. This dialog also supports advanced print options such as print all, print a selected page range, or print a selection, so that users can print selected parts of their documents.

The PrintDocument Component

Just like the PrintDialog component, the PrintDocument component doesn't have much application in the context of VSTO or VBA programming. This component is used to set the properties that determine what will be printed and how it will be printed. It is typically used in connection with the PrintDialog component to control all aspects of document printing.

The PrintPreview Control

The PrintPreview control is used to display a PrintDocument as it will appear when printed. Again, since we usually deal with documents whose parent application provides the printing capabilities, this control doesn't have much application for VSTO or VBA. The PrintPreview control has no user interface elements, and is used only if you wish to write your own print preview user interface. The control's key property is the Document property, which sets the document to be previewed. The Columns and Rows properties of the PrintPreview control determine the number of pages displayed horizontally and vertically on the control. The Antialiasing property can be set to True to make the text appear smoother, but it can also make the display slower.

The ProgressBar Control

The Windows Forms ProgressBar control (shown in Figure 13-27) is used to indicate progress by displaying a series of rectangles in a horizontal bar from left to right. The

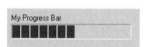

Figure 13-27: The ProgressBar control

progress bar is "filled" when progress reaches 100%. Progress bars are typically used to notify users of a slow process that requires a wait period.

The key properties of the ProgressBar control are the Value, Minimum, and Maximum properties. The Minimum and Maximum properties set the maximum and minimum values that the progress bar can display. ProgressBars are usually controlled within a loop structure that allows the Value property to be incremented at certain intervals. The Value property represents the progress that has been made toward completing the given operation. Since the progress is represented with rectangles, the actual progress can only be shown as an approximation.

The RadioButton Control

A RadioButton control (shown in Figure 13-28) presents two or more mutually exclusive choices to the user. Radio buttons are used to query the user for a specific choice, in contrast to check boxes, which allow the user to select one or many choices.

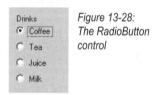

Figure 13-28:
The RadioButton
control

When a user selects a radio button, the Click event handler is fired and the control's Checked property is set to True. The CheckedChanged event is raised if the value of the Checked property changes. The default AutoCheck property automatically clears all other buttons in a group when the user selects a given radio button. The AutoCheck property should be used sparingly, and is only set to False when manual validation code is necessary to make sure the button selected is an allowable option.

The SaveFileDialog Component

The SaveFileDialog component (shown in Figure 13-29) allows you to display the Windows SaveFileDialog. This control inherits from the CommonDialog class. When developing in VBA, programmers commonly utilized the application's Save dialog via the Dialogs object, or made use of the Windows Common Controls. You can open a file in read/write mode using the OpenFile method. When a SaveFileDialog is added to a form, it appears in the tray at the bottom of the Windows Forms Designer.

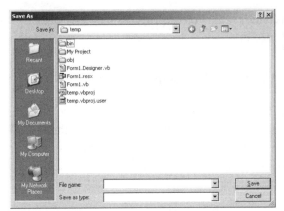

Figure 13-29: The SaveFileDialog component

The Splitter Control

The Splitter control allows users to resize run-time controls. It is often used on forms with controls that have varying lengths of data to present. If the width of the information can vary at run time, you may want to use a splitter control so the user can resize the control to fully view the information. The user can position the mouse over the undocked edge of a control and resize it by pulling the edge forward or backward. The splitter control resizes the docked control that is immediately before it.

The Tab Control

Adding tabs to a Windows Form can be achieved using the Tab control (shown in Figure 13-30). This control allows multiple tabs, similar to the VBA MultiPage and TabStrip controls. The Tab control is very robust in that the tabs can contain just about any other control. The most important property of the Tab control is the TabPages property, which contains the individual tabs. Each individual tab is a TabPage object. When a tab is clicked, it raises the Click event for that TabPage object.

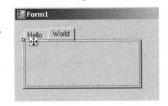

Figure 13-30: The Tab control

The TextBox Control

Text boxes are used to get input from the user or to display text. The TextBox control (shown in Figure 13-31) is generally used to allow a user to edit text found within the TextBox control; however, these text

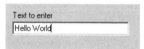

Figure 13-31: The TextBox control

boxes can also be made read-only. Text boxes do not allow font manipulation such as bolding, italics, or underlining. These manipulations are reserved for the more robust RichTextBox control. Text boxes can display multiple lines, wrap text to the size of the control, and add basic formatting. The TextBox control provides a single format style for text displayed or entered into the control.

The primary difference between a Windows Form text box and a VBA text box is that in the Windows Form version, you access the control's displayed text through the Text property. The default text box can contain up to 2,048 characters, but you can increase that value by setting the MultiLine property to True. This expands the value so that the text box can contain up to 32 KB of text.

The Timer Component

The Timer component specifies the length of the interval by setting the value of the Interval property, which is measured in milliseconds. The Tick event is fired at every interval and can be set to execute code at specific times. The key methods of the Timer component are Start and Stop, which turn the timer on and off, respectively. The Timer is reset when it is switched off. Keep in mind that there is no way to pause a Timer component.

The ToolBar Control

One of the limitations of VBA UserForms is that they could not display a menu at the top of the form. Although this was basic functionality, MSForms didn't provide the ability without making numerous API calls. The ToolBar control (shown in Figure 13-32) of the Windows Form displays a row of drop-down

Figure 13-32: The ToolBar control

menus and buttons that activate commands. These buttons can be set to appear and behave as push buttons, drop-down menus, or separators. These toolbars can be used to model your application after traditional Windows applications where menus (such as File, Edit, View, etc.) are provided to allow quick access to an application's most frequently used functions and commands.

The ToolBar control is dockable and can be moved from the top of its parent window to any side of the window. The ToolBar control also supports tooltips, which are displayed when the user positions the mouse pointer over a toolbar button. The toolbar's appearance is controlled via an Appearance property that allows the toolbar buttons to appear either three-dimensional or flat. When set to Flat, the buttons appear three-dimensional when the mouse is positioned over the them. Toolbar buttons can be divided into logical groups by using separators. A separator is simply another button with the Style property set to Separator, which makes it appear as an empty space or a line on the toolbar.

The ToolTip Component

The ToolTip component (shown in Figure 13-33) displays text when the user places the cursor above a control in a Windows Form. This text is displayed in a shadowed box and can be associated with any control on the form. Tooltips allow you to provide the user with a hint about the control's use while still conserving space on the form.

A ToolTip component provides a ToolTip property for multiple controls on a Windows Form. The key methods of the ToolTip component are SetToolTip and GetToolTip. You can use the SetToolTip method to set the tooltips displayed for controls.

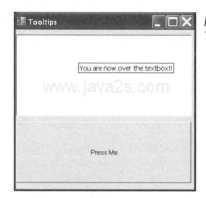

Figure 13-33: The ToolTip component

The TrackBar Control

The TrackBar control (shown in Figure 13-34) allows users to navigate a large set of information easily. Visually, the control looks like a slider on the form

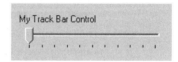

Figure 13-34: The TrackBar control

and can be used to visually adjust a numeric setting. The TrackBar control is comprised of a sliding indicator (also referred to as a thumb) and incremental tick marks. The sliding indicator's position along the tick marks corresponds to the Value property. Tick marks are placed at specific intervals and provide a visual indicator of the control's relative value.

The key properties of the TrackBar control are Value, TickFrequency, Minimum, and Maximum. Minimum and Maximum are the smallest and largest values that can be represented on the track bar. TickFrequency is the property that sets the spacing of the ticks.

The TreeView Control

The Windows Forms TreeView control (shown in Figure 13-35) has many improvements over its VBA counterpart. This TreeView control displays a hierarchical set of nodes similar to Windows Explorer in both look and feel. Each node can contain other child nodes, and parent nodes can be displayed as expanded or collapsed. In addition, if the

CheckBoxes property of the TreeView control is set to True, the TreeView will display check boxes next to the nodes.

Figure 13-35: The TreeView control

The primary properties of the TreeView control are Nodes and SelectedNode. The SelectedNode property sets the currently selected node, while the Nodes property contains the list of top-level nodes in the tree view. The TreeView control also supports icon images that are displayed next to the nodes. These images are taken from an associated ImageList control, which can be set in the TreeView's ImageList property.

Conclusion

Although Visual Basic for Applications is a powerful tool, we can extend our developmental skills beyond VBA by using Visual Basic 9.0, which is used in Visual Studio 2008. Visual Studio offers a full-fledged development environment that enables the developer to do things that VBA simply does not offer. This chapter served to compare and contrast the many similarities and even more differences between VBA and Visual Basic 9.0. Namely, this chapter looked at the IDE (Integrated Development Environment), language, and forms offered by both environments and briefly discussed the properties, syntax, and general discrepancies found between the two offerings.

Chapter 14

Understanding .NET

Introduction

In the previous chapter we compared the various similarities and differences between Visual Basic for Applications and Visual Studio. After going through the multitude of features offered by Visual Basic through Visual Studio 2008, you can see that developing with Visual Basic 9.0 in Visual Studio 2008 can give you much more control over your code and many more features as well. However, before we begin building Visual Studio 2008 Office applications, it's important to have a solid understanding of the Microsoft .NET Framework and how it interacts with COM applications such as those of Office. With the introduction of the .NET Framework, tremendous change was brought to the development of Windows applications. In this chapter we will look at the inner workings of the .NET Framework to help you get a more complete understanding of developing Office 2007 applications through Visual Studio 2008.

Microsoft .NET

At its core, Microsoft .NET is a set of software components that exist inside a structure. This structure is referred to as a framework, which is used for building and running software. The Microsoft .NET Framework not only includes traditional software, but it also includes web-based applications, smart client applications, and XML components. The .NET Framework is an integrated Windows component for building and running modern software applications and web services. The .NET Framework supports over 20 different programming languages and also enables developers to focus on the core business logic code, making it easier than ever before to build, deploy, and administer applications. At its core, the .NET Framework is composed of the Common Language Runtime and a unified set of class libraries. In the following sections, we will take an in-depth look at these components.

The Common Language Runtime of .NET

One of the most basic elements of the .NET Framework is the Common Language Runtime (CLR), which is illustrated in Figure 14-1. The CLR utilizes a run-time environment for the execution of code written in any of the .NET languages. The CLR is in charge of managing the execution of .NET code, as well as memory and object lifetime management. In addition to these management services, the CLR allows developers to perform debugging, exception handling, and inheritance across multiple languages. Performing these tasks requires that the language compilers follow the Common Language Specification (CLS), which describes a subset of the data types supported by the CLR that are common to all of the languages used in .NET.

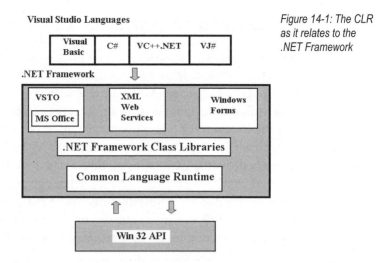

Figure 14-1: The CLR
as it relates to the
.NET Framework

The CLR introduced some improvements over previous Microsoft development foundations. One of the biggest improvements is that the CLR enables cross-language object inheritance and exception handling. This means that objects aren't bound to a single language, which can greatly improve developer productivity. You can write code in any supported language that targets the .NET runtime and the objects you create can be inherited seamlessly by other languages. Likewise, any exceptions raised in those objects will appear exactly like native exceptions because they all conform to the .NET error-handling standards.

The CLR also greatly improves the handling of memory management tasks, which means that developers no longer need to worry about memory allocation. The CLR is now responsible for allocating the memory required by an object and utilizes automatic garbage collection to release resources when they're no longer used. Cross-language integration results in more easily reusable code, and automatic resource management results in more robust programs.

The Microsoft Intermediate Language

After interpreting your code, the compiler of the .NET Framework turns your code into a language called Microsoft Intermediate Language (MSIL, or IL for short). When the code is first executed, the just-in-time (JIT) compiler evaluates the IL and turns it into executable machine code for the target machine. Optionally, IL assemblies may be compiled to native code by the CLR at install time using a utility called Native Image Generator (Ngen.exe). Although at some cost to performance due to optimizations available during JIT compilation, compiling to native code can improve startup time. Figure 14-2 gives a visual illustration of how VB .NET code is converted into machine code.

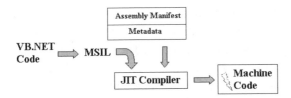

Figure 14-2: Flow chart of VB .NET code to machine code process

Any code that is compiled to IL and managed by the CLR is referred to as *managed code*. The reason behind this naming is because the CLR takes responsibility for managing the execution of the code, including the instantiation of objects, allocation of memory, and garbage collection of objects and memory.

Applications can be written in any .NET-supported language and compiled into managed code that is executed by the CLR. These types of application components are referred to as .NET managed assemblies, or more commonly as just *assemblies*. Conceptually, an assembly is very similar to a COM component. The difference is that COM components utilize type libraries that describe their interface. Assemblies use a file called a manifest to describe their interface. This manifest contains a set of metadata that describes the contents of the assembly.

An important benefit of the manifest is that it is physically a part of the assembly and also helps to describe it. Assemblies do not need to be registered in order to work on a machine (assuming all other prerequisites are met).

The metadata associated with an assembly describes the dependencies and version information associated with the assembly. Not only does this make it much easier to ensure that all necessary dependencies of an assembly are met, but it is now possible for multiple versions of the same assembly to run side by side on the same computer without conflict. This was a major design goal of the .NET Framework and helped eliminate the DLL issues that were common problems that plagued COM developers for many years. However, there should be no such problems in using .NET. As long as the consuming application knows which version of an assembly it's designed to use, it can locate the correct version among multiple versions of the same assembly by querying the assembly's metadata.

Assemblies

In the previous section we briefly mentioned what an assembly is. Now let's take a closer look at assemblies and the benefits they provide. What follows in this section is a brief introduction to .NET assemblies and how they can be used for your VSTO projects. One of the biggest changes when Microsoft moved to the .NET Framework was the departure from stand-alone executables and to the introduction of assemblies. The term "assembly" was not new when Microsoft introduced .NET; the concepts underlying the framework had been around for several years.

Simply put, an *assembly* is the smallest unit of versioning, security, deployment, version control, and reusability of code in .NET Framework. An assembly can contain one or more files. A single file assembly contains all the requirements of that assembly in a single file. On the other hand, a multi-file assembly contains a number of .NET modules and is used for large-scale applications.

At its essence, an assembly is the .NET equivalent of the longtime standard known as the executable file. When working with .NET, the end result of an assembly will be an .exe or .dll just like with VB 6 and other languages. However, the file extension is about the only thing that remains the same. The internal organization of the .NET assembly is entirely different from traditional executables. Most notably, in the .NET world, executables are actually comprised of an MSIL program (unless you are using Ngen.exe to create a native code executable).

When you execute a .NET assembly, you're really just invoking the CLR, which compiles the assembly into native code just before it's executed. This is called the .NET just-in-time (JIT) compiler.

This new architecture has several advantages over the previous platform. For example, in previous platforms, you had to create full installation packages for even the smallest of components. With this new architecture, you can "install" components by simply copying them to a new location. There is no need to worry about registering components on a client's machine. In previous versions of Visual Basic (up to VB 6), programmers had to consider how to properly register their applications and COM components in the Windows Registry. It was a common to see new versions "breaking" end-user machines because a component was overwritten with a later version that omitted earlier functionality.

The .NET architecture keeps track of every component with a unique version number. When developing an assembly, you can target specific versions of a component. Another major benefit is that these components can be programmed using different languages. After they're compiled into an assembly, they all look the same to the CLR. This has an enormous impact, as different programmers working on the same project can use different languages.

Yet another benefit is that "resources," such as graphic files, can be embedded right in the assembly for ease of updating, deploying your system, and adding security measures so that the resource doesn't get altered or replaced with something else. Assemblies can even utilize several individual files if necessary. Figure 14-3 illustrates a .NET assembly and its corresponding pieces.

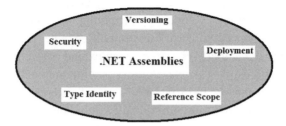

Figure 14-3: The pieces that comprise a unit that is a .NET assembly

In contrast to this method, in traditional COM programming, shared components were usually stored in the System directory and "registered" in Windows so other programs could locate them. This was the primary reason why the Windows Registry became corrupt or installing one application would inadvertently break another. The .NET architecture eliminated this issue. The .NET architecture still uses the Registry, but not to identify components. In .NET, every assembly contains a manifest, which provides the same functionality that was formerly placed in the Registry. The manifest contains metadata that tells the CLR what it needs to execute the assembly instructions.

The CLR needs the specific version number of components used by the assembly. If you reference your own component, you'll need to specify the versioning and security to ensure that the right component is used. This is why you can run several instances of the .NET Framework and the COM-based Visual Studio 6 side by side. Each version uses only the components designed and tested for it.

The main reason that COM located most resources in the Windows System directory was to provide a central location for all applications. Although this works for components that are shared by many different programs, if the solution is custom developed, COM still requires the same type of registration and possible access by other applications. The .NET architecture allows you to easily locate the components in the application's root directory.

The .NET Framework Class Library

The .NET Framework class library is designed to support Visual Basic developers by providing base classes from which developers can inherit. Functionality can be inherited from other developers' classes or even extend base classes provided by Microsoft. This class library is a hierarchical set of .NET classes that developers can use in order to implement both basic and advanced functionality into their own applications. These classes are referred to as namespaces, and are an integral part of programming in Visual Basic 9.0. As the name implies, all class names with a given namespace must be unique.

Namespaces utilize a dot notation syntax scheme to describe a hierarchical organization. This naming convention allows developers to easily organize related classes and extend their functionality. Namespaces adhere to the following naming pattern: companyname.technology. Microsoft components all follow this convention. For instance, the Microsoft Win32 namespace (a Microsoft-created namespace) contains classes that enable an application to access the Win32 API set. Another example of this naming scheme within the .NET Framework is the System.Data namespace, which is the root level of the ADO.NET classes (a class we will discuss in a bit).

Namespaces in .NET

The .NET Framework makes it easy for you to implement advanced functionality in your application by making use of the different .NET namespaces and classes in your code. To use the classes contained in a given namespace, all you have to do is include an import directive in your application. Knowing which namespace provides support for what type of functionality is the most difficult part of using the .NET Framework class libraries.

By default, your VSTO applications (in fact, all .NET applications) include the System namespace, which provides basic support for variables and data types like objects, bytes,

Int32, and strings, as well as the Exception classes that provide structured error handling. However, to provide support for other functions, you need to include various namespaces from the .NET Framework class libraries.

ADO.NET is a set of computer software components that can be used by programmers to access data and data services. This is defined in the System.Data namespace. Using this namespace to provide database access for your VSTO solution is a great example of accessing data and data services. You will need to include the System.Data namespace in your VSTO solution in order to use ADO.NET and access databases. This will enable your solution to take advantage of the data access classes and methods provided by the ADO.NET technology.

Microsoft Namespaces

The entire set of functionality in .NET is built on top of different namespaces. In fact, the languages supported by the .NET Framework each have their own namespace. The following table provides an overview of the different Microsoft programming language namespaces provided as part of the .NET Framework. To make you more productive, these language namespaces are provided as part of .NET and Visual Studio. It's entirely possible to write .NET applications without the use of Visual Studio.

Namespace	Description
Microsoft.CSharp	Contains the classes required to compile C# source code.
Microsoft.JScript	Contains the classes required to support the JScript runtime.
Microsoft.VisualBasic	Contains the classes required to compile Visual Basic .NET source code as well as the Visual Basic runtime.
Microsoft.Vsa	Provides classes that enable you to integrate the .NET scripting interface in your applications.
Microsoft.Win32	Contains the classes that enable your application to handle events that are raised by the system, as well as classes that enable your application to read and write to the Registry.

The following table provides an overview of the different namespaces provided by the System namespace in the .NET Framework class library.

Namespace	Description
System	The most fundamental of all the .NET Framework namespaces; it must be used by all applications, and it contains the classes that represent the basic data types.
System.CodeDom	Contains classes that are used to represent a source code document.
System.Collections	Contains classes used to manage collections of objects.
System.ComponentModel	Provides classes that control the design-time and run-time behavior of components and controls.
System.Configuration	Contains classes that enable your application to access the .NET Framework configuration settings.
System.Data	Provides support for ADO.NET and its database access classes and data types. The basic ADO.NET data management classes contained in the System.Data Namespace are the DataSet and DataTable classes that enable disconnected data access for Windows and web-based applications.
System.Diagnostics	Contains classes that enable your application to manage system processes as well as read the system event logs and performance monitor counters.
System.DirectoryServices	Contains classes that enable your application to access the Active Directory via the ADSI (Active Directory Services Interface).
System.Drawing	Contains classes that access the system's GDI+ functions, which provide graphics support.
System.EnterpriseServices	Contains classes that provide access to COM+ for *n*-tiered enterprise application support.
System.Globalization	Contains classes that enable National Language Support (NLS) as well as support for Calendar objects.
System.IO	Contains classes that enable your applications to read and write to data streams either synchronously or asynchronously.
System.Management	Contains classes that provide access to the WMI (Windows Management Interface) infrastructure to provide systems monitoring and management support.

Namespace	Description
System.Messaging	Contains classes that enable your application to read and write messages for the Microsoft Messaging Queuing technology.
System.Net	Contains classes that enable your application to conduct network communications using HTTP, as well as TCP and UDP sockets.
System.Reflection	Contains classes that enable the application to read the metadata of a loaded assembly.
System.Resources	Contains classes that enable your application to store and load regional-specific resources.
System.Runtime.CompilerServices	Contains classes that allow compiler developers to control aspects of the runtime behavior of the CLR.
System.Runtime.InteropServices	Contains classes that enable your .NET applications to interface with COM (Component Object Model) objects and native Win32 APIs (application program interfaces).
System.Runtime.Remoting	Contains classes that enable your application to manage remote objects required for developing distributed applications.
System.Runtime.Serialization	Contains classes that allow your applications to store and load objects by converting them into a sequential stream of bytes (serialization).
System.Security	Contains classes that enable your application to control .NET Framework security features. These classes can manage security features such as permissions, policies, and cryptography.
System.ServiceProcess	Contains classes that allow your applications to create, install, and manage Windows services.
System.Text	Contains classes that represent ASCII, Unicode, UTF-7, and UTF-8 character sets.
System.Threading	Contains classes that enable you to develop multithreaded applications.
System.Timers	Contains classes that permit your application to raise an event following a specified interval of time.
System.Web	Contains a set of classes that define ASP.NET. These classes essentially provide support for web browser to web server interaction. For example, different classes contained in this namespace support web hosting, mail, security, and user interface components.

Namespace	Description
System.Windows.Forms	Contains the classes that enable the development of Windows-based applications.
System.Xml	Contains a set of classes that enable your application to work with XML documents.

Office Primary Interoperability Assemblies (PIAs)

In order to develop Visual Basic 9.0 Office solutions, it's necessary to first have a good understanding of how the .NET-based languages interface with Office applications. The underlying structure of Office applications is based in COM, which was the predecessor to .NET technology. When you are creating VSTO solutions, you are working with managed code. These managed assemblies interface with Office applications via the use of Office Primary Interop (short for Interoperability) Assemblies, or PIAs.

These PIAs are a .NET technology that essentially wraps the native COM Office Application objects in managed code. The underlying Office applications are all written in unmanaged code and expose traditional COM interfaces. The PIAs allow your managed code (written in Visual Studio) to interact with the unmanaged Office application code. These PIAs are just a set of .NET classes that have been compiled into the PIA. Figure 14-4 shows how PIAs fit into the scheme of having your code interact with Office application code.

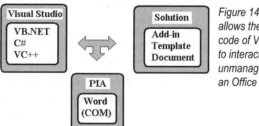

Figure 14-4: PIA allows the managed code of Visual Studio to interact with the unmanaged code of an Office application.

It's important to note that you could simply use the Type Library Importer (TLBIMP) to work with the objects in Office applications. TLBIMP is used to convert the type definitions found within a COM type library into equivalent definitions in a common language runtime assembly. (You can find out more about TLBIMP at http://msdn2.microsoft.com/en-us/library/tt0cf3sx(VS.80).aspx.) The actual command-line syntax to use TLBIMP is simply "tlbimp.exe (switches)". The output of TLBIMP is a binary file (an assembly) that contains run-time metadata for the types defined within the original type library. Essentially, in using TLBIMP, you'd be creating your own interop assembly. Keep in mind that any interop assembly you create yourself will not be as robust or as finely tuned as the officially supported PIA supplied by Microsoft. The PIA distinction is reserved for the Microsoft created and supported interop assemblies.

In previous versions of Visual Studio, it was necessary to install the PIAs separately and customize them through the Office Installation Wizard; however, these PIAs are created by default with Visual Studio 2008.

A computer on which the CLR is installed has a machine-wide code cache called the Global Assembly Cache (GAC for short) that stores those assemblies that specifically need to be shared by several applications. The GAC exists as part of the Assembly subdirectory of the Windows directory and is where PIAs are housed. We will discuss the GAC further in the next section.

As a general guideline, assembly dependencies are private, and assemblies should be stored in the application directory (unless it is required to share an assembly, such as the PIA). It is also not necessary to install assemblies into the GAC to make them accessible to COM, interop, or unmanaged code.

The Global Assembly Cache

To provide an overall organizing medium for components that really need to be shared among programs, utilize the Global Assembly Cache (GAC). Windows offers several customized ways of working with the GAC. You can simply browse to the Assembly subdirectory of the Windows directory using Windows Explorer, as shown in Figure 14-5.

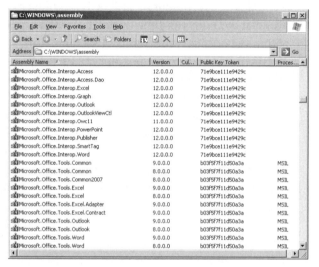

Figure 14-5: To reach the GAC, browse to the Assembly subdirectory of the Windows directory.

You may notice that the Paste option isn't available while browsing the Assembly subdirectory. This is because, rather than just copying files to this directory, assemblies must be properly installed in the GAC. The subdirectory structure is also hidden in the Windows Explorer view of the GAC. In order to browse the GAC's directory structure and view the assemblies, you'll need to bypass the Windows Explorer shell extension that controls the default GAC view. You can get to a more accessible version of the GAC by selecting **Start | Run** and typing **%systemroot%\assembly\GAC**. This is illustrated in Figure 14-6.

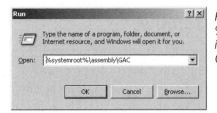

Figure 14-6: Type
%systemroot%\assembly\GAC
in the Run dialog to browse the
GAC.

Once you have run the previous statement, you'll notice that the assemblies appear as ordinary files and you are free to browse the GAC. Figure 14-7 shows the VSTO PIAs as they are stored in the GAC. You can explore the PIA subfolders to see what is stored inside them.

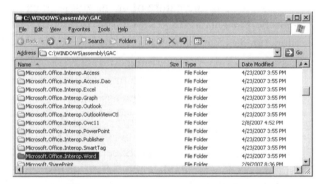

Figure 14-7: Office's PIAs being displayed in the GAC

When installing .NET, some additional tools are installed in Windows to help you manage .NET and assemblies. These tools can be accessed by selecting **Start | Control Panel | Performance and Maintenance | Administrative Tools | Microsoft .NET 2.0 Configuration**. (Note that XP omits the Performance and Maintenance option.)

You can use this tool to view the existing components or install a component into the GAC. Before allowing copying functionality, the tool forces you to give the component a strong name. Using the .NET 2.0 configuration tool allows you to target a specific version of a component. Just select the particular component you want to be used and specify the range of versions that should use it.

Using the .NET Assembly

In this section we will examine the executable programs contained in the .NET namespaces. As previously discussed, assemblies are just a new way of packaging and describing executable code. Just as they were with programs produced by earlier compilers, the file extensions for .NET assemblies are typically .exe or .dll. However, unlike earlier programs that contain native x86 machine instructions, the output executables of the .NET compilers contain a combination of MSIL (Microsoft Intermediate Language), metadata, and resources such as bitmaps.

Because of the nature of an assembly, it cannot run without the presence of the .NET CLR. Proper execution is also dependent upon the metadata information that's stored in the assembly. This information is known as the *manifest* (we will discuss these shortly). These manifests contain information about the resources within the assembly, as well as its dependencies. The executable code, or MSIL, is a platform-independent, intermediate language that is on a higher level than the native machine code produced by older compilers. Unlike standard x86 executable code, MSIL utilizes the concept of objects. MSIL has native instructions that can instantiate and access object properties. Additionally, MSIL has functionality to raise and catch exceptions.

Also mentioned before, an assembly can contain a wide range of resources, including bitmaps, icons, and other binary files that are used by the application. Assemblies can also be broken into multiple files. For instance, an assembly could be split into three different files where one contains the metadata, another contains the MSIL, and another contains the resources and bitmaps used by the application.

Additional Assembly Features

In addition to containing the executable program instructions, assemblies occupy several important roles in the .NET Framework. First, assemblies define a security boundary. The assembly is the default unit to which .NET permissions are granted. This security information enables a very granular level of security that was never possible with Win32 applications. .NET security can restrict and grant access at the function level of an application.

Next, the assembly's manifest contains versioning information. This versioning information both identifies the current assembly and defines the version requirements for any required assemblies. Because each assembly carries its own version identification, as well as the version information of all dependent components, there is no possibility of an older versioned component or a similarly named component being accidentally installed and used. Yet another important job that assemblies take is that the assembly limits the scope of the types it contains. Each type is contained within the physical boundary of the assembly to which it belongs. Although types in different assemblies are identically named, they are completely different from the perspective of the CLR.

Assemblies are also the basic unit of deployment for a .NET application. When deploying a .NET application, you essentially just need to copy the assembly to the target system. The assembly's metadata is responsible for finding any required components.

You can create assemblies by specifying them as either private or shared. Private assemblies are used by a single application where only the same application domain can access them. These private assemblies are housed in the application's folder. The assemblies that we create are private by default unless we specifically make them shared. The shared or global assemblies have globally unique names and are stored in the GAC, which can be accessed by multiple applications.

Assemblies can be static or dynamic. Static assemblies are stored on disk as physical files while dynamic assemblies are not saved to disk before execution and are executed directly from memory. A static assembly resides in a PE (portable executable) file that's stored as an on-disk structure. A dynamic assembly is created and executed directly in memory.

Assembly Manifests

As mentioned earlier, the metadata in an assembly is called an assembly manifest. This manifest contains information about the types and resources that are externally visible outside the assembly. Furthermore, the metadata contains information about any dependencies that the assembly has. This information includes name, location, and version number information of a dependent assembly. The following table shows the various metadata found in an assembly's manifest.

Metadata	Description
Assembly name	The assembly name provides narrative text describing the assembly's name.
Culture	This is used to provide language-specific information that the assembly supports.
Information on referenced assemblies	This provides a list of other assemblies that are referenced within the assembly. It provides a mechanism to include information about the dependent assembly's name, metadata, and public key if the assembly is strong named.
List of all files in the assembly	This metadata provides a hash of each file contained in the assembly and a file name. It's important to remember that all files that make up the assembly must be in the same directory as the file containing the assembly manifest.
Strong name information	When an assembly has a strong name, this metadata includes public key information from the publisher.
Type reference information	This metadata is used by the runtime to map a type reference to the assembly. It contains the explicit type declaration and implementation usage of the assembly.
Version number	This includes both a major and minor version number, and a revision and build number. These numbers are used by the Common Language Runtime (CLR) to enforce version policy.

Including the metadata information as a part of the assembly has a couple of important advantages. The manifest architecture is the structure that finally eliminated the "DLL hell" that continues to plague COM-based Windows applications and also frees the application from dependencies on the Windows

Registry. DLL hell describes an all-too-common scenario experienced by Windows applications where new software installations inadvertently replace required application components such as DLLs with similarly named but incompatible components from a different version.

When this scenario occurs, the new application typically works, but it breaks an existing application that depend on the old component. Reinstalling the old software to restore the original component breaks the new application, and the cycle continues. Maintaining this versioning information in the metadata makes it possible to have side-by-side deployment where multiple versions of an assembly can be used simultaneously.

Because the metadata specifies exactly which version of the component is required and where that component is located, assemblies can load the dependent assemblies needed without fear of using an incompatible component. Because assemblies are self-describing, using the Registry isn't necessary to locate any of the dependent assemblies used in an application. Registering an assembly during installation is also unnecessary. This vastly simplifies the installation process and essentially enables an xcopy style of deployment, where assemblies can simply be copied to their destination system and executed. (Read more about xcopy at http://technet.microsoft.com/en-us/library/bb491035.aspx.) When using xcopy, you'll want to make sure you use the "/O" command-line switch to preserve security and ownership information. Otherwise, you'll copy it without security to another location and you could compromise your system.

Using Assembly Tools

Now that you are more familiar with assemblies, let's switch gears a bit and look at some important tools relating to assemblies. There are five basic utilities available when working with assemblies: MSIL Assembler (Ilasm.exe), MSIL Disassembler (Ildasm.exe), Strong Name (Sn.exe), Assembly Linker (Al.exe, which is not discussed here as it is outside the scope of this book), and Global Assembly Cache (Gacutil.exe). To access these tools, you need to either navigate to the appropriate directory in the .NET Framework or set your path to include the directory so that you can run these commands from anywhere on the command line. For example, if you're running Framework 3.5, the typical command would be (include the quotes because of the spaces in the name):

```
"C:\Program Files\Microsoft Visual Studio .NET
2005\SDK\v1.1\Bin\ILDASM.exe"
```

Microsoft provides a batch file to set the PATH to include the Framework SDK directory. The batch file opens a DOS console, sets the path for that window only, and closes it again. Remember that this is a command-line utility, so you can't just double-click it in Windows Explorer. A typical command to execute this batch file (named SDKVARS.bat) would be:

```
"C:\Program Files\Microsoft Visual Studio
9.0\SDK\3.5\Bin\SDKVARS.bat"
```

The MSIL Assembler and Disassembler Utilities

In some cases, you will want to either assemble or disassemble applications from the command line. Microsoft offers two convenient command-line utilities. To assemble applications, you can use the MSIL Assembler utility (Ilasm.exe). The MSIL Disassembler utility (Ildasm.exe) is used to disassemble an application and inspect the internals of an assembly. These utilities begin with "IL" because they deal with Microsoft Intermediate Language, the language used for all code within .NET assemblies.

If you've ever taken a class in assembly language, you understand why this is called "intermediate" language. Each type of processor supports a given instruction set. In assembly language, you are working at the most granular level available as far as programming goes. Assembly is a "low-level" language and in it you write statements such as "put" and "mov" to execute commands.

At the opposite end of the spectrum is VB.NET. VB.NET is a high-level language that abstracts many things away from the developer. Right in between VB.NET and assembly language is the IL. It's a low enough level language that it can be interpreted very fast, but it is also much more user friendly than assembly in that you can reasonably understand what the program is attempting to do by reading the code. You can run Ildasm.exe from the command line, as shown in Figure 14-8.

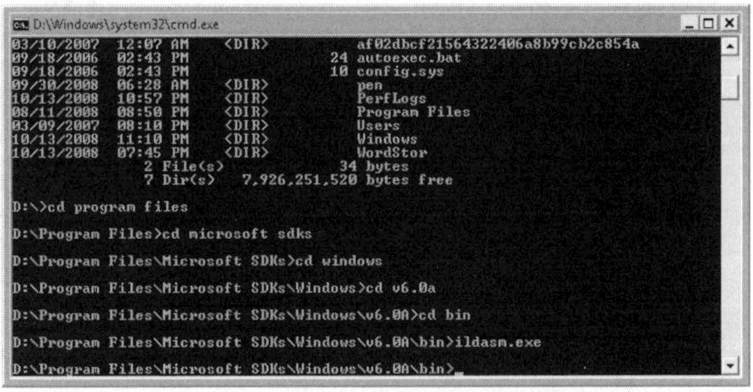

Figure 14-8: Running ILDASM from the command line

The MSIL Disassembler tool is one of the most useful tools for discovering exactly what is in your VB.NET assembly. ILDASM runs from the command line, but it opens a regular window to display results. Figure 14-9 shows the tool's evaluation of the permissions calculator. You can double-click the manifest (or any of the subsidiary items) to bring them up in a separate window. Like your assembly, the information reported by Ildsam.exe is in two sections: the manifest and the rest of the program. Figure 14-10 shows some of the metadata that is contained in the manifest. You can double-click the window shown in Figure 14-9 to display the assembly information in a separate window, as shown in Figure 14-10.

Figure 14-9: Running Ildasm.exe against the permissions calculator

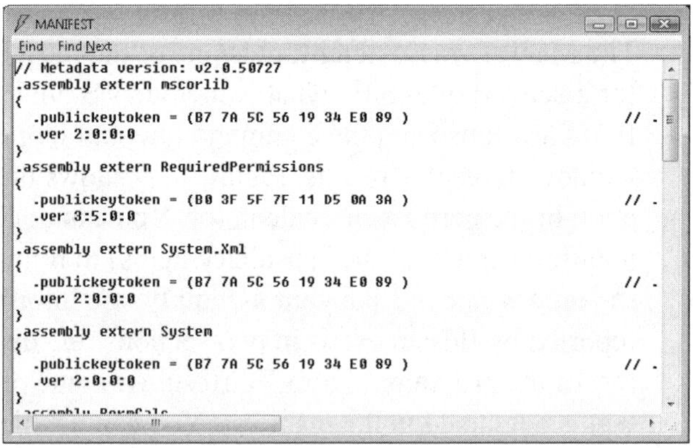

Figure 14-10: Assembly information

You can also use MSIL Disassembler to evaluate your own code. The tool converts the executable (.exe or .dll) created by a Visual Basic build into CIL source code. Let's take a look at an example of how to do this. To start, we'll need to write some VB.NET code at the command line. Simply start the command-line editor by typing **edit** at the command line to open a window like the one shown in Figure 14-11.

```
D:\Windows\system32\cmd.exe - edit                              _ □ ×
    File  Edit  Search  View  Options  Help
                              UNTITLED1
 Imports System
 Module TestProgram
         Sub Main()
                 Console.WriteLine("ILDasm Example")
                 Console.ReadLine()
         End Sub
 End Module_




 F1=Help                                      Line:7      Col:11
```

Figure 14-11: Using the command-line editor

In the editor, type the following code and use the Alt+F key combination to expand the drop-down so you can use the SaveAs functionality. By default, it will want to save the file in the current directory, but you may save the file wherever you like. Figure 14-12 shows the Save As dialog box that appears.

```
Imports System
Module TestProgram
Sub Main()
Console.WriteLine("ILDasm Example")
Console.ReadLine()
End Sub
End Module
```

Figure 14-12: The Save As dialog box

Once you've saved your VB file, you'll still need to compile it. You can also do this from the command line using the Visual Basic compiler (VBC.exe). This tool is not in the same directory, but if you already ran SDKVARS.bat you should be able to access it via the command line. If you can't, then simply do a search for "vbc.exe" and run the command from the appropriate directory for your version of the Framework. This will create a portable executable (PE) file called TestProgram.exe. Figure 14-13 shows the IL we just created, while Figure 14-14 shows the result of running Ildasm.exe against the executable file.

Figure 14-13: TestProgram CIL source code

Figure 14-14: Running Ildasm.exe against the TestProgram executable

The Strong Name Utility

Shared assemblies must have a "strong name" consisting of the name of the assembly, the version, a 64-bit hash of a public key (called a "token"), and the culture. You can think of a strong name as the .NET Framework equivalent of the old COM GUID. To provide a recognized strong name for an assembly, you can use the Strong Name utility (Sn.exe). The file it creates will also contain the public and private keys that an application would use.

Figure 14-15 shows how this utility can be run directly from the command line. In this case, we are simply creating an *.snk file, which we can then utilize in an assembly.

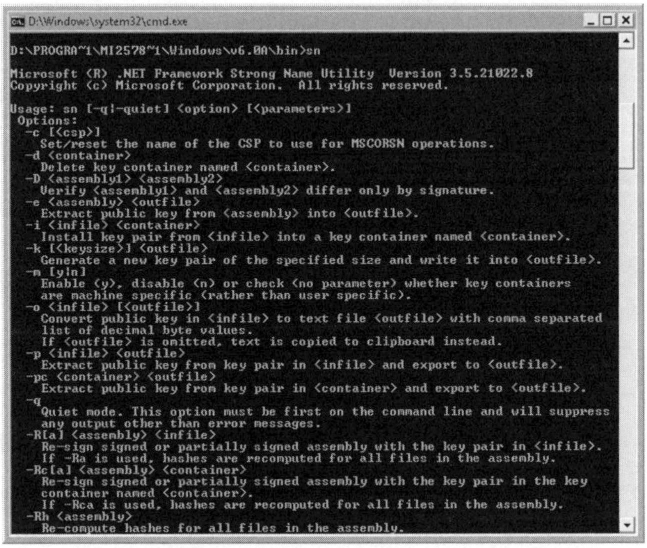

Figure 14-15: Using the Strong Name utility

The GAC Utility

The GAC utility (Gacutil.exe) is used to store assemblies into the Global Assembly Cache (GAC). Once in the GAC, the assembly will be globally shared and available for applications. You can run the Gacutil.exe utility from the command line to make the assembly testprogram.dll globally accessible, as shown below:

```
gacutil /i testprogram.dll
```

While it is true that assemblies in the GAC must have a strong name, the inverse is not true. A strong named assembly can also be placed somewhere other than the GAC; for example, it can be stored in the application's directory.

Assembly Security

Assembly security is controlled by policies that are enforced by the CLR. Basically, when an assembly is invoked, the CLR checks its policy settings to ensure that the code is safe to run in the given environment. It ensures this safety by checking the user, machine, application, and domain where the assembly is located. If it finds an appropriate policy, it will let the code execute.

In .NET, the assembly security information is referred to as "evidence." Evidence includes the assembly's publisher, its site, and its zone. Of course, this is a greatly simplified view of assembly security.

Setting Permissions

An administrator can define the security policies for a .NET application by using the .NET Framework Configuration tool (shown in Figure 14-16). This tool is a Microsoft Management Console (MMC) snap-in that's included with the .NET Framework. The permissions set by the .NET Framework Configuration tool will be in place once the application is actually deployed by an administrator. These permissions will control the application's run-time behavior. It's important to note that security settings are not created during the development.

In addition, the .NET Framework Configuration tool can set security policies based on an enterprise-based policy, a machine-based policy, or a user-based policy. You can access the tool by selecting **Start | Control Panel | Administrative Tools** or by **selecting Start | Programs | Microsoft Visual Studio .NET | Visual Studio .NET Tools | Visual Studio Command Prompt**. From this command prompt, you can type **mscorcfg.msc** to access the Configuration tool, but note that the Control Panel allows you to run the tool for specific versions of the .NET Framework visually.

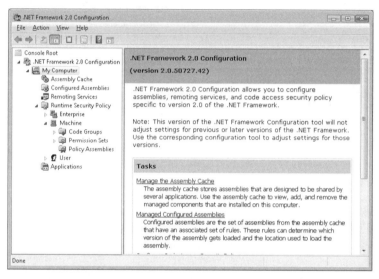

Figure 14-16: The .NET Framework Configuration tool

Conclusion

This chapter served as an introduction to the .NET Framework and how it interacts with COM applications such as those in Office. Further, we learned about various components of the .NET Framework such as the Common Language Runtime (CLR) and the various namespaces that .NET provides. We took an in-depth look at assemblies, discussing its features and the benefits of using a manifest to store metadata. This chapter also went over a few utilities that deal with assemblies such as Ilasm.exe and Ildasm.exe, which assemble and disassemble applications to expose their internals.

Chapter 15

Practical Concerns in Word Programming

Introduction

Office 2007 introduced many important new features, one of which is the interface known as the Ribbon. You'll need to understand the new Office 2007 Ribbon user interface in order to develop Office 2007 applications. In this chapter, we'll take a look at both ways you can customize the Ribbon: using XML and using the RibbonX Designer directly in Visual Studio. We will also cover the project templates for document-level customizations and application-level add-ins for VSTO. You will need to choose one of these methods to develop your Office solutions. We'll discuss exactly how each option works so you can make an informed decision.

Customization of Office 2007

Office 2007 introduces a plethora of new features, including the biggest advancement in Office history: the new Ribbon user interface. The Ribbon UI also introduces a new way of customization. The new version of Office has raised the bar over previous Office applications that relied on basic custom toolbars, menus, and code buttons. In this new version you'll have to either resort to third-party customization applications or learn the XML-based RibbonX language.

The new mechanism for controlling user customizations is the Quick Access Toolbar (QAT). As part of Microsoft's research into user usability, they discovered that the vast majority of users never changed more than three buttons on any given Office application. The response to this research was to create the QAT, so that users could easily add their favorite functionality to a spot accessible directly from the top level of the application. The following table shows the components of the new Office Ribbon UI.

UI Element	Description
Context menus	These are the same right-click context menus that we all know and love from previous versions of Office. In the Office 2007 release, RibbonX does not apply to context menus, but they can be extended and customized using the CommandBars object model just as they could in the past.
Contextual tabsets	When objects such as pictures or tables are selected inside the document, contextual tabsets appear and contain all the UI elements for dealing with those objects. RibbonX add-ins can alter the visibility of built-in tabsets and add custom tabs to them.
Groups	Tabs contain sets of groups, which in turn contain individual UI controls. RibbonX add-ins can alter the visibility of built-in groups and create custom groups.
MiniToolbar	The MiniToolbar is a collection of common formatting commands that appears above text selections and right-click context menus. RibbonX add-ins cannot modify the contents of the MiniToolbar, but they can disable or repurpose the built-in commands on it.
Office button	This button drops the Office menu, which is the rough equivalent of the File menu in previous releases of Office.
Quick Access Toolbar	This toolbar contains commonly used commands and is the main location for end-user customizations. Users can right-click on any Ribbon control and add it to the Quick Access Toolbar.
Ribbon	The large rectangular region above the document is known as the Ribbon. It contains the title bar, the Office button, the Quick Access Toolbar, and the tabs.

UI Element	Description
Status bar	The status bar contains several handy new controls, such as word count and the view slider. The status bar cannot be customized by add-ins in the 2007 Office system, but it can be hidden.
Tabs	The tabs make up the main content of the Ribbon and contain UI controls that deal with the content of the document at hand. RibbonX add-ins can create their own custom tabs and alter the visibility and labels of the built-in tabs.
Task panes	Several task panes still exist in the 2007 Office system, and it's now possible to have more than one open at a time. COM add-ins can now create custom task panes that host content.

The QAT takes the lowest-common-denominator approach. This, however, makes life a little more difficult for the advanced Office user or developer who desires a great deal of customization. In Office 2007 you must use RibbonX to tell the host application what you want the Ribbon to look like. The good news is that you'll find working with RibbonX is convenient in that you only need to describe the changes to the Ribbon. In other words, you don't have to tell the application all the details concerning the tab — only the changes you desire. The application then applies the changes you specify to the default setting of the tab.

RibbonX changes can be loaded either by creating an add-in or by using a regular document, workbook, or template. Before we look at using Visual Studio to customize the Ribbon, we'll take a quick look at how you can manually customize it with RibbonX. This will give you a greater understanding of the new interface as we continue working with the specific applications.

The RibbonX Language

RibbonX is an Office 2007 customization language created by Microsoft. The language is entirely XML based and can be edited manually or by utilizing third-party editors. The Ribbon consists of the Office button, the QAT, and the tabs and their associated controls. Figure 15-1 shows the default components of the Ribbon UI.

Figure 15-1: The Office Ribbon

RibbonX is an XML-based UI declaration. Instead of writing complicated code that builds up the UI using a series of object model calls, you can create an XML file that specifies the appearance of the UI in a structured markup form. For the add-in writer, this has several advantages.

One of the advantages of the XML-based UI is that the Ribbon allows you to separate your custom UI enhancements from the code behind any of the events. Previously, add-ins tied all changes to the same file using customized menus and code behind. Now, with RibbonX you can control the UI entirely separate from your code. In fact, if you choose to load the Ribbon's XML from an external file, the UI can be modified without even recompiling the add-in. This essentially eliminates the cycle of editing and recompiling the code.

A second advantage is that the add-in's UI is separated not only from the default Office UI but from any other add-in as well. Previous versions of Office had no means to associate toolbars and menus to a specific add-in. The result was a mélange of UI customizations that could inadvertently break other add-ins. All of these UI modifications used COM calls, which had the disadvantage of not being able to be traced to specific add-ins.

Another advantage of this new UI is that Office can now clean up an add-in's UI automatically. Previously, add-ins needed special code that deleted their menus and toolbars on shutdown or uninstalls. When these previous add-ins crashed or failed to clean up properly, they would leave useless buttons in the UI. Now that Office 2007 cleans up add-ins' UIs automatically, there's no need to write any cleanup code and no possibility that orphan controls will clutter the UI.

The lack of versioning of add-ins found in the Command-Bar object often broke the program using that object when newly upgraded add-ins were released to Office. This was due to the fact that the Add-Ins tab was unable to distinguish which controls belonged to which add-in. Valid XML files contain an xmlns namespace declaration that identifies the schema to which they apply. This provides RibbonX with version information for a particular add-in and allows it to map the UI appropriately. Office can now control the changes that might have occurred between versions.

Finally, XML is widely understood and has a wide variety of associated tools. You can use many different applications (including Word 2007) to create and customize a Ribbon XML file given the RibbonX schema. As opposed to the older definition format of DTD, this new schema is in the form of an XSD.

Many companies are struggling with the decision of whether or not to deploy Office 2007. Previous Office versions were more or less the same (as far as the UI is concerned) and they required little training. However, for the first time since the initial release of Office, the UI has been changed dramatically. The result is that many long-time Office users initially dislike the new Ribbon UI.

Through extensive research, Microsoft found that users were frustrated with the Office UI. For example, in previous Office versions, the image-editing toolbar appeared when pictures were inserted into a Word document. Microsoft discovered that most people closed the toolbar to get it out of the way. Minutes later, they would become frustrated when they couldn't figure out how to edit the image or move pictures to correct their placement inside a document.

When Microsoft first created the new Ribbon UI, they gave early Office 2007 software to a handful of testers from Fortune 500 companies in the Seattle area. At the time, Office 2007 had the basic framework and concepts in place. Although users found the changes overwhelming at first, they grew to prefer them over the traditional interface after completing five months of testing. Most users have expressed the why-did-they-move-that displeasure that should be expected.

However, once they've used the new applications for a couple weeks, the new benefits and ease of use greatly outweigh any attachment to the old look and feel.

XML Ribbon Enhancements

The easiest way to create RibbonX markup is to use a validating XML editor. If you can provide the necessary schema (XSD) file, Microsoft Visual Studio 2008 provides such an editor that you can use. In this case, you need a current copy of customUI.xsd, which is readily available and may have been installed already if you have installed Visual Studio 2008.

Now let's take a look at creating a Ribbon enhancement in Visual Studio. Once you have a project open, start by creating a new XML file by going to **File | New | File** to launch the New File window, as shown in Figure 15-2.

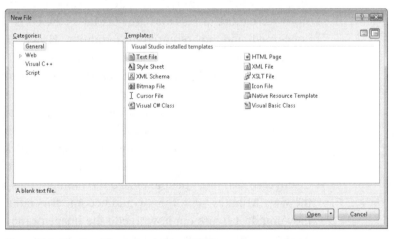

Figure 15-2: The New File window in Visual Studio

An XSD schema essentially defines a test that an XML document must pass in order to be valid according to that XSD. Validity is a step above and beyond the basic XML well-formedness rules (refer to Chapter 11 for more information about XML). Although you can enter the schema reference directly into the XML, Visual Studio provides an easy mechanism to associate an XSD with the current XML file. As you can see in the Properties window (shown in Figure 15-3), the Schemas line does not contain any references. You can display the Properties window once you have the file open to edit by right-clicking the body of the document and choosing Properties.

Figure 15-3: The Properties window of the XML file

When you initially click on the Schemas property, you'll be presented with a long, hierarchical list of all the schemas that Visual Studio knows about. One of the schemas of interest is the CustomUI schema that defines exactly how your RibbonX XML file should look. Once the association is made, you'll also be able to take advantage of IntelliSense directly inside the IDE. This makes writing your RibbonX customization much easier than attempting to develop this customization in a utility such as Notepad. Figure 15-4 shows a sample representation of the many schemas available to Visual Studio.

Although the CustomUI is installed by default, in the event that the CustomUI schema is not listed, you can add it manually. Associating the schema is as easy as navigating to the file location and selecting the file. This will set the Schemas property to include the customUI.xsd file. This then enables you to take advantage of Microsoft IntelliSense technology as you enter XML content into the file. You might also find the XML Notepad 2006 download, which is available from the Microsoft Download Center, useful. This tool enables you to edit and view XML content in a tree-based format.

Using IntelliSense is a convenient way to access descriptions of functions and particularly their parameter lists. This speeds up software development by reducing the amount of keyboard input required and by giving you quick and easy access to information about the functions. Figure 15-5 shows how IntelliSense can help you develop a RibbonX XML file that conforms to the CustomUI schema.

Use	Target Namespace	File Name	Location
▼		DotNetConfig20.xsd	D:\Program Files\
		DotNetConfig30.xsd	D:\Program Files\
		DotNetConfig.xsd	D:\Program Files\
	DeclarativeConditions	declarativeconditionsxoml.xsd	D:\Program Files\
	http://microsoft.com/schemas/VisualStudio/TeamTest/2006	vstst.xsd	D:\Program Files\
	http://schemas.microsoft.com/AspNet/AdRotator-Advertisement-File-1.2	adrotator.xsd	D:\Program Files\
	http://schemas.microsoft.com/AspNet/AdRotator-Schedule-File	adrotator1_0.xsd	D:\Program Files\
	http://schemas.microsoft.com/AspNet/SiteMap-File-1.0	SiteMapSchema.xsd	D:\Program Files\
	http://schemas.microsoft.com/AutomationExtensibility	addinschema.xsd	D:\Program Files\
	http://schemas.microsoft.com/developer/2004/01/bootstrapper	Package.xsd	D:\Program Files\
	http://schemas.microsoft.com/developer/msbuild/2003	Microsoft.Build.xsd	D:\Program Files\
	http://schemas.microsoft.com/developer/vscontent/2005	vscontent.xsd	D:\Program Files\
	http://schemas.microsoft.com/developer/vstemplate/2005	vstemplate.xsd	D:\Program Files\
	http://schemas.microsoft.com/dsltools/SyncDesigner	SyncDesignerSchema.xsd	D:\Program Files\
	http://schemas.microsoft.com/linqtosql/dbml/2007	DbmlSchema.xsd	D:\Program Files\
	http://schemas.microsoft.com/office/2006/01/customui	customUI.xsd	D:\Program Files\
	http://schemas.microsoft.com/VisualStudio/2004/03/SmartDevices/XMTA.xsd	xmta.xsd	D:\Program Files\
	http://schemas.microsoft.com/VisualStudio/2005/CodeSnippet	snippetformat.xsd	D:\Program Files\
	http://schemas.microsoft.com/Visual-Studio-Intellisense	vsIntellisense.xsd	D:\Program Files\
	http://schemas.microsoft.com/xsd/catalog	catalog.xsd	D:\Program Files\
	http://schemas.xmlsoap.org/soap/envelope/	soap1.1.xsd	D:\Program Files\
	http://schemas.xmlsoap.org/wsdl/	wsdl.xsd	D:\Program Files\
	http://schemas.xmlsoap.org/wsdl/soap/	wsdlSoap11Binding.xsd	D:\Program Files\
	http://schemas.xmlsoap.org/wsdl/soap12/	wsdlSoap12Binding.xsd	D:\Program Files\
	http://www.w3.org/1999/xhtml	xhtml.xsd	D:\Program Files\
	http://www.w3.org/1999/xlink	xlink.xsd	D:\Program Files\
	http://www.w3.org/1999/XSL/Transform	xslt.xsd	D:\Program Files\
	http://www.w3.org/2000/09/xmldsig#	xmlsig.xsd	D:\Program Files\
	http://www.w3.org/2001/04/xmlenc#	xenc.xsd	D:\Program Files\
	http://www.w3.org/2001/XMLSchema	xsdschema.xsd	D:\Program Files\
	http://www.w3.org/2003/05/soap-envelope	soap1.2.xsd	D:\Program Files\
	http://www.w3.org/XML/1998/namespace	xml.xsd	D:\Program Files\
	urn:schemas-microsoft-com:datatypes	xdrtypes.xsd	D:\Program Files\
	urn:schemas-microsoft-com:rowset	XdrRowset.xsd	D:\Program Files\
	urn:schemas-microsoft-com:xml-data	xdr.xsd	D:\Program Files\
	urn:schemas-microsoft-com:xml-msdata	msdata.xsd	D:\Program Files\
	urn:schemas-microsoft-com:xml-msdatasource	DataSource.xsd	D:\Program Files\
	urn:schemas-microsoft-com:xml-wcfservicemap	ServiceMapSchema.xsd	D:\Program Files\
	urn:schemas-microsoft-com:xslt	msxsl.xsd	D:\Program Files\

Figure 15-4: Partial listing of the schemas available to Visual Studio

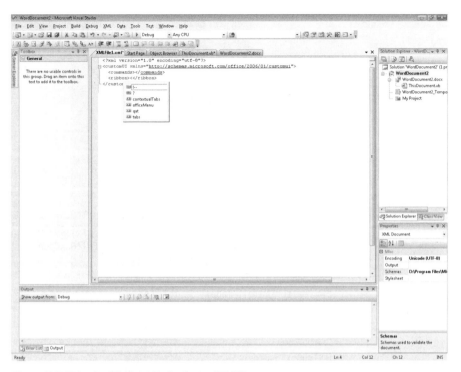

Figure 15-5: Using IntelliSense with the CustomUI XSD

Now that you've seen how to utilize IntelliSense to create your RibbonX file, please enter the XML that appears in the following code.

Note: You can download this file from the book's companion sites: www.wordware.com/files/word2007 and www.docbuilder.com.

This XML adds several custom controls to the Office Ribbon. You can see the tab definitions as well as several controls, including a toggle button, check box, edit box, combo box, and dialog launcher. You can also see that code definitions are defined in the body of the XML file. These code definitions define which code will be executed upon the particular event defined in the XML file.

```
<?xml version="1.0" encoding="utf-8"?>
<customUI xmlns="http://schemas.microsoft.com/office/2006/01/
customui">
    <ribbon>
```

```
            <tabs>
                <tab idMso="TabHome">
                    <group idMso="GroupFont" visible="false" />
                </tab>
                <tab id="CustomTab" label="My Tab">
                    <group id="SampleGroup" label="Sample Group">
                        <toggleButton id="tgbButton" size="large"
                            label="Large Toggle Button"
                            getPressed="ThisDocument.tgbButtonCode"
                            onAction="ThisDocument.tgbButtonCode"  />
                        <checkBox id="chkCheckbox" label="A CheckBox"
                            screentip="This is a check box"
                            onAction="ThisDocument.CheckboxCode" />
                        <editBox id="edbEditBox" getText="ThisDocument.EditBoxCode"
                            label="My EditBox" onChange="ThisDocument.EditBoxCode"/>
                        <comboBox id="cboComboBox" label="My ComboBox"
                            onChange="ThisDocument.ComboBoxCode">
                            <item id="Name1" label="Scott" />
                            <item id="Name2" label="Debra" />
                            <item id="Name2" label="Connor" />
                        </comboBox>
                        <dialogBoxLauncher>
                            <button id="lncLauncher" screentip="My Launcher"
                                onAction="ThisDocument.LauncherCode" />
                        </dialogBoxLauncher>
                    </group>
                    <group id="MyGroup" label="My Group" >
                        <button id="btnButton1" label="Large Button"
                            size="large" onAction="ThisDocument.ButtonCodeOne" />
                        <button id="btnButton2" label="Regular Button"
                            size="normal" onAction="ThisDocument.ButtonCodeTwo" />
                    </group >
                </tab>
            </tabs>
        </ribbon>
    </customUI>
```

Once you've created the sample RibbonX file, create a folder in which to store the file. For this example, we will save this file as **customUI.xml** in a folder named **customUI** on the desktop. After this has been done, create a document in Word, Excel, or PowerPoint and save it with an Office Open XML Format file extension (.docx, .docm, .xlsx, .xlsm, .pptx, or

.pptm). If you want to add code that reacts when the user interacts with the Ribbon customization, you must save the document in code-enabled format. Files that contain codes have an "m" suffix in their extension and can contain procedures that can be called by RibbonX commands and controls. Documents with this code functionality include the .docm, .xlsm, and .pptm formats. For our example, we'll save an Excel file as shown in Figure 15-6.

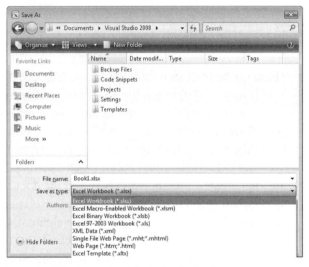

Figure 15-6: Saving an Excel file for the CustomUI

Exit the Office application once you've saved the file. You can open the file using a program such as WinZip (shown in Figure 15-7), or you can use Windows Explorer to rename the file with a .zip extension. If you rename the file, you can double-click the file to open it as a compressed folder. Add the customization file to the container by dragging the customUI folder (from the desktop in our case) to the compressed folder.

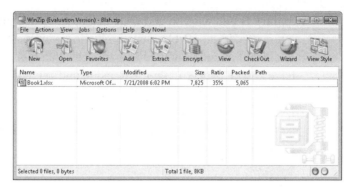

Figure 15-7: The Excel file as displayed in WinZip

There is one final step after you've added your XML file. You'll need to define the file so that the Office application (Excel in our case) knows about the relationship. Drag the _rels folder containing the .rels file from the newly created zip file to the desktop (or any other location). Open the folder and open the .rels file in a text editor (such as Notepad). Add a line that creates a relationship between the document file and the customization file between the final <Relationship> element and the closing </Relationships> element. Ensure that you specify the folder and file names correctly (the Id attribute supplies a unique relationship ID for the customUI — its value is arbitrary). Figure 15-8 shows the highlighted line as it should appear in the file. Following is the exact line that should be added:

```
<Relationship Type="http://schemas.microsoft.com/office/2006/
relationships/ui/extensibility" Target="/CustomUI.xml"
Id="customUIRelID" />
```

Figure 15-8: Modifying the .rels file

Once you've saved the .rels file, add it back (replacing the existing .rels file) into the _rels folder in the compressed file. Next, remove the .zip extension from the container file. Now, when you open the file in the Office application, the UI appears with your customizations. Depending on your application settings, if you use the markup from the previous section in this example, you might receive several warning messages as you open the document. Figure 15-9 shows how Excel will look once you've made the Ribbon enhancements.

Figure 15-9: The customized Ribbon in Excel

The VSTO Ribbon Designer

From the previous section, you've seen that creating XML to control the Office UI is relatively easy. The newly introduced VSTO Ribbon Designer includes a visual designer and an extensibility object model that gives you an even easier method of controlling the Office UI. This tool makes it straightforward for developers to create, configure, and debug the Ribbon UI. You can drag and drop controls onto the design surface and set properties through the Properties window. It works much the same as the Windows Forms designer in that you can create event handlers for your new Ribbon items by double-clicking them. In addition, Office callbacks are mapped to the events on the VSTO Ribbon objects, so developers write event handlers instead of callback methods.

The Ribbon Designer uses drag-and-drop functionality, so you can drag controls from the Office Ribbon Controls tab of the toolbox. Supported Ribbon controls include tabs, groups, and buttons. In the following example, we have added two groups to the Ribbon. In working with Ribbon controls, you use groups as an organizational mechanism, so within each group we have added buttons and images. Figure 15-10 shows how to edit a control's properties.

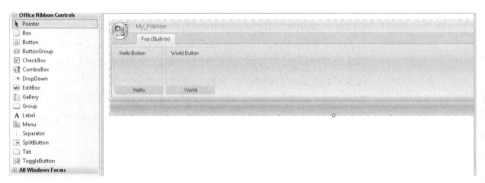

Figure 15-10: Using the Ribbon Designer

A VSTO customization is constructed within a specific hierarchical structure of Ribbon objects. A typical VSTO Ribbon customization consists of one or more Ribbon objects, where each object contains one or more Tab objects that contain one or more Group objects, and so on. You can then add one or more group controls to the tab and add buttons, toggle buttons, and menus to the group. There are, however, limitations within any given menu, as you can only go five levels deep.

You'll also want to add event handlers to execute your code. With a custom Ribbon now built, you can add event handlers to the Ribbon elements. You add an event handler to an individual Ribbon control basically the same way you do it with other controls — by double-clicking the control. Visual Studio then automatically adds a Click event and opens the source code view for you to enter your event handler code.

VSTO Templates on a Document or Application Level

VSTO contains project templates for document-level customizations and application-level add-ins. According to your specific solution, you will need to decide which type of project you need. In considering, think about whether you want your code to run only when a specific document is open, or whether you want the code to be available whenever the Office application is open.

Support for document-level customizations was not provided in the previous version of VSTO (VSTO 2005 SE). Currently, document-level customizations are still only available for the Word and Excel applications. Document-level customizations are comprised of an assembly associated with a specific document, workbook, or template. This associated assembly is loaded when the associated document is opened. Likewise, the features you create are only available when the associated document is open. Another important implication is that these customizations cannot make application-wide changes. If you want to work at the root application level, you'll need to work with an add-in.

An application-level add-in is comprised of an assembly that is associated with a Microsoft Office application. This model is almost identical to the legacy Office add-in, but with subtle differences. The primary difference is that an application add-in is developed directly in Visual Studio and has its own specific project type. Although you could still create COM-based add-ins, the VSTO model is much easier to work with and much more robust. Application-level add-ins use the Shared Add-in technology. This not only gives better access to the object model, but there is no need to use the confusing Shim as an interface between the COM Office application and your .NET code.

Application add-ins are launched when the associated application is started. Users can also load add-ins once the application is running. The best thing about add-ins is that all the features you create are available to the application itself. In other words, you don't need to have a specific document open.

Application-Level Add-in Creation

To create an application-level add-in, let's start by creating a new project from the File menu in Visual Studio. In the Project Types pane, expand the Office tree, which is situated under the node for VB. Now, depending on which version of Office you are using, select the 2003 or 2007 folder. In the Templates pane, select an add-in project. Add-in projects have the name *<application>* Add-in, where *application* is the name of the particular Office application.

If you want to use the default Setup project to deploy your add-in, the project name cannot contain Unicode characters. VSTO projects support using Unicode characters in the project name, but Setup projects do not. By default, the name of the Setup project for add-ins includes the name of the add-in project. Also, if you plan to deploy the solution for use online, you must give the project a name using characters that fit the HTTP protocol specifications. The different projects available for Office 2007 add-ins are shown in Figure 15-11.

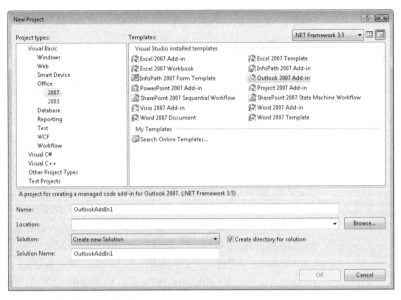

Figure 15-11: Office 2007 add-in projects

By default, add-in projects are always saved when they are created. They cannot be created as temporary projects because a solution can contain only one temporary project. Add-in solutions contain two projects: the add-in project and the Setup project. In the Location box, enter a location where you want to create the project. You can use absolute and Universal Naming Convention (UNC) paths. Do not use HTTP, FTP, or other protocol paths for the project.

Locations have the following formats:

▼ [drive]:\

▼ \\<Server>\<Share>

These characters are invalid in the location:

▼ Asterisk (*)

▼ Vertical bar (|)

▼ Colon (:) (except following the drive letter)

▼ Double quotation mark (") (paths that contain spaces do not need quotation marks)

▼ Less than (<)

▼ Greater than (>)

▼ Question mark (?)

▼ Percent sign (%)

A Closer Look at Application Add-ins

After you've created your application add-in you will need to build the solution. In the process of building an application-level project, the application manifest and a program database (PDB) file are created. The build process for application-level projects also creates a set of Registry entries on the development computer that are required to load the add-in.

When you use VSTO to build an add-in, you create a managed code assembly that is loaded by a Microsoft Office application. After the assembly is loaded, the add-in can respond to events that are raised in the application, such as a user's button click. The add-in can also call into the object model to automate and extend the application, and it can use any of the classes in the .NET Framework.

The Created Registry Entries

VSTO creates all required Registry entries on the development computer when building your solution so that you can debug and run your add-in. The way Microsoft Office applications find add-ins is by looking for a set of Registry entries. Most of the Registry entries are the same for Microsoft Office 2003 and the 2007 Microsoft Office systems, but one key is different: Office 2007 applications look for the manifest entry (that specifies the full path of the deployment manifest) under:

```
HKEY_CURRENT_USER\Software\Microsoft\Office\<application
name>\Addins\<add-in ID> key
```

or

```
HKEY_CURRENT_USER\Software\Microsoft\Visio\Addins\<add-in ID> for
Visio
```

Conversely, Microsoft Office 2003 applications look for the ManifestName and ManifestLocation entries (that specify the location and name of the application manifest) under:

```
HKEY_CURRENT_USER\Software\Microsoft\Office\<application name>\Addins\<add-in ID>
key
HKEY_CURRENT_USER\Software\Microsoft\Office\application name\Addins\add-in ID
HKEY_CURRENT_USER\Software\Classes\add-in ID\CLSID HKEY_CURRENT_USER\Software\
Classes\CLSID\{add-in CLSID}
HKEY_CURRENT_USER\Software\Classes\CLSID\{add-in CLSID}\InprocServer32
HKEY_CURRENT_USER\Software\Classes\CLSID\{add-in CLSID}\ProgID
HKEY_CURRENT_USER\Software\Classes\CLSID\{add-in CLSID}\Programmable
HKEY_CURRENT_USER\Software\Classes\CLSID\{add-inCLSID}\VersionIndependentProgID
```

or

```
HKEY_CURRENT_USER\Software\Microsoft\Visio\Addins\<add-in ID> for Visio)
```

You can deploy a VSTO add-in for Office 2003 so that it is available to all users of a computer by creating the Registry keys under HKEY_LOCAL_MACHINE instead of HKEY_CURRENT_USER. However, you cannot deploy a VSTO add-in for Office 2007 Office system to all users of a computer by registering the add-in under HKEY_LOCAL_MACHINE. Applications under Microsoft Office 2007 only recognize VSTO add-ins that are registered under HKEY_CURRENT_USER.

The Deployment and Application Manifests

Add-ins use deployment manifests and application manifests to identify and load the most current version of the add-in assembly. The deployment manifest points to the current application manifest while the application manifest points to the add-in assembly and specifies the entry point class to execute in the assembly. A difference to note between Office versions is that the deployment manifest is optional for Microsoft Office 2003 add-ins, but it is required for add-ins for the 2007 Microsoft Office system.

Document-Level Customization Creation

To create a document-level customization, start by creating a new Visual Studio 2008 project by going to the File menu and selecting New project. Under the node for VB in the Project Types pane, expand Office. Select either the 2003 or the 2007 folder and select the appropriate Word or Excel project. The available document-level projects are Excel workbook, Excel template, Word document, and Word template.

Next, provide a name in the Name box and select Create a new document if you want to create a new document in the solution or select Copy an existing document if you want to use an existing document in the solution. If you create a new document, specify the name in the Name box, and choose the format of the document from the Format box. Figure 15-12 shows the available Office 2007 document projects.

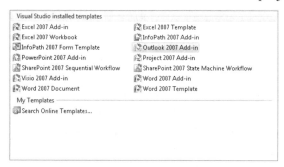

Visual Studio installed templates

Excel 2007 Add-in	Excel 2007 Template
Excel 2007 Workbook	InfoPath 2007 Add-in
InfoPath 2007 Form Template	Outlook 2007 Add-in
PowerPoint 2007 Add-in	Project 2007 Add-in
SharePoint 2007 Sequential Workflow	SharePoint 2007 State Machine Workflow
Visio 2007 Add-in	Word 2007 Add-in
Word 2007 Document	Word 2007 Template

My Templates

Search Online Templates...

Figure 15-12: Office 2007 document projects

Document-level customizations are designed to work at a lower level than application add-ins and are generally concerned with creating a particular file. In working with document-level customizations, you can work with custom task panes and use Smart Tag technology. Document-level customizations also provide data islands/data cache functionality.

Document-Level Projects

In this section we will look at the fundamental aspects of how the document-level projects are created and how they work. Keep in mind that we are only talking about Word and Excel when discussing document-level customizations, as they are the only applications that currently support this feature. The project assembly and all referenced assemblies have their Copy Local property set to True. When these projects are built, the document is copied and the copy is placed in the output directory with the assemblies.

An important thing to note is that VSTO does not include a project template for creating a Word document-level customization based on a WordProcessingML file. Another important note is that Excel workbook and template projects do not allow you to change either the output path or the working directory. If you set the working directory option in the Debug pane of the Project Designer to a different location, Excel will change it back to the default at run time when the document is opened. However, for Word solutions, you can change the output path normally. In both cases, when you build a document-level project, a few things are included in the project output: the application manifest (embedded in the document), a program database file, and a copy of the project document.

If you base your solution on a document that was originally created in a version of Word or Excel that is earlier than the version specified by the project template, VSTO will update the format to the version specified by the project template. You should design managed code extensions only for documents in the supported formats. Otherwise, certain events might not be raised when the document opens in the application. The following list describes the document formats you can use in document-level customizations for Excel and Word.

- ▼ Excel 97-2003
  - ▼ Excel workbook (.xls)
  - ▼ Excel template (.xlt)
- ▼ Excel 2003-Excel 2007
  - ▼ Excel workbook (.xlsx)
  - ▼ Excel code-enabled workbook (.xlsm)
  - ▼ Excel binary workbook (.xlsb)
- ▼ Excel 97-2003 workbook (.xls)
  - ▼ Excel template (.xltx)
  - ▼ Excel code-enabled template (.xltm)
- ▼ Word 97-2003
  - ▼ Word document (.doc)
  - ▼ Word template (.dot)

- ▼ Word 2003-Word 2007
  - ▼ Word document (.docx)
  - ▼ Word code-enabled document (.docm)
- ▼ Word 97-2003 document (.doc)
  - ▼ Word template (.dotx)
  - ▼ Word code-enabled template (.dotm)

The VSTO Loader

A general understanding of the VSTO loader is needed to understand exactly how VSTO solutions work. The VSTO runtime includes a loader component that performs most of the work required to load the customization assembly. This loader has different file names, depending on the version of Microsoft Office in use. Customizations for the 2007 Microsoft Office system use a loader named VSTOLoader.dll, while a loader named otkloadr.dll is used by Office 2003 customizations. When a user opens a customization, the loader starts the CLR and loads the assembly. This assembly can capture events that are raised in the document or workbook. Note that a customization must be secure in order for it to run on an assembly. Figure 15-13 illustrates the general security process that VSTO utilizes.

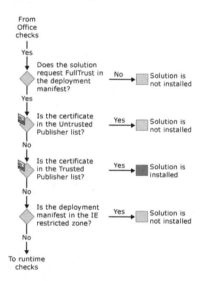

Figure 15-13: The general VSTO security process

In addition to the security process, there are many steps that occur when a Microsoft Office document with managed code extensions is opened:

1. The document is checked to see if there are any managed code extensions associated with it by the VSTO loader.

2. The VSTO Office runtime is started if there are any managed code extensions associated with the document.

3. An application domain is created by the VSTO runtime, which then sets the policy for the application to not trust the "My Computer zone."

4. Validation of the evidence presented by the assembly is done by the .NET Framework. If the validation comes back clear, then the process continues. However, if it fails, then an error is raised.

5. Utilizing the application and deployment manifests, the VSTO runtime checks for any assembly updates. Updates are performed if they are available.

6. The assembly is loaded into the application domain by the VSTO runtime.

7. The startup event handler in your customization assembly is loaded by the VSTO runtime.

8. The VSTO loader creates a separate application domain for each document.

Having a separate application domain for each document makes the solution more robust. It also ensures that when the document is closed, all the code is shut down and the assemblies are unloaded from memory. Document-level customizations are designed to work with a single document in a single application domain. They are not designed for cross-document communication.

VSTO Runtime

When running an Office 2007 application, the application uses the deployment and application manifests to locate and load the most current version of the add-in assembly. End-user computers must have the VSTO runtime in order to run add-ins that are created using VSTO. There are different versions of the VSTO runtime that work with add-ins for each version of Office. All versions of the VSTO runtime also include a component that ensures that the correct version of the VSTO runtime is loaded for the version of Microsoft Office that is loading the add-in. This component is named VSTOEE.dll. Although multiple versions of the VSTO runtime can be installed on the same computer, only one instance of VSTOEE.dll is installed at a time.

Options in Deploying VSTO

One of the greatest improvements of Visual Studio 2008 is the introduction of the ClickOnce deployment technologies. VSTO solutions that use applications in Office 2007 can be deployed using this technology. ClickOnce deployment enables self-updating solutions that can be installed and run with minimal user interaction. VSTO automatically checks the deployment location to see whether there is an update every time a user (connected to a network) opens a document or application that contains a ClickOnce Office solution. If an update is found, VSTO downloads and installs the updated solution. You can update or roll back versions of a solution by updating the manifests and solution files at the deployment location.

The main deployment considerations include the following elements:

▼ ClickOnce Office solution requirements

▼ ClickOnce manifests and the Publish Wizard

▼ Installing a ClickOnce Office solution

▼ Running a ClickOnce Office solution

▼ ClickOnce cache

A ClickOnce Office solution consists of the following components:

▼ The assembly that contains the compiled custom code and any dependent assemblies, such as resources, satellites, or helper libraries

▼ The application manifest

▼ The deployment manifest

End users must have the following software installed on their computer:

▼ The Microsoft .NET Framework 3.5

▼ The VSTO runtime

▼ The necessary Office applications, including the primary interop assemblies (PIAs)

The ClickOnce deployment architecture is based on two XML manifest files: an application manifest and a deployment manifest. These manifests are generated and deployed automatically when you use the Publish Wizard (more on the Publish Wizard below).

The application manifest describes the ClickOnce Office solution itself, including:

▼ The assemblies

▼ The dependencies

▼ The files that make up the solution

▼ The entry points into the solution

▼ The permissions the solution will request at run time

The deployment manifest describes how the solution is deployed, including:

▼ The location of the application manifest

▼ The current version of the solution

The Publish Wizard

The Publish Wizard uses information you enter to generate the ClickOnce manifests and copy the required files to the specified locations. This information includes the deployment location and the installation method. After the manifests and solution files have been copied to the deployment location, end users can download and install the solution.

When you update the deployed solution, you can use the Publish Wizard to generate a new application manifest (pointing to the location of the new version of the solution) and copy the new files to a deployment location — usually a subfolder of the original solution deployment folder.

Security and Manifest Certificates

Application and deployment manifests must be signed with a certificate to pass the security checks that VSTO performs before loading a solution. When a VSTO project is created, a temporary certificate is generated that can be used to sign the application and deployment manifests. This temporary certificate should be used only during development. After development is finished, use an official certificate for deployment. An administrator can add the official certificate to the Trusted Publisher certificate store on the end user's computer. After the Publish Wizard has copied the solution to the deployment location, end users can download and install it.

In VSTO, you can install solutions only by running VSTOInstaller.exe at a command prompt. VSTOInstaller.exe is stored by default in the root VSTO install directory. When running VSTOInstaller.exe, the only required parameter is the location of the deployment manifest. The location of the deployment manifest can be a web site, a UNC share, or in a file path. After a ClickOnce Office solution is installed, it is loaded from the ClickOnce cache by its host application the next time the host application is run.

All ClickOnce Office solutions are stored on the client computer in a ClickOnce application cache. The ClickOnce cache is a family of hidden directories that holds all of the solution's files, including the assemblies, configuration files, application and user settings, and data directory. ClickOnce Office solutions use the same cache as Windows Forms ClickOnce applications.

Conclusion

When creating Office projects in Visual Studio 2008, there are many practical considerations to think about, ranging from creating document-level or application-level templates to deployment methods. In this chapter we discussed some of the Ribbon customization options of the new Ribbon UI. Additionally, we discussed document-level templates versus application-level templates, and how to determine which one is right for you according to your solution. Finally, this chapter visited the topic of the new ClickOnce deployment and how VSTO projects are loaded under Windows. In the next chapter, we will look at programming Word via VSTO.

Chapter 16

VSTO Document Assembly

Introduction

Throughout the book, we have seen the power, flexibility, and plethora of features of Microsoft Word 2007. And as we have learned from the previous chapters, you can access almost all of these features using VSTO, meaning that you have almost 300 objects in your programming arsenal. In addition, there are more than 4,500 properties and methods at your disposal for these objects.

Note: To see a comprehensive list of the objects and their relative properties and methods, visit the Word Object Model Reference at: http://msdn2.microsoft.com/en-us/library/bb244515.aspx.

In previous chapters, we looked at Visual Studio Tools for Office (VSTO) and how it relates to programming Office applications such as Word in Visual Studio. This chapter will focus on automating Word through VSTO. For most of the chapter we will be taking a look at the various objects, properties, and methods of the Application and Document objects. At the end of the chapter we will implement these objects in a small project.

Automating Document Assembly in Word

Before learning how to automate document assembly in Word, a solid foundation of how Word works is required. Word is highly extensible and allows you to execute almost all of the same commands that you can access from the Ribbon UI. (Refer to Chapter 15 for more information about the Ribbon.) In starting this solid foundation of knowledge on the inner workings of Word, we need to look at the two most important Word objects: the Application object and the Document object. Because there are way too many Word objects to cover in one chapter, we'll discuss only the most commonly used document assembly objects and their properties and methods. Figure 16-1 shows how the Document object is related to the Application object.

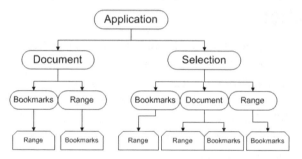

Figure 16-1: The basic Word object hierarchy

The Word Object Model

As you can see from Figure 16-1, the Word object hierarchy is fundamentally simple; however, beneath this simple initial hierarchy is a vast multitude of features. As mentioned in the previous section, the most important Word objects are the Application object and the Document object. The Application object represents the actual Word application, and is the parent of all of the other objects. Its members usually apply to the Word application as a whole in that you can use its properties and methods to control the Word environment. In turn, the Document object is central to programming Word. When you open an existing document or create a new document, you are essentially creating a new Document object that is added to the Word Documents collection.

The Application Object

In order to understand the Application object, let's create a simple project that we can use to demonstrate code along the way. Start Visual Studio and create an Office 2007 Word document project with a name of your choice. Next, drag a command button from the toolbox directly onto the document, as shown in Figure 16-2.

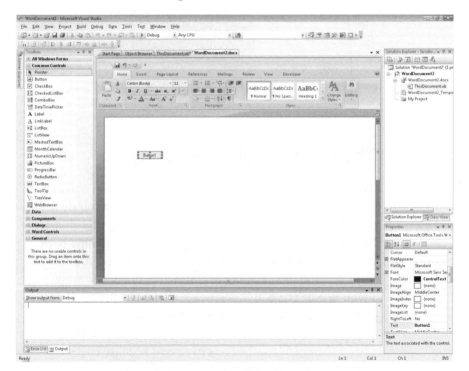

Figure 16-2: Adding a button directly to Word

Once this is done, simply double-clicking the button creates the event stub (a placeholder for event-driven code) for the button's Click event. Once you've double-clicked the button, you will automatically be taken to the ThisDocument.vb file, where the code shown below should appear.

```
Public Class ThisDocument

    Private Sub ThisDocument_Startup(ByVal sender As Object,
ByVal e As System.EventArgs) Handles Me.Startup

    End Sub

    Private Sub ThisDocument_Shutdown(ByVal sender As Object,
ByVal e As System.EventArgs) Handles Me.Shutdown

    End Sub

    Private Sub Button1_Click(ByVal sender As System.Object,
ByVal e As System.EventArgs) Handles Button1.Click

        'Your code will go here

    End Sub
End Class
```

The ActiveDocument Property

The ActiveDocument property of the Application object returns a Document object that represents the currently active document in a Word session. Sometimes using this object can be a little tricky. For example, say a user is switching back and forth between documents. As the developer, you may think a particular document is the active document when in fact it is not. The better practice is to programmatically control the creation or addition of documents and then assign the new document to a Document object variable. That way, the active document confusion is bypassed because each document can have a unique variable name.

To illustrate a simple usage of the ActiveDocument property, let's enter a simple message box showing the active document's name behind the Click event we created above. The code for this should be the following:

```
MsgBox(Application.ActiveDocument.Name)
```

Note: This syntax is subtly different from the very similar VBA syntax. In VSTO you're forced to use the Application qualifier even though ActiveDocument is a global property within Word. In this case, however, you're working outside the context of Word (inside Visual Studio) and you need to qualify your property call.

After adding this line of code, your Click event should now look like this:

```
Private Sub Button1_Click(ByVal sender As System.Object, ByVal e
As System.EventArgs) Handles Button1.Click
    'your code will go here
    MsgBox(Application.ActiveDocument.Name)
End Sub
```

You can begin executing your program just as you would any other Visual Studio project. You can press the Play (Run) button, or you can simply press F5, which will build the project and cause Visual Studio to create an instance of Word with your document project. The button you've created should be the only item visible on the document. When you click the new button, you should be prompted with the message box we created, as shown in Figure 16-3.

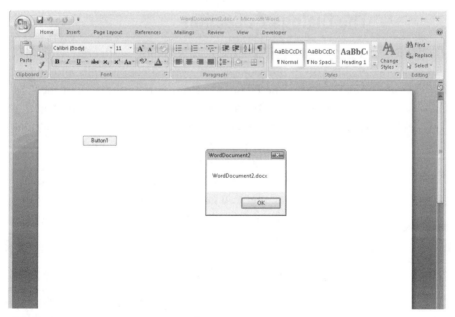

Figure 16-3: Displaying the ActiveDocument.Name property in a message box

The Template Object

The Template object represents a template in Word. Much like the Documents collection, the Template object is a collection object that contains all available Word templates at a given point in time. This collection includes all templates that are currently open as documents, all global templates (as shown in the Add-ins dialog box), all templates attached to any open document, and the Normal template.

The OpenAsDocument and Save methods are the only methods of the Template object. The OpenAsDocument method is important because it allows you to access certain properties and methods that are not available when a template is *acting like a template*. The following line of code will display the currently attached template of the ActiveDocument:

```
MsgBox(Application.ActiveDocument.AttachedTemplate())
```

The Template object provides a way for you to work with a Word template, which is the foundation object of a Word document.

The Dialogs Collection

A good understanding of Word's Dialogs collection will enable you to intercept Word's built-in commands and add functionality. The Dialogs collection represents all of the built-in dialog boxes in Word. There are over 200 built-in dialog boxes that you can access from the Word object model. You can see the complete list at http://msdn2.microsoft.com/en-us/library/bb214033.aspx.

These built-in dialog boxes can be displayed to get user input. You'll see that you can control almost every aspect of the Dialogs collection through the many methods and properties of the collection.

Arguments of a Dialog Box

Unless you become accustomed to checking Help and finding the arguments for a specific dialog box, working with dialog boxes can be especially frustrating. The Help topic for Dialog box arguments is "Built-in dialog box argument lists," and if you start Help by pressing F1 with Dialogs selected, it's no less than three layers of Help away. This can be annoying if you're in the middle of a project and you need to find a particular argument. Figure 16-4 shows the Help dialog box with the arguments for the File Open dialog box.

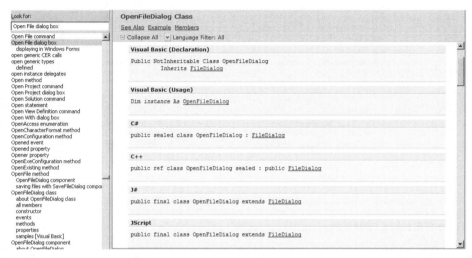

Figure 16-4: Dialog object arguments

Once you are working with the appropriate Dialog object, you can use arguments to set options in the dialog box. In most cases, the name of the argument will correspond closely to one of the options on the actual Word dialog box; however, checking these dialog boxes can eliminate the headaches of trying to guess the right argument in your code. You control dialog box settings in a very similar manner to the way you return them. The following snippet sets the .Name argument of the File Open dialog box instead of returning it, as shown in Figure 16-5.

```
With Application.Dialogs(Word.WdWordDialog.wdDialogFileOpen)
    .Name = "VSTO is Fun!"
    .Display()
End With
```

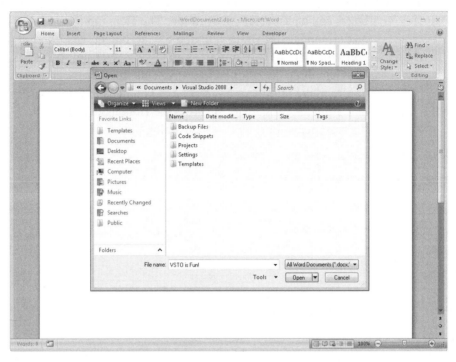

Figure 16-5: Setting a dialog argument

Return Values of a Dialog Box

A return value is generated every time a user clicks a button on a dialog box. This value indicates which button was clicked to close the dialog box. Once again, the following code displays the File Open dialog box, and then displays a message box indicating which button was clicked. The possible return values are shown in the table.

Return Value	Description
–2	The Close button.
–1	The OK button.
0 (zero)	The Cancel button.
> 0 (zero)	A command button: 1 is the first button, 2 is the second button, and so on.

```
Dim x As Integer
x = Application.Dialogs(Word.WdWordDialog.wdDialogFileOpen)
Select Case x
Case -1
  MsgBox "Open"
Case 0
  MsgBox "Cancel"
End Select
```

As mentioned before, you can control almost every aspect of the Dialogs collection through its many methods and properties. In the following sections, we'll take a look at the most important methods and properties and discuss how they can be implemented.

The Show Method

The Show method of the Dialog object can be used if you simply need to display a particular dialog box to the user and do not want to add any functionality. This method will display the dialog according to the wdWordDialog constant that you use and will execute any action taken just as if Word displayed it. When utilizing Dialog objects, the easiest way to ensure the proper syntax is to use IntelliSense. Figure 16-6 shows how to select the fully qualified name of the dialog box using IntelliSense to avoid syntax errors when typing the name.

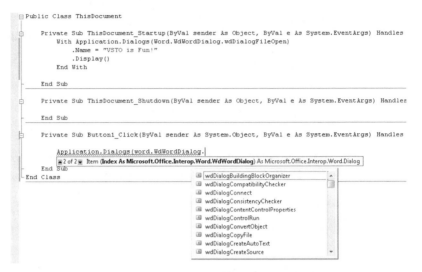

Figure 16-6: IntelliSense displaying dialog constants

The following code snippet displays the SaveAs dialog box:

```
Application.Dialogs(Word.WdWordDialog.wdDialogFileSaveAs).Show()
```

Once this line of code is executed, the Show method will display the SaveAs dialog box. The user can then enter a new file name and click OK, and the file will be saved. If you need to display a particular tab to the user, you can set the Default Tab property. You can also rely on IntelliSense to display a list of the available options tabs. For example, if you wanted to display the General tab of the Office button | Word Options dialog box, you could use the following code:

```
With Application.Dialogs(Word.WdWordDialog.wdDialogToolsOptions)
    .DefaultTab = wdDialogToolsOptionsTabGeneral
    .Show
End With
```

The Show method also has an optional TimeOut parameter. This parameter takes an argument of long variable type and represents the length of time (in milliseconds) the dialog box will remain displayed.

The Display Method

The Display method is used to display a dialog box without enabling the actions that are built into that dialog box. Any changes made by the user will not be applied unless we use the Execute method of that dialog box. The Display method can be useful if you need to prompt the user with a built-in dialog box and return the entered settings. This is also the method you will be using to intercept a user's commands and carry out your own execution.

The following code will display the File Open dialog box and return a message box to the user with the name of the file that was selected. Remember, although the File Open dialog box is being used, the file will not actually be opened when the Display method is used because the Execute method has not been called. In our sample project, change the Click event as follows:

```
Private Sub Button1_Click(ByVal sender As System.Object, ByVal e
As System.EventArgs) Handles Button1.Click
    'your code will go here
    With Application.Dialogs(Word.WdWordDialog.wdDialogFileOpen)
        .Display()
        MsgBox(.Name())
    End With
End Sub
```

As previously mentioned, in order to open the file after displaying the message box in the previous example, you can use the Execute method. The following example displays the File Open dialog box, displays a message box showing the chosen file name, and opens the file (given that the Name property is not empty). The Execute method will execute the appropriate actions of the dialog box based on the settings even if the dialog box is not displayed.

```
Private Sub Button1_Click(ByVal sender As System.Object, ByVal e
As System.EventArgs) Handles Button1.Click
    'your code will go here
    With Application.Dialogs(Word.WdWordDialog.wdDialogFileOpen)
        .Display()
        MsgBox(.Name())
        If .Name <> "" Then .Execute
```

```
      End With
End Sub
```

The CompareDocuments and MergeDocuments Functions

When you need to programmatically compare and/or merge multiple Word documents, the CompareDocuments and MergeDocuments functions, new to Word 2007, can be particularly useful. Each function takes several parameters as shown in the following table, but you can think of each function in much the same manner as you would if you were working directly with the Word user interface.

Name	Description
CompareCaseChanges	This determines whether to mark differences in case between the two documents. Default value is True.
CompareComments	This determines whether to compare differences in comments between the two documents. Default value is True.
CompareFields	This determines whether to compare differences in fields between the two documents. Default value is True.
CompareFootnotes	This determines whether to compare differences in footnotes and endnotes between the two documents. Default value is True.
CompareFormatting	This determines whether to mark differences in formatting between the two documents. Default value is True.
CompareHeaders	This determines whether to compare differences in headers and footers between the two documents. Default value is True.
CompareTables	This determines whether to compare the differences in data contained in tables between the two documents. Default value is True.
CompareTextboxes	This determines whether to compare differences in the data contained within text boxes between the two documents. Default value is True.
CompareWhitespace	This determines whether to mark differences in white space, such as paragraphs or spaces, between the two documents. Default value is True.

Name	Description
Destination	This determines whether to create a new file or to mark the differences between the two documents in the original document or in the revised document. Default value is wdCompareDestinationNew.
FormatFrom (only merge)	This determines the document from which to retain formatting.
Granularity	This determines whether changes are tracked by character or by word. Default value is wdGranularityWordLevel.
IgnoreAllComparisonWarnings (only compare)	This determines whether to ignore warnings when comparing the two documents.
OriginalDocument	This determines the path and file name of the original document.
RevisedAuthor	This determines the name of the person to whom to attribute changes when comparing the two documents.
RevisedDocument	This determines the path and file name of the revised document to which to compare the original document.

The CompareDocuments function compares two documents and returns the result as a Document object. Closely related to CompareDocuments is MergeDocuments, which merges two documents and returns a Document object that represents a separate document that contains the differences between the two documents. These differences are marked using tracked changes.

The following code demonstrates how to use MergeDocuments to merge two fictitious documents together. If you have downloaded the sample files, you should be able to use the code shown below in the Click event of the previously created document project. Replace the existing code and insert the following in the Click event:

```
Dim origDoc As New Word.Document
Dim newDoc As New Word.Document
Dim resultDoc As New Word.Document

origDoc = Application.Documents.Open("C:\Scott\VSTO\Original Contract.docx")
newDoc = Application.Documents.Open("C:\Scott\VSTO\New Contract.docx")
resultDoc = wrdApp.MergeDocuments(origDoc, newDoc)
resultDoc.Application.Visible = True
```

This example jumps ahead in terms of the objects involved in the code, but it is useful to illustrate the MergeDocuments function. First, we begin by declaring three Document variables. You can see by the assignment of these variables that one is used to represent the original contract document, the second is used to represent the amended contract document, and the third is used to contain the resultant document returned by the MergeDocuments function. If you have the sample files installed, you should see the resultant document as shown in Figure 16-7.

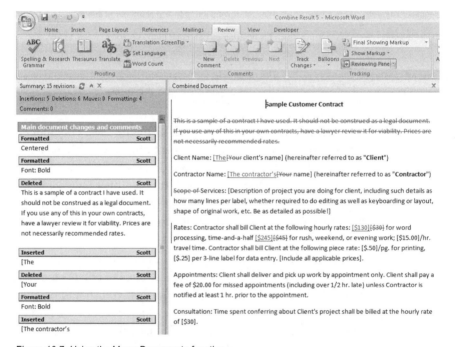

Figure 16-7: Using the MergeDocuments function

The SynonymInfo Property

The practical application of the SynonymInfo object may seem a little elusive without some creative thinking. Typically, if a user is interacting with Word, he has the option of using the Thesaurus functionality from the Ribbon tab. From a programmatic standpoint, the SynonymInfo object returns arrays, so a search-and-replace type function is out of the question unless you were to arbitrarily choose an index value (which would have spurious results at best). Let's take a closer look at the inner workings of the SynonymInfo property.

The Application object's SynonymInfo property returns a SynonymInfo object. The SynonymInfo property applies to the Range object. You'll need to specify the lookup word or phrase and a proofing language ID when the SynonymInfo object is accessing the SynonymInfo property at the application level. If the SynonymInfo object is returned from a range, Word uses the specified range as the lookup word. The following table shows the SynonymInfo object's properties.

Name	Description
AntonymList	Returns a list of antonyms for the word or phrase. The list is returned as an array of strings.
Application	Returns an Application object that represents the Microsoft Word application.
Creator	Returns a 32-bit integer that indicates the application in which the specified object was created.
Found	True if the thesaurus finds synonyms, antonyms, related words, or related expressions for the word or phrase.
MeaningCount	Returns the number of entries in the list of meanings found in the thesaurus for the word or phrase. Returns 0 (zero) if no meanings were found.
MeaningList	Returns the list of meanings for the word or phrase. The list is returned as an array of strings.
Parent	Returns an object that represents the parent object of the specified object.
PartOfSpeechList	Returns a list of the parts of speech corresponding to the meanings found for the word or phrase looked up in the thesaurus. The list is returned as an array of integers.
RelatedExpressionList	Returns a list of expressions related to the specified word or phrase. The list is returned as an array of strings.
RelatedWordList	Returns a list of words related to the specified word or phrase. The list is returned as an array of strings.
SynonymList	Returns a list of synonyms for a specified meaning of a word or phrase. The list is returned as an array of strings.
Word	Returns the word or phrase that was looked up by the thesaurus.

Many of the properties of the SynonymInfo object return an object that contains an array of strings. To see the elements in the returned object's array, you can assign the returned array to a variable and then index the variable.

The following code shows an example of using the SynonymInfo object in case you want to include Word's thesaurus-like functionality in other custom applications. With very little code you can include a great deal of functionality to your existing applications or cross-application VSTO projects. The following example also shows how to use a new feature of VB 9.0, implicit variable assignment, using a function return value. Figure 16-8 shows the hierarchical structure of the data retrieved in the nested loops.

```
Dim sInfo As Word.SynonymInfo

sInfo = wrdApp.SynonymInfo("blank")
'implicit variable assignment - Meaninglist returns an Array
Dim sMeanings = sInfo.MeaningList
Dim sSyns As Array
Dim sWord As String
Dim i = 1
Dim s As String

For i = 1 To sInfo.MeaningCount
   sSyns = sInfo.SynonymList(sMeanings(i))
   sWord = sMeanings(i)
   s = s & sWord & vbNewLine
   For y = 1 To UBound(sSyns)
      s = s & vbTab & sSyns(y) & vbNewLine
   Next
Next
MsgBox(s)
```

Figure 16-8: Using the SynonymInfo object

The AutoSummarize Function

An often overlooked feature in Word is the AutoSummarize function. AutoSummarize grabs the key points of a document and puts them in an abstract or line-by-line summary. This can be an invaluable tool when you are working with a new document that is very long.

Word's AutoSummarize function attempts to condense a document to a concise summary. While it is subjective whether the function's summary is perfect or not, it is a great function that you can use creatively when necessary. The following code shows how to loop through a directory of documents, open them, AutoSummarize them, and save the results to a separate directory.

```
Dim sDir As String = "C:\Scott\vsto\testdocs\"
Dim dDir As New System.IO.DirectoryInfo(sDir)
Dim docFile As System.IO.FileInfo
Dim sumDoc As New Word.Document
For Each docFile In dDir.GetFiles()
    Dim tempDoc As New Word.Document
```

```
    tempDoc = wrdApp.Documents.Open(sDir & docFile.Name, False,
True)
    sumDoc = tempDoc.AutoSummarize(40,
Word.WdSummaryMode.wdSummaryModeCreateNew)
    sumDoc.SaveAs("C:\Scott\vsto\testdocs\output\" & docFile.Name)
    tempDoc.Close(True)
Next
```

The CleanString Function

When working with HTTP requirements, file names, text processing, or even saving strings to certain data types in a
database, they often must be parsed and cleaned. A great function of the Word Application object to carry out this task is
the CleanString function. This function removes or changes to
a white space (character code 32) nonprinting characters
(character codes 1–29) and/or special Microsoft Word characters from the specified string. An example usage of the
CleanString function is shown below:

```
Application.CleanString("string")
```

When working outside of Word, you must often create your
own CleanString function to accomplish this task. Although
you wouldn't want to invoke Word just to use this function,
Word's CleanString function works quite well and can prove
to be quite efficient when working in the context of a Word
VSTO project.

The Document Object

The Document object represents a Word document and
resides inside the Documents collection. You can access
members of the Documents collection by name or by their
respective index value. You can also iterate over the entire
Documents collection easily by using a For...Each loop. The
Document object is so fundamental to Word programming
that you really can't avoid using it. In order to use the Document object, you'll need to understand the basics such as
adding, deleting, opening, and accessing documents.

However, in order to write any document automation or document assembly routines you'll probably require a deeper understanding.

The BuiltInDocumentProperties Object

The purpose of document properties is to provide a common way to describe any document. Document properties are details, or metadata, about a file that help identify it. Details such as a descriptive title, the author name, the subject, and keywords that identify topics or other important information in the file are just a few examples. Custom properties extend this functionality by allowing you to define your own properties.

There are four main types of document properties: Automatically updated properties, Preset properties, Custom properties, and Document Library properties. The Automatically updated properties include statistics that are maintained for you by Office programs, such as file size and the dates files are created and last modified. The Preset properties already exist (such as author, title, and subject), but you must add a text value. The Custom properties are properties you define. You can assign a text, time, or numeric value to custom properties, and you can assign them the values "yes" or "no." You can also choose from a list of suggested names or define your own. And finally, the Document library properties are for files in a document library on a web site or public folder. When you design a document library, you define one or more document library properties and set rules on their values.

The following example illustrates how to use the BuiltInDocumentProperties object to display the list of authors for each document in a given directory.

```
Private Sub Button1_Click(ByVal sender As System.Object, ByVal e
As System.EventArgs) Handles Button1.Click
    'your code will go here
    Dim sDir As String = "C:\Scott\vsto\testdocs\"
    Dim dDir As New System.IO.DirectoryInfo(sDir)
    Dim docFile As System.IO.FileInfo
```

```
Dim s As String
For Each docFile In dDir.GetFiles()
    Dim tempDoc As New Word.Document
    tempDoc = wrdApp.Documents.Open(sDir & docFile.Name, False,
True)
        s = s & vbNewLine & tempDoc.BuiltInDocumentProperties(Word.
            WdBuiltInProperty.wdPropertyAuthor).Value
    Next
    MsgBox(s)
End Sub
```

If you've downloaded the companion files, you should be able to run this code in our current project and see the message box displayed in Figure 16-9.

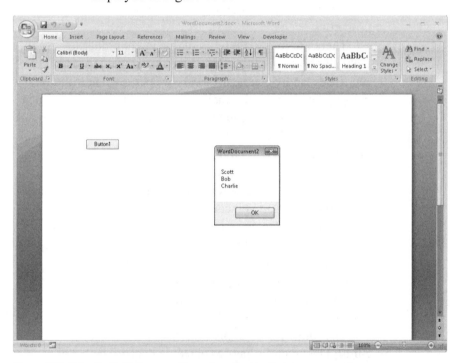

Figure 16-9: Using the BuiltInDocumentProperties object to display a message box

In this example, the sDir variable holds a hard-coded path to the test documents. We then use a fully qualified call to the System.IO (you could also import this) DirectoryInfo function and iterate the files in that directory using a For...Each loop. The results are concatenated into a single string variable using the vbNewLine constant to display a list. As you can see, we must programmatically open the Document object in order to access the BuiltInDocumentProperties.

There are several different constants associated with BuiltInDocumentProperties that you may need to access depending on your specific project. Be sure to use the appropriate object for your organization as these properties are different from the CustomDocumentProperties. The syntax and behavior of the two objects are very similar except that CustomDocumentProperties uses an arbitrary name while BuiltInDocumentProperties uses predefined constants. The following table shows the constants used by Word.

Member Name	Description
wdPropertyAppName	Name of application
wdPropertyAuthor	Author
wdPropertyBytes	Byte count
wdPropertyCategory	Category
wdPropertyCharacters	Character count
wdPropertyCharsWSpaces	Character count with spaces
wdPropertyComments	Comments
wdPropertyCompany	Company
wdPropertyFormat	Not supported
wdPropertyHiddenSlides	Not supported
wdPropertyHyperlinkBase	Not supported
wdPropertyKeywords	Keywords
wdPropertyLastAuthor	Last author
wdPropertyLines	Line count
wdPropertyManager	Manager
wdPropertyMMClips	Not supported
wdPropertyNotes	Notes
wdPropertyPages	Page count
wdPropertyParas	Paragraph count
wdPropertyRevision	Revision number

Member Name	Description
wdPropertySecurity	Security setting
wdPropertySlides	Not supported
wdPropertySubject	Subject
wdPropertyTemplate	Template name
wdPropertyTimeCreated	Time created
wdPropertyTimeLastPrinted	Time last printed
wdPropertyTimeLastSaved	Time last saved
wdPropertyTitle	Title
wdPropertyVBATotalEdit	Number of edits to VBA project
wdPropertyWords	Word count

The Fields Collection

The most robust set of items available to a Word document is the Fields collection. The Field object represents an individual field in a Word document, while the Fields property returns a Fields collection. The Fields collection contains all of the fields that currently exist in a document.

You can use fields in much the same manner as bookmarks, and for inserting text into a document. There are several fields that will also populate information without writing code. Take the Date field for instance. You can easily add the current date to a document without writing a single line of VB.

You can also use fields to build intelligence into the document using conditional statements. This covers adding additional documents, if necessary, and using language dependencies. The following table shows the methods associated with Word Field objects.

Name	Description
Copy	Copies the specified field to the clipboard.
Cut	Removes the specified field from the document and places it on the clipboard.
Delete	Deletes the specified field.

Name	Description
DoClick	Clicks the specified field.
Select	Selects the specified field.
Unlink	Replaces the specified field with its most recent result.
Update	Updates the result of the field. Returns True if the field is updated successfully.
UpdateSource	Saves the changes made to the results of an IncludeText field back to the source document.

The following table shows the properties associated with Word Field objects.

Name	Description
Application	Returns an Application object that represents the Microsoft Word application.
Code	Returns a Range object that represents a field's code. Read/write.
Creator	Returns a 32-bit integer that indicates the application in which the specified object was created. Read-only long.
Data	Returns or sets data in an AddIn field. Read/write string.
Index	Returns a long that represents the position of an item in a collection. Read-only.
InlineShape	Returns an InlineShape object that represents the picture, OLE object, or ActiveX control that is the result of an IncludePicture or Embed field.
Kind	Returns the type of link for a Field object. Read-only WdFieldKind.
LinkFormat	Returns a LinkFormat object that represents the link options of the specified field. Read-only.
Locked	True if the specified field is locked. Read/write Boolean.
Next	Returns the next object in the collection. Read-only.
OLEFormat	Returns an OLEFormat object that represents the OLE characteristics (other than linking) for the specified field. Read-only.
Parent	Returns an object that represents the parent object of the specified Field object.
Previous	Returns the previous object in the collection. Read-only.
Result	Returns a Range object that represents a field's result. Read/write.
ShowCodes	True if field codes are displayed for the specified field instead of field results. Read/write Boolean.
Type	Returns the field type. Read-only WdFieldType.

Adding Fields to a Collection

Adding fields to a document is accomplished by using the Add method of the Fields collection. The Add method has four parameters, two of which are required. The Range parameter is the range where you want to add the field. The Type parameter is the type of field as defined by the Word.WdFieldType constant. The optional Text parameter is any additional text necessary for a particular field. The optional PreserveFormatting parameter is set to True to have the formatting preserved when the field is inserted. The syntax of the Add method is shown below.

```
FieldObject.Add(Range, Type, Text, PreserveFormatting)
```

We'll take an in-depth look at adding fields to a document in the document assembly project at the end of this chapter. While adding fields is important, a far more common situation involves the deletion of fields from a document in order to cleanse metadata.

Deleting Fields from a Collection

Fields are actually metadata. Because of this, you should avoid using them to contain sensitive information or at least make sure you clear them out before the document is shared with others. There is no exact VB equivalent of the UI's Home tab | Editing group | Replace method for globally deleting all fields in a document. You can accomplish the same thing using VB code, but you must iterate through each StoryRange of the document in order to delete every field. StoryRanges are a collection of Range objects that represent stories in a document. Stories are simply a mechanism by which Word organizes a document into its associated components.

The following example procedure can be used to delete all of the fields in a document:

```
Sub DeleteAllFields()
Dim rngDel As Word.Range
rngDel = Application.ActiveDocument.Range
```

```
Do
    With rngDel.Fields
    While .Count > 0
        .Item(1).Delete()
    End While
    End With
    rngDel = rngDel.NextStoryRange
    Loop Until rngDel Is Nothing
End Sub
```

Let's say that you only want to delete a particular type of field. After bookmarks, the DocVariable field is probably the number two method of inserting text into a document. You should know, however, that DocVariable fields can contain a great deal of metadata that is not visible on the *face* of the document. From an end user's perspective, search and replace simply wouldn't work because the DocVariable information may have been created programmatically and may not exist on the actual document itself. The following example procedure will delete all DocVariable fields in a document:

```
Sub DeleteDocVariables()
    Dim rngDel As Word.Range
    Dim oFld As Word.Field

    For Each rngDel In Application.ActiveDocument.StoryRanges
        Do
            For Each oFld In rngDel.Fields
                Select Case oFld.Type
                    Case Word.WdFieldType.wdFieldDocVariable
                        oFld.Delete()
                    Case Else
                        'Do nothing
                End Select
            Next
            rngDel = rngDel.NextStoryRange
        Loop Until rngDel Is Nothing
    Next
End Sub
```

The Paragraphs Collection

When working with the organization or structure of a Word document, the Paragraphs collection is one of the most convenient mechanisms to utilize. You can programmatically add paragraphs or manipulate a paragraph's text using either the Range or the Selection objects.

Word also provides styles, which allow you to format both paragraphs and individual characters in your document. These styles can greatly simplify the consistent application of formatting across an entire document. You may need to determine the name of the style applied to a particular paragraph. You can do that by using the Style property of a Paragraph object, where the argument "i" represents the numeric identifier of an individual paragraph in the Paragraphs collections. The following line of code is an example of determining a particular style name of a paragraph and assigning it to a variable:

```
sStyle = Application.ActiveDocument.Paragraphs(i).Style
```

There are also tasks that you can programmatically achieve that are impossible by using just the Word UI. For instance, a user may want to find all bulleted paragraphs in a lengthy document. This task seems easy enough; however, keep in mind that you cannot use Word's search feature to find bulleted paragraphs. Word doesn't provide a way to search for the *bulleted* attribute. Word also does not allow you to search for the actual bullet character.

One approach to this task would be to make sure you always use styles to apply your bullets to paragraphs. This would allow you to quickly search for paragraphs formatted with a specific style. The following example provides a quick mechanism to search for the first occurrence of a bulleted paragraph and take the user directly to it. You can easily extend this type of functionality to match your needs.

```
Sub FindBulletedParagraphs()
    Dim rngTarget As Word.Range
    Dim oPara As Word.Paragraph
```

```
rngTarget = Application.ActiveDocument.Range
With rngTarget
    Call .Collapse(Word.WdCollapseDirection.wdCollapseEnd)
    .End = Application.ActiveDocument.Range.End

    For Each oPara In .Paragraphs
        If oPara.Range.ListFormat.ListType =
Word.WdListType.wdListBullet Then
            oPara.Range.Select()
            Exit For
        End If
    Next
End With
End Sub
```

The FormFields Collection

Although InfoPath and simple web programming have greatly
diminished the value of Word's simple FormFields, there are
still quite a few documents out there that use FormFields. You
can use the FormFields property to return the FormFields collection. The following code counts the number of text box
form fields in the active document:

```
Dim count As Integer
    For Each aField In Application.ActiveDocument.FormFields
        If aField.Type = Word.WdFieldType.wdFieldFormTextInput Then
count = count + 1
    Next aField
    MsgBox("There are " & count & " text boxes in this document")
```

You can programmatically add FormFields to a document
using the object's Add method. The following example adds a
check box at the beginning of the active document.

```
Application.ActiveDocument.FormFields.Add( _
    Range:=ActiveDocument.Range(Start:=0, End:=0), _
    Type:=wdFieldFormCheckBox)
```

Bookmarks

The Word bookmark is simply a name associated with a specific range of text or a single insertion point. This aspect is

perhaps the most important thing to understand when working with bookmarks. Word has two types of bookmarks: place-holder bookmarks and enclosure bookmarks. When working with bookmarks, you'll want to turn on display of bookmarks by going to **Office button** | **Word Options** | **Advanced** and selecting **Show Bookmarks**. This makes it easier to see what's actually happening as a result of your code. Figure 16-10 shows how the two different bookmarks actually appear in the Word UI.

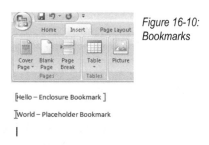

Figure 16-10:
Bookmarks

A placeholder bookmark is indicated by an I-beam-shaped mark, while an enclosure bookmark appears enclosed in square brackets. The following line of code illustrates a simple use of a bookmark for document assembly. You can set the Text property of a bookmark's Range object to insert text at the bookmark's location.

```
Application.ActiveDocument.Bookmarks("name").Range.Text = "Johnny
Carson"
```

You can also add a Bookmark object to the Bookmarks collection by using the following syntax:

```
Application.[Document].Bookmarks.Add(Name, Range)
```

Bookmarks are probably the most utilized method of pro-grammatically inserting text into a document. Bookmarks are flexible in that they can mark either a single insertion point or an entire paragraph (or more) if necessary. If you are using bookmarks as placeholders for dynamic text in a boilerplate document, you'll want to create a subroutine that inserts the appropriate text so that you don't have to write code each time you want to insert text.

The best way to insert text at a bookmark without losing the bookmark is to set a Range variable to the bookmark's range. The following example code provides a simple UpdateBookmark procedure that you can utilize to insert text into a document. The function takes the name of the bookmark and the text to be inserted as parameters.

```
Sub UpdateBookmark(ByVal bookmarkName As String, ByVal insertText
As String)
    Dim rngBookmark As Word.Range
    rngBookmark = Application.ActiveDocument.Book-
marks(bookmarkName).Range
    rngBookmark.Text = insertText
    Application.ActiveDocument.Bookmarks.Add(bookmarkName,
rngBookmark)
End Sub
```

The previous procedure works great if you know that the bookmark parameter is valid and is within the scope of the document. However, if you do not know the validity of a given bookmark, the Exists method can be used to check for its existence. If you attempt to access bookmarks that do not exist, you'll trigger an error. For example, you could add the following conditional statement to the UpdateBookmark procedure:

```
If Application.ActiveDocument.Bookmarks(bookmarkName).Exists Then
'code to execute
End If
```

Document Shapes and InlineShapes

Each Word document has two graphical layers: the text layer and a drawing layer. If you've ever used Adobe's Photoshop you should be familiar with virtual layers. You can simply think of layers as transparent sheets over a white background. A Shape object is a Word object that is placed on the drawing sheet, which in turn lies on top of the text sheet.

Shape objects are anchored to a specific range. This results in the often-frustrating experience of changing nearby text and inadvertently moving the shape. InlineShape objects, on the other hand, are shapes that are placed onto the text sheet of the document.

Shapes utilize a Z-order property in much the same way as controls on a form are ordered. Z-order can be set in the following four ways: move the shape to the front, move the shape to the back, move the shape one step forward, and move the shape one step backward.

You can programmatically convert shapes from one type to the other. The following code converts each InlineShape object in the active document to a Shape object.

```
For Each iShape In Application.ActiveDocument.InlineShapes
    iShape.ConvertToShape()
Next iShape
```

You can use the New method of the InlineShape object to create a new picture as an inline shape. You can use the AddPicture and AddOLEObject methods to add pictures or OLE objects and link them to a source file. The Count property for this collection in a document returns the number of items in the main story only. To count items in other stories, use the collection with the Range object. When you open a document created in an earlier version of Word, pictures are converted to inline shapes.

Templates and Documents

Every Word document is based on a template. Templates are distinguished in the file system by the extension (.dot, .dotm, or .dotx, depending on the version of Word). Documents have a .doc, .docm, or .docx extension. Every time that you create a new document, it maintains a link to the template that created it. This association can be changed, but a document cannot exist without an accompanying template. New documents are created based on the Normal.dot default template unless you specify a custom template. This template is created when Word is installed and will be recreated upon launching Word if it is inadvertently deleted. There are two basic types of templates: global templates and document templates. Global templates are available to all documents and are typically referred to as template add-ins. In order to use settings from another template, you must either load the other template as a global template or attach a reference to the other template. If a template is loaded as a global template, items stored in that template are available to all documents. Figure 16-11 provides a simple illustration of how a document may access both its associated parent template and numerous potential add-in templates.

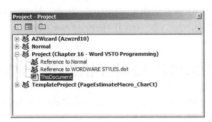

Figure 16-11: The interaction of documents and templates

There are two areas where document templates can reside in order to appear in the Templates list when you choose **Office button | New**. The User templates and Workgroup templates directories are specified in Word under **Office button | Word Options | Advanced | File Locations**. These directories, and any subdirectories containing templates, appear in the New Document window when you choose **Office button | New**. This is where any organization templates should reside. It is important to note that the My Templates list displays templates appearing in both locations.

The most common global template is the Normal template. This is the default template from which all blank documents are created. Templates contain settings that are available only to documents attached to that template. A document created from a template can use the settings from both the template and the settings in any global template. Word provides numerous document templates and there are thousands available on the Internet for free. You can also create your own templates.

The Normal.dotx Template

The Normal.dotx template is global in scope and thereby available to every document you create. For VSTO solutions, the best approach is to create customized templates for specific applications. Documents created using your custom template still have access to the settings contained in any corporate or organization-specific default Normal.dotx template. In fact, you can attach a document to more than one custom template in addition to Normal.dotx if you want.

Programming Code Behind Documents

You are not limited to templates as containers for customized styles and code. You can also create a Word Document project to customize and write code in individual documents without affecting the content of the parent template. When Word invokes your code, it uses the fully qualified reference of the source. This way, the choice of a document or template project is based entirely upon the actual usage, rather than a technical limitation of either type.

Document Assembly Project Using VSTO

As mentioned at the beginning of the chapter, in this section we implement what we have learned in this chapter in a small project. We'll look at how we can programmatically assemble a single document based on a variety of documents contained in a single folder. We'll do this in a very linear, straightforward manner by inserting a series of fields.

This project relies on sample files that represent fictitious pieces of a business plan. We assemble these document pieces into a single business plan template in the ThisDocument Startup event using the methods we discussed earlier in this chapter. You will need to change the paths according to your directory structure, but Figure 16-12 shows the five files that comprise the foundation directory. Each file represents a discrete section of the business plan.

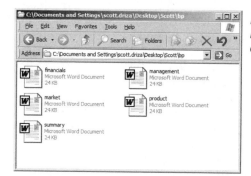

Figure 16-12: Files in the business plan component directory

The first step is to create a new Word template project and choose to create a new document when prompted by the dialog box shown in Figure 16-13. Using VSTO code, we add the component documents utilizing Word's IncludeText field and update the fields to show the subsidiary documents.

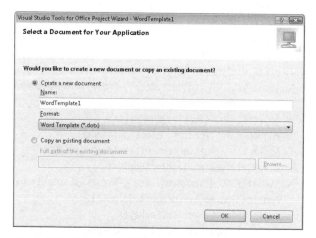

Figure 16-13: Using a new Word document for the template project

Next, we create a variable to hold the range of the ActiveDocument. Every time a template is launched, it will create a document that is attached to the template. This association is the reason we are working with the ActiveDocument rather than ThisDocument.

The code then collapses to the beginning of the document to make sure we are at the very beginning. After this, we add fields to the document and pass in a directory location (which you will need to change to accommodate your settings) for the subsidiary documents. The following code demonstrates using the Startup event of a template:

```
Private Sub ThisDocument_Startup(ByVal sender As Object, ByVal e
As System.EventArgs) Handles Me.Startup
    Dim rngDoc As Word.Range
    rngDoc = Application.ActiveDocument.Range
    rngDoc.Collapse(Word.WdCollapseDirection.wdCollapseStart)
    Application.ActiveDocument.Fields.Add(rngDoc,
Word.WdFieldType.wdFieldIncludeText,
"C:\Scott\VSTO\BPlan\intro.docx", PreserveFormatting:=True)
    Application.ActiveDocument.Select()
    Application.Selection.EndKey()
    rngDoc = Application.Selection.Range
    Application.ActiveDocument.Fields.Add(rngDoc,
Word.WdFieldType.wdFieldIncludeText,
"C:\Scott\VSTO\BPlan\exec.docx", PreserveFormatting:=True)
    Application.ActiveDocument.Select()
    Application.Selection.EndKey()
    rngDoc = Application.Selection.Range
    Application.ActiveDocument.Fields.Add(rngDoc,
Word.WdFieldType.wdFieldIncludeText,
"C:\Scott\VSTO\BPlan\desc.docx", PreserveFormatting:=True)
    Application.ActiveDocument.Select()
    Application.Selection.EndKey()
    rngDoc = Application.Selection.Range
    Application.ActiveDocument.Fields.Add(rngDoc,
Word.WdFieldType.wdFieldIncludeText,
"C:\Scott\VSTO\BPlan\prod.docx", PreserveFormatting:=True)
    Application.ActiveDocument.Select()
    Application.Selection.EndKey()
    rngDoc = Application.Selection.Range
    Application.ActiveDocument.Fields.Add(rngDoc,
Word.WdFieldType.wdFieldIncludeText,
"C:\Scott\VSTO\BPlan\mgmt.docx", PreserveFormatting:=True)
End Sub
```

When you run this project, Word navigates to the folder you've specified and creates the IncludeText fields as shown in Figure 16-14. The resultant document at this point contains fields that represent the individual component documents as a single document. The Selection object ensures that we are adding the subsidiary documents in the correct order. After selecting the entire range (after each field addition), the

EndKey method moves the cursor location to the end of the document. Notice that we are not adding a hard return; in this example, the hard returns and physical structure of the document are contained by the subsidiary templates.

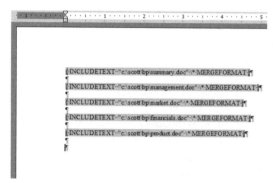

Figure 16-14:
IncludeText fields
created by VSTO

The resultant document looks correct, but there is one important caveat to mention. The document still contains the actual field codes rather than the resultant text. In most cases, you'll want to create a complete document so that the users aren't worried about whether they are working in the context of a Word field or whether they are actually interacting directly with the Word document.

In order to detach the text from the source fields, you'll need to update the field to get the latest result and unlink to force the resultant text into the document. The following procedure highlights the code to accomplish these two tasks. The resulting document is shown in Figure 16-15.

```
Private Sub ThisDocument_Startup(ByVal sender As Object, ByVal e
As System.EventArgs) Handles Me.Startup
    Dim rngDoc As Word.Range
    rngDoc = Application.ActiveDocument.Range
    rngDoc.Delete()
    rngDoc.Collapse(Word.WdCollapseDirection.wdCollapseStart)
    Application.ActiveDocument.Fields.Add(rngDoc,
Word.WdFieldType.wdFieldIncludeText,
"C:\Scott\VSTO\BPlan\intro.docx", PreserveFormatting:=True)
    Application.ActiveDocument.Select()
    Application.Selection.EndKey()
    rngDoc = Application.Selection.Range
```

```
            Application.ActiveDocument.Fields.Add(rngDoc,
        Word.WdFieldType.wdFieldIncludeText,
        "C:\Scott\VSTO\BPlan\exec.docx", PreserveFormatting:=True)
            Application.ActiveDocument.Select()
            Application.Selection.EndKey()
            rngDoc = Application.Selection.Range
            Application.ActiveDocument.Fields.Add(rngDoc,
        Word.WdFieldType.wdFieldIncludeText,
        "C:\Scott\VSTO\BPlan\desc.docx", PreserveFormatting:=True)
            Application.ActiveDocument.Select()
            Application.Selection.EndKey()
            rngDoc = Application.Selection.Range
            Application.ActiveDocument.Fields.Add(rngDoc,
        Word.WdFieldType.wdFieldIncludeText,
        "C:\Scott\VSTO\BPlan\prod.docx", PreserveFormatting:=True)
            Application.ActiveDocument.Select()
            Application.Selection.EndKey()
            rngDoc = Application.Selection.Range
            Application.ActiveDocument.Fields.Add(rngDoc,
        Word.WdFieldType.wdFieldIncludeText,
        "C:\Scott\VSTO\BPlan\mgmt.docx", PreserveFormatting:=True)
            Application.ActiveDocument.Fields.Update()
            Application.ActiveDocument.Fields.Unlink()
        End Sub
```

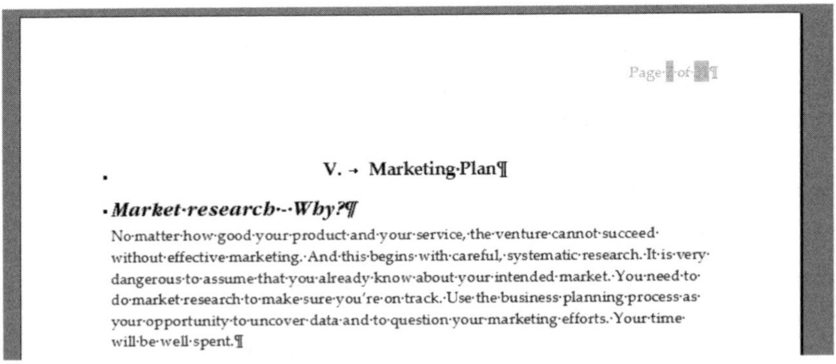

V. → Marketing·Plan¶

Market·research·--·Why?¶

No·matter·how·good·your·product·and·your·service,·the·venture·cannot·succeed·
without·effective·marketing.··And·this·begins·with·careful,·systematic·research.·It·is·very·
dangerous·to·assume·that·you·already·know·about·your·intended·market.·You·need·to·
do·market·research·to·make·sure·you're·on·track.·Use·the·business·planning·process·as·
your·opportunity·to·uncover·data·and·to·question·your·marketing·efforts.·Your·time·
will·be·well·spent.¶

Figure 16-15: The resultant document

Conclusion

In this chapter we learned about automating document production in Word 2007. Since a solid understanding of the inner workings of Word is necessary in order to undertake such a task, we looked at the Application and Document objects of Word 2007 and their various methods and properties. The Application object essentially represents the actual Word application. Through various methods and properties, we can programmatically control the application to do things even beyond the controls of the UI. The Document object is crucial to programming Word documents. Essentially, every document in Word *is* a Document object. After familiarizing ourselves with the more important methods and properties of the Application and Document objects, we then implemented a simple project in order to apply what we learned in this chapter. In the next chapter, we will take a step further and look at some of the advanced options of VSTO.

Chapter 17

Advanced Word VSTO Options

Introduction

The last chapter familiarized us with the basics of Word VSTO. Beyond the fundamentals, VSTO offers a vast number of advanced features. Since a complete discussion of all of the ways to utilize these features is beyond the scope of this book, in this chapter we will take a look at a few of the advanced aspects of VSTO.

There are many ways to interact with the end user. In this chapter we will focus on controls and event handling for Windows Forms and using controls in a document or template. Next, we will continue looking at the Word Application object model by discussing the Range and Selection objects. Word 2007 offers a wide range of functionality to control the appearance of text and many ways to programmatically insert text into a document. This large feature set can be managed more easily once you understand the most commonly used features. The starting point for almost any text formatting is either the Range or Selection objects, which we cover in the last half of the chapter.

User Interaction

Although Word has a huge selection of built-in dialog boxes for gathering user input, VSTO opens the doors to using Windows Forms and Windows Forms controls with your Office solutions. There are several ways you can interact with a user in Word using VSTO. In this section we focus on using Windows Forms and placing controls directly on a document or template.

VSTO and Windows Forms

As mentioned in Chapter 13, Windows Forms are completely different from the MSForms UserForms that are part of VBA. Windows Forms are founded in the System.Windows.Forms.Form class supplied by the .NET Framework. There are three basic ways you can work with Windows Forms in your VSTO solution. The first way is to display a custom Windows form, which requires input from the user. This method lets you control the size of the UI and prevent the user from hiding or deleting the form's controls. The second way is to put Windows Forms controls onto a document or template. In this way, the controls are always displayed and are in line with the data in the document. This method also allows users to enter data directly into the document. And finally, you can put the Windows Forms controls onto a custom task pane. This provides contextual information to the user and ensures the controls do not get printed with the document. Using this method ensures that the view of the document will not be obstructed by the UserForm UI.

VSTO projects display Windows Forms just like any other Visual Studio project. In this section we'll take a brief look at creating a form, adding controls, and responding to events. Finally, we'll look at adding controls directly to the face of a document or template.

When Visual Basic became part of the .NET platform, it added a feature called "inheritance" that allowed it to become an object-oriented programming language. Visual Basic programmers can rapidly build VSTO applications while seamlessly using Windows Forms. The System.Windows.Forms namespace provide types that you need to build a Windows Form. To create a form, you simply add it to your project. To insert a new Windows Form into your VSTO project, choose **Project | Add Windows Form**. You will then be prompted with the Add New Item dialog box as seen in Figure 17-1.

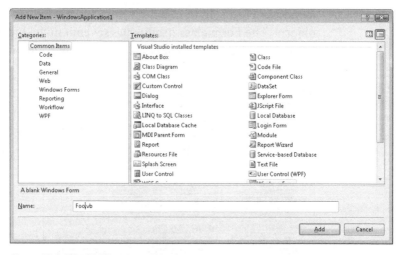

Figure 17-1: The Add New Item dialog box

After adding a Windows Form to your project, two new tabs will be created in the Visual Studio IDE. The first tab is for the design time layout of the form. The second is the actual *.vb file to which you will add your code. If you double-click the form in design mode, it will take you over to the Code window and create an event stub for the Load event of the form. The actual code should appear as:

```
Public Class myForm
    Private Sub myForm_Load(ByVal sender As System.Object, ByVal e
As System.EventArgs) Handles MyBase.Load
    End Sub
End Class
```

When working with forms you will be using classes from the System.Windows.Forms namespace. You can import namespaces to avoid having to type the namespace in front of every class you use. For instance, if you wanted to import the System.Windows.Forms namespace, you could type:

```
Imports System.Windows.Forms
Public Class myForm
    Inherits System.WinForms.Form
End Class
```

Windows Forms, in turn, inherit from several higher level objects. The Form class itself is the seventh in the hierarchy. Figure 17-2 shows the actual hierarchy of the Windows Forms.

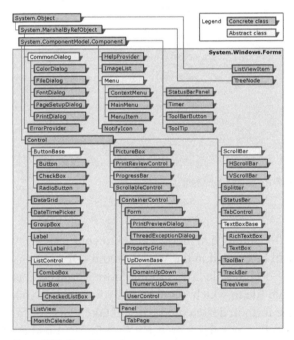

Figure 17-2: Form hierarchy

When working with traditional Windows Forms in a VSTO project, you'll need to decide whether you want the display to be Modal or Modeless. Modal forms require user interaction, and control is only given back to the document once the user clicks OK, Cancel, or Close on the actual form. Modeless forms float alongside your document and can be repositioned to allow the user to concurrently interact with the document while working in the document.

Adding Controls to Windows Forms

Windows Forms are not really useful without controls. You can add controls at design time using the Control designer and dragging and dropping them directly onto the form's surface. You can also create them at run time. Instantiating a control at run time is like instantiating any other object in that you use the New keyword. Once you have an instance of the control, you can add that object to the form.

Because the Form class has no such method as Add(Control), you can't add a control directly to it. However, the Form class inherits the Controls property from the Control class. You can use the Controls property to obtain the System.Windows.Forms.Form.ControlCollection object of the form. The Form.ControlCollection class represents the collection of controls contained within a form. You can use its Add method to add a control to the form and its Remove method to remove a control from the form. The following code shows an example of adding a button to a Windows Form:

```
'Declare the button
Dim Button1 As System.Windows.Forms.Button
'Instantiate the button
Button1 = New System.Windows.Forms.Button()
'Add the button to the form
Me.Controls.Add(Button1)
```

To obtain a desired behavior and the look and feel, you can set the control's many properties. You can set these properties before or after adding the control to the form, but only after the control is instantiated. For its size and position, a control has properties such as Left, Top, Width, and Height. The Button control also has the Text property, which sets the text shown on the actual button. The following example code adds a Button and a TextBox to the control:

```
Public Class Form1

    Private Sub Form1_Load(ByVal sender As System.Object, ByVal e
As System.EventArgs) Handles MyBase.Load
        ' Control declaration: a Button and a TextBox
        Dim Button1 As Button
        Dim TextBox1 As TextBox

        Me.Text = "VSTO Form"
        Me.Width = 400
        Me.Height = 300

        Button1 = New Button()
        TextBox1 = New TextBox()

        Button1.Left = 200
        Button1.Top = 200
        Button1.Width = 100
        Button1.Height = 40
        Button1.TabIndex = 0
        Button1.Text = "Click Me"

        TextBox1.Left = 200
        TextBox1.Top = 30
        TextBox1.Width = 150
        TextBox1.Height = 40

        Me.Controls.Add(Button1)
        Me.Controls.Add(TextBox1)
    End Sub
End Class
```

Event Handling for Windows Forms

All versions of VB are event-driven and you can easily write code that responds to a specific event. For instance, if you want a button to respond to the user click, all you need to do is to create an event procedure. For example, if we had a button named Button1, we would create an event procedure called Button1_Click (actually Visual Studio does this for you). Once you draw your control in design mode, you can double-click it to tell Visual Studio that you want to write an event procedure.

The Form class and all the control classes inherit the events from the Control class. If you look up the .NET Framework reference for the System.Windows.Forms.Control class, you will see that this class has numerous events, including Disposed, Click, DoubleClick, GotFocus, LostFocus, KeyUp, and KeyDown, to name a few. The following is a list of the various events that pertain to a Windows Form.

AutoSizeChanged	Layout
BackColorChanged	Leave
BackgroundImageChanged	LocationChanged
BackgroundImageLayoutChanged	LostFocus
BindingContextChanged	MarginChanged
CausesValidationChanged	MouseCaptureChanged
ChangeUICues	MouseClick
Click	MouseDoubleClick
ClientSizeChanged	MouseDown
ContextMenuChanged	MouseEnter
ContextMenuStripChanged	MouseHover
ControlAdded	MouseLeave
ControlRemoved	MouseMove
CursorChanged	MouseUp
Disposed	MouseWheel
DockChanged	Move
DoubleClick	PaddingChanged
DragDrop	Paint
DragEnter	ParentChanged
DragLeave	PreviewKeyDown
DragOver	QueryAccessibilityHelp
EnabledChanged	QueryContinueDrag
Enter	RegionChanged
FontChanged	Resize
ForeColorChanged	RightToLeftChanged
GiveFeedback	SizeChanged
GotFocus	StyleChanged
HandleCreated	SystemColorsChanged
HandleDestroyed	TabIndexChanged
HelpRequested	TabStopChanged
ImeModeChanged	TextChanged
Invalidated	Validated
KeyDown	Validating
KeyPress	VisibleChanged
KeyUp	

Controls within a Document or Template

The design experience of adding controls to your document or template is identical to that of adding them to a Windows Form. You can simply select the control and draw it at the appropriate location in the document. An important point to note when you are working with controls is that the toolbox may obscure a good portion of the document sometimes, but this can be controlled with the autohide features.

When you add a control to a Word document, the control is added in line with text. If you want to change the style of the control, choose **Format | Control** and select a wrapping style in the Layout tab of the Format Object dialog box. If you open a Word template in the Visual Studio designer, controls on the template that are not in line with text might not be visible because Visual Studio opens the template in Normal view. You can view these controls by selecting **View | Microsoft Office Word View | Print Layout**.

There are a number of limitations when using Windows Forms controls directly on a Word document or template. Some methods and properties of Windows Forms controls do not work the same way on a document and should not be used. The following methods and properties of Windows Forms controls are unsupported for Word: Hide, Show, Anchor, Dock, Location, TabIndex, TabStop, TopLevelControl, and Visible.

Control Location within a Document or Template

The placement of Word controls is affected by the insertion settings in the Word Options dialog. Controls can only exist in the main body of the document and cannot be placed in the header, footer, or a subdocument. Depending on your needs, controls can operate as either a Shape or an InlineShape. This means that a control can be inserted in line with the text so that if the text flow of the document changes, the control is repositioned. Controls can also be inserted in front of the text so that they essentially float over the document and maintain an absolute position. Figure 17-3 shows the settings for the default insertion style in the Word UI.

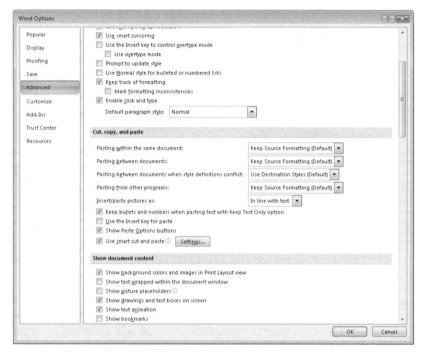

Figure 17-3: Default insertion style

If you need to add multiple controls to your Word documents, it can be cumbersome to position these controls correctly. Thankfully, you can quickly set the alignment of all of the selected controls by using the Paragraph group on the Home tab of the Ribbon. This toolbar has a number of buttons that enable you to arrange multiple controls on the document, including Align Lefts, Align Centers, Align Rights, Align Tops, Align Middles, Align Bottoms, Make Horizontal Spacing Equal, and Make Vertical Spacing Equal.

You may have noticed that a good number of controls do not show up in the Controls toolbox. Microsoft intentionally excluded these controls due to erratic behavior when placed on the document or template surface. In some cases, this omission was due merely to design time limitations. This means that you can still add the controls at run time.

Adding Controls to a Document or Template Dynamically

Controls added programmatically to a document become part of the Controls collection. This collection can be used to iterate through all of the controls in your document, including the controls you added at design time (static controls). You can remove dynamic controls from the collection by passing either the control or the name of the control to the Remove method of the Controls collection. However, note that you cannot remove static controls at run time. Attempting to remove a static control at run time will result in an exception being thrown. At run time, if you programmatically add a control and specify a range for the location, the control is added in line with text.

VSTO has made it easier to add controls to your document dynamically. The most common controls have a helper method so that you don't have to work with the AddControls method, which can be tricky. Generally, each helper function can place the control at the start of a specified range or at a specific insertion point. When you add a control programmatically, you must provide the location to place the control and a name that uniquely identifies the control. Each of the helper methods is overloaded so that you can pass either a range or specific coordinates for the location of the control. The available helper methods are shown in the following list:

AddButton	AddMonthCalendar
AddLabel	AddDomainUpDown
AddLinkLabel	AddNumericUpDown
AddTextBox	AddTrackBar
AddCheckBox	AddRichTextBox
AddRadioButton	AddDataGridView
AddPictureBox	AddHScrollBar
AddComboBox	AddVScrollBar
AddListView	AddPropertyGrid
AddTreeView	AddWebBrowser
AddDateTimePicker	

You can still add controls that aren't supported by the helper methods, but you must use the generic AddControl method and pass the correct parameters. The AddControl method takes three parameter arguments: the actual control, a location for the control, and a name that uniquely identifies it. The AddControl method returns an OLEControl in Word. The following example code demonstrates how to dynamically add a DataGrid control to ActiveDocument.

```
Private Sub ThisDocument_Startup(ByVal sender As Object, ByVal e
As System.EventArgs) Handles Me.Startup
    Dim customControl As New DataGrid
    Dim rng As Word.Range
    rng = Application.ActiveDocument.Range
    Dim dynamicControl As Microsoft.Office.Tools.Word.OLEControl =_
        Me.Controls.AddControl(customControl, 10, 50, 100, 200,
"dynamicDataGrid")
End Sub
```

A Further Look at the Word Object Model

In the previous chapter we were introduced to the Word object model and its multitude of properties and methods. Although there are numerous properties and methods within the Word object model, don't be intimidated, as most of these properties and methods are not used often in Word programming. You can always refer to the Help system to find the correct syntax of a less-frequently used property or method. The following sections focus on providing a good, general understanding of a few of these objects and how they work in Word programming. The two primary objects we'll be looking at toward the end of this section are the Range and Selection objects, also mentioned in the previous chapter. These two objects provide control over the fine details that you'll need to work with Word.

Characters, Words, and Sentences as Collection Objects

One of the neatest things about working with Word is that an individual character in a Word document is actually an object. Characters, words, and sentences are all Collection objects in Word. As you can see by the following syntax, accessing these objects is quite simple.

```
Application.ActiveDocument.Range.Characters.[property]
Application.ActiveDocument.Range.Words.[property]
Application.ActiveDocument.Range.Sentences.[property]
```

As Collection objects, characters, words, and sentences can utilize all the typical Collection properties. You can access an individual instance of an object within a collection using the Item method. You can iterate through these items using a loop until the upper limit has been reached. You can also easily access the beginning and end items using the First and Last properties. General properties and methods of Collection objects include Application, Count, Creator, First, Item, Last, and Parent.

The Find Object

A very common operation in Word is to search and replace text in the body of a document. Word provides a very robust interface that allows your VSTO project to utilize this same functionality in the Find object. There are several properties to work with when using the Find object and you may find that it is easier to obtain the correct syntax by simply recording a macro in VBA and converting the code to VB syntax.

The actual process of searching for text or formatting is as simple as assigning values to the appropriate properties of the Find object and launching the Execute object. Keep in mind that Find is an object and not a method. The Find object has 25 properties that can be set for any given search. As a demonstration in using the Find object, the following code utilizes the Find object to search for all instances of the word "[Company]" and replace it with "Microsoft."

```
Private Sub Button1_Click(ByVal sender As System.Object, ByVal e
As System.EventArgs) Handles Button1.Click
    'your code will go here
      Dim rng as Word.Range

      rng.Find.ClearFormatting()
      rng.Find.Replacement.ClearFormatting()
   With rng.Find
      .Text = "[Company]"
      .Replacement.Text = "Microsoft"
      .Forward = True
      .Wrap = wdFindContinue
      .Format = False
      .MatchCase = False
      .MatchWholeWord = False
      .MatchWildcards = False
      .MatchSoundsLike = False
      .MatchAllWordForms = False
   End With
rng.Find.Execute(Replace:=wdReplaceAll)

End Sub
```

If you've ever searched for something in Word, you've probably encountered the Wrap property. In a manual search, you
are prompted with a dialog box that lets you know you've
reached the end of the document and asks you whether you
wish to continue searching from the beginning. This scenario
is essentially the Wrap property in action. Wrap takes the following constants: wdFindAsk, wdFindContinue, and
wdFindStop.

In searching for a string combination, you may not want
to actually replace the text for which you are searching. To
find the number of instances of a particular word, you can
simply search for a word and replace it with the same word to
see the number of occurrences. Programmatically, the Find
object returns a Boolean value to show the result of the
search. If the search is successful, the Range variable is
updated so that it contains the result of the search. If Find is
being used from a Selection object, the selection will be
changed (the actual highlighting in the Word document or
template will change) to include the results of the search.

Figure 17-4 shows the resultant message box when I searched and replaced the word "the" in the current document.

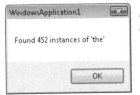

Figure 17-4: Counting instances of a particular word

The Range Object

The Range object often acts as a means to access other objects. Although it may appear as though you are working with properties of the Range object, you are really just using Range to qualify a child object. A good example to illustrate this is the Font object that can be accessed through the Range object as shown here:

```
Application.ActiveDocument.Paragraphs(1).Range.Font
```

The Font object cannot be accessed directly from a Paragraph object, and would result in a syntax error if this is attempted. The following line of code produces a syntax error:

```
Application.ActiveDocument.Paragraphs(1).Font
```

The Range object is simply a block area of a document and everything contained inside that block. Ranges have a single starting character position and a single ending character position. Furthermore, there can be multiple Range objects in a single document. Range objects can be anything from a single character to the entire document. In addition, you can create variables to represent a range and have numerous range variables overlapping within the same document. Range objects have the following characteristics:

▼ The Range object can represent an area other than the current selection.

▼ The Range object is a creature of code and exists only while the code that creates it is executing.

▼ When you insert text at the end of a range, Word automatically expands the range to include the inserted text.

▼ The Range object can consist of a single character, a block of text, or the entire document.

▼ The Range object includes nonprinting characters such as tab characters, spaces, and paragraph marks.

Using the Range Object

Word projects often utilize more than one Range object at a time. You can create multiple Range type variables that represent multiple ranges. And although it's not a good practice, these ranges can even overlap if necessary. Conversely, there can only be one Selection object per Application object at any given time. This is one of the major advantages the Range object has over the Selection object. There are numerous ways to create a Range object. The following table shows the common ways of creating a Range object.

Range Object	Description
Entire document	Range is a child of a Document object and can return a range that consists of the whole document.
Range method and Range property	Both of these return a Range object for the parent object that calls them.
FormattedText property	This property returns a Range object that represents both the formatting and the text of a particular object.
Characters, words, sentences and paragraphs	Each of these provides a Range property.
GoTo method	Returns a Range object that corresponds to the insertion point of the GoTo result.
ConvertToText method	This method belongs to the Table object and some of its children. It returns a Range object that represents the resultant text.
Find object	If executed successfully, a Range object is returned.
Field object	Using either Code or Result returns a Range object.
TextRange property	This property is used with frames.

Using the Range Object to Insert Text

The Range object provides a great way to insert text into a document by setting the object's Text property. Furthermore, when you need to see the text of a certain range, you can retrieve this text property as well. When inserting text using this method, unless you want to replace the entire range you've chosen, you'll probably want to make sure that the range represents a single insertion point in the document. You can easily move to the beginning or end of a Range object using the Collapse method, as shown below.

```
Range.Collapse(Direction)
```

The Collapse method allows you to collapse to the end or to the start of the current range using the constants Word.WdCollapseDirection.wdCollapseStart and Word.WdCollapseDirection.wdCollapseEnd.

Once you've collapsed the Range object, you can simply assign the desired text to the Text property to insert it into the specified range. Let's take a look at this in the context of a simple project. Simply create a Word document or template project in Visual Studio, drag a button onto the document, and double-click it to begin the Click event code.

Enter the following into the Click event. Then dimension a Range variable and assign the ActiveDocument.Range to it. This will cause the variable to contain the entire document. You can then collapse the range either back or to the start and assign some text to the variable's Text property. When you run the code, you should see something similar to that shown in Figure 17-5.

```
Private Sub Button1_Click(ByVal sender As System.Object, ByVal e
As System.EventArgs) Handles Button1.Click
    'your code will go here
    Dim rngDoc As Word.Range
    rngDoc = Application.ActiveDocument.Range
    rngDoc.Collapse(Word.WdCollapseDirection.wdCollapseStart)
    rngDoc.Text = "VSTO Document Assembly" & Chr(13)
End Sub
```

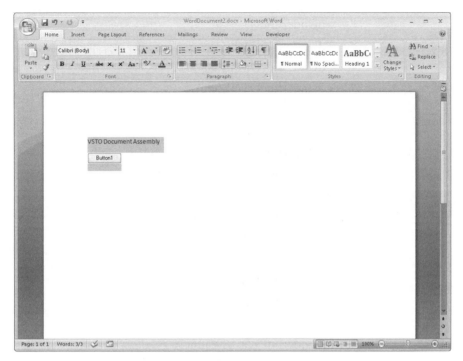

Figure 17-5: Inserting text with the Range object

Applying Bold, Italic, and Underline to the Range Object

Most of the properties we are discussing apply to both the Range and Selection objects. However, the Range object has a few format-related properties that the Selection object does not have. Both objects have a Font object that can be used to control the font details, but the Range object can also access the Bold, Italic, and Underline properties of the Font object directly.

The Bold and Italic are pretty straightforward in that their properties can be set to True, False, or Word. The return value for Bold and Italic can be True, False, or Undefined (if there is a mixture in the current range).

The Underline property, however, is a little more complex in that it has several associated constants as listed:

▼ wdUnderlineDash

▼ wdUnderlineDashHeavy

▼ wdUnderlineDashLong

▼ wdUnderlineDashLongHeavy

▼ wdUnderlineDotDash

▼ wdUnderlineDotDashHeavy

▼ wdUnderlineDotDotDash

▼ wdUnderlineDotDotDashHeavy

▼ wdUnderlineDotted

▼ wdUnderlineDottedHeavy

▼ wdUnderlineDouble

▼ wdUnderlineNone

▼ wdUnderlineSingle

▼ wdUnderlineThick

▼ wdUnderlineWavy

▼ wdUnderlineWavyDouble

▼ wdUnderlineWavyHeavy

▼ wdUnderlineWords

The following code and Figure 17-6 demonstrate how to apply the different possible values for underlining. You'll notice that these same options are available when working through the Word user interface.

```
oPara.Range.Underline = Word.WdUnderline.wdUnderlineDashLong
```

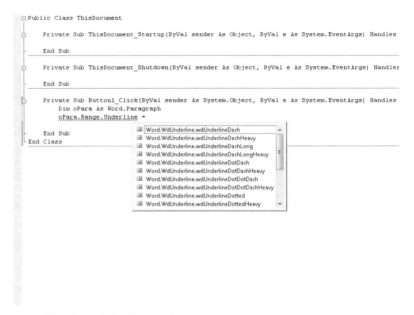

Figure 17-6: The Underline format options

The Selection Object

The Selection object simply represents the area of the document that is currently selected. When you select an area of a document using the mouse or keyboard, you are actually setting the boundary of the Selection object. The Selection object is not a result of code; it always exists and there may only be one Selection object at any given time. If nothing is selected, the Selection object represents the insertion point where the cursor is located. The Selection object can also be multiple noncontiguous blocks of text (when several different items are highlighted).

Using the Selection Object

Although the Selection object is conceptually very similar to the Range object, the procedure for creating a Selection object is a bit different. You can create Selection variables just as you can Range variables, but remember that there can only be one selection at a time in a given Application object. To set the Selection object, use the Select method of the appropriate object that will set the selection. The object can be a Paragraph object, a Bookmark object, a Field object, and so on. For instance, just as with the Range object, executing Application.ActiveDocument.Select causes the selection to represent the entire document.

Another important thing to note is that the Selection property applies only to the Application, Pane, and Window objects. At first this may seem a bit strange, but this is because there can only be a single selection at any given point in time (per window). As a practical matter, you'll work with the application's Selection object most of the time. There are several objects that contain the Select method, as shown below.

Bookmark	Cell	Column
Columns	Document	Field
FormField	Frame	InlineShape
MailMergeField	OLEControl	PageNumber
Range	Row	Rows
Selection	Shape	ShapeRange
Subdocuments	Table	

The Selection object has most of the same functionality we discussed above for the Range object. However, there are a few important differences. One of the differences is that the Selection object has several sub Select methods that the Range object does not. These methods are:

▼ SelectColumn
▼ SelectCurrentAlignment
▼ SelectCurrentColor
▼ SelectCurrentFont
▼ SelectCurrentIndent
▼ SelectCurrentSpacing
▼ SelectCurrentTabs
▼ SelectRow

Additionally, the Selection object has several Type methods that the Range object does not. These methods are:

▼ TypeBackspace

▼ TypeParagraph

▼ TypeText

And finally, unlike the Range object, the Selection object can be very important when interacting with a user as it will contain whatever the user has highlighted.

GoTo Method

The Range, Selection, and Document objects all have a GoTo method. GoTo returns a Range object that represents the starting position of the GoTo target. The syntax of GoTo is as follows with *expression* being a Range, Selection, or Document object.

```
Expression.Goto(What, Which, Count, Name)
```

The *What* parameter of the GoTo method identifies the type of object that the GoTo method is trying to find. Following is a list of the GoTo constants in regard to the *What* parameter. Keep in mind that these would all be preceded by the appropriate qualifier (Word.WdGoToItem.[constant]) so that VSTO knows exactly what you are working with.

wdGoToBookMark	wdGoToLine
wdGoToComment	wdGoToObject
wdGoToEndNote	wdGoToPage
wdGoToEquation	wdGoToPercent
wdGoToField	wdGoToProofreadingError
wdGoToFootnote	wdGoToSection
wdGoToGrammaticalError	wdGoToSpellingError
wdGoToGraphic	wdGoToTable
wdGoToHeading	

The optional *Which* parameter identifies the specific target among the potentially numerous items identified by the above constants. It has six potential constants, listed below, that help identify the target. The constants are all preceded by the curiously named syntax Word.WdGoToDirection.[constant].

▼ wdGotoAbsolute

▼ wdGoToFirst

▼ wdGoToLast

▼ wdGoToNext

▼ wdGoToPrevious

▼ wdGoToRelative

The *Count* parameter identifies the relative number among a series of potential targets. And lastly, the *Name* parameter pertains to those items that have relative names, such as bookmarks, fields, comments, and objects.

Conclusion

In this chapter, we looked at some advanced aspects of VSTO programming. Namely, we looked at how to interact with the user by way of Windows forms, documents, and templates. We can add controls to these forms, documents, and templates and programmatically add events through each control's event handler. In the latter part of the chapter, we took a closer look into the Application object model by discussing a few of its advanced features such as the Range object and the Selection object. Simply put, the Range object is a block area of a document and everything contained inside that block, while the Selection object represents the area of the document that is currently selected.

Appendix

Word Commands

Command Name	Modifiers	Key
About		
Accept All Changes in Doc		
Accept All Changes Shown		
Accept Changes and Advance		
Accept Changes or Advance		
Accept Changes Selected		
Activate Object		
Add Caption		
Add Digital Signature		
Add Record Default		
Add to Contacts		
Addr Fonts		
Address		
Adjust List Indents		
Advanced Brightness Contrast		
Advertise Publish As		
Align Bottom		
Align Center Horizontal		
Align Center Vertical		
Align Left		
Align Right		
Align Top		
Alignment Tab		
All Caps	Ctrl+Shift+	A

Command Name	Modifiers	Key
Annot Ink Eraser		
Annot Ink Pen		
Annotation	Alt+Ctrl+	M
Annotation Edit		
Annotations		
App Maximize	Alt+	F10
App Minimize		
App Move		
App Restore	Alt+	F5
App Size		
Apply Heading1	Alt+Ctrl+	1
Apply Heading2	Alt+Ctrl+	2
Apply Heading3	Alt+Ctrl+	3
Apply List Bullet	Ctrl+Shift+	L
Apply QFSet Initial		
Apply QFSet Template		
Arrange All		
Arrange Side By Side		
Auto Caption		
Auto Correct		
Auto Correct Caps Lock Off		
Auto Correct Days		
Auto Correct Exceptions		
Auto Correct HECorrect		
Auto Correct Initial Caps		
Auto Correct Manager		
Auto Correct Replace Text		
Auto Correct Sentence Caps		
Auto Correct Smart Quotes		
Auto Fit Content		
Auto Fit Fixed		
Auto Fit Window		
Auto Format	Alt+Ctrl+	K
Auto Format Begin		
Auto Format Style		
Auto Manager		
Auto Mark Index Entries		
Auto Scroll		
Auto Sum		
Auto Summarize		

Command Name	Modifiers	Key
Auto Summarize Begin		
Auto Summarize Close		
Auto Summarize Percent of Original		
Auto Summarize Toggle View		
Auto Summarize Update File Properties		
Auto Text		F3
Auto Text	Alt+Ctrl+Shift+	V
Automatic Change		
AW		
Back History Item		
Background Color		
Background Fill Effect		
Background More Colors		
Background Watermark		
BBProperties Dlg		
Bib Insert Source		
Bibliography		
Bibliography Bibliography to Text		
Bibliography Citation to Text		
Bibliography Create Source		
Bibliography Edit Citation Button		
Bibliography Edit Citation Toolbar		
Bibliography Edit Source		
Bibliography Edit Source Button		
Bibliography Edit Source Toolbar		
Bibliography Filter Languages		
Bibliography Source Manager		
Blog Blog Account Options Dlg		
Blog Blog Insert Categories		
Blog Blog Insert Category		
Blog Blog Open Blog Site		
Blog Blog Open Existing Dlg		
Blog Blog Publish		
Blog Blog Publish Draft		
Bold	Ctrl+	B
Bold	Ctrl+Shift+	B
Bold Run		
Bookmark	Ctrl+Shift+	F5
Bookshelf Define Reference		
Bookshelf Lookup Reference		

Command Name	Modifiers	Key
Border All		
Border Bottom		
Border Color Picker		
Border Horiz		
Border Inside		
Border Left		
Border Line Color		
Border Line Style		
Border Line Weight		
Border None		
Border Outside		
Border Right		
Border TLto BR		
Border Top		
Border TRto BL		
Border Vert		
Borders		
Borders and Shading		
Bottom Align		
Bottom Center Align		
Bottom Left Align		
Bottom Right Align		
Break		
Bring Forward		
Bring to Front		
Browse Next	Ctrl+	Page Down
Browse Prev	Ctrl+	Page Up
Browse Sel	Alt+Ctrl+	Home
Building Block Begin Document		
Building Block Begin Section		
Building Block End Document		
Building Block End Section		
Building Block Footer		
Building Block Header		
Building Block IP		
Building Block Organizer		
Bullet Default		
Bullet List Default		
Bullets and Numbering		
Bullets Gallery		

Command Name	Modifiers	Key
Bullets Numbering Style Dialog		
Bullets Numbers		
Calculate		
Callout		
Cancel		Esc
Cancel Highlight Mode		
Caption		
Caption Numbering		
Cell Options		
Center Align		
Center Para	Ctrl+	E
Change Byte		
Change Case	Shift+	F3
Change Case Fareast		
Change Kana		
Changes		
Char Left		Left
Char Left Extend	Shift+	Left
Char Right		Right
Char Right Extend	Shift+	Right
Char Scale		
Char Scale Dialog		
Character Clear Formatting		
Character Remove Style		
Chart		
Check Box Form Field		
Check Compatibility		
Check Document Parts		
Check For Updates		
Checkin		
Checkout		
Citation		
Clear		Del
Clear All Formatting		
Clear Form Field		
Clear Formatting		
Clear Table Style		
Close		
Close All		
Close or Close All		

Command Name	Modifiers	Key
Close or Exit	Alt+	F4
Close Pane	Alt+Shift+	C
Close Para Above		
Close Para Below		
Close Preview		
Close Reading Mode		
Close Up Para		
Close View Header Footer		
Code		
Color		
Column Break	Ctrl+Shift+	Return
Column Select	Ctrl+Shift+	F8
Column Width		
Columns		
Combine Characters		
Comma Accent		
Compare Documents Combine		
Compare Documents Compare		
Compare Documents Last Major		
Compare Documents Last Minor		
Compare Documents Version		
Compare Translation Base Documents		
Compare Versions		
Compat Chkr		
Condensed		
Confirm Conversions		
Connect		
Consistency		
Consistency Check		
Contact Us		
Content Control Building Block Gallery		
Content Control Combo Box		
Content Control Date		
Content Control Dropdown List		
Content Control Group		
Content Control Picture		
Content Control Rich Text		
Content Control Text		
Content Control Ungroup		
Contents Arabic		

Command Name	Modifiers	Key
Context Help		
Continue Numbering		
Control Properties		
Control Run		
Convert All Endnotes		
Convert All Footnotes		
Convert Notes		
Convert Object		
Convert Text Box to Frame		
Copy	Ctrl+	C
Copy	Ctrl+	Insert
Copy As Picture		
Copy Format	Ctrl+Shift+	C
Copy Ink As Text		
Copy Text	Shift+	F2
Create Auto Text	Alt+	F3
Create Auto Text Block from Sel		
Create Bibliography from Sel		
Create Building Block from Sel		
Create Common Field Block from Sel		
Create Cover Page Block from Sel		
Create Directory		
Create Envelope		
Create Equation Block from Sel		
Create Footer Block from Sel		
Create Header Block from Sel		
Create Labels		
Create Layout Block from Sel		
Create Page Num Bottom from Sel		
Create Page Num from Sel		
Create Page Num Page Block from Sel		
Create Page Num Top from Sel		
Create Shared Workspace		
Create Subdocument		
Create Table		
Create Table Block from Sel		
Create Table of Contents from Sel		
Create Task		
Create Text Box Block from Sel		
Create Water Mark Block from Sel		

Command Name	Modifiers	Key
Cross Reference		
Css Links		
Customize		
Customize Add Menu Shortcut	Alt+Ctrl+	=
Customize Keyboard		
Customize Keyboard Shortcut	Alt+Ctrl+	Num +
Customize Menus		
Customize Remove Menu Shortcut	Alt+Ctrl+	-
Customize Toolbar		
Cut	Ctrl+	X
Cut	Shift+	Del
Database		
Date Field	Alt+Shift+	D
Date Time		
Decrease Indent		
Decrease Paragraph Spacing		
Default Char Border		
Default Char Shading		
Default Condensed		
Default Expanded		
Define New Bullet		
Define New List		
Define New List Style		
Define New Number		
Delete All Comments in Doc		
Delete All Comments Shown		
Delete All Ink Annotations		
Delete Annotation		
Delete Back Word	Ctrl+	Backspace
Delete Cells		
Delete Column		
Delete General		
Delete Hyperlink		
Delete Row		
Delete Style		
Delete Table		
Delete Word	Ctrl+	Del
Demote List		
Demote to Body Text		
Diacritic Color		

Command Name	Modifiers	Key
Dictionary		
Display Details		
Display Document Management Pane		
Display Final Doc		
Display For Review		
Display Original Doc		
Display Shared Workspace Pane		
Distribute Column		
Distribute General		
Distribute Para	Ctrl+Shift+	J
Distribute Row		
Do Field Click	Alt+Shift+	F9
Do Not Distribute		
Doc Close	Ctrl+	W
Doc Close	Ctrl+	F4
Doc Encryption		
Doc Export		
Doc Inspector		
Doc Maximize	Ctrl+	F10
Doc Minimize		
Doc Move	Ctrl+	F7
Doc Restore	Ctrl+	F5
Doc Size	Ctrl+	F8
Doc Split	Alt+Ctrl+	S
Document Actions Pane		
Document Map		
Document Map Reading Mode		
Dot Accent		
Dotted Underline		
Double Strikethrough		
Double Underline	Ctrl+Shift+	D
Download Pictures		
Draft		
Draw Align		
Draw Align Distribute Relative to Canvas		
Draw Align Distribute Relative to Container		
Draw Align Distribute Relative to Diagram		
Draw Align Distribute Relative to Org Chart		
Draw Align Distribute Relative to Page		
Draw Align Distribute Relative to Selection		

Command Name	Modifiers	Key
Draw Attach Text		
Draw Auto Format Diagram		
Draw Auto Layout Diagram		
Draw Auto Layout Org Chart		
Draw Bring in Front of Text		
Draw Callout		
Draw Change to Cycle		
Draw Change to Pyramid		
Draw Change to Radial		
Draw Change to Target		
Draw Change to Venn		
Draw Close Freeform		
Draw Compress Pictures		
Draw Delete All Ink Comments		
Draw Delete Diagram Node		
Draw Delete Freeform Segment		
Draw Delete Org Chart Node		
Draw Diagram Style		
Draw Disassemble Picture		
Draw Distribute Horizontally		
Draw Distribute Relative to Page		
Draw Distribute Vertically		
Draw Duplicate		
Draw Edit Picture		
Draw Edit Word Art		
Draw Exit Ink Mode		
Draw Expand Canvas		
Draw Expand Diagram		
Draw Expand Org Chart		
Draw Eyedropper		
Draw Fill Color		
Draw Fill Toggle		
Draw Fit Canvas to Contents		
Draw Fit Diagram to Contents		
Draw Fit Org Chart to Contents		
Draw Flip Horizontal		
Draw Flip Vertical		
Draw Group		
Draw Insert Accent Border Callout1		
Draw Insert Accent Border Callout2		

Command Name	Modifiers	Key
Draw Insert Accent Border Callout3		
Draw Insert Accent Border Callout4		
Draw Insert Accent Callout1		
Draw Insert Accent Callout2		
Draw Insert Accent Callout3		
Draw Insert Accent Callout4		
Draw Insert Arc		
Draw Insert Arrow		
Draw Insert Balloon		
Draw Insert Bent Arrow		
Draw Insert Bent Up Arrow		
Draw Insert Bevel		
Draw Insert Block Arc		
Draw Insert Border Callout1		
Draw Insert Border Callout2		
Draw Insert Border Callout3		
Draw Insert Border Callout4		
Draw Insert Brace Pair		
Draw Insert Bracket Pair		
Draw Insert Bulls Eye Chart		
Draw Insert Callout1		
Draw Insert Callout2		
Draw Insert Callout3		
Draw Insert Callout4		
Draw Insert Can		
Draw Insert Chevron		
Draw Insert Circular Arrow		
Draw Insert Cloud Callout		
Draw Insert Cube		
Draw Insert Curve		
Draw Insert Curved Down Arrow		
Draw Insert Curved Down Ribbon		
Draw Insert Curved Left Arrow		
Draw Insert Curved Right Arrow		
Draw Insert Curved Up Arrow		
Draw Insert Curved Up Ribbon		
Draw Insert Cycle Chart		
Draw Insert Diagram		
Draw Insert Diagram Shape		
Draw Insert Diamond		

Command Name	Modifiers	Key
Draw Insert Donut		
Draw Insert Double Arrow		
Draw Insert Double Wave		
Draw Insert Down Arrow		
Draw Insert Down Arrow Callout		
Draw Insert Drawing Canvas		
Draw Insert Explosion1		
Draw Insert Explosion2		
Draw Insert Filled Freeform		
Draw Insert Filled Polygon		
Draw Insert Flowchart Alternate Process		
Draw Insert Flowchart Collate		
Draw Insert Flowchart Connector		
Draw Insert Flowchart Decision		
Draw Insert Flowchart Delay		
Draw Insert Flowchart Display		
Draw Insert Flowchart Document		
Draw Insert Flowchart Extract		
Draw Insert Flowchart Input Output		
Draw Insert Flowchart Internal Storage		
Draw Insert Flowchart Magnetic Disk		
Draw Insert Flowchart Magnetic Drum		
Draw Insert Flowchart Magnetic Tape		
Draw Insert Flowchart Manual Input		
Draw Insert Flowchart Manual Operation		
Draw Insert Flowchart Merge		
Draw Insert Flowchart Multidocument		
Draw Insert Flowchart Offline Storage		
Draw Insert Flowchart Offpage Connector		
Draw Insert Flowchart Online Storage		
Draw Insert Flowchart Or		
Draw Insert Flowchart Predefined Process		
Draw Insert Flowchart Preparation		
Draw Insert Flowchart Process		
Draw Insert Flowchart Punched Card		
Draw Insert Flowchart Punched Tape		
Draw Insert Flowchart Sort		
Draw Insert Flowchart Summing Junction		
Draw Insert Flowchart Terminator		
Draw Insert Folded Corner		

Command Name	Modifiers	Key
Draw Insert Freeform		
Draw Insert Heart		
Draw Insert Hexagon		
Draw Insert Home Plate		
Draw Insert Horizontal Scroll		
Draw Insert Ink Space		
Draw Insert Isosceles Triangle		
Draw Insert Left Arrow		
Draw Insert Left Arrow Callout		
Draw Insert Left Brace		
Draw Insert Left Bracket		
Draw Insert Left Right Arrow		
Draw Insert Left Right Arrow Callout		
Draw Insert Left Up Arrow		
Draw Insert Lightning Bolt		
Draw Insert Line		
Draw Insert Moon		
Draw Insert No Smoking		
Draw Insert Notched Circular Arrow		
Draw Insert Notched Right Arrow		
Draw Insert Octagon		
Draw Insert Org Chart		
Draw Insert Org Chart Assistant		
Draw Insert Org Chart Coworker		
Draw Insert Org Chart Subordinate		
Draw Insert Oval		
Draw Insert Parallelogram		
Draw Insert Pentagon		
Draw Insert Plaque		
Draw Insert Plus		
Draw Insert Polygon		
Draw Insert Quad Arrow		
Draw Insert Quad Arrow Callout		
Draw Insert Radial Chart		
Draw Insert Rectangle		
Draw Insert Rectangular Callout		
Draw Insert Ribbon		
Draw Insert Ribbon2		
Draw Insert Right Arrow		
Draw Insert Right Arrow Callout		

Command Name	Modifiers	Key
Draw Insert Right Brace		
Draw Insert Right Bracket		
Draw Insert Right Triangle		
Draw Insert Rounded Rectangle		
Draw Insert Rounded Rectangular Callout		
Draw Insert Scribble		
Draw Insert Seal16		
Draw Insert Seal24		
Draw Insert Seal32		
Draw Insert Seal4		
Draw Insert Seal8		
Draw Insert Smiley Face		
Draw Insert Stacked Chart		
Draw Insert Star		
Draw Insert Striped Right Arrow		
Draw Insert Sun		
Draw Insert Trapezoid		
Draw Insert Up Arrow Callout		
Draw Insert Up Down Arrow		
Draw Insert Up Down Arrow Callout		
Draw Insert UTurn Arrow		
Draw Insert Venn Diagram		
Draw Insert Vertical Scroll		
Draw Insert Wave		
Draw Insert Word Art		
Draw Insert Word Picture		
Draw Layout Org Chart Horizontal1		
Draw Layout Org Chart Horizontal2		
Draw Layout Org Chart Vertical1		
Draw Layout Org Chart Vertical2		
Draw Line Color		
Draw Line Toggle		
Draw Marquee Objects		
Draw Menu Shadow Color		
Draw Menu3 DColor		
Draw More Colors Lines		
Draw More Size		
Draw Move Diagram Shape Backward		
Draw Move Diagram Shape Forward		
Draw Nudge Down		

Command Name	Modifiers	Key
Draw Nudge Down One Pixel		
Draw Nudge Left		
Draw Nudge Left One Pixel		
Draw Nudge Right		
Draw Nudge Right One Pixel		
Draw Nudge Up		
Draw Nudge Up One Pixel		
Draw Open Freeform		
Draw Org Chart Fit Text		
Draw Org Chart Select All Assistants		
Draw Org Chart Select All Connectors		
Draw Org Chart Select Branch		
Draw Org Chart Select Level		
Draw Org Chart Style		
Draw Pen		
Draw Pen Style		
Draw Picture Fill		
Draw Picture Automatic		
Draw Picture Black and White		
Draw Picture Grayscale		
Draw Picture Inline		
Draw Picture Less Brightness		
Draw Picture Less Contrast		
Draw Picture More Brightness		
Draw Picture More Contrast		
Draw Picture Reset		
Draw Picture Watermark		
Draw Point Add		
Draw Point Auto		
Draw Point Corner		
Draw Point Delete		
Draw Point Smooth		
Draw Point Straight		
Draw Regroup		
Draw Reset Word Picture		
Draw Reshape		
Draw Reverse Diagram		
Draw Rotate Left		
Draw Rotate Right		
Draw Run Cag		

Command Name	Modifiers	Key
Draw Run Cag For Movies		
Draw Run Cag For Pictures		
Draw Run Cag For Shapes		
Draw Run Cag For Sounds		
Draw Segment Curved		
Draw Segment Straight		
Draw Select All		
Draw Select Multi Objects		
Draw Select Next		
Draw Select Previous		
Draw Send Behind Text		
Draw Set Arrow Style		
Draw Set Fill Color		
Draw Set Fill Effect		
Draw Set Line Color		
Draw Set Line Pattern		
Draw Set Transparent Color		
Draw Shadow Color		
Draw Shadow Customize		
Draw Shadow Nudge Down		
Draw Shadow Nudge Left		
Draw Shadow Nudge Right		
Draw Shadow Nudge Up		
Draw Shadow Semi Transparent Toggle		
Draw Shadow Toggle		
Draw Show Auto Shapes and Drawing Toolbars		
Draw Snap to Grid		
Draw Text Box		
Draw Text Box2		
Draw Toggle Canvas Resize		
Draw Toggle Canvas Scale		
Draw Toggle Canvas Toolbar		
Draw Toggle Crop Mode		
Draw Toggle Diagram Resize		
Draw Toggle Diagram Scale		
Draw Toggle Edit Points Mode		
Draw Toggle Ink Annotation Toolbar		
Draw Toggle Ink Toolbar		
Draw Toggle Layer		
Draw Toggle Org Chart Resize		

Command Name	Modifiers	Key
Draw Toggle Org Chart Scale		
Draw Toggle Picture Toolbar		
Draw Toggle Rotate Mode		
Draw Toggle Select Object Mode		
Draw Toggle Word Art Toolbar		
Draw Ungroup		
Draw Unselect		
Draw Vertical Text Box		
Draw Vertical Text Box2		
Draw Word Art Align Center		
Draw Word Art Align Left		
Draw Word Art Align Letter Justify		
Draw Word Art Align Right		
Draw Word Art Align Stretch Justify		
Draw Word Art Align Word Justify		
Draw Word Art Auto Format		
Draw Word Art Kern		
Draw Word Art Rotate Characters		
Draw Word Art Set Characters to Same Height		
Draw Word Art Spacing Loose		
Draw Word Art Spacing Normal		
Draw Word Art Spacing Tight		
Draw Word Art Spacing Very Loose		
Draw Word Art Spacing Very Tight		
Draw Word Art Stretch to Fill		
Draw3 DColor		
Draw3 DCustomize		
Draw3 DDepth Infinite		
Draw3 DDepth0		
Draw3 DDepth1		
Draw3 DDepth2		
Draw3 DDepth3		
Draw3 DDepth4		
Draw3 DLighting Flat		
Draw3 DLighting Harsh		
Draw3 DLighting Normal		
Draw3 DParallel		
Draw3 DPerspective		
Draw3 DSurface Matte		
Draw3 DSurface Metal		

Command Name	Modifiers	Key
Draw3 DSurface Plastic		
Draw3 DTilt Down		
Draw3 DTilt Left		
Draw3 DTilt Right		
Draw3 DTilt Up		
Draw3 DToggle		
Draw3 DWire Frame		
Drawing		
Drawing Advanced Layout		
Drawing Object		
Drawing Object Wrap Behind		
Drawing Object Wrap Front		
Drawing Object Wrap Inline		
Drawing Object Wrap None		
Drawing Object Wrap Square		
Drawing Object Wrap Through		
Drawing Object Wrap Tight		
Drawing Object Wrap Top Bottom		
Drop Cap		
Drop Down Form Field		
Em Space		
Email Attachment Options		
Email Check Names		
Email Choose Account		
Email Envelope		
Email Flag		
Email Focus Introduction		
Email Focus Subject		
Email Message Options		
Email Options		
Email Save Attachment		
Email Select Bcc Names		
Email Select Cc Names		
Email Select Names		
Email Select to Names		
Email Send		
Email Signature Options		
Email Source		
Email Stationery Options		
En Space		

Command Name	Modifiers	Key
Enclose Characters		
End of Column	Alt+	Page Down
End of Column	Alt+Shift+	Page Down
End of Doc Extend	Ctrl+Shift+	End
End of Document	Ctrl+	End
End of Line		End
End of Line Extend	Shift+	End
End of Row	Alt+	End
End of Row	Alt+Shift+	End
End of Window	Alt+Ctrl+	Page Down
End of Window Extend	Alt+Ctrl+Shift+	Page Down
End Review		
Endnote Area		
Endnote Cont Notice		
Endnote Cont Separator		
Endnote Now	Alt+Ctrl+	D
Endnote Separator		
Eng Writing Assistant		
Envelope Setup		
Envelope Wizard		
Envelopes and Labels		
Equation		
Equation Align At Equals		
Equation Align This Character		
Equation Array Expansion		
Equation Auto Professional Format		
Equation Bar Location		
Equation Centered As Group Justification		
Equation Centered Justification		
Equation Change Style		
Equation Decrease Alignment		
Equation Decrease Argument Size		
Equation Delete Argument		
Equation Delete Column		
Equation Delete Row		
Equation Equation Array Spacing		
Equation Expansion		
Equation Grouping Character Location		
Equation Horizontal Center		
Equation Horizontal Left		

Command Name	Modifiers	Key
Equation Horizontal Right		
Equation Increase Alignment		
Equation Increase Argument Size		
Equation Insert		
Equation Insert Argument After		
Equation Insert Argument Before		
Equation Insert Column After		
Equation Insert Column Before		
Equation Insert Empty Structure		
Equation Insert Row After		
Equation Insert Row Before		
Equation Insert Structure		
Equation Insert Symbol		
Equation Left Justification		
Equation Limit Location		
Equation Linear Format		
Equation Linear Fraction		
Equation Manual Break		
Equation Match Delimiters		
Equation Math Auto Correct		
Equation Matrix Spacing		
Equation Nary Limit Location		
Equation No Bar Fraction		
Equation Normal Text		
Equation Professional Format		
Equation Recognized Functions		
Equation Remove Structure		
Equation Remove Subscript		
Equation Remove Superscript		
Equation Right Justification		
Equation Script Alignment		
Equation Script Location		
Equation Show Hide Border BLTRStrike		
Equation Show Hide Border Bottom		
Equation Show Hide Border Horizontal Strike		
Equation Show Hide Border Left		
Equation Show Hide Border Right		
Equation Show Hide Border TLBRStrike		
Equation Show Hide Border Top		
Equation Show Hide Border Vertical Strike		

Command Name	Modifiers	Key
Equation Show Hide Closing Delimiter		
Equation Show Hide Lower Limit		
Equation Show Hide Opening Delimiter		
Equation Show Hide Placeholders		
Equation Show Hide Radical Degree		
Equation Show Hide Upper Limit		
Equation Skewed Fraction		
Equation Stacked Fraction		
Equation Stretch Delimiters		
Equation Stretch Nary Operator		
Equation Toggle	Alt+	=
Equation Vertical Bottom		
Equation Vertical Center		
Equation Vertical Top		
Equations Options		
EServices		
Excel Table		
Exit		
Expanded		
Extend Selection		F8
Fax Service		
Field		
Field Chars	Ctrl+	F9
Field Codes	Alt+	F9
File		
Fill Color		
Fill Color Picker		
Fill Policy Label		
Find	Ctrl+	F
Find Reading Mode		
Fit Text		
Fix Me		
Font	Ctrl+	D
Font	Ctrl+Shift+	F
Font Color		
Font Color Picker		
Font Size		
Font Size Select	Ctrl+Shift+	P
Font Substitution		
Footer		

Command Name	Modifiers	Key
Footer Only		
Footnote		
Footnote Area		
Footnote Cont Notice		
Footnote Cont Separator		
Footnote Now	Alt+Ctrl+	F
Footnote Separator		
Footnotes		
Form Field		
Form Field Options		
Form Shading		
Format Cell		
Formatting Pane	Alt+Ctrl+Shift+	S
Formatting Pane Current		
Formatting Properties	Shift+	F1
Formatting Restrictions		
Formula		
Forward History Item		
Frame		
Frame or Frame Picture		
Frame Properties		
Frame Remove Split		
Frame Split Above		
Frame Split Below		
Frame Split Left		
Frame Split Right		
Frameset TOC		
Frameset Wizard		
Freeze Layout		
Getting Started Pane		
Go Back	Shift+	F5
Go Back	Alt+Ctrl+	Z
Go To	Ctrl+	G
Go To		F5
Go to First Pg		
Go to Footer		
Go to Furthest Read Pg		
Go to Header		
Go to Header Footer		
Go to Last Pg		

Command Name	Modifiers	Key
Go to Next Comment		
Go to Next Endnote		
Go to Next Footnote		
Go to Next Page		
Go to Next Section		
Go to Previous Comment		
Go to Previous Endnote		
Go to Previous Footnote		
Go to Previous Page		
Go to Previous Section		
Goto Comment Scope		
Goto Next Linked Text Box		
Goto Prev Linked Text Box		
Goto Table of Contents		
Gram Settings		
Grammar		
Grammar Hide		
Graphical Horizontal Line		
Greeting Sentence		
Gridlines		
Grow Font	Ctrl+Shift+	.
Grow Font One Point	Ctrl+	]
Hanging Indent	Ctrl+	T
Head Foot Diff First Page		
Head Foot Diff Odd Even Page		
Header		
Header Footer Link	Alt+Shift+	R
Header Only		
Heading Numbering		
Headings		
Help		F1
HHC	Alt+Ctrl+	F7
Hidden	Ctrl+Shift+	H
Hide Outline		
Highlight	Alt+Ctrl+	H
Highlight Color Picker		
Horizontal in Vertical		
Horizontal Line		
Hyperlink	Ctrl+	K
Hyperlink Open		

Command Name	Modifiers	Key
Hyphenation		
Hyphenation Auto Off		
Hyphenation Auto On		
Hyphenation Manual		
Ichitaro Help		
Ignore All Consistence Error		
Ignore Consistence Error		
Imager Scan		
IMEControl		
IMEReconversion		
Increase Indent		
Increase Paragraph Spacing		
Indent	Ctrl+	M
Indent Char		
Indent First Char		
Indent First Line		
Indent Line		
Index		
Index and Tables		
Ink Annotation Eraser		
Ink Annotations		
Ink Comment		
Ink Split Menu		
Insert Cells		
Insert Column		
Insert Column Right		
Insert General		
Insert Row		
Insert Row Above		
Insert Row Below		
Insert Table		
Italic	Ctrl+	I
Italic	Ctrl+Shift+	I
Italic Run		
Japanese Greeting Closing Sentence		
Japanese Greeting Opening Sentence		
Japanese Greeting Previous Greeting		
Join to Previous List		
Jump to Heading		
Justify Para	Ctrl+	J

Command Name	Modifiers	Key
Justify Para High		
Justify Para Low		
Justify Para Medium		
Justify Para Special		
Justify Para Thai		
Label Options		
Language		
Learn Words		
Left Para	Ctrl+	L
Letters Wizard JToolbar		
License Verification		
Line Color		
Line Color Picker		
Line Down		Down
Line Down Extend	Shift+	Down
Line Num Continuous		
Line Num Off		
Line Num Reset Section		
Line Num Rest Page		
Line Num Suppress		
Line Spacing		
Line Up		Up
Line Up Extend	Shift+	Up
Links		
List		
List Commands		
List Indent		
List Num Field	Alt+Ctrl+	L
List Outdent		
Load Oss Theme from Template		
Lock Document		
Lock Fields	Ctrl+	3
Lock Fields	Ctrl+	F11
Lock Policy Label		
Lower Text Baseline		
Lowered		
Ltr Para		
Ltr Run		
LTRMacro Dialogs		
Macro	Alt+	F8

Command Name	Modifiers	Key
Magnifier		
Mail As HTML		
Mail As Plain Text		
Mail As RTF		
Mail Check Names		
Mail Hide Message Header		
Mail Merge		
Mail Merge Address Block		
Mail Merge Ask to Convert Chevrons		
Mail Merge Check	Alt+Shift+	K
Mail Merge Clear Document Type		
Mail Merge Convert Chevrons		
Mail Merge Create Data Source		
Mail Merge Create Header Source		

Index

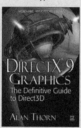

Professional MEL Solutions for Production
1-59822-066-7 • $44.95
6 x 9 • 576 pp.

Essential LightWave v9
Steve Warner
Kevin Phillips
Timothy Albee
1-59822-024-1 • $49.95
6 x 9 • 992 pp.

Essential ZBrush
WAYNE ROBSON
1-59822-059-4 • $44.95
6 x 9 • 768 pp.

3ds max Lighting
Nicholas Boughen
1-55622-401-X • $49.95
6 x 9 • 432 pp.

LightWave v9 Lighting
1-59822-039-X • $44.95
6 x 9 • 616 pp.

LightWave v9 Texturing
Nigel Reeves
1-59822-029-2 • $44.95
6 x 9 • 648 pp.

The Art of Flash Animation: Creative Cartooning
1-59822-026-8 • $34.95
6 x 9 • 480 pp.

Maya 8.0 Character Modeling
1-59822-020-9 • $44.95
6 x 9 • 504 pp.

The Mechanics of Anime and Manga
STUDIO IMOGHIS
1-59822-019-5 • $29.95
7.25 x 10.25 • 328 pp.

Design First for 3D Artists
1-55622-085-5 • $49.95
9 x 7 • 336 pp.

Advanced Lighting and Materials with Shaders
1-55622-292-0 • $44.95
9 x 7 • 360 pp.

Polygonal Modeling: Basic and Advanced Techniques
MARIO RUSSO
1-59822-007-1 • $39.95
6 x 9 • 424 pp.

Modeling, UV Mapping, and Texturing 3D Game Weapons
CHRISTIAN CHANG
1-55622-870-8 • $39.95
6 x 9 • 368 pp.

LightWave 3D 8 Cartoon Character Creation Vol. 2: Rigging & Animation
Jonny Gorden
1-55622-254-8 • $49.95
6 x 9 • 440 pp.

LightWave 3D 8 Cartoon Character Creation Vol. 1: Modeling & Texturing
Jonny Gorden
1-55622-253-X • $49.95
6 x 9 • 496 pp.